STREETWISE

STREETWISE

GETTING TO AND THROUGH GOLDMAN SACHS

LLOYD BLANKFEIN

ORION
IGNITE

First published in Great Britain in 2026 by Orion Ignite,
an imprint of The Orion Publishing Group Ltd
Carmelite House, 50 Victoria Embankment
London EC4Y 0DZ

An Hachette UK Company

The authorised representative in the EEA is Hachette Ireland,
8 Castlecourt Centre, Dublin 15, D15 XTP3,
Ireland (email: info@hbgi.ie)

1 3 5 7 9 10 8 6 4 2

Copyright © Lloyd Blankfein 2026

Published by arrangement with Penguin Press, an imprint of
Penguin Random House LLC.
First published in the United States in 2026.

No part of this book may be used or reproduced in any manner
for the purpose of training artificial intelligence technologies or systems.
This work is reserved from text and data mining
(Article 4(3) Directive (EU) 2019/790).

The moral right of Lloyd Blankfein to be identified as
the author of this work has been asserted in accordance
with the Copyright, Designs and Patents Act of 1988.

All rights reserved. No part of this publication may be
reproduced, stored in a retrieval system, or transmitted
in any form or by any means, electronic, mechanical,
photocopying, recording, or otherwise, without the
prior permission of both the copyright owner and the
above publisher of this book.

A CIP catalogue record for this book is
available from the British Library.

ISBN (Hardback): 978 1 398 72548 5
ISBN (Export Trade Paperback) 978 1 3987 2549 2
ISBN (Ebook) 978 1 3987 2551 5
ISBN (Audio) 978 1 39872 552 2

Printed in Great Britain by Clays Ltd, Elcograf, S.p.A.

www.orionbooks.co.uk

For Laura, Alex, Jonathan, and Rachel

Contents

Preface		ix
1.	**Advantages**	1
2.	**Getting Out**	16
3.	**Glimpses Beyond**	32
4.	**Lawyer, Briefly**	40
5.	**Gold Mettle**	49
6.	**From Gold Man to Goldman**	64
7.	**Breaking Through**	74
8.	**De-Vals and Re-Vals**	83
9.	**Innovation**	92
10.	**Howdy, Partner!**	106
11.	**Paranoia Is a Job Requirement**	114
12.	**My First "Crisis of the Century"**	124
13.	**How I Earned My Reputation for Being Difficult**	133
14.	**Lloyd of London**	141

15.	To IPO or Not to IPO	149
16.	The Unforeseen	173
17.	Succession	187
18.	Is He Completely Housebroken?	198
19.	A Modern Merchant Bank	211
20.	The Partnership Culture	223
21.	The Storm Before the Storm	240
22.	Don't Get Dead	260
23.	How to Survive a Crisis	279
24.	*How Did You Do It?*	291
25.	Just a Few More Calamities	315
26.	Notes on an Illness	327
27.	Goodbye to All That	337
28.	Risk Is Risky	344
	Epilogue: Life After Goldman	359
	Acknowledgments	365
	Image Credits	369
	Index	371

Preface

As I decompressed following my retirement from Goldman Sachs at the end of 2018, I spent a few months doing very little. In forty years, I'd never taken a break longer than a two-week vacation, and every vacation had been punctuated by calls and haunted by thoughts of what I had to do when I got back to work. Now, for the first time since I was in my twenties, I could luxuriate in having free time and a lack of responsibilities.

Soon I settled into a new kind of rhythm. My days were now spent on a balance of commercial stuff (trading/investing, advising, and punditry); nonprofit stuff; and personal stuff (exercise, random intellectual interests, family, and travel). I felt alternately busy and bored.

During the "bored" period, I thought, *I know, I'll write a memoir! A gift to the world!* I had an unlikely journey into the world of finance, rising to the highest position at a storied investment bank. The career I had was improbable, and in retrospect hardly seems possible. How likely was it that I would go from public housing in Brooklyn to the Ivy League and get a big job anywhere? And that I would get hired as a salesman at a relatively small trading firm focused on a niche international market? And that the trading firm would happen to get acquired by the most iconic firm on Wall Street? And that this would all occur at just the moment when trading was taking off and cross-border activity beginning to explode? I wanted to look back at my improbable story in part to explain to myself, *How did all that happen?*

Beyond reexamining my own journey, I thought my experience might just hold some relevance for people trying to understand the way finance and the economy had evolved over the past several decades. My career at Goldman Sachs corresponded with a decades-long bull market in financial assets, a march toward globalization, important applications of new technologies in financial services, and the rise of alternative asset managers like hedge funds and private equity funds, as well as the growth of complex risk-apportioning financial instruments like credit default swaps and securitized mortgages.

If you look at a forty-year chart, the market-performance graphs are smooth and rising. But living through this period on the ground, there were many moments of terror when it seemed the world was coming to an end: the 1987 stock market crash; the 1994 bond market crisis; the Asian debt crisis of 1997; Russia's default and the collapse of Long-Term Capital Management in 1998; and the bursting of the dot-com bubble in 2000. It all culminated in the defining politico-economic disaster of the modern era, the 2008 financial crisis. What had I learned from those experiences that might be valuable to others? Had markets and the world absorbed the right lessons?

And so I went at it and wrote a few chapters, starting with my early years. That part was easy. There was no public record I had to take account of, and few people alive, or at least compos mentis, who could challenge my memory. But it got harder as my history started to overlap with History. As time ticked by following my departure from Goldman, I began to feel less relevant. I questioned whether anyone would or should care about my story. I put my pen down and put the manuscript in a drawer. It would be four years before I picked it up.

Why did I pick it up again?

First, I realized that the events I witnessed, and perhaps slightly influenced, remained at the center of political conflict and change. The global financial crisis and its aftermath continue to reverberate. Would we have as polarized a society, would we have a Donald Trump, had we not had the crisis, the bank bailouts, the reaction, and the reaction to the reaction? There were many, many accounts of these events from the perspectives of policymakers and economists. But there was almost nothing describing what that experience felt like from inside the financial world.

Second, I wanted to share what I learned at Goldman Sachs. Goldman holds a unique place in the world of finance, and a uniquely distorted place in the imaginations of many people. I accumulated a lot of experience managing and leading a firm that attracts top talent and top egos, that affects and is affected by other industries and macro-events around the world. I recruited and led ambitious people and managed and responded to risk. I did that in tough times when there was often no choice to make, and in good times, which were sometimes harder because there were difficult choices to be made and a lack of urgency about making them. I learned the hard way about reputational risk, how to deal with the politics, the press, and the public, all while keeping the firm on mission and maintaining morale. In the process, I discovered resilience in myself, my colleagues, and the institution.

Third, I felt the human urge to express myself. I continue to enjoy good relationships with my old colleagues. I like it when they ask my advice, and I enjoy giving it. What seems to resonate with them is my different perspective. In tough and stressful times I see irony and humor. Ironically, that has sometimes hurt me and led to my least humorous moments. But I do have a way of framing things that seems to stick with people. After I left Goldman, my colleagues put together a catalog of "Lloydisms"—things I said that they remembered because they were clever or shocking or at least a little blunter and more honest than most of what you usually hear from people in finance. Why not share my indiscretions with a larger audience?

If my story, the one I wanted to tell, has wider implications, it's because it's really about striving, humility in the face of an unknowable future, resilience after disappointment, resolve and optimism in crisis, and the universality of human nature—even among the very rich and successful.

Is it relevant? I hope so, but I leave it to the reader to judge.

STREETWISE

CHAPTER 1

Advantages

When I go into a room full of people, I have to decide whether I'm going to be the member of the establishment or the kid from Brooklyn.

I am a product of East New York, Brooklyn, where I grew up in the projects, and I still see the world through those eyes. To this day, I have to concentrate to say *rather* and not *rath-uh*. I can't compare myself with people I've worked with who overcame really severe disadvantage, like broken homes, civil wars, extreme poverty, or forced emigration. But growing up in public housing, in a family that was just getting by, and attending public schools that were failing, left its mark on me. I struggle with ambivalence. I spend half my time wanting to give stuff to my kids, the other half tormenting them for having stuff I gave them that I didn't have.

My earliest memories are from the South Bronx, where my family lived in a tenement building on Leggett Avenue. I used to love watching the coal that heated the building get delivered. It made a roar as it poured from the truck down a chute into the cellar. Another memory: the organ-grinder who sometimes played on the sidewalk outside our apartment. My mother wrapped a coin in paper and threw it out the window for his monkey to pick up.

When I was three, we moved from the Bronx to East New York, in search of a better life—which, for a time, we found. The year was 1957 and the city hadn't yet finished paving the streets of the new public housing development we were moving into, the Linden Houses, run by the New York City Housing Authority. This was subsidized housing for the working class, with buildings arrayed in an irregular pattern bordered by bits of landscaped greenery. They were not yet "the projects." At the time, it must have seemed like Shangri-la to my parents. Everything was clean and new. Children had an actual playground, with swings and monkey bars to climb. The neighborhood was reasonably safe. Those nineteen largely identical redbrick high-rises were not yet blighted in the ways they would be by the time I was in high school.

My mother, my father, my sister, my grandmother, and I occupied a small apartment with two bedrooms and a bathroom, maybe eight hundred square feet, on the fourth floor of a fourteen-story tower at 243 Wortman Avenue. My sister, Jacky, and I shared a bedroom, while my grandmother, Lilly, slept on a foldout couch in the living room. It was tight but neat. You weren't allowed to sit on a bed—beds were for sleeping, not sitting, according to my mom. There were plastic slipcovers on every piece of furniture that anyone could sit on or lean against. When we got our first TV, a big console set that I watched every afternoon and evening while lying on the living room floor, my mom made me rotate to different places on the floor so I wouldn't wear out the rug unevenly. When my parents retired to Florida decades later, the furniture they left behind was in pristine condition.

My Blankfein ancestors were Yiddish-speaking Jews who emigrated in the 1880s from a shtetl that was then in Russia and is now part of Poland. Isaac Blankfein, my paternal great-grandfather, worked as a tailor on Delancey Street, on the Lower East Side. He started a wholesale garment business that moved around Lower Manhattan, first to Greene Street—long before that neighborhood was called SoHo—then to Bleecker Street in Greenwich Village, then to East 14th Street. My grandfather Saul, who died when I was six, was the youngest of Isaac's five sons, and the only one who stayed involved in the family business.

When that business went bad during the Depression, our branch of the family became the poor relations. Over the years, as I became more famous (or notorious), I've heard from various Blankfeins descended from the other four brothers. They ended up as professionals—teachers, doctors, and lawyers. Not our side of the family. My dad worked as a clerk in the post office, while his younger brother, my uncle Sheldon, worked as a cutter in the Garment District.

After my grandfather Saul died, my grandmother Hannah Blankfein stayed in their apartment in a brownstone in the South Bronx, which I remember surrounded by rubble-strewn vacant lots as the neighborhood declined. On the long drive from Brooklyn to visit her, I would sleep, or pretend to sleep, stretched out in the back seat of our car. Because Hannah's mother was from Austria and spoke German rather than Yiddish, I understood that she was from a slightly higher social class among descendants of Jewish immigrants. A voluble, outgoing woman, my grandmother was uneducated but might have been the most accomplished person in our family. She was active in Bronx politics, served as a district leader, and even attended the 1964 Democratic Convention in Atlantic City as an alternate delegate.

My mother Blanche's family, the Krellmans, came to the United States a little later, around the turn of the twentieth century. They were also from the Pale of Settlement at the western edge of the Tsarist Empire. My mother's parents had a bitter divorce when she was young, and she broke off relations with her father, who subsequently remarried and had another family. My mom stuck with her mother, my grandmother Lilly, so I never knew my grandfather on my mother's side. When I shared a room with her as a kid, Grandma Lilly never talked about him. She worked at S. Klein, a department store on Union Square in Manhattan, which was a long ride on the 2 train from New Lots Avenue. Her job at Klein's was "floorwalker," which meant helping lady customers find the right size dresses and assisting the regular salespeople.

My mother was an extrovert and a schmoozer, always engaging strangers in conversation—an instinct she passed along to her children.

But while she projected a lot of warmth to the outside world, she was all business at home, where she was the principal decision-maker about everything in our crowded household. During the day, she worked as a receptionist at a burglar alarm company—one of the few growth industries in the neighborhood. Other than watching TV in the evening, her main form of recreation was playing mah-jongg with women friends. She was only nineteen in 1940 when she married my father, Seymour, who was five years older. They met while working in the same dry-goods store in the Bronx. When he was drafted into the army in 1942, he was sent to Omaha, Nebraska, to work as a mechanic at the Army Air Corps base there. My mom moved there to be with him. My older sister was conceived there and was born on V-J Day, September 2, 1945.

My father was a big man—223 pounds at the time of his enlistment, according to his army records—but quieter than my mother and somewhat overshadowed by her. My dad liked to point to new car ads and say, "I can't wait to buy that car in six years." I inherited both his sense of humor and his anxiety. He was a constant worrier who never let the gas gauge on our secondhand Pontiac fall below three quarters full. I remember him taking that car, with its old style divided windshield, to be checked out at a garage before the longest drive we'd take every summer, to Weiner's Hotel, a Jewish-owned resort in Moodus, Connecticut. Part of the "Connecticut Catskills," the hotel had cabins and a kind of musty main building. As I write this, I can still smell the mildew. You didn't really want to unpack. There was a shared bathroom on every floor.

My dad worked nights as a mail sorter at the post office because it meant a 10 percent pay boost above the day shift. We all had to be quiet during the day while he slept. In our world, nobody's father, if he had a job, went to work in a suit. No one I knew had a parent who had gone to college. My friends' fathers worked for the government, drove taxis, or were store clerks. I knew kids whose parents were Holocaust survivors, or "refugees" as they were called back then. My father was content with his job at the post office, or at least glad he had a secure job. Earlier, when I was very young, he was laid off from his job as a delivery driver for a dry-goods company. He was unemployed for a while, and the atmosphere at home was miserable and anxious. He never wanted that to happen again, hence his attachment to the civil service.

I had never been to the place where my father worked. He retired while I was in law school, and his coworkers threw a small party for him on his last day, at their station at the General Post Office in Brooklyn. Our family was invited. I remember going in, seeing the cramped space where letters moved by on a conveyor belt and the guys sorted them into slots. I remember thinking, *How soul-destroying.* But it got worse. Behind my dad and his colleagues was a large piece of equipment, literally in a plastic wrapper. I asked what it was. It was a machine that could sort mail at hyperspeed via an "electronic reader." It was meant to perform the same job held by my dad and his coworkers, only a lot faster, more cheaply, and better. But the government wouldn't deploy the machine and displace the workers until they retired. Imagine performing that mindless job when you knew it didn't even need to be performed. I still feel so sad when I think about the waste of my dad's brains and effort.

There was always tension and fighting at home about the lack of money, the lack of privacy, the need to be quiet, and miscellaneous stresses, like whose turn it was to use the bathroom and how long someone was taking. Cutting "cents off" coupons from newspapers for grocery items was the arts-and-crafts project I remember. A searing memory for me as an eight- or nine-year-old kid was breaking my glasses while roughhousing with friends. I didn't get yelled at, but I was made to feel that new glasses were budget breaking. My folks did the best they could, and I loved them, but we didn't always get along.

Even more than my mother, my sister, Jacky, was a people person—we used to say she could talk to a lamppost. Nine years older than me, she was in some ways more of a parent than a sibling. She was my co-conspirator, the person with whom I could always laugh about our lives. Jacky was the one who took me to the World's Fair in Flushing in 1964. We rode Walt Disney's "It's a Small World" ride and watched a life-size animatronic Abraham Lincoln deliver excerpts from the Gettysburg Address. My strongest memory is of a futuristic technology you could try inside a bubble-shaped "Family Phone Booth": the speakerphone. To ten-year-old me, it seemed like a contraption from *Dick Tracy*.

Jacky, cut from the same cloth as me, was a victim of the attitudes of the 1950s and early 1960s. At school, she was channeled into a "commercial" diploma, which meant studying stenography and typing instead of history and English. She married at twenty, mostly, I think, to get out of our house. That turned out to be a costly mistake. She had a baby within a year, right after her husband, a bookkeeper, was discovered to have stolen from his employer. She moved back into our apartment with her baby, which meant that I had to share a room with my grandmother in the slightly larger apartment we were assigned in one of the other towers. My sister's divorce was ugly, and the police were often called to mediate disputes over child custody.

Because my father worked nights, we seldom had family dinners together. My mom put everything in the toaster oven, even hamburgers, and we ate a lot of Birds Eye frozen dinners. Corn and spinach, as far as I knew, came from cans, not the ground. Sometimes my grandmother would cook something slightly more effortful. Our kitchen table wasn't exactly a lively intellectual environment. I don't remember my parents having any political conversations, unless you count the constant cursing of Mayor Lindsay because of the deterioration of the neighborhood. But like everyone else in our world, my parents voted Democratic. We got the *Daily Mirror*, a Hearst tabloid that folded in 1963, and later the *New York Daily News*. I would play the Jumble word puzzle, perhaps a precursor to the *New York Times* Spelling Bee, which I'm addicted to these days, but a great deal easier. The *Times* never made an appearance in our household, and I doubt that anyone in my immediate family had even heard of *The Wall Street Journal*.

For kids in the projects, there were no organized sports or teams—no Little League or junior football. There were cement playgrounds, where children could play street games like skelly, where you flick bottle caps into squares outlined with chalk, or stickball, which you played with a rubber Spaldeen or a handball. Ring-a-levio was a game of team tag. I was the best at Chinese handball, which we played against the side of P.S. 190 on Sheffield Avenue. In the fall, we played touch football in a mostly deserted parking lot, using the parallel lines as yard markers. If the Battle of Waterloo was won on the playing fields of Eton, as Wellington is supposed to have said, a lot of personalities and characters were shaped playing those street games in Brooklyn.

We kids sorted ourselves out—there were no adults supervising. I was slightly chubby in those days, not a great athlete, not great eyesight, and I tended to get picked nearly last. Joining the local Y swim team and later the swim team in high school got me in better shape. But I was funny, and I made friends like Felice Yurkiewicz and Richard Kalb, whom I've been close to my whole life. When I'm with them, my Brooklyn accent comes back in full force. At school, my report cards usually identified me as the class clown.

Felice, who lived on the second floor of our building, was a friend throughout our childhoods. We both taught ourselves to read from DC and Action Comics. We used to quiz each other: *Where does Superman keep the Bottle City of Kandor? In his Fortress of Solitude.* At seven or eight, I'm not sure we understood the concept of solitude, but we knew the answer. As my tastes matured, I came to like Batman better. Superman didn't earn his superpowers. He got them by virtue of being born on the planet Krypton—a nepo baby if there ever was one. Batman, on the other hand, was a regular guy, albeit from a wealthy family, who through smarts and hard work became the peer of other superheroes with supernatural advantages.

A new comic book cost ten cents, and Felice's parents, both Holocaust survivors, had even less money than mine to buy us the latest installments. I had the idea to sell our lightly used comic books in front of our building at a 50 percent discount. Soon I was buying and selling from other kids on the secondary market, ending up with a large inventory and a pocketful of coins. That was my first commercial venture, to be followed by a brisk trade in baseball cards.

When we turned seven, we got New York Public Library cards and could take three books a week out of the branch library at New Lots Avenue. Another pastime, as we got older, was movies. One of my favorites was *Gone With the Wind*, especially the scene where those left at Tara Plantation are starving amid the devastation of the Civil War. Under a moonlit sky, the desperate Scarlett O'Hara yanks a raw radish from the decimated garden, gags on it, and falls to her knees in despair. "As God is my witness," she declares to the heavens, "they're not going to lick me. I'm going to live through this, and when it's all over, I'll never be hungry again."

"As God is my witness," I proclaimed, "I'll never share a bedroom again—unless, of course, it's with someone I *want* to share a bedroom with." I knew that getting out of my crummy neighborhood was going to take effort. Around that time—approximately seventh grade—I started taking school more seriously.

While I was growing up, there were regular teacher strikes, the longest of which occurred in 1968, when I was in ninth grade, and lasted from September into November. Because of that, my parents, who were not at all observant, almost enrolled me in a yeshiva, a Jewish religious day school. They did send me to the nearest synagogue for afternoon Hebrew school. Every day after school—first P.S. 190, then George Gershwin Junior High School 166 on Van Siclen Avenue—I went to B'nai Israel on Hendrix Street with other kids from the projects.

Rabbi Avner German, who presided at that Orthodox synagogue, was a charismatic leader who wanted to get his mostly secular students more interested in Judaism. He was probably the first person I ever met who wore a suit (plus a black fedora), but that didn't stop him from rolling up his shirtsleeves and playing ball with us kids. On certain Jewish holidays, Rabbi German would farm us out for a weekend with Orthodox families in Crown Heights to give us a feel for religion that he hoped would stick. I remember one Passover seder where we didn't eat until 2:00 a.m. That was it for me. Eventually, when there were no longer enough Jewish families in the old neighborhood to sustain a congregation, Rabbi German opened a yeshiva for the newer influx of Russian immigrants, many of whom were totally unfamiliar with Jewish life. He touched an extraordinary number of people.

My studies led to my bar mitzvah, when, around my thirteenth birthday, I read from the Torah. (I can still chant my haftarah portion on request.) Some of my friends were having big parties and I really wanted one too, even though my parents couldn't afford it. In hindsight I feel bad that I put them in that situation, but I was only twelve years old. We had the reception at the Astoria Manor in Queens, a banquet facility, which seemed pretty impressive to me. My bar mitzvah should have been the start of my religious education. But for me, as for a lot of Jewish kids from secular families, it was the end of it.

I was a good student and competed in the Brooklyn-wide spelling bee. The word that knocked me out in the final round was *yawl*. I was not familiar with sailboats and thought the word must be *y'all*, the second-person plural pronoun of the Southern states.

New York City had a program that let strong students skip the eighth grade, and so I did. At that point, I could have applied to a more rigorous magnet school. There were three main ones: Bronx High School of Science, Brooklyn Tech, and Stuyvesant, which was in Manhattan. Brooklyn Tech was closest, but still much more than an hour commute each way by bus and subway, and the subway was dangerous. Also, I was not a science/engineering type. But if I'm honest, I was also being a bit calculating. At Jefferson, the undistinguished neighborhood high school, I thought I might have a better shot at getting great grades and thus at getting into an out-of-town college. Escaping the neighborhood was, at that point, my primary ambition in life. It didn't dawn on me that actually reading books and learning things in high school also might be positives for a college application.

Overcrowded Jefferson ran on triple session, which meant students went to school for a few hours in the early morning, middle of the day, or late afternoon into early evening. We took only the major state-required courses, no electives, no PE—the gymnasium had been taken over to be a police station. I finished the requirements for graduating by my junior year, when I was fifteen. I stayed another year because I thought I was too young to get accepted by a decent college. Senior year, I competed on *It's Academic*, the local NBC quiz show hosted by Art James. I was good—there were three of us on the Jefferson team, and our coach said I was the only one allowed to hit the buzzer. We won a couple of episodes, one of them by identifying the Colossus of Rhodes as one of the Seven Wonders of the Ancient World. I'd never heard of the Colossus of Rhodes, but it seemed the most likely of the three choices offered. I was awarded a pen. In another round, our team won a desk encyclopedia. It was not a big-budget show.

Jefferson High School was mostly Black and Hispanic, which probably helped develop my ability to talk easily to different kinds of people. It was designated a Title I school because of the high proportion of families who lived below the poverty line. That meant you got a free lunch and waivers of the fees to take the SATs and to submit college applications. I attended after-school programs at the local United Jewish Appeal–supported Y and summer day camp when I was younger. Growing up in that world, you develop an expectation that you will get stuff "on scholarship." It is the furthest thing from your mind to give money away. It required an adjustment on my part when I started to earn a lot and had to learn to enjoy donating some of it. Jefferson High School was shut down in 2007 due to low graduation rates. The building was repurposed as four schools focused on teaching trades.

Each of the public housing projects in New York City was designated for a specific income level, with a limit on how much you could earn and still live there. Howard Schultz, the founder of Starbucks, grew up in a development in the nearby neighborhood of Canarsie that was upscale compared with mine. The Linden Houses were for lower-lower-middle-class families. In the less evolved era when the project was built, the New York City Housing Authority (NYCHA) was reserving 70 percent of the units for white families. There were "unofficial" separate waiting lists depending on your race.

In 1964, the housing authority announced that it was dropping that discriminatory policy, one that would be unimaginable today. When it did, the neighborhood began changing more quickly—*white flight* was the term everyone used. White families were moving out, mostly to Long Island or to safer sections in Brooklyn. The other term urban sociologists brought into vogue was *tipping point*. Once the nonwhite population rose to a certain level, the evacuation by white families would accelerate dramatically. In 1960, East New York was 85 percent white. By 1966, it was 80 percent Black and Hispanic—a remarkably fast transformation.

Unlike many of our Jewish neighbors, we stayed as the area around the Linden Projects got rougher. Shootings, knifings, vandalism, and deliberately set fires in abandoned buildings were common. In the summer of 1966, when I was eleven, there were a couple of "riots"—the first a street fight between Italian and Puerto Rican teenagers, the second between whites and Blacks. I didn't go outside much, other than to school and to my odd jobs. I didn't go out at night at all. In 1968, major riots close to my home after the assassination of Dr. Martin Luther King Jr. really put us on the map.

I went to Jefferson by city bus and was warned to stay on it and ride it back around whenever there was a crowd or commotion in front of the school. In my three years there, I don't think I ever went to the bathroom or left a classroom except during "passing," when all students shuffled between classes. Because I was on the swim team, the pool was a safe zone for me, and I could use the bathroom there. I was mugged at knifepoint for pocket change several times, threatened but never hurt. Once, I got held up in the stairway of my own apartment building. The mugger approached me from behind, and when I turned around, we recognized each other—we lived on the same floor. My memory is that we dealt with the awkward situation by both just walking away.

I had several part-time jobs, including as a delivery boy, a lifeguard, and a tutor—a babysitter, really. I was expected to contribute $20 a week toward household expenses. My best job was working as a vendor at Yankee Stadium in the Bronx, a very long commute from Brooklyn. I got the job when I was thirteen, which was the earliest age you could get working papers." Given the hazards of taking the subway or walking home after dark, I worked only day games on weekends. I walked around the stadium hawking souvenirs, hot dogs, or sodas that I carried with me. Passing through the bleachers was like wading through a river packed with piranhas, because kids would try to strip you of your goods. I got paid a 13 percent commission on sales. The stands in the old Yankee Stadium were steep. Hot dogs, with the water tray I carried them in, were heavy. I would get signaled by some guy at the top of the upper deck who would expect me to walk all the way up. For 13 percent of forty cents, i.e., a fraction over a nickel. Never a tip. Did I climb those steps, risking my life, for five cents? You bet I did.

For two summers I worked at the swimming "club" in a LeFrak housing development called Arcadia, in Coney Island. My job was to set up deck chairs and watch over the pool as a lifeguard. It was moms and kids during the week and full families on the weekends. I made friends with some of the young marrieds in their thirties and early forties who used the pool—I sometimes kept it open so they could have cookouts after hours, and they'd give me a ride home if it was after dark. These people had jobs in fields like accounting or sales. Coming from my narrow world, their lifestyles seemed aspirational— a standard of living I might attain if I did really well in life. It was one of my first previews of what it might be like to live in a world beyond East New York. In the coming years, I would continue to assimilate— and often misinterpret—such glimpses.

The following summer I had my eyes opened a bit further. Ron Leiser, a well-liked high school gym teacher at Jefferson, was the head waterfront counselor at an upscale summer camp. This was Raquette Lake Boys Camp in the Adirondacks, where he gave me a job the summer after eleventh grade. I was fifteen (but said I was sixteen), and the oldest campers were my age. I only got paid $100 for the summer, but it got me out of the city and exposed me to new scenery and to people who were different from those I knew. The kids who went to this camp were the children of lawyers, doctors, and businesspeople. They came to camp with miniature TVs, small stereos, and their own tennis rackets and canoe paddles. It was my first experience with kids whose parents had gone to college and who lived in the suburbs in houses with lawns. They also had years of coaching and playing sports and were competent at athletics, whether they were talented or not. I only knew stickball and street games and felt like an alien. You could say that summer left me with a bit of a chip on my shoulder, a prerequisite for a striver.

That chip sometimes activates when people assume that the CEO of Goldman Sachs must have come from a life of privilege. I remember Bill de Blasio, when he was mayor of New York City, convening a breakfast meeting for business leaders at Gracie Mansion. When he finished lecturing us about how ignorant we were about the lives of ordinary people, I raised my hand. *I'm from East New York*, I said, *and my dad worked in the post office. You're from Boston, and your father went to Yale.* We bantered back and forth, good-naturedly, and I challenged him to a competition. *I bet I can name more subway stops in Brooklyn than you can. Name the line*, I said, *and I'll tell you where it goes.* I didn't change his view of capitalism, but de Blasio was a little kinder about me after that.

Some of my childhood friends remember the Linden Houses and Jefferson High School with a nostalgic glow. My own feelings are a mix, a combination of sad and happy memories. I think about everything we missed out on and the obstacles we faced, but also about the way that pushed me to get ahead. When I was growing up, I didn't feel deprived; I felt motivated and curious about people and things outside my bubble. Even today, at a dinner party, I'd rather be seated next to someone I don't already know, for the opportunity to learn something new. Overall, that experience helped to develop my drive and resilience. Being from a place I was in a hurry to leave fueled a restless ambition that has served me well. At the same time, it wasn't the kind of childhood I wanted for my own kids. For them, I wanted the benefits I missed out on—coaching in sports, music lessons, travel to interesting places, intellectual challenges at an early age, and experiences with people from a wide range of backgrounds.

I'm always a bit reluctant to dwell too much on the disadvantages I faced, for a few reasons. Perhaps because I didn't have much exposure to more prosperous families, other than on TV, I didn't feel bad about my situation at the time. And later in life, working for a global company, I got to know people who faced real deprivation, like struggling to survive in and escape from countries torn by conflict and civil war. I grew up with two working parents who were married to each other, a roof over my head, and enough to eat—am I really in a position to complain? When I hear people talk about having to walk three miles to return a library book, uphill in both directions, it can sound like a humblebrag—*look at how much I overcame*. Also, if I spent the first twenty years of my life with less privilege than most Americans, I've spent the subsequent fifty years on the highly fortunate side of the ledger. Once you've joined the 1 percent, it seems like whining to complain about the time before you got there.

Perhaps more important, life has left me with a sense of the advantages that my comparatively disadvantaged childhood gave me. Being an outsider helped foster my street smarts, which I would define as the ability to see myself objectively and apply that same perception to others. I developed a knack for sizing up different kinds of people quickly—not always with perfect accuracy, but faster and more accurately than most. If I could read people, I could figure out how to be useful to them and get them to help me. These reflexes would become a great asset for me in the years ahead. Coming from the projects in East New York, I had more to escape, more to prove, and more to gain than a lot of people I subsequently encountered. Succeeding simply mattered more to me than it did to them. My working-class background also saved me from some of the blind spots that seem to come with growing up in more privileged environments. I don't assume people are stupid just because they aren't educated, or they have a notable accent, or they lack other refinements. I think about where the subway trains go when they leave Manhattan for the outer boroughs, and the lives of the working people who live out near the end of the line. I'm not surprised when someone without polish or academic credentials turns out to be really smart. I'm surprised that other people are surprised.

I'm still close to people from those days. Friends from kindergarten were at my son Alex's wedding. A larger group keeps in touch on the East New York Facebook page. Many of the kids I grew up with lead regular lives, teaching, working for the government, or in the service economy. I still feel comfortable with them because I think the same way they do. I know that a large part of what determined my progression, as well as theirs, was just luck, not greater virtue or brains or talent. Because I'm still that kid from Brooklyn, I still identify with the waiter more than the customer, with the cab driver more than the guy in the back seat.

CHAPTER 2

Getting Out

I know a lot of folks who were probably voted "most likely to succeed" in kindergarten. I wasn't one of them. I hope that as a result, what I gave up in confidence, I made up in resilience.

Growing up, my biggest goal in life was to get out of East New York. I always knew that I would go to college, even though no one in my family had. I got excellent grades in high school and was my class valedictorian, but Jefferson wasn't very competitive. I had good, not great, standardized test scores—nearly perfect in math but mediocre in verbal, which is ironic given how much I talk and how little I add. I thought that getting admitted to a top out-of-town school I could afford was a long shot. But after I attended a college fair at Midwood, another big public high school in a nicer neighborhood, I applied not only to Brooklyn College and SUNY Binghamton but also to several of the Ivies, and got interviews.

My memory of getting an interview at Harvard stands out because it was such a big name, even in Brooklyn. I can still see the stationery of the letter inviting me; it had a watermark of the university crest. I was given the interviewer's name and a time and place to show up. I had tremendous anxiety about not being late—an inheritance from my father that I suffer from to this day and that I've passed on to my son Alex. I'd made the subway journey to a Manhattan destination no more than half a dozen times, including twice to the Radio City Christmas show. I built in so much extra time for every element of the trip—bus to the subway, waiting for the train, transferring, getting lost looking for the building—that I arrived two hours early. I spent the time walking circles around the block until I thought I wouldn't look too stupid going in.

The place turned out to be the Harvard Club, a nineteenth-century McKim, Mead & White building that is one of the grandest interior spaces in New York. I was ushered into a huge hall with portraits of grandees, big-game trophies on the walls that later I learned were Teddy Roosevelt's, and overstuffed leather couches and chairs all around. I didn't know what a "club" was and had never seen anything remotely like it. I didn't think it was the place my interviewer lived, but I thought he probably lived in someplace like it. Sizing up this bow-tied WASP in his grand salon, I had an instinct for how to present myself to impress him. Some Brooklyn—but not *too* Brooklyn. This subconscious calibration, sometimes called code-switching, came to me by instinct. A chameleon doesn't have to think about how to blend in with its surroundings—it just does. Later, when I volunteered as an interviewer, I met my interviewees in a coffee shop.

Yale passed on me—their loss. But then I came home from school one day to find an envelope with the Harvard crest on the living room table where we put the mail. My dad was in the next room.

"You got another college letter," he said.

I dropped my backpack, ran into another room to be alone, and ripped open the envelope, my heart thumping. I'd applied to Harvard almost as a joke, in a moment of either bravado or sheer fantasy. I scanned it quickly, picking out the key words and phrases: *pleased to inform you, accepted, and congratulations*. I read the letter again more carefully, then a third time, just to be sure I hadn't misunderstood. No, it was there in black and white. Harvard wanted me.

When I told my dad, he didn't say anything. Was he thrilled for me? Conflicted that my path would separate me from the family? Reflecting on his own disappointments? I remember his expression as blank, probably because he was feeling all of those things and more, the way that pure white light is what you get when you mix every color at once.

I was not ambivalent. To say this was one of the happiest moments in my life doesn't begin to do it justice. I thought about my dad's monotonous nights in the post office, my mom's fatigue when she kicked her shoes off at the end of the day, my sister's struggle to start her life over with a toddler, and our whole cramped, confined existence—our living room with its mirrored wall and furniture encased in plastic, the cooking smells in the hallway, the triple locks on the door. That world was about to become my past.

Harvard was almost another planet, one of brilliance, privilege, and financial ease. And here it was, offering me a bridge, welcoming me in. But then the anxiety kicked in. Would street smarts get me through? How would I explain to family and friends after I flunked out in a few weeks? My thoughts were a mixture of exhilaration and terror. My life was going to be different in a way it wouldn't have been if I were heading off to one of the SUNY campuses. Harvard was offering a financial aid package that covered full room and board and tuition. As part of the package, I would have to earn money by working during the school term and over the summer, and also take out loans. Even with all that, it would be a stretch.

I didn't know anyone who'd ever gone to an Ivy League school. My mental pictures of college life were clichés from dated movies, like *Where the Boys Are* with George Hamilton and Paula Prentiss. It seemed like a good idea to actually see the place for myself. So my sister generously volunteered to take me. At twenty-five, Jacky had taken on a lot of responsibilities, working, raising her son, and practically coparenting me. At that point she was more than just a sister—she was my supporter, but one whose life was dealing her a different set of cards.

We got a Greyhound bus from Port Authority in Manhattan. As we settled into our seats amid families, students, and regular commuters, I understood that this was, in a sense, a one-way trip. Even though I'd be back in Brooklyn that night, I knew that Harvard would change me in ways that would make it all seem different. It was a long ride, maybe four and a half hours. We left early, ate the sandwiches Jacky had packed for us, and got to Cambridge at midday.

Strolling toward the heart of Harvard Yard, we were greeted by a sight straight out of a postcard—redbrick buildings, ornate iron gates, and sprawling lawns. The campus buzzed with students rushing back and forth, but there wasn't anyone there we knew. We didn't know what anything was, and we had told no one we were coming. In front of the iconic John Harvard statue, we awkwardly posed for photos. I stumbled upon that snapshot recently. There I stand, looking utterly pitiful in a light-brown rain jacket outgrown by one of the kids of my parents' friends. (My idea of new clothes at that point was another batch of hand-me-downs from the Goldbergs.) It was about as breathable as a plastic trash bag.

Soon after our impromptu photo shoot, we turned around and caught the bus home. I remember the ride back as a bit melancholy. At sixteen, my world revolved around me and only me. I didn't think about how Jacky, so much like me, must have felt watching doors swing open for me while her own dreams lay dormant. She should have been off chasing her ambitions, attending college herself. Instead, she found herself navigating single parenthood under her parents' roof, juggling a good-for-nothing ex-husband alongside attempts at dating and clocking hours at a clerical job just to make ends meet. On this particular day, she had taken time off work to accompany me—an act of unwavering support amid her chaotic life. What audacity did I possess to chase after something so far beyond her grasp? My departure for college wouldn't ease her burdens any. If anything, my absence would add another layer to her already heavy load.

My parents wanted to support me, but this was all new to them too. They took me to the Male Shop on Ralph Avenue in Brooklyn, where you got a whole wardrobe—a suit, a sport jacket, a pair of slacks, a raincoat, a shirt, two neckties, and socks for $99. Plus a transistor radio. I have a picture of myself in one of the outfits: a burnt-orange double-breasted jacket with powder-blue pants. My uncle Sheldon pitched in by taking me to the garment factory where he worked to pick out a sport coat of my choice. I selected the most conservative one on the rack, in a blue and maroon check pattern. This was in 1971, with the Vietnam War and the counterculture in the background.

In September, my parents drove me to school in our new (to us) car, a maroon 1967 Buick LeSabre. My dorm room was number 32 in Weld Hall, a nineteenth-century Victorian building in Harvard Yard that had recently been renovated. As if the whole experience weren't foreign and intimidating enough, Harvard listed the prior occupants of dorm rooms and, sure enough, an earlier occupant of Weld number 32 was John F. Kennedy, when he was a freshman. All freshmen lived in the Yard, and the Yard was all men—the integration of the Yard with Radcliffe women happened in the class after mine.

I had two roommates. Greg Marsella was a skinny wrestler who played the guitar. He was from Cranston, Rhode Island, and had gone to Moses Brown, a prep school known for feeding into Brown. Robert Lazarsfeld, whose father was a famous sociologist, had gone to private school in New York City. They were okay guys, but we were from different planets, and we really went to different Harvard Universities at the same time. Everything they did and said contributed to my insecurity—sometimes on purpose. They both signed up for Math 55, a very advanced course, while I took Math 1A, Introduction to Calculus. "Baby math," they called it, somewhat cruelly. It probably didn't help that I was so young for a first-year student—still sixteen when the school year started. This was not because I was any kind of prodigy but because the New York City Department of Education's policies were designed to push kids through overcrowded schools and an overburdened system as quickly as possible.

On the first day after I arrived, three or four of us were walking to the freshman dining hall for lunch, and I blurted out, "Wow, you guys who get to Harvard are really tall!"

"We're not tall," came the response. "You're short."

I was? In Brooklyn, whether because of a healthy ego or because I grew up with dwarfy Jewish kids, I never thought of myself as short.

At Harvard, I was short.

Also completely lost. Everyone else hit the ground running. They seemed to know a code I didn't—what clubs and extracurricular activities to try out for, how the athletic teams worked, how to dress for various occasions. I couldn't even understand a lot of what my classmates were getting involved in. What was the *Lampoon,* anyway? The *Crimson* I understood, but I believed you had to be able to write to be on it. Many of my new classmates had brothers and sisters who were at Harvard or had gone there previously. They all seemed to have come with high school classmates or to have known previous graduates from their high schools. There was definitely no one else there from Jefferson. Roy Geronemus, who became a close friend (and later a top dermatologist in New York), said later that when we met at Harvard, I seemed like the person in our class least likely to succeed.

The private-school kids complained about the dining hall food. I thought the food was unbelievably great—and you could have as much of it as you wanted! After sharing a room with my grandmother, my dorm could have been the White House. At my reunion twenty-five years later, I took my wife, Laura, and our three kids to see what I remembered and had described to them as my beautiful and palatial freshman dorm room, with its wood-burning fireplace and built-in bookshelves. My jaw dropped when I opened the door into a glorified closet.

Working fifteen hours a week putting dirty plates into dishwashers in the dining hall served to differentiate strivers like me even more clearly from the preppy kids whose biggest problem was finding a parking spot for their convertibles. In the years since, quite a few nonscholarship students have written me into their college memories—revisions of personal history that I'm happy to play along with. But the real friends I made that year were from working-class backgrounds parallel to mine. One of the kids in my entryway was David Grizzle, a big guy from Lithonia, Georgia. His dad stacked stone at a quarry. Dave's thick Southern accent and clothes from the sale rack at Sears marked him out as "not from here" just as clearly as mine did me. He came to Harvard on a Greyhound bus with a green footlocker and a tuba. Not surprisingly, we hit it off. My other friends were also mostly from public schools and the first in their families to go to college. We met girls by going to mixers at the Boston women's colleges, not at the Hasty Pudding or the Harvard final clubs.

Naively, I went to an open tryout for the swim team, which was the only extracurricular activity I could relate to. What I didn't understand was that Harvard had a serious, top-notch swimming program. Coach Don Gambril was on his way to being a coach of the US Olympic team in 1972, and all his swimmers were recruited. Several of them made it to the Olympics. My swimming event at Jefferson was distance, so I joined a bunch of kids in a thousand-yard practice race. The whistle blew and we dove in. By the time I finished, the other guys were practically showered and dressed. I toweled off quickly, put my street clothes on over my wet bathing suit, and escaped as quickly as I could.

Next I tried rowing. I hadn't known what "crew" even was, but they sent out letters soliciting participation. Both Grizzle and I decided to try out—he was heavyweight crew, I was lightweight. When I got to the river, the coach pointed to a boat and told us all to get in. I'd never seen a rowing shell before, and I promptly put my foot through the bottom of the fragile hull. "Didn't you see the sign?" the coach yelled at me. "It's printed on the bottom: DO NOT STEP." It was my first week of college, and my first thought was that I couldn't pay for the damage.

A lot of the ordinary behavior on the rowing team shocked me. To keep the sweat out of their eyes, my crewmates made headbands by ripping towels into strips. How could people be so cavalier about destroying school property—and with the coaches watching? Where I came from, you used a towel for approximately forty years. Here people didn't husband everything or feel that they always had to defer gratification. These were more data points in my emerging comprehension of the other half and how it lived.

In hopes of surviving, and because I'd had only the basics in high school, I registered for mostly entry-level courses. My roommates mocked me for taking the biology course for humanities students and not the biology course for future doctors and scientists. The only required course was Freshman Expository Writing, which gave me my first homework assignment. We had to write a 250-word paper to turn in the following week. That is about a single page of double-spaced text, but they might as well have asked me to write *War and Peace*. I remember counting every word, every preposition, over and over. I would later become a fluid writer, but I could not think of 250 words to put into the topic, whatever it was. I spent a week working on it and lost sleep over it, but I got there. I can't even begin to describe the effort and angst I put into that nothing assignment that wasn't even graded. That was typical of the year. I killed myself and got mostly A-minuses.

Desperate to fit in, I went out and spent some of the meager pay from my student job on a Lacoste shirt—crimson, with the alligator logo—and a normal blue blazer that was neither a garish plaid nor double-breasted. With the addition of a blue crewneck sweater from the Harvard Shop, I was outfitted like a fresh graduate of Andover, ready to dazzle everyone at the next college mixer. Not knowing anything and doing my own laundry for the first time, I put the wool sweater in the wash, and it came out of the tumble dryer suitable for Mickey Mouse. It made me sad every time I looked at it, but I kept it anyway. I wasn't paying for another one.

What embarrasses me when I think about it today is not that I was trying to assimilate into this strange, new environment—who doesn't at that age? It's the shame I felt about where I was from. When friends from college visited me back home in Brooklyn, I was mortified about everything. The first thing you saw when you got off the subway at the stop closest to our apartment was the storefront of an exterminator business, its window display dramatizing the death of a big, ugly cockroach—cringe. My father's powder-blue polyester leisure suit with the shirt collar extending almost to the shoulders—cringe. When some of my high school friends came to visit me at Harvard that fall, I remember their overpowering Brooklyn accents, like something from *My Cousin Vinny*—cringe.

I made a point of wearing my alligator shirt at home for the holidays.

I can still hear my pomposity, gushing about my dorm room with the fireplace, rowing crew, and my whole new world, as far as possible from East New York. I proudly told my dad that I'd read Harvard grads earned an average salary of $90,000 a year. My father, who might have been making $15,000, was impressed. Harvard was doing its job of distinguishing me from my parents. When they finally left the Linden Houses in 1972, they were among the last Jewish families to go. They moved to a tiny apartment in Starrett City, an enormous private apartment complex just off the Belt Parkway in Brooklyn, near Jamaica Bay.

Dave Grizzle came home with me over spring break. He'd never stayed in anyone else's home before, let alone a Jewish family's, and was terrified of saying the wrong thing. He was amazed that we had crates of seltzer delivered—just like milk. Dave enjoyed his first taste of gefilte fish and has been fishing for them ever since, without success. He became fast friends with my sister and completely won over my parents, who always asked me about him thereafter. Eventually, they moved to a retirement community west of Fort Lauderdale, which was their dream, though I wish they'd had more time to enjoy sitting around the pool before they passed away.

My new life also created distance from Jacky, who had been so supportive and kind to me. She used to joke when introducing me to someone, "This is my older brother, Lloyd. He used to be my younger brother." While her life was difficult, my sister was in many ways an older twin. Talk about street smarts. You could throw Jacky into any job or situation, and she would figure out how to succeed. At the computer company Wang, she started as a secretary but was such a good communicator and so smart and good with people that she ended up training business clients in using their systems.

With her infectious personality, Jacky made friends everywhere she went. Much later, secretaries and assistants at Goldman Sachs would come up to me to say, "I know your sister from Staten Island" (where she lived with her Italian American second husband) or "I knew your sister in Florida" (where her husband pursued his no-show job with the NYC Transit Authority). She loved jobs where she could be sociable and flirtatious, like working as a blackjack dealer at an Indian casino in Boca Raton. Though she smoked when she was younger—we all did in those days—I'm convinced that the tobacco haze in her workplace led to her lung disease. I tried to get her out of there, and offered to replace her salary, but she liked the social part of the job too much to retire. She died young, at sixty-four.

I GOT THROUGH MY FIRST YEAR AT HARVARD, BUT AT A STEEP COST IN anxiety and insecurity. The result was that in my sophomore year, I blew up. I couldn't maintain the intensity of fear that had driven me as a freshman. I went into an honors major that I wasn't equipped for and didn't enjoy, and my grades suffered. I quit rowing but had to continue working. My new work-study job was caddying books to and from the library for the political scientist Seymour Martin Lipset, a great man I managed to ignore. I know working part time through college is supposed to be character building, but I really couldn't see it at the time, maybe not even now. All the money that I've since given to Harvard and other schools has been for financial aid, with the thought that less privileged students shouldn't have to face the kind of disheartening choice I did, between rowing crew and cleaning crew.

That tailspin lasted my whole second year, fueled by certain friends I would describe as bad influences. I was in a suite in Leverett House, living in a room by myself, and it was lonely. Though finances constrained my excesses, there was plenty of weed and hash around, and I did inhale. My low point academically was getting a C in an undergraduate constitutional law class my sophomore year—not ideal for someone interested in going to law school. In that era of grade inflation, it took an effort to get a C. I had a panic attack and froze during the exam, even though it was open book.

I had classes with great professors and didn't do them justice. My freshman seminar leader and adviser was Martin Peretz, a streetwise outer-borough Jew like me, but one who was wealthy (by marriage), fashionably left-wing, and fabulously well connected. Peretz had supported Eugene McCarthy's presidential campaign in 1968 and at that point was trying to get McCarthy to run again in 1972. I got into his class off the wait list—the story of my life. I wrote one of my better papers for Peretz on the Gulf of Tonkin Resolution and the beginning of the Vietnam War. I remember when I needed a recommendation for social studies, which was an honors major, he handed it to me directly rather than mailing it in. He described me as "a diamond in the rough"—a cliché, but I liked it.

In social studies, I came across the sociological concept of anomie—a feeling of alienation that comes from a gap in social standards or belief systems. It was a fancy term for what I was experiencing on a daily basis but didn't have a way to express. The Brooklyn world I came from and the Havard world I lived in were unbridgeably distant. I was in a small political philosophy seminar with the legendary conservative thinker Harvey Mansfield, who people used to joke knew Machiavelli personally. My main memory of it is straining to stay awake. Osmosis must have worked, though, because I learned and remember the material—including Hobbes and Locke—pretty well. I can still almost visualize the page numbers of certain passages. But while much of what I read stuck, I'm still mad at myself for wasting the opportunity to get to know such an important thinker, or to engage more deeply with the material.

The times—the late Vietnam era—added to the general malaise. I went to sleep every night listening to the chanting in Harvard Yard: *"US OUT OF VIETNAM, HARVARD OUT OF GULF!"* (Gulf being a major oil company that later merged into Chevron.) During one protest, demonstrators ransacked the Center for International Affairs—where Henry Kissinger had been a fellow—and did a lot of damage. The police cleared them out of Harvard Square with tear gas that wafted into the yard. I somewhat regretted arriving at Harvard in 1971, after most of the drama of the antiwar movement was over, so I was grateful for the prestige of being (very mildly) tear-gassed.

Those days were a window of time when the drinking age was lowered to eighteen, on the theory that if you were old enough to be drafted and die in a war, you were old enough to drink. It started to go up again as people realized that old enough to drink also meant old enough to die in a drunk-driving accident. Once I turned eighteen, I was eligible for the draft; I remember watching the lottery on TV with Dave Grizzle in our dorm room. Both of our birthdays translated to high numbers, and we had no risk of being drafted. With Nixon's Vietnamization policy, the demand for young men was quickly going down, and the draft would soon end entirely. But people from my neighborhood didn't have doctors to sign letters attesting to their obscure disabilities, such as bone spurs. My political views were liberal, and I was against the war. But if I'd been drafted, I would have gone.

What weighed on me more heavily than politics was the lack of money. My student loans and work in the dining hall barely filled the gap between my scholarship and tuition plus room and board. At one point, I went into the financial aid office and told them I was flat broke. No big deal—they gave me a form to fill out that was like a P&L statement, with income on one side and expenses on the other. I wrote my expenses generously and my income conservatively, producing a shortfall of $500. Right there, they wrote me a check for $500, no other questions asked. Harvard was my first experience in life of not being nickel-and-dimed. I remain grateful to this day, both for the money and for the lesson about how to give.

During the summer, I made money by working in the Borscht Belt, at the Brickman Hotel in the Catskills. They liked having kids from the Ivy League, in part because school started so much later for us—mid-September instead of before Labor Day for state schools. At night, I worked as a waiter in the bar. By day I was a lifeguard. One afternoon, the tummler who was entertaining the guests by the pool decided to incorporate me into his act. While he sat at the end of the high diving board, I was supposed to try to grab him but instead jump over him into the water. The diving board has gotten higher and higher in my memory. In reality, it might have only been twelve feet, but just climbing up the ladder was traumatic for me. The leap into the water didn't kill me, but it sure didn't cure my fear of heights.

Back at Harvard, I was eventually helped to regain positive momentum by Dave Grizzle and another friend who had lived across the hall from me freshman year. Both of them were religious Christians. They didn't take drugs and they were serious about their studies and lives. Junior year, they invited me into their roommate group, which meant switching houses, from Leverett to Winthrop House—something that was hardly ever done. I had enough residual sense to be grateful for the invitation and to do it. There were three bedrooms for four people, so we were supposed to alternate semesters sharing the room with a bunk bed. I started out with one of the single bedrooms. True to my *Gone With the Wind* pledge to never share a bedroom again, I managed to avoid taking a turn in the double.

My new roommates came from backgrounds very different from mine, but in a way comparable. Mark Campisano was from a Catholic family in Walpole, Massachusetts, famous for being the site of the state's maximum-security prison. He went on to become a Marshall Scholar, an editor on *The Yale Law Journal*, and a clerk for Supreme Court justice William Brennan. Grizzle was head of photography for the yearbook and graduated magna cum laude. He took one of the few pictures of me that I have from those days. I'm sitting in a window, pretending to read a book. After law school, he went into the aviation industry, becoming a senior executive at Continental Airlines, and later, chief operating officer of the FAA.

Our fourth roommate, Charlie Overfelt, was also religious but from a wealthy family in Kansas City—one of his grandfathers was a minister. A graduate of St. George's School near Newport, Rhode Island, he seemed to have a new pair of Adidas every week and bought a seventy-gallon aquarium for our room. I was fascinated by the discus fish he bought, both because they seemed gratuitously expensive and because they would jump out of the water when you fed them. Dave remembers being woken up one night by my shouting that one of the fish had jumped clear out of the tank and that it wasn't my fault. Like a lot of prep school kids, Charlie seemed to have peaked early. He couldn't get the hang of anything, kept taking classes that were just beyond his abilities, and dropped out of sports because the practices were too hard for him. He was a wonderful person who could never find his place. He later borrowed money he couldn't pay back for a business he started in Kansas City, and ten years after graduation his life ended in a federal prison, where he was serving a sentence for kiting checks.

The rest of my college career was not spectacular but pretty good. Senior year, the school reminded me that there was a language requirement for graduation. I learned how to introduce myself and ask directions in four languages before eventually passing basic French. I worked on a senior thesis about the rise of professionalism through guilds and voluntary associations in nineteenth-century America. I was excited about the topic, but my adviser, Abigail Thernstrom, a political scientist, didn't show much interest or monitor my progress. I missed submitting it in time to complete the requirements for the honors Social Studies major. And if I didn't hand it in soon, I wasn't going to graduate at all.

Dave and his girlfriend, now his spouse of fifty years, Anne Fletcher, formed an assembly line to type it up as we raced against the deadline for me to qualify for a Harvard diploma. They alternated three-hour shifts while I furiously hand-wrote the final pages. Saved again by the God Squad. While the paper may have been good, I'm not sure any professor ever read it. Forty years later, Thernstrom was still complaining that I'd blown off the assignment, mentioning it in an interview she gave to *The Atlantic*. I graduated in the default major of General Studies, exiting with honors—along with 93 percent of my class.

When I reflect on my college years, I realize how much I took away from them that was valuable—a love of history, an engagement with current events, and friendships that have lasted my whole life. I learned to write fluently and developed my confidence. But I'm disappointed that I didn't take fuller advantage of the opportunity. I was too young, too insecure, and so focused on survival that I didn't manage to have a breakthrough intellectual experience or feel the stirrings of a lifelong intellectual pursuit. Nor did I have a deep relationship with a mentor or professor. The closest I came to that was getting to know William Schneider, whose course on voter behavior I took senior year. Bill, just ten years older than me, was a public-school kid from Portsmouth, Virginia, who got shipped north when his high school closed for a year in protest over the racial integration required by the *Brown v. Board of Education* decision. He was a gracious and supportive teacher, and we kept in touch for a while after I graduated. For many years he was a fixture of political analysis on CNN, where he always stood out for his fair-mindedness and geniality.

Even an imperfect liberal arts education left me with an appreciation of its value. I strongly disagree with the technology investor Peter Thiel, who has offered cash grants to budding entrepreneurs if they opt out of college and found start-up companies instead. To succeed in a career, you have to know the technical minutiae of your field, of course. But you also need to be a complete person—the kind of person other people want to engage with. Your undergraduate years are your best opportunity to make yourself uncomfortable in a way that can help make you more curious and interesting. If further justification is needed, general knowledge of science, history, and culture is good for almost any career. You can get whatever specialized training you need once you're finished with college, on the job.

As grateful as I am to Harvard for all it made possible for me, I survived it more than I enjoyed it and would never have the validation of feeling "of it," as opposed to someone who made his way through. When asked, I tell people that, depending on the kid, Harvard may or may not be the best place to go, but for the doors it opens, it is always the best place to have gone. And the "going" to college is for only four years, while the "have gone" is for decades. Years later, my kids got to experience Harvard College the way I didn't. When he was at Harvard, my oldest son, Alex, told me that his classmates at the Fly Club, where he was a member, were inviting parents to come talk about their different careers. They'd love to hear from the CEO of Goldman Sachs.

I'd be happy to do it, I said, but would prefer to speak at his dorm, Adams House, so that kids who weren't in the club—and maybe couldn't afford to be in the club—could attend too. I'd never even set foot in a final club when I was at Harvard. I was happy that Alex found so many close friends there, but I wasn't comfortable participating in an event that would be exclusive to more privileged kids. It was the Fly Club or nothing, so I passed.

While I've become a big donor and an honored alum, one who gets invitations to speak at classes or events, I still remain something of an alien at Harvard in my own mind. I love the place but am not sure it fully reciprocates. I'm welcome but don't fully belong. I feel the same way when I walk into certain exclusive clubs today. In my mind, I'm still wearing that alligator shirt, wondering whether it's working.

CHAPTER 3

Glimpses Beyond

For a long time, I thought of myself as "disadvantaged" because of my background. But after Harvard College and Harvard Law and a job at a prestigious law firm, I had to face the fact that I was by then in the upper range of "advantaged."

While waiting to hear about my applications to college, I was hopeful, but I wasn't nervous. I had no expectations. I really had no idea how much was at stake for me. While waiting to hear about my applications to law school, by contrast, I was very nervous and ran to the mailbox every morning to check. By that time, I was no longer naive about the importance of getting into a top law school. Once again, Yale decided that it could carry on without me. The hell with them! I got into Harvard, which placed a finger on the scale in evaluating candidates from the college. Of around 560 students in my law school class, nearly 100 had been Harvard undergraduates. It was a rolling admissions process, and I think I was one of the last to make it in, well after my roommate Dave Grizzle. Once again, I'd cleared the bar, barely.

I started law school in September 1975, when I was just twenty. In addition to being one of the youngest members of the class, I was still pretty insecure in those days. I imagine that Harvard Law would have been an intimidating place for even the most self-assured of college graduates. The movie *The Paper Chase* had come out a couple of years earlier, in 1973. It was about the dynamic between a young Harvard Law student and the scowling, old-school Professor Kingsfield, who interrogates his students like hostile witnesses. In class, Kingsfield flips a dime to a student who stammers his way through a series of questions. "Call your mother and tell her there is serious doubt about your becoming a lawyer," he says.

Now I don't know if Kingsfield, as portrayed by John Houseman, was always the archetype of Harvard Law professors. But once the movie became popular, he turned into the role model for many of them, in the same way that the fictional characters in *The Godfather* influenced a generation of real mobsters. I got there just in time for this exercise in professional vanity and intimidation. Employing the so-called Socratic method, professors would call on students at random to question them about the day's material. If you hadn't done the work and you got called on, they'd embarrass you in front of your whole section of 140 students. If you weren't prepared one day, you had the option of sitting in the back row. But if you back-benched too frequently, they'd kill you for that.

If you'd asked me then, I probably would have said that my goal was to get decent grades, get a good job at a law firm, and after that, who knows. The students I hung out with mostly hated law school. Business school is about networking; law school is about grinding. MBA programs have always seemed fundamentally contentless to me, finishing schools for the corporate world. But a law degree, as hard as the work is, has real content and value as training for business. It grounds you in an understanding of basic principles and of how rules evolve to accommodate social and technological change. Studying law inculcates habits of care and precision. And it makes you appreciate the fundamental need for compromise, because so many of the problems you study involve arbitrating between competing values, not right versus wrong.

I didn't appreciate the gratuitous brutality of the first year of law school, well covered in the book *One L*, written by Scott Turow, a fellow member of my Harvard Law class of 1978. But I actually liked the content, which was a feast for someone who loves history. The first year focuses on common law, which embeds social history much in the way the human genome includes strands of DNA from the precursors to *Homo sapiens*. The feudal origins of today's property laws are evident in *quiet enjoyment, rule against perpetuities, deed of seisin,* and so on. Studying contracts, torts, and criminal law, you come to understand their pragmatic evolution from those medieval roots. I learned to appreciate the way that the common law continually evolved over time in response to changing societal needs and pressures. If you were to apply strict liability to everything, we never would have had railroads or automobiles, or much else. So courts developed doctrines like contributory negligence and comparative negligence that made technological progress legally possible.

Second- and third-year courses, on the other hand, are mostly about legislatively drafted laws, reflecting the political trade-offs of a particular moment. Outcomes are not always logical or elegant; you just have to follow the compromise rules of the legislation. I liked those courses less. But I read fast, grasped matters quickly, and, unlike some of the hapless students in *The Paper Chase*, had the mental flexibility to apply what I learned to various hypothetical scenarios. I got mostly A-minuses and B-pluses, not quite law review material, but good enough. After four years crossing Harvard Yard, I knew my way around, and didn't feel anything like the anomie and disorientation of my undergraduate years. I was more voluble, and classmates might have described me as a personality—cynical and quick with a wisecrack. But as in college, I felt I never quite got the rhythm until the end. If I could go back, I'd work harder to get to know professors and to take advantage of the opportunities outside class.

It took effort to develop a social life at law school, mostly because a lot of the people there were, like me, straight from college and narrowly focused on academics. I lived in Story Hall, a featureless dormitory designed by the Bauhaus architect Walter Gropius, with 120 square feet to call my own. My room was off a narrow passageway that served as the hallway to the shared bathroom as well as the main thoroughfare for residents coming and going. It felt a little like bunking in a train station.

The first week, I took my initiative and law books over to Wellesley College, where in those carefree days anyone could walk in and take a seat in the library. My motivation was obvious. After a couple of failed attempts—*Would you like a cup of coffee?*—I met Susie, my first serious girlfriend, a nice Jewish girl from Kansas City. Who knew there were Jews in Kansas City? While she was three years younger than me, Susie was more worldly than I was, having attended private school and studied piano seriously.

So that we could be together that summer, I got out the Martindale-Hubble directory and sent letters to thirty-five law firms in and around Kansas City. Charles Egan, who had been a lawyer to the Hall family, founders of Hallmark Cards, and was now Hallmark's general counsel, wrote back and offered me a job. The summer associate work that year was going through file cabinets looking for documents responsive to a discovery request in a long-forgotten Federal Trade Commission inquiry. But if the legal work at a greeting card company was a little boring, the people there were incredibly nice to me. When there were some documents that needed to be sent to New York, they offered to let me deliver them in person so I could see the bicentennial Fourth of July weekend—the tall ships in New York Harbor and the fireworks.

Susie ended up taking a summer music course at Harvard, and I didn't see all that much of her in Kansas City. I did spend time with her family, who were extremely kind. I enjoyed taking her little brother to the movies. Her mother saw the need and took me shopping for some better clothes. Her father was a lawyer, and their lifestyle was again at the outer limit of the success I could imagine. I'd never lived in the suburbs or even been to a country club like the one they belonged to. What was commonplace for them seemed exotic to me. Alas, my relationship with Susie didn't work out after I returned to Cambridge.

She ended up marrying a very nice guy, a Jewish doctor. Her mother must have been thrilled.

My second year, I lived off campus in a house in working-class Somerville and, toward the end of it, ended up getting together with Debbie, one of my housemates. Debbie was a fellow New Yorker, albeit from a completely different New York from the one where I grew up. I remember driving from Cambridge to New York City and dropping her off at her parents' place on Park Avenue on my way to Brooklyn. She asked me up to meet her folks, and when the doorman asked Debbie which floor of the duplex she wanted the elevator to go to, I was momentarily baffled. I didn't know apartments could have two floors.

They invited me to stay for dinner. We were served by a cook and a maid, and when we were ready to eat, Debbie's mother rang a little bell. The first course looked like the top of a pineapple, and I picked off leaves and started eating with everyone else. I chewed and chewed and wasn't getting anywhere. Everyone was looking at me. It turns out I was trying to chew and swallow the leaves of an artichoke, which I had never seen before. Eventually I was given some guidance as to what on my plate was and wasn't edible, and I got through the meal. But my sense of being an urban hick was reinforced. I could tell her parents didn't think I was good enough for Debbie—and they were probably right. They kept asking me to do things they knew were outside my comfort zone, like opening a bottle of champagne. When the cork shot out of the bottle, I almost lost an eye, to everyone else's amusement.

Another time at her home, at a fancy reception attended by Mayor Abe Beame and some prominent people from Wall Street firms like Lazard Frères, we were in the kitchen and Debbie reached for something on a tray of hors d'oeuvres. "Debbie, don't eat that—it's raw!" I said, slapping it out of her hand. My introduction to steak tartare.

Debbie's family was, in truth, incredibly nice to me. I stayed with them most of that summer, while I was working for Proskauer Rose, a firm with a specialty in labor law. That was the summer of the Son of Sam serial killer, and beyond the walls of their co-op, it was a grim, scary time in New York City. The news was a steady drumbeat of misery and chaos about a city overwhelmed by rats, crime, fiscal insolvency, and fear. A few typical headlines:

> POWER FAILURE BLACKS OUT NEW YORK;
> THOUSANDS TRAPPED IN THE SUBWAYS;
> LOOTERS AND VANDALS HIT SOME AREAS

> 100,000 LEAVE NEW YORK OFFICES
> AS BOMB THREATS DISRUPT CITY;
> BLASTS KILL ONE AND HURT SEVEN

> HOBO COLONY LIVES MOLE-LIKE IN AN
> INFERNO OF PIPES UNDER PARK AVENUE

And that was *The New York Times*. It's hard to imagine now, but you didn't stroll freely around the Upper West Side. You avoided side streets and tried to walk on blocks where there were doormen. Central Park was a no-go zone.

Back at Harvard Law School for my final year, I took a lot of tax courses. I don't know what I was thinking. Tax is a hard, complex, intricate pursuit. It has lots of rules, that, because of the way they evolved, are not always logical. The practice of tax law doesn't rely heavily on the personality of the practitioner. Among a team of corporate lawyers, the tax lawyer structures transactions in the way a structural engineer determines whether a building as designed will stand. Unlike the architect and builder, you hear about the structural engineer only if something goes very wrong. Yet the skills are necessary for the overall project.

Actually, I do know what I was thinking in going into tax law. I was thinking about getting a well-paying job. When I graduated, I'd be only twenty-three, and I figured I'd get big-firm experience, earn a good income, pay back my student loans, and after a few years be qualified and ready to do something else if I wanted to. Tax law was an elite practice and a very marketable skill. There was a tranche of the class that pursued clerkships. I wasn't Supreme Court material, but I might have gotten a lower court. I didn't pursue one, however, and I wasn't going to do public interest work or work for a federal agency either. My student loans were payable beginning nine months after I graduated.

So I applied to the tax departments of a few of the large New York firms. The interviewing process is always strange, but this was the 1970s, when everyone wore ripped jeans to class but put on suits for the on-campus interviews. (I imagine now you can wear ripped jeans to both.) One interview I won't forget was with a snooty Davis Polk partner who, right off the bat, asked me what my father did for a living. They didn't make me an offer.

There was still a bifurcation in those days, even among prestigious law firms, between the white-shoe establishments like Davis Polk and younger Jewish, or "ethnic," firms. You would find a few Jews at those fancy New York firms in the 1960s, but they were Jackie Robinsons—notable for being extraordinary, at least until the 1980s. The real test of openness isn't when the member of a minority group can break through. It's when someone from a minority only has to be marginally better than others, not soar above and beyond, to get a job.

I did get offers from a few good firms, including Paul, Weiss (a lot of Jews) and Donovan, Leisure (a lot of Irish Catholics). Paul, Weiss was the most prestigious of the firms that would take me, so in the spring of my final year at law school, I accepted a job in their tax department. A month or so later, before I started, I got a call from the head of the tax department, Alfred Youngwood, who matter-of-factly advised me that they had overhired and were transferring me to their corporate department. So much for all those tax courses in law school. Though startled, I had the presence of mind to ask how many new tax associates they had hired.

"Five," he said.

"How many openings did you have in tax?"

"Four," he said.

"Let me get this straight. I am fifth on your list of four?"

"Well, we don't see it that way..."

There was no other way to see it, so I said that under the circumstances, I couldn't accept the job. I had some pride. Without delay, I got on the phone to Donovan, Leisure and asked if their offer was still good. It was.

Youngwood, who ranked me last of five at Paul, Weiss, didn't do badly either. He eventually moved up to become head of the firm—his brilliance went even beyond his astute assessment of my potential as a tax lawyer. Over the years we have run into each other. He remembers the story the way I do, and we always laugh about it.

Looking back on law school, I can see that at that stage, I was still holding myself back—not aiming for the law review or a clerkship, or pursuing a more exciting legal specialty. Why was I underestimating my ability, underperforming my smarts? I think the truth is that coming from where I did, I still felt like an impostor. There was that chip on my shoulder, always looking for someone to knock it off. In certain rooms I felt, and still feel, illegitimate. Other people are the real grown-ups—I'm not. As I'm writing this, I'm waiting for a repairman to come to fix our broken ice maker. The ice cubes are coming out small and wet, because the machine is overheating, freezing and melting the ice at the same time. As I prepared to enter the working world, I was experiencing the first flush of success at what I was doing—and throwing off a lot of heat in the process.

CHAPTER 4

Lawyer, Briefly

I liked tax law because it was intricate and complicated. Then I started to hate it because it was intricate and complicated.

fter my job was settled, I still had to take the bar exam, as did my girlfriend, Debbie. If law school was about learning how to think like a lawyer, and where tests were open book, the bar was more about memorizing arcane rules that would spill out of your brain the moment you shook your head after the exam.

While waiting for our results, we rewarded ourselves with a trip to Europe. It was my first time out of the country and probably Debbie's hundredth. In a concession to my impecunious circumstances, we bought seats on the cheapest flight to an overseas destination we could find. Thanks to airline deregulation and Freddie Laker, that was London—around $100 for a standby ticket. You had to be in line at the airport at 4:30 a.m. to have a chance of getting a seat. Once we got overseas, we stayed in youth hostels and avoided anywhere fancy. After some days in London, we found a cheap flight to Madrid. I learned to drive stick shift by trial and error in a rental car on the way to Andalusia. You never quite forget that feeling of stopping at a traffic light and rolling backward down the hill. Eventually, I got the hang of it. From Spain we caught a ferry to Tangier. My main memory of Morocco is spending two hours haggling over a rug for my apartment.

Like most exotic souvenirs, it didn't look so good when I unrolled it at home.

Tax wasn't the most important part of Donovan, Leisure, which was predominantly a corporate litigation firm. No matter, I had pretty interesting work and a lot of responsibility for my level. I was routed into tax litigation and assigned to work on a series of tax refund claims filed by record companies for the investment tax credit. In those days, in order to spur investment, a corporate taxpayer was allowed a 10 percent tax credit for investing in tangible property—equipment used in its manufacturing processes and sales in the US. The tax credit did not apply to intangible property like intellectual rights, except that in calculating the cost of qualifying tangible property against which the credit could be taken, associated intangible costs could be included. So if the purchase of a tool or die included the cost of a license or patent, those costs could be included for the credit.

In those days before digital music, original sound recordings were embedded in metallic disks called "mothers," which were used to stamp polyurethane into the "LPs" that those over a certain age used to play on their "stereos." Our record company clients argued that those stamps or mothers were tangible property eligible for the credit. Also, they argued that the cost basis for those mothers should include not only the physical materials they were made from but also the costs paid to recording artists for the creation of the music imprinted on the mothers, i.e., the royalties that would be paid on record sales. The position of the IRS was that the mothers were not really like a tool or die, and that even if they were, the royalties were intangible, separate from the mothers, and ineligible for the credit. It was a long litigation with a lot at stake. The material cost of the mothers was minimal, but the royalties paid were huge. The size of the potential refund for any one of the record companies was in the several tens of millions—in 1970s dollars.

Our clients included Capitol Records, MCA, Disney, and PolyGram. Although the litigation was occurring in the late seventies and early eighties, the tax years at issue and the years the recordings had been made were the sixties and early seventies. The case was laborious, in part because, while cost information was available, it was not kept in a usable form. These were prespreadsheet days, or at least pre–my use of spreadsheets. Outside it was 1979, but at my desk it was 1967. I was collecting scraps of information to reconstruct the costs of Beach Boys recordings. It didn't matter what was going on in the real world or what was written in the daily newspapers. Current events were irrelevant to the litigation at hand. All of the facts had already happened, and I had to organize and work within those stale facts. There was law to fight over too: What was the correct interpretation of the investment tax credit rules in the Internal Revenue Code? I researched and wrote a large part of the briefs. The legal problem was even more complicated, because there are three different courts that adjudicate tax claims—Tax Court, the Court of Claims, and federal district court. We pursued most of our case in a California district court because it looked like the most promising audience for our case. In law, that's known as forum shopping.

My apartment was in New York City, but our clients, the jurisdiction, and the relevant files were all in Los Angeles. So the firm rented an apartment and a bright-red Ford Mustang for me in LA. For two years I mostly lived there, shuttling back to New York City every few weeks on a 747 jumbo jet, the one with the upstairs bubble lounge. On the one hand, it was heady stuff for a twenty-five-year-old associate. Being involved in big-money cases was exhilarating. On the other hand, it was tough and lonely putting in sixteen-hour days in a city where I had few friends apart from my coworkers. My social life was mostly after-work dinners in Chinatown, near the firm's downtown office, with my colleague Greg Ho. My apartment was in Westwood, not far from the UCLA campus. My neighbors were students and other young people trying to make it in LA's principal industry, film. Even on weekends, I would leave my apartment for the office, stepping around young women lounging by the pool in bikinis. If they noticed me at all, they must have thought, *Who's the nerd?*

My boss, John Baity, was a young but prominent partner in the firm, a natural leader, and an important figure in my professional evolution. We were very different people, but he took an interest in me, and I was fascinated by him. John, whose father was a director of Standard Oil of Indiana, dressed elegantly and drove a Mercedes 300D sedan. I remember the car because he once gave me a lift but asked me to drop him off and park it myself because we were late for a client meeting in Beverly Hills. I was terrified that I would scratch it on the way into the garage. Later on, he divorced his wife and dated a fellow law associate of mine at the firm. They've now been married for forty years.

This was the first job where I had to wear a suit and tie, and John took me aside to tell me that I needed collar stays to keep my shirt collars from popping out. This was the kind of stuff my dad would have taught me, except that he never went to work in a suit and tie and didn't know it himself. The advice kept coming. *I'm not trying to spend your money*, John said, *but instead of those polyester ties, you should go buy an Hermès tie, and then, when you can afford it, buy a few more.* John took me along to lunches and dinners at upscale restaurants and sometimes to clubs that were restricted and that even today I might not be able to join. I had a negative reaction to some of it, but I learned a lot and appreciated his investment in me. That feeling of being somewhere you don't quite belong can be an advantage. Hyperconscious of how others saw me, I became more empathetic about the sensitivities and vulnerabilities of other people. John, who was even shorter than me, must have been insecure too, because he reveled in those memberships in clubs that he knew his guests couldn't join—and he knew his guests knew.

Thinking back on my time as a law associate also reminds me just how much digital technology has changed a profession like law—and makes me think about how much more AI will surely change it in the future. For a young associate, a huge part of the job was Shepardizing—reviewing volumes of cases and published supplements to see whether and how courts around the country had commented on precedents we were relying on. What part of a case had courts overruled? What had they criticized? Finding the citations was laborious and could take days and days in a law library. Today, you use a database like

LexisNexis or Westlaw and gather all the relevant references in seconds. Back then, legal drafts had to be typed and retyped, proofread and proofread again and again. Printing houses entertained law associates with platters of shrimp and crab claws to cultivate their valuable business. At the one we used for typesetting our briefs in LA, there were pinball machines and video games so that we could amuse ourselves while waiting for the next round of page proofs. Word processing put an end to all that.

I worked on that tax case for two years. We won and garnered large judgments for our clients. I liked the teamwork and the combativeness of litigation. But there was a lot of process and drudgery and arcane arguments about how money should be allocated from events that had happened years before. The technology around recording had already changed so that records were no longer stamped by mothers. Music was by then being transferred digitally. The law was also changing. First Congress clarified it to make clear how much of a record's costs were eligible for the investment tax credit, and eventually the investment tax credit provision was deleted entirely. So while the fight over tax refunds was important to the parties involved, there was no continuing relevance. The cases I worked on were worth a lot of money to our clients, but they had no real impact on their business, or anything else, going forward.

It all brought me back to thinking about my dad's job at the post office, which could have been automated way earlier. Though the stakes were higher, I had the same feeling of irrelevance and futility.

THE RECORDING INDUSTRY CASES OVER, I MOVED BACK TO NEW YORK and settled into work at Donovan, Leisure's offices at 30 Rockefeller Plaza. It was 1981 and the city was not in great shape, still reeling from its debt default a few years earlier. It was suffering from dangerous streets, an infestation of drugs, poor services, and a declining population. But it was still very much the business and finance capital of the country. So while the top law firms did well, rents in Manhattan were surprisingly affordable. Even as a junior associate, I could afford a one-bedroom apartment in a doorman building in the very nice neighborhood of Murray Hill, just off Park Avenue.

At the firm's office at 30 Rock, I shared my space with another tax associate, Emily Sherman. In close quarters we got to know a lot about each other. Emily was dating another law associate, whom she would soon marry. She offered to set me up with dates. My relationship with Debbie hadn't survived my moving to LA while she remained in New York, clerking for a judge. She ended up marrying a fellow law clerk in the same office, a very nice Jewish fellow. Her mother too must have been very happy.

My LA relationships also didn't survive my move back to New York City, so I appreciated Emily's help. Ever the good lawyer, she was systematic and thorough. We flipped through her Rolodex looking for possibilities, and she made calls with me sitting there. For those under fifty, a Rolodex is a physical card file of contacts. My last one sits gathering dust next to my slide rule. While Rolodexes existed, cell phones did not, and for the first few calls we made, there was no answer at the office or home numbers. We made it all the way to *J* before finding life. Laura Jacobs.

Laura was too stunned by the effrontery to turn down the opportunity, and we had our first date later in the week at a Chinese restaurant. It remains one of her favorite stories. When she got up to use the bathroom, I ordered for both of us—and I do tend to order a lot of food. When she got back to the table, the food didn't come and didn't come. Finally, we asked the waiter where it was. They were waiting for the other guests they assumed must be joining us. Well, here we are, more than forty years, three kids, four grandkids, and decades of my overeating later.

Laura had been Emily's roommate at Georgetown Law School. Her childhood involved obstacles different from the ones I faced, but she has a similar resilience bred by adversity. Her father, Norman Jacobs, was a left-wing academic and intellectual who edited a journal for the Foreign Policy Association. His proudest moment was being called before Joe McCarthy's House Un-American Activities Committee. Laura's mother died when she was just six years old, and her father remarried a Frenchwoman who didn't show much warmth to her stepchildren—Laura and her two brothers, who were eight and six years older. While a bit better off than my family, they lived in a small apartment in the Bronx and weren't quite comfortable either. The family car was a VW Beetle. At Fieldston, a tony private school that accepted Laura and her brothers on scholarship, mean girls left notes in her locker mocking her for having only five outfits, one for each day of the week, and the wrong style at that. Her stepmother was strict in a European way and not very sympathetic. Laura would later make up for her lack of maternal attention by lavishing it on our kids.

Laura went through Barnard on student loans. She graduated from law school a year behind me and was an associate at a different firm, Phillips, Nizer, Benjamin, Krim & Ballon. (Nizer was the legendary First Amendment and celebrity lawyer Louis Nizer, who represented clients like Muhammad Ali and Elizabeth Taylor.) For two overworked associates at New York law firms, dating was organized around our time constraints. We'd leave our respective offices around dinnertime, meet at a restaurant (at firm expense up to $15 or $20), and then return to one or the other's law firm library, where we'd both work till midnight or so. Romantic, huh?

I'd like to say that I got down on one knee and proposed. What actually happened was that it was still brutally hot in September, and Laura's apartment in the Village, unlike mine, had air-conditioning. After I'd taken advantage of it for some time, she laid down the law. No more free air-conditioning without a ring. Not that I had any doubts. Laura and I were in love and ready to sign up as life partners. She had abundant smarts and common sense. Thanks to her, I now had a real life outside work—plans to meet other couples for dinner, weekend excursions to FDR's home in Hyde Park and the like. In addition to being a force for stability, she shared a lot of my interests and appreciated my sense of humor. Some of my happiest memories of that time are the mornings we would wake up at her place and take the

Sixth Avenue bus to work together, Laura dressed in her 1980s-era power suit and pussy-bow blouse, like Melanie Griffith in *Working Girl*. I would kiss her and hop off at Rockefeller Center. Her law office was two stops farther uptown.

MY JOB, HOWEVER, WAS BECOMING LESS AND LESS FUN. I WAS WELL liked and made plenty of friends at the firm. And I was successful, judged by my work for the record companies and my close relationship with John Baity. But when I got back after spending two years litigating tax cases in LA, it was put to me that if I was to be promoted at the firm, I would have to make it in either the tax department or the litigation department. There was no "tax litigation" department. I chose the tax route, and for a year I plumbed the depths of the tax code and engaged only with people who were doing the same. Tax law was hard, complicated, and very technical. It meant knowing all the rules and arguing over their application with great precision. Slight variations in a corporate structure with no economic significance could result in dramatically different tax outcomes.

Soon enough, I came to hate it. That wouldn't have deterred me, as I had plenty of capacity for pain. What stopped me was the realization that I'd never be as good as the other tax associates I was working with, like my brilliant friend Tim O'Neill, who was hired at Donovan, Leisure a year or two after me and somehow knew as much about tax law as the senior partners. Tim actually liked the content! Every month, in those preinternet days, a collection of recently decided tax cases from all over the country would be distributed to law firms by mail. I dreaded the arrival of these "advance sheets" because I would be expected to pick out relevant cases and read and understand them. Meanwhile, my colleagues—Tim and the other born tax lawyers—were waiting breathlessly by their mailboxes.

I was having a prelife crisis, looking down the road toward a life that would be comfortable, boring, and to me not that meaningful. I remember Truman Bidwell, a distinguished partner at Donovan,

Leisure, taking me out to dinner and afterward asking me if I minded briefly stopping by a big, fancy social event for New York City private-school kids. He had to deliver a message to his daughter, who was attending. Laura had gone to Fieldston, so I didn't think I was a complete bumpkin about that world. But my jaw must have been hanging open at the sight of so many well-dressed teenagers, because Truman said to me, "I know this is foreign to you. But it won't be foreign to your kids."

Earning $60,000 a year in my twenties did require a shift in mentality. Growing up, we were takers, not givers. I remember the first time I was asked to contribute to a scholarship fund at Harvard, my attitude was *I get scholarships; I don't give scholarships.* But now, as a young lawyer at a New York firm, I was starting to be in a different position. I remember saying to Dave Grizzle, who was also doing well as an associate at Dewey, Ballantine, "If this keeps up, we're going to have to start giving things away instead of getting them."

And then one weekend, Laura and I went to a law firm party at the Long Island house of one of the partners she worked for. Her senior colleagues were not that interesting. I remember thinking that if you became a partner in a big law firm, this was the kind of life you would have. It seemed so horrible and bourgeois to me. I just thought, *I can't aspire to this—it looks deadly.*

I kept thinking about the end of the movie *The Heartbreak Kid*, one of the great existential comedies of the 1970s. The lead character, a newlywed sporting goods salesman played by Charles Grodin, neglects his wife on their honeymoon in Miami while chasing after the dazzling young Cybill Shepherd. Overcoming all obstacles, he leaves his new wife and marries Shepherd. In the last scene, at the wedding reception, he's sitting by himself, perplexed. To me, the look on his face said, *I got what I wanted. But now that I have it, what was the point?*

CHAPTER 5

Gold Mettle

After three years of law school and four-plus years of practice, I called a career mulligan. It was such a bold move, I barely recognized myself.

From the first day of work at a big law firm, you start hearing from headhunters, who get paid to move young people from one job to another. They serve a useful job market "liquidity" purpose, to be sure. But their clients are the employers, not the employees, and they get paid for churning people. When I ran a company that was a target, I thought headhunters were parasitic and not serving the best interests of the young professionals. But when I was a young professional myself, I found the engagement flattering. It's always nice to be told how great and in demand you are, sincerity optional.

Around three or four years out of law school, the calls from headhunters start to come in faster. It's a sweet spot: You are a bit trained up but still relatively cheap and, in your twenties, still flexible with respect to your career path. Many in my young associate cohort were interviewing around, and several people I knew quit, usually to go to law firms that were indistinguishable from the ones they were leaving. A few bold kids went to consulting firms or to Wall Street firms to become investment bankers.

I knew nothing about Wall Street. Nothing. I didn't invest, I hadn't taken finance courses, I didn't read *The Wall Street Journal*. My practice at Donovan, Leisure didn't touch finance, except for some mind-numbing reviews of boilerplate for lease-financing transactions, whose economics I wasn't asked to understand or review. Frankly, I didn't know what investment banks did. I wasn't qualified for business other than by being a bright, ambitious kid, and there were a lot of us around. A few big Wall Street firms hired from law firms for entry-level jobs, which was shrewd. In a pool of fourth-year law associates, you got kids who were smart, a bit older than fresh graduates, and used to having very little life outside work. Law firm associate work was so joyless and oppressive, in fact, that almost anything else would be an uptick.

Naturally, I responded to the headhunters who called me. But after a while, realizing that a move to another tax department at another firm was pointless, I told the callers I would be open only to nonlaw jobs for the time being. The calls slowed but didn't stop completely. I applied and got interviews at the investing banking departments of several big Wall Street firms. I remember Morgan Stanley, Dean Witter (before it merged into Morgan Stanley), and Goldman Sachs. At Goldman, I never made it past the IIR gatekeepers. After eventually getting into Goldman through the back door, I avoided the people who had dinged me. Later, as I rose in the firm, they avoided me.

My rejection by Wall Street was disheartening but, in hindsight, understandable. I didn't know anything about the businesses I was trying to join and, more indicting, I made no effort to learn enough in advance of the interviews to make a better impression. I wasn't lazy, just stupid about the whole thing.

Then I got a call from a headhunter asking if I would interview at J. Aron, a firm I had never heard of, other than from Dave Grizzle, who had interviewed there a year earlier. It was a commodity trading firm, whatever that meant. Sure, why not? Thus began a series of interviews that took place over many weeks in glass-walled offices off J. Aron's trading floor in Lower Manhattan.

That trading floor on Water Street was a madhouse, all noise and movement. This was still a world of rotary phones and handwritten trade tickets. Nearly everyone sat in the same big room. Traders and salespeople sat at desks behind screens, which at that point in the technology cycle were bulky boxes stacked one on top of another. There were squawk boxes, clanking telex machines, overflowing ashtrays, and clouds of cigarette smoke over the desks. Today trading floors are smoke-free and quiet. Back then, communication was by shouting. You couldn't always tell if people were doing actual business on the phone or fighting with their wives—the traders were all men, with one or two exceptions. There was no privacy and seemingly no sensitivity to the lack of it.

Apart from the frenetic sights and sounds, I was struck by the kind of people who worked at J. Aron. The Aron crowd was far from Ivy League. Most people sat on the trading floor and didn't have glassed-in offices. They rose based on performance, not their résumés. Some entered the firm as drivers, clerks, or secretaries who over time stepped up into producer roles. Frankly, I thought that many of the people I spoke to during endless rounds of interviews were not that impressive, and I assumed I must be missing something. In fact, I was. While the Aron people were not as a rule burdened by broad curiosity, I would come to appreciate that they were miles deep in knowledge related to their narrow business functions. In any case, I was there to get the job by answering questions, not by asking them.

More impressive were a couple of Ivy League guys my age, Richard Witten, who was general counsel, and Steve Hendel, who ran a commercial marketing group dealing with metal-mining companies and industrial users. That business wasn't just buying and selling from an office. It involved mastery of a global supply chain, something that wasn't being managed at any meaningful scale at many other commodity trading firms. The metals team had to secure refining space, arrange for shipment, deal with storage in multiple locations, and handle delivery and insurance—all with the goal of being the highest-quality, lowest-cost middleman. It was an early glimpse for me of what an effective logistics team looks like and of Aron's deep confidence around the execution of its business, despite the Wild West atmosphere. Witten was a classmate of mine at Harvard Law School and Hendel was a Yale graduate and also a lawyer. It was the early success of those two young law school graduates—who later went on to become important Goldman partners—that encouraged Aron to recruit other young associates from law firms. This was the dragnet that missed Dave Grizzle and caught me.

After months of talking to different people, I eventually worked my way to a partner, Dennis Suskind, who ran the bullion-trading operation that was said to generate most of J. Aron's profits. Dennis is a big, bearded extrovert, kind of person who is quick to tell you he didn't go to college but ends up as a trustee or chairman of the board at every institution or organization he gets near—the Chicago Mercantile Exchange, where he still serves with many of his old cronies; the Marymount School of New York, which his daughter attended; the Town Council of Southampton, where he has a vacation house; the Deer Valley ski resort, where he goes skiing; the Atlantic Golf Club, where he plays golf; and so on. He is the most affable guy I've ever known, generous, smart, and practical. He's very proud of having started his career as a shoe salesman.

"How you doin', College Boy?" Dennis said when I entered his office.

I'm sure we spoke for a while, but the only other thing I remember is him pointing to the chaotic trading floor outside his office.

"So, College Boy, do you think you could work in this kind of place?"

"Work in it?" I responded. "Where I grew up, I went home to it every day."

I was offered the job. And that complicated my life in a way I hadn't really anticipated. I spent so much of my effort getting Aron to like me that I didn't focus much on whether I liked them. In fact, I wasn't entirely sure that they did like me that much. I soon learned that they hired a lot of young people every year in the hope that one or two would make it, and they'd quickly get rid of the rest. It was their "mud down a sluice" hiring strategy. If they came up with a nugget or two, that would be great—an appropriate metaphor for a company that traded gold. But foolishly, I'd gone through the entire interviewing cycle without coming away with a clear idea of what they did, how they made money, or what my own responsibilities and prospects would be once I joined. Of course, if I'd asked about my future career path, Dennis would have just laughed.

Although I didn't understand J. Aron and wasn't sure I loved the people I'd met, there were many elements that attracted me: the energy and the pace of markets, the impact of current events, the rapid decision-making, and the immediate gratification (or disappointment) of outcomes. I had no kids and no mortgage and decided that if I was going to make a switch, this was the time. I certainly didn't make the move for money. When the issue of compensation came up, Dennis asked me what I had been making at my law firm—the answer was $60,000—and agreed to match it. Coincidentally, a few days later Donovan raised the salaries of the associates in my class to $65,000, so I went back to Dennis. He declined to match the raise. So I was actually going to be taking a pay cut. Then I asked what my title would be.

"Title? What title? Call yourself contessa if you want to!"

Laura and I were going to get married. And now I was coming home to tell her I was going to work at a commodities company—doing what, I wasn't sure. To say this news was poorly received would be an understatement. We were both lawyers, we were planning to start a family, and I was leaving a prestigious position where I was liked—to trade gold? Actually, to sell gold bars and coins. What did that mean? Willy Loman with heavy bags?

Laura didn't believe I would quit my law job for this. Literally didn't believe it. I had to put my closest Donovan friend, Greg Ho, on the line with her to tell her I had actually done it. And when it finally sank in, she started to cry. My mother felt the same way. I was throwing away my education and my future. *FOR THIS YOU WENT TO HARVARD?*

At Donovan, they were shocked I was leaving. After a bit more than four years there, it seemed like a dumb move to them. But they were great to me. The firm gave me a going-away bonus (unheard of for a "leaver") and told me that I would be welcomed back when I came to my senses. John Baity threw me a going-away party at his home in Westchester.

At J. Aron, it was a different story. When I arrived on the trading floor at 160 Water Street, just before Thanksgiving 1982, it felt like they were surprised to see me.

I WAS SO OBLIVIOUS THAT I DIDN'T EVEN REALIZE THAT J. ARON HAD recently been acquired by Goldman Sachs. It didn't register with me and probably not with many of the folks who worked for J. Aron, other than the senior people who were enriched by the deal, and a few others who thought they should have been made rich but were disappointed. Postacquisition, the firm continued to run independently. The full Goldmanization of J. Aron would take many years. Much later, some would view the process that had taken place as the Aronization of Goldman. Both perspectives contain elements of truth.

I was met by someone from the personnel department who told me I would be working for Marcy Grau, vice president in charge of the precious metals sales desk. Marcy, who had started as Dennis's secretary, was the first and at that point the only woman manager at J. Aron. To get promoted, she'd had to overcome the objections of men who came up with any pretext to oppose her being there—her voice wasn't loud enough; women were "too emotional" for the work. Marcy dealt with that kind of sexism with a combination of niceness and toughness. We hit it off right away. In the New York City-is-a-small world department, Marcy's husband, Bennett, who became Aron's first foreign-currency trader in the 1970s, was from Canarsie and graduated from Jefferson High School five years ahead of me. Laura and I became their close friends and remain so to this day.

Looking out across that huge trading floor, with people seemingly tethered to their desks in long rows, the image that popped into my head was the Roman galley scene from *Ben-Hur*. I was now one of scores of oarsmen, chained to their benches and rowing in sync to the beat of a drum. *We keep you alive to row this ship. So row well—and live.* But how could Oarsman 41 not just survive but break out from all the others? How could you do something that would move the needle at a company as big as Goldman Sachs?

Marcy says that people at Aron were initially doubtful about me because I didn't open my mouth for the first few weeks. "You know, if he doesn't start talking more, this isn't going to work out," one of the partners told her. This was surely the only time in my life that anyone ever complained about my saying too little. I must have been experiencing a kind of culture shock as I absorbed this adrenaline-driven and chaotic new environment. It took me a little while to comprehend that when managers and colleagues on the gold desk said "Good morning" and asked how I was doing, they weren't interested in my health, my mood, or my home life. They wanted to know whether I was making money for the firm.

I sat next to Marcy at a U-shaped desk with the perimeter populated by precious-metals salespeople. Inside the U were a senior trader and a few junior traders, each standing with a phone to each ear, barking out "two-way" prices in gold, i.e., a price at which they'd buy physical gold and a price at which they would sell it. At the other end of the phones were the exchanges where gold futures were traded, the main one being the COMEX, located in the World Trade Center. COMEX was an open-outcry market where traders would jostle one another in a pit, buying and selling gold and silver futures via hand signals. For the J. Aron traders, the futures price could be converted to a price for physical gold by adding or subtracting a factor, the factor varying with the quality of the physical gold (standard or extra fine .9999 gold), the date when it would be delivered, the location of delivery, and the form of the gold (coins, kilo bars, or larger bars).

The discipline was answering phones quickly, attracting a trader's attention, relaying any transaction accurately, and recording and confirming trades. My training consisted of Marcy and other, more senior people yelling or banging the desk if I didn't answer the phones fast enough, or made a mistake, or was slow in relaying information. Or if

I got distracted by all the yelling and chaos. The whole place felt like Penn Station at rush hour. The head silver trader, my soon-to-be-close-friend Jim Riley, had a wastepaper basket set up next to his desk to catch the water dripping from an air conditioner over his head. Quite a change from having my own office, a secretary, and a law library so quiet you could hear the pages of the law books turning. It was like going from Harvard back to Brooklyn.

My morning chores and daily responsibilities began to take shape, and after a few weeks, I apparently started speaking again. I had to write and send out a short market summary via telex, proofread trade confirmations, and call a list of clients I was made responsible for. Those clients were for the most part professional traders working in international gold markets whose job was executing trades for investors. I called customers in Riyadh, Zurich, London, and Johannesburg. Rarely did I speak to anyone in the United States. The customers I spoke to, essentially desk execution people, weren't so different from me, except that they likely had been performing their functions for a few years already. And they weren't wasting a law degree from Harvard.

My job was to get people who were going to buy gold from someone to buy it from me. I would call and chat them up on my views of gold, supported by research that a J. Aron analyst would write on "supply and demand" fundamentals that always trended bullish. But what really drove purchases in a mostly speculator's market was news—government statistical reports, especially on inflation; pronouncements by pundits; threats of war; or interest rate changes. Because trading took place by voice over the phone, my job was to make sure I was on the line with a client at the very moment relevant news was announced. Then he or she would be trapped into dealing with me.

I learned to dial those foreign telephone numbers—in Saudi Arabia, Switzerland, the UK, South Africa—on my rotary phone so that the first twelve digits would click and the phone would ring just as an inflation report or money supply figures were released. None of this was highly intellectual. The skill set required was rapid dialing; keeping people on the phone for longer than they wanted to be (something I was pretty good at); adding a spread to or subtracting a spread from a trader's price; and making sure you reflected accurately whether your client had bought or sold. Oh, and proofreading "confirms" before sending them, which turned out to be very stressful. It was easy to make a mistake, and the adverse consequences could be great. God help you if you sent a confirm to the Central Bank of the Republic of China (Taiwan) that was meant for the Central Bank of the People's Republic of China (Beijing). You could easily lose money and blow up relationships. Or worse, if the confirm incorrectly reported a sale instead of a purchase. Instead of books in balance at the end of the day, you could have a large position going the wrong way.

Now I was talking plenty. But I couldn't help noticing that some of the business didn't make any commercial sense. There were scores of people covering producers, covering consumers, moving metal around, reviewing refining contracts, and so on. They surely made some margin on the spread, but it hardly seemed like enough to cover the costs of those operations. Whether it did or not, I'm not sure the J. Aron people had the metrics or the tools to really know. What I didn't understand at the time was the ultimate significance of the global connections and the commercial instincts embedded in J. Aron's trading culture—a network built on street smarts. This outer-borough DNA would prove to be the real value of the acquisition and a tremendous advantage for Goldman in the years ahead.

One of my clients was Dean Witter, fondly remembered for not hiring me. Dean Witter had a network that on occasion recommended gold to its clients. The only physical gold that a US citizen could effectively buy in those days was gold coins, because only gold coins that were legal tender somewhere could avoid sales tax. At Dean Witter there was a desk that would execute the purchase and sale of those coins for its customer network, and I covered that desk. They would buy Canadian Maple Leafs or South African Krugerrands (the latter later excluded as a result of boycotting South Africa while apartheid prevailed), sometimes ten or twenty at a time. The total volume would be small. We would charge a few dollars over our cost, say $5 each on twenty coins or $100 total gross margin. For this I would call on the clients regularly and sometimes take people on their trading desk out to dinner. How could this possibly be profitable?

Never mind—gold fever, ignited by the oil shock and inflation of the 1970s, was still in the air. More as a conversation piece than as an investment, I bought a kilogram of gold myself. Gold is incredibly dense and heavy. A cube that weighs a ton is only fourteen inches on each side. A kilo is surprisingly small for its weight—slightly bigger than a Hershey bar. The one I bought cost around $15,000. For many years, the price went nowhere, losing value from inflation. But I got a lot of pleasure passing it around at dinner parties. Holding the gold bar, people would become slightly mesmerized. No one ever wanted to let go of it. Even in the age of Bitcoin, aka "digital gold," the real thing retains its elemental power over the human psyche.

Another account I covered from early on was the South African Reserve Bank. The Reserve Bank was to the gold market what the Saudi Arabian Oil Ministry was to oil. They were by a large measure the biggest producer. I was too junior to be in charge of the overall relationship, but I was at the right level to be responsible for getting them on the phone and trading every time there was bullish news and the price of gold "popped." They were only and always sellers whose single objective was to sell gold at a high price. (All the South African mining companies were obligated to sell their gold to the central bank for South African rands. The central bank then resold the gold for dollars in the international market.) Everyone in the gold market pandered to them, and they could afford to be quite curt and difficult on the phone. I was very eager. I got good at talking to them, and I called them nonstop.

Apparently, they liked dealing with me, because the main trader on their gold desk, Johan Detmann, called my boss and told him to send me to Pretoria to meet with them. Other than that summer trip to Europe after law school and maybe a visit to Club Med in the Bahamas, I had never left the country, so this was an exciting invitation. It was a major trip. You had to change planes in London and stop again to refuel in Cape Verde. When I got to Pretoria after more than twenty-four hours of travel, my hosts couldn't have been nicer. South Africa was far away and becoming a pariah in the international markets, so it didn't get many visitors. They showed appreciation to those who came. When I arrived, I was invited to dinner at Johan's home, with some other colleagues and his family. We ended late, but as I was leaving for my hotel and an early-morning flight back to New York City, he said, "Don't get too settled. We're coming to pick you up in a couple of hours and we'll drive you to Kruger Park. You can sleep in the car. Trust me, it will be all right with your boss."

And so I went on safari for a couple of days with one pair of jeans and a couple of T-shirts that I had traveled with. (I had packed only two days' worth of business clothes.) We saw lions and elephants and everything we were supposed to. On the trip home, I tried to process what I'd seen on my brief visit. Competing against the warmth I felt from the people in the bank was the brief exposure I had to apartheid, where Blacks and whites would walk down the streets and look through one another, never interacting. I hadn't given the issue much thought previously, and it shocked me.

South Africa was a weird, morally compromised place, but also beautiful and fascinating. Not long after my trip, J. Aron/Goldman Sachs joined the boycott of South African trade, and we stopped selling Krugerrands. I made subsequent visits to South Africa before the African National Congress took over and the boycott ended, but not to transact, only to maintain relationships with all constituencies for the day when business would normalize under a new constitution. We later hosted training for a cadre of senior ANC leaders who were slated for high financial positions in the new government.

Whatever my own views, the gold business meant dealing with the central banks and treasuries of repressive governments and foreign powers hostile to the United States—China, the Soviet Union, and the Soviet vassal states of Eastern Europe. For those countries, gold and the metals that are often found with gold, such as platinum, palladium, and rhodium—needed for catalytic converters on newer cars—were a principal source of foreign exchange. For that reason, the Soviet Union, unlike Russia after the fall of communism, was absolutely scrupulous about honoring its contracts and paying its debts. Bad actors on the international stage were some of the most reliable customers in the gold market.

Another relationship I supported at the sales desk was with the Bank for Foreign Trade in Moscow, the official outlet through which the Soviet Union sold its gold. J. Aron also had a commercial relationship with Almaz, the distribution outlet for platinum outside the Soviet Union. Dennis Suskind graciously invited me to accompany him to Moscow to meet with the principals of the Bank for Foreign Trade and Almaz. In preparation for the trip, he told me to buy cartons of Marlboros and rock CDs. (Bruce Springsteen's *Born in the USA* was popular and seemed appropriate.) This was the currency we would use to get around, and for gifts.

We flew to Moscow and checked into our rooms at the Cosmos Hotel, a concrete and glass colossus built for the 1980 Olympics (the one that the US boycotted in the wake of the Soviet invasion of Afghanistan). The concierge on the fifth floor was an old woman sitting at a computer terminal. But the "computer" was just for show—if you looked from the side, you could see that the monitor was an empty shell. An encouraging thought: Maybe their missiles were hollow too?

My memory of that trip is only in black and white. The cars were all the same: clunky black Lada sedans. The drivers in black leather jackets all looked the same too. Everyone smoked all the time. Dennis and I tried to get our official driver to take us to Dzerzhinsky Square, where Jewish refuseniks had been arrested for protesting, but the driver either didn't understand us or pretended not to. I don't remember much about the business meetings—my knack for making a quick study of people hit a brick wall with these stolid Soviet bureaucrats. What I do remember is a lunch where our host filled everyone's tall water glasses with vodka and made a big deal about everyone having to drink. Our hosts didn't care so much about our finishing ours, so long as they could finish theirs.

That evening, Dennis announced that he was taking me to the circus. We didn't have our car, so we went to the front of the hotel and he waved a US ten-dollar bill at a taxi driver while yelling, "Circus, circus!" Understanding that much, he drove us there. When we arrived, we told the driver to "wait, wait," but apparently that point didn't get through. We enjoyed the show, but when we got out, there was no car where we had left it. It was November and snowing. These were assuredly pre-Uber days, and pre-Americans-on-their-own days. So Dennis stepped into the road and flagged down a random passenger car. He waved some dollars in front of the driver and said, "Cosmos, Cosmos," and in we jumped. I thought I'd never get home alive, yet here I am today.

A veteran traveler to Moscow, Dennis also had the inspiration to buy a couple of kilos of the best caviar from a kitchen worker at the hotel restaurant for $50. It was highly illegal to use dollars, even for goods that weren't stolen. I thought it was an even worse idea for me to risk smuggling caviar through Russian customs so that Dennis could impress his friends in New York. I didn't want to go to the Gulag for the sake of a dinner party I wasn't going to be invited to anyway. So I told Dennis he was on his own with the caviar. I knew he had accomplished his purpose when he got on the plane and asked the stewardess to put his carry-on bag in a refrigerator in the plane's galley.

MY BOSSES AT J. ARON WERE OBSESSED—NOT TOO STRONG A WORD— with having balanced books. As arbitrage traders, they never wanted to be long or short gold or silver at the end of the day. Sometimes when they'd find a discrepancy, they'd shut down trading altogether until they could figure out which idiot had confused a buy with a sell. This conservatism was bred in the bone, going back to J. Aron's founding as a coffee-trading company in New Orleans in 1898. Jack Aron, son of the firm's original founder, was famous for saying that "our plan of operation calls for being long or short up to a maximum of twenty seconds."

The customer business that I and other members of the sales force pursued made a small contribution to the P&L, at least in theory. With customers who regularly transacted, we could earn a spread by buying on our bid and selling on our offer—classic market making. There were also commercial deals to do: The firm got paid to move metal around and to refine one type of gold into another.

There was more profit to be made from an interest rate arbitrage strategy involving cash (spot) gold and gold futures. When you owned cash gold, you had to pay for it up front, which meant there was a cost to financing that position. This cost was the price for having exposure to the physical commodity, and it included financing fees, with additional costs like storage and insurance. On the other hand, when you bought a gold future on the COMEX, you needed to put up only a small amount of cash, using margin to gain exposure to the commodity.

The financing cost of holding physical gold was built into the price of the futures contract, causing the future price to be higher than the cash price on the spot market. This difference is known as the carrying cost, or "contango." The cash gold market typically attracted long-term holders, like me with my 2.2-pound Hershey bar, while the futures market attracted speculators. When the speculative market was optimistic, futures would be priced higher, trading at a premium to the spot price plus the embedded financing costs. In that case, Aron could buy cash gold and sell futures to hedge, essentially lending money to the futures market at a high rate of interest. When the market was bearish, like after the gold boom, futures would trade at a discount. In that scenario, Aron could sell gold for cash and hedge by buying futures at a lower price, effectively borrowing money from the market at a low rate. This strategy was a form of interest rate arbitrage with some complexities. The risk of interest rate changes could be easily hedged. A bigger challenge was finding sources from which we could borrow gold for short sales.

To do that, Aron turned to central banks, the ultimate long-term holders of gold. For the central banks that held gold as part of their reserves, anything they got to compensate for their storage costs and earn a small lease rate—perhaps twenty-five or fifty basis points—was gravy. For us, the availability of physical gold to borrow was the key to the operation.

The central banks that delivered this key weren't the major ones you'd think of but the smaller central banks of countries like Hungary, Czechoslovakia, and Austria. Most of their gold reserves were held on deposit beneath the Bank of England in London or a few blocks from our office, in a vault built into the bedrock of Manhattan, eighty feet below street level at the Federal Reserve Bank of New York. While the Unites States' own gold reserves are held in Fort Knox and at West Point, the New York Fed earns a fee for storing gold belonging to many other countries. When you leased that gold, you had to physically move it in a Brinks truck from 33 Liberty Street to another vault at Citibank, which would hold it on deposit for private firms like ours.

The gold arbitrage that was driving most of the profits of J. Aron was simple, elegant, and disconcertingly easy for others to replicate. That was what made people at Aron so secretive. They didn't want anyone to know how they made their money.

CHAPTER 6

From Gold Man to Goldman

I've learned as much from negative examples as from positive ones.

 number of factors were driving the gold boom at the start of my career at J. Aron. The enabling condition was the new right of private citizens to own gold. In April 1933, at the start of the New Deal, Franklin D. Roosevelt signed an executive order criminalizing the hoarding of gold in the United States. This was necessary to increase the money supply and increase federal spending during the Depression. Because the dollar was still convertible into gold, the Federal Reserve couldn't print more money unless it forced the conversion of more gold coins and bullion into paper notes. Exceptions to the prohibition were made for dentists and rare coin collectors. In 1971, President Nixon closed the so-called gold window by taking the dollar off the gold standard. A few years later, in 1974, Gerald Ford signed a bill allowing ownership and trade of gold in its various forms.

The oil crisis and inflation of the 1970s made precious metals, whose prices had long been fairly stable, look appealing as both an inflation hedge and a speculative vehicle. Prices for commodities of all kinds became much more volatile and in the case of precious metals increased dramatically. In a few years, gold jumped from a fixed rate of $35 per ounce into the triple digits, peaking at a high of $850 in 1980. In the same period, silver went from around $6 to a high of $49 in late 1981, thanks to an attempt by the Texas-based Hunt brothers to corner the market. People were melting jewelry and candlesticks to sell into the precious metals bubble.

The new prominence of commodities traders was underscored by a series of high-profile deals. In 1981, Donaldson, Lufkin & Jenrette acquired ACLI, another venerable New Orleans coffee brokerage that had branched out into other commodities. That same year, Philipp Brothers, or Phibro, another German Jewish commodities firm that dated back to the turn of the twentieth century, acquired Salomon Brothers and took on its name. Salomon was a Goldman Sachs rival, so that increased the pressure on Goldman to acquire its longtime client J. Aron. Not only had the firms worked closely together for many years, but Aron was incredibly profitable (shhh). In 1981, it made $60 million in profit on capital of only $100 million. It had a higher profit margin than Goldman, it had a much smaller staff, and it took very measured market risk. It looked, in other words, like a terrific business, and Goldman decided to buy it.

The timing for the acquisition was in fact terrible for Goldman—but not for the astute traders at J. Aron. Thanks to Fed chairman Paul Volcker, inflation was already being tamed, and the long bear market in stocks was about to end. The silver bubble popped shortly after the J. Aron acquisition closed, bringing the price back down to $5 per ounce in the summer of 1982. Gold settled into a fairly narrow trading range, anchoring itself around $400. When I was interviewing in 1982, the newly acquired J. Aron was still making money, but the opportunities had leveled off—it earned just $30 million that year, half of what it had the previous year. In 1983, my first full year at the firm, it earned no profit at all. The acquisition of J. Aron would ultimately prove a good deal for Goldman, but not in the way it was expected or intended to be. What the Goldman partners may not have fully appreciated at that point was the importance of the international connections and mercantile culture that came with J. Aron. Where Goldman's business was 85 percent domestic, Aron's was the reverse. Aron had deep contacts all over the world, and real skill not just in paper trading but in the complex logistics required to successfully trade physical commodities.

The commodity/interest arbitrage that had been driving profits was relatively simple, and the firm had evolved a lot of activities around it, such as trying to buy at a bid price and sell at an offer price to earn a spread. But the big profits available when speculators were driving up gold futures were waning. Falling interest rates took the volatility out of the metals market and with it the opportunity to execute riskless arbitrage at any meaningful scale. The partners of J. Aron must have understood what was happening, but as an apprentice salesman, I didn't have a clue. Certainly, Goldman Sachs didn't see the change coming, because it paid $130 million for J. Aron, big bucks for a partnership to lay out in those days and the biggest acquisition that Goldman made until 2000, when it bought the NASDAQ-focused trading firm Spear, Leeds & Kellogg for $6.5 billion at the height of the dot-com bubble.

As the metals business declined, it became much more competitive. Citibank and J.P. Morgan were now doing metals sales and arbitrage too. Some of the new competition came from senior J. Aron traders who had not been made partners of Goldman at the time of the acquisition and defected to Drexel Burnham Lambert to set up their own operation, dubbed Drexel Trading. They knew about leasing gold from obscure central banks and offered a higher fee for doing so.

This made the J. Aron partners increasingly paranoid that others in the company might split off and create even more competition, and they became furtive and squirrelly around their own people. They used code names for clients and compartmentalized information on a need-to-know basis. The National Commercial Bank of Jeddah had the code name Channel 4, because its initials, NCB, sounded like the local NBC channel. There were serious reasons for such practices.

The Central Bank of the Republic of China (Taiwan) surely didn't want the Central Bank of the People's Republic of China (Beijing) to find out about its transactions because traders were shouting orders across a trading floor in New York. Trying to be a nugget and not mud sliding down the sluice, I was scrupulous about the protocols. But all the secrecy meant that I was excluded from meetings and information flow that would have allowed me to learn the business. I was caught in a vicious circle of not being invited to engage in discussions because I had little to contribute and never having anything to contribute because I wasn't permitted to expand my knowledge. It seemed that my role would forever be calling up accounts and asking them to "please do your precious metals business with me today." Maybe it wasn't too late to start over somewhere else. I started daydreaming about the good old fourteen-hour days studying tax rulings as an associate at the law firm.

Nor were the senior J. Aron people natural mentors. I had to be at my desk at 7:00 a.m., when the London market would already be active. The COMEX closed at 3:00 p.m., so working late meant staying until 5:00 p.m. I stayed late most days. My hope was that when the place thinned out, I could trap anyone senior who was left into a conversation. I had nothing to do anyway until Laura finished up work at her law firm, where the day ran much later. I remember hanging around late one afternoon because the head gold trader, Richard Pront, was still doing his paperwork. I had been at Aron for several months, and he never gave me the time of day. Finally, as Richard was leaving, he turned and asked me if I lived in the Village, which I did, and he offered me a ride. Eureka, my breakthrough at last! On the way uptown, he said he needed to stop at Balducci's, a grocery famous for overpriced prepared food. Legal parking was impossible, and he asked me to wait in his double-parked car. When he returned with his bags, he got in and said that since he was in a hurry, would I mind making my own way home? I swallowed hard and got out of the car, realizing what my value to him was.

At the big Wall Street firms, the commodities bubble was giving way to buyer's remorse. Within a few years, Donaldson, Lufkin & Jenrette would cut its losses and sell off ACLI, which had been losing money. Eventually, the Salomon people pushed out the Phibro people who had notionally acquired them, restoring what the Salomon executives viewed as the proper order of the universe. And at Goldman, the senior partners, who had always regarded commodities as somewhat déclassé, were coming to realize that they had acquired a business that wasn't the profit machine they had thought they were buying—and that perhaps they had been duped or outtraded in the transaction. It began to dawn on me that I had gone to work for a company that was in decline and under tremendous pressure to deliver better results. When John Whitehead retired as cochairman to work under George Shultz as deputy secretary of state, *The New York Times* noted, "One of Goldman's few black marks in recent years was the 1981 purchase of J. Aron and Company."

The unhappiness was fueled on both sides by the vast gap in culture between the two firms. Where Goldman was a "paper" trader, the Aron people were "physical" traders. Goldman was an established firm with Jewish roots. J. Aron had Jewish roots too, but it wasn't "Our Crowd." Goldman was Ivy League / Harvard Business School; Aron was a lot of "streety" folks, most of whom had gone through the SUNY or CUNY system, if they'd gone to college at all. The Goldman people were articulate and had polished presentation skills. The Aron people cursed and slammed telephones—and one another—when things didn't go their way.

Most people within Goldman knew J. Aron through its coffee-importing business, which was the largest in the country. As in its earliest days in New Orleans, the coffee operation included industrial roasting machines and a tasting room, where master tasters graded the coffee by quality. This was done behind a glass wall, in a room with an elaborate ventilation system—roasting coffee smells delicious from a distance but less so up close. The head taster had been at J. Aron since 1937. While he was there, he was helped by his son, who succeeded him in the top tasting job around the time I arrived and stayed for another twenty years—until Goldman finally exited the coffee business in 2001. Investment bankers would bring their clients to gawk at the coffee-tasting operation, which involved the taster swirling sips of coffee around in his mouth and spitting them into the kind of cuspidor that you'd find next to a dentist's chair. I had a feeling that J. Aron was regarded as something of a zoo or a theme park. Whatever it was, it didn't feel like finance.

Wall Street was a pretty heady place in those go-go days, though not necessarily at the J. Aron commodities division at Goldman Sachs. New hires would sometimes rotate through our floor as part of their training program. One such junior analyst was Jim Cramer, later of CNBC fame, a great popularizer of financial markets to the retail crowd. Jim is quite brilliant and a great communicator. I knew him slightly because we overlapped at Harvard College and Harvard Law School. In college, Jim was editor of the *Crimson*, a position once held by FDR and others who went on to greatness. Unfortunately, Jim made the mistake of giving a quote to *The New York Times* in a 1986 article about the high compensation of even junior people on Wall Street.

"'There isn't anything I see in a store that I can't buy,' said James Cramer, a thirty-one-year-old retail broker at Goldman Sachs & Company."

He was gone from the firm shortly thereafter. Years later in a *New York* magazine piece where famous New Yorkers talked about other New Yorkers they admired, Jim was very complimentary about me because I was nice to him during his brief tour at Aron. I feel guilty taking credit, because we didn't get many Goldman visitors, and I was just grateful for his genuine interest.

With its coffee-scented trading floor at 160 Water Street, and later on its separate floors in Goldman's new building at 85 Broad Street, J. Aron continued to evolve apart from the Goldman Sachs culture, the way many animals in Australia evolved differently from species on other continents. J. Aron and Goldman Sachs did not really begin to cross genes until much later. Years after the move into the new building, I was still calling Goldman Sachs "Goldman," and J. Aron "us."

The culture gap was on vivid display at lunch. At Goldman, investment bankers would head out to nice meals with their clients, often involving the midday consumption of alcohol, if the client was so inclined. If you were a trading partner, the catering staff would bring you lunch from the partners' dining room on a silver tray. At J. Aron, traders couldn't leave their desks while the market was open. So lunch was ordered at eight thirty in the morning from whatever restaurants people wanted. Takeout menus littered the floor like the lobby of a New York apartment building without a doorman. Some traders, unsure what they'd feel like eating when the lunch hour rolled around, would order three or four meals—Italian, Chinese, Mexican—and the food would remain available for snacking until the overnight cleaning crew tossed the leftovers. The carryout containers attracted an active population of unwanted creatures.

There were battles over lines of business that J. Aron and Goldman traders both wanted, such as bond futures arbitrage. To J. Aron, this seemed a lot like gold or silver futures arbitrage—short the futures contract, go long the underlying security, or vice versa. To Goldman, it was simply a species of fixed-income trading—one of its established client-facing activities. Goldman won that fight—no surprise. And that defeat, along with various other slights, as well as the problem of not making much money anymore, increased the feelings of resentment at J. Aron. At the end of my first year, the J. Aron crew had our picture taken for Goldman's annual report. Dennis bought red suspenders for us all to put on, to mock our betters upstairs. I don't think any of them even noticed.

Had I made a huge mistake in taking this job? Some of the Aron people were actual college graduates, for crying out loud, some of us with law degrees even. Marcy Grau was a cultured person who had studied French and Russian literature at the University of Michigan and graduated Phi Beta Kappa. And here we were, waving our arms and shouting orders like characters in the Eddie Murphy movie *Trading Places*.

I was thus feeling a sense of precariousness about my professional future when Laura and I got married in June 1983. We were both still paying off our student loans and didn't have any financial help from our families. And so the reception was a modest affair at the Westbury Hotel, sixty people for drinks and hors d'oeuvres. To keep costs down, we had the wedding at 3:00 p.m. on Father's Day—the cheapest time slot available. Laura picked up flowers in the Manhattan Flower District on the way to the ceremony. Given the limits of our budget and what she could carry, the arrangements were sparse. The hotel manager took pity on us and sent up the lobby floral display to adorn the bare-looking room for a few hours. Our band consisted of one person playing a flute.

Most of my friends at our wedding were from my earlier life. Greg Ho, my pal from Donovan, Leisure, was best man. The only new J. Aron friends there were Marcy and Bennett Grau. They gave us a gold coin as a wedding gift.

My only regret is that Laura and I pushed for a *New York Times* wedding announcement. In interviewing us for the article, the editor asked what our parents did. Laura said that her dad worked for a foreign policy quarterly supported by the Rockefeller Foundation. That sounded pretty upscale. I said my dad worked for the government.

"Where in the government?"

"The post office."

"What does he do in the post office?"

"He's a clerk."

Even as I said it, I knew it would make my parents feel bad, but it couldn't be undone.

The future bride's father, the item read, "was editor in chief of the publications of the Foreign Policy Association in New York." The groom's father "was a clerk with the Postal Service in Manhattan." It looked like I'd gone out of my way to embarrass my parents. I didn't want that, of course, but I had wanted my wedding announcement in the *Times*. It was another Lacoste shirt, another step in the gentrification of Lloyd.

I WAS IN FOR ANOTHER AWAKENING AT BONUS SEASON. I HAD COME from a law firm where all members of a class who started at the same time were paid the same, the amount was known, and the environment was professional. At J. Aron, I was told that comp was a process, a negotiation, and that complaining was expected and often effective. Bonus time was like haggling in a bazaar. All the human emotions were on full display. A person would go into a room and be asked what he thought his bonus should be. If his boss agreed to the number, he knew he had asked for too little. People would come out with a big smile or an aggrieved look and then go back in a bunch of times to push for more. The mainframe computer at Aron couldn't process a check larger than $99,999.99. So when the mail cart came around at bonus delivery time, you could make a decent guess at how someone had done that year by the number of envelopes delivered to their desk. Direct deposit took away all that fun.

Within Goldman Sachs, and on Wall Street generally, there was a hierarchy of prestige. Investment bankers were at the top of the food chain, higher than traders. Within the community of traders, equity (stock) traders were more important than traders in fixed income (bonds). Within fixed income, longer-duration bond traders were more important than short-duration traders (e.g., money markets). But anyone in any fixed-income business was more important than currency or commodity traders.

There was also a prestige gap between the traders who took the risk and recorded the profits and the salespeople who brought in the customer activity. At least in equities, salespeople generated commissions. In fixed income, currency, and commodities, there were no commissions, and the traders had to capture a spread to profit. A perennial question was: How much value did a salesperson contribute? The uncertainty always diminished the contribution. Salespeople were at the bottom of the food chain.

So in the Goldman Sachs universe, I was in a trading division in a banking culture; a commodities person at the bottom of the industry hierarchy around equities, fixed income, currency, and commodities; and a salesman, not a trader. In other words, I was the lowest of the low in an underperforming part of a very successful firm that was determined to stay that way. I didn't understand any of this when I took the job. Often after I called all my accounts, there was simply nothing to do. I was told to hold a phone to my ear and pretend to be busy, especially when there were senior people around, and even more especially when Goldman Sachs partners were walking around.

One morning in the fall of 1983, when I had been there for a year, everyone around me seemed upset. People were getting called into the partners' offices, and it didn't take long for even me to realize that they were getting fired. The guy to my left and the guy to my right were called in and then gone. By the end of the next day, about a hundred of the three-hundred-person J. Aron staff had been laid off.

After two days of terror, there was a lull and I was summoned into Dennis's office. To me and the other survivors he was delivering a set of talking points: *Markets are tough, and we are overstaffed. But the layoffs are over, and your job is now safe. We are optimistic about the opportunities ahead and the team we have.*

I thanked him and didn't have much else to say.

"You must have been nervous," he said.

No, I wasn't. I figured I was brighter and cheaper and willing to work harder than most of the people on the floor. Dennis looked at me as if he were disappointed by my answer.

"Of course, you could have been fired. We were thinking about it."

"Oh, then I'm really relieved."

This was getting nutty. What was obviously planned as a set of meetings to put the survivors of the layoffs at ease ended with his trying to stoke my anxiety after I acted too much at ease! Life went on, but it did occur to me that I might need a new job. The division wasn't growing, I wasn't being given new responsibilities, and I had trouble keeping busy after 3:00 p.m.

CHAPTER 7

Breaking Through

In a good culture, you can accomplish anything from any seat in the organization.

I did manage to do something that garnered positive attention from the Goldman folks.

One of the accounts I covered was code-named 27B. It was Al Rajhi, a large Saudi bank based in Riyadh. Years later, Al Rajhi became an entirely Islamic bank following sharia law. After the September 11 attacks, it was implicated in terrorist financing (and ultimately exonerated). But back in the early 1980s, I knew Al Rajhi simply as a bank that was buying and selling gold on behalf of its private clients. Some of them sat in the bank's office and speculated on gold as a communal activity, watching the market like they were at a sporting event and placing bets. My contact who described this world to me was K.V. Thomas, an Indian national who ran the Al Rajhi trading operation. I was curious about this world, and he seemed to enjoy telling me about it. In a way, we were both outsiders studying it.

Through my phone conversations with K.V., I began to learn about Islamic financing. In Islam as practiced in conservative Saudi Arabia, charging interest was not permitted. But investment income was allowed. An objective for a wealth adviser in the kingdom was thus to find opportunities that would provide close to a guaranteed return (like an interest rate) but that involved enough risk and other investment characteristics to be certified halal under Islamic law. So there was a divide to be bridged between Arabian oil sheikhs who were restricted in their trading opportunities and Goldman traders who could help solve their problem but weren't engaged with it. While I was growing more conversant in the lingo of finance, I still had enough of a Wall Street outsider's perspective to think beyond the more familiar lines of business. The problem was similar to creating a tax shelter, the kind of thing I'd done as an attorney at Donovan, Leisure. If investment income qualified as a capital gain rather than interest, it would be taxed at a lower rate. This was an analogous problem, but with the Quran in place of the Internal Revenue Code. How could you legitimately classify an ongoing investment yield as a gain?

Transactions like the gold arbitrage at J. Aron appeared at first to fill the bill. The problem, I was told, is that gold is "money" and that a return on gold did not pass muster as an Islamically permitted transaction. There were other commodities where arbitrage against a futures market might have worked. Unfortunately, the sizes of the overall markets were too small to be relevant to Saudi princes.

But what about equity futures? The S&P 500 futures contract, a way to bet on the future price of the stock market, was still relatively new. The cash-and-carry yield—the return on buying the stock index at its current price and simultaneously selling it forward at the higher future price—was substantial. Why were people willing to pay more than the current price of the stock index for a contract to buy it in six or twelve months? Because it was a way to speculate on a rising stock market with borrowed money. As with gold futures, speculators would pay what amounted to a relatively high effective interest rate to finance their positions at prices well above the current cash price for the same shares. During the long bull market of the 1980s, they often made out very well by doing so.

Over several weeks, K.V. and I discussed how his clients could take the opposite side of the futures speculation via the exchange. I proposed that they put up the cash to buy shares in the S&P 500, short the future contract on the exchange, and earn a high return for the period their cash was outstanding. As described, the transaction would be low risk, but there were some complications. K.V. advised that among the companies in the S&P 500, shares of banks and shares of companies involved in the liquor business would have to be excluded for religious reasons. Thus there would be "tracking risk" because the stock positions wouldn't exactly match the five hundred companies embedded in the futures contracts.

    K.V. got his approvals and I took the idea to Bob Rubin, a senior and powerful partner at the firm whose background was in equity arbitrage. Rubin was supportive and connected me with the equities division. That got me involved for the first time with people at the "real" Goldman Sachs. If the metaphor for recruiting at J. Aron was mud down a sluice, Goldman picked from the top of the heap, with an acceptance rate that Harvard would have envied. It might have been only a few floors away, but it was a different civilization up there. Rubin's imprimatur meant that the Goldman stock traders took me seriously as we worked through the analyses and execution details. The first order was for $100 million of the stock basket—probably the largest such transaction up to that time. I remember a tremendous feeling of relief when we filled the order: Oarsman 41 served the ship and was going to live. The net for the client was something like a 17 percent annualized yield with about a 5 percent tracking risk (the risk that being underweight banks and spirits companies would move the needle up or down by 5 percent). It was very satisfying to all concerned, and more, larger trades followed.

    At Goldman, even though I was the most junior person, I got tutorials and execution help the whole way through from relatively senior people, and for something that seemed far-fetched until it was done. My J. Aron bosses knew only vaguely what was happening. Separate from the polish and professionalism of the Goldman people, working with them gave me an early insight into the importance of a good culture, where you could accomplish anything from any seat in the organization. It was also an illustration of the way that innovative ideas often come from younger people who have no existing business to rely on and aren't trapped by convention.

When I later visited clients in Saudi Arabia and Kuwait, I got a better sense of the people I was dealing with. I experienced the value Arabs place on hospitality, which didn't seem in any way lessened when the guest happened to be a Brooklyn Jew. Big groups would gather in their homes to meet me, everyone wanted to talk, and the cultural barriers seemed to melt away. The conversations were followed by impressive banquets. Engaging with the Saudi merchant families opened my eyes to a lot of new things. The patriarchs I met those evenings had mostly grown up in real poverty—I remember the head of the central bank telling me that he went around barefoot as a boy. Only after the 1973 OPEC embargo drove up the price of oil did the flow of petrodollars bring a wave of development, the opening of many luxury auto dealerships, and young Saudis studying in Britain and the United States. My approach was to be very open in my curiosity and candid about my opinions, and I was surprised how many of them were shared—at least by this nonrepresentative community of merchant princes. In 1986, the US bombed Libya in response to Mu'ammar Gaddhafi's sponsorship of a series of terrorist attacks that killed American citizens in Europe. I remember talking about the bombing and noting that the Saudis hadn't allowed our F-111s fly over their airspace. Their perspective was less that they opposed Reagan's military retaliation than that it would be politically impossible in their country to openly support it.

IT WAS INCREASINGLY EVIDENT THAT THE OLD, UNSCALABLE COMMODIties arbitrage business that had fueled J. Aron's large profits wasn't coming back. But the culture at Aron at that point didn't encourage innovation, let alone the kind of dramatic reinvention that the business needed if it was going to survive.

The watershed event for J. Aron postmerger, and for me, was the arrival of Mark Winkelman. Mark was a blond, blue-eyed Dutchman with a lean and hungry look. He had come to the US to get a graduate degree at Wharton and planned to go back to Holland afterward. Instead he met his future wife, Dorinda, who was an administrator at the school, and ended up remaining in the US.

Mark told me he made the choice to stay partly because businesses in Europe were more highly structured and hierarchical than in the US. On Wall Street, he thought he would have a better chance of advancing faster. And that proved to be the case. After a brief stint working for Robert McNamara at the World Bank in Washington, Mark took a job at Goldman Sachs in fixed income in 1978. Widely regarded as brilliant, he made partner four years later on the strength of his early application of computer analysis to government bond arbitrage, which he turned into a meaningful profit center for the firm.

Mark had been opposed to Goldman's acquiring J. Aron. He thought Goldman could build its own commodities business more cheaply and effectively. Soon enough, fixing J. Aron was *his* problem. In 1982, Bob Rubin, who shared responsibilities as chief operating officer, inserted Mark into J. Aron to be the Goldman guy on the scene, and ultimately to sort out Goldman's failing investment. The move also served the purpose of separating Mark from Jon Corzine, his rival and near contemporary who was the other rising star in the fixed-income division. Getting Aron straightened out was also an important test for Rubin, who was widely expected to run the firm at some point. His background in trading, as opposed to investment banking, made him the natural person to oversee it.

Goldman had a lot of smart people, but Mark was exceptional: strategic, methodical, and one of the few partners who cared about operations and technology. For a guy who wanted to get away from the rigidity of the European system, he seemed pretty stiff and European himself. But while he could be a bit of a cold fish, Mark radiated competence and wisdom and had a strange kind of charisma. To the brightest of the rising Goldman professionals, among whose ranks I was trying to be included, he had a certain aura. We hung on his every word and killed ourselves for his approval, even as the compliments fell from him like he was made of Velcro. He later told me I impressed him when he saw me push away a trader who was trying to wrestle my phone away from me so that he could yell at my client—ordinary behavior at J. Aron in those days. The trader was mad because the client had caused him to lose money on a transaction. But yelling at the client wasn't going to do any good and would have undone months of relationship building on my part.

Mark formed a to-do list to revamp J. Aron and systematically checked all the boxes. He played a significant role in the winnowing of the J. Aron population that I survived. Most fundamentally, Mark converted J. Aron into a risk-taking "principal" business that traded for its own account—a significant change in mentality for an operation that had always fixated on the risk-free part of risk-free arbitrage.

Mark brought rigorous analytics and new technology to the business. He played a key role in the emergence of the Wall Street "quant." At Goldman, he and Rubin recruited Fischer Black, famous for codeveloping the Black–Scholes model used to price options. Rail thin, oft married, and a smoker of hand-rolled cigarettes, Black died young in 1995. Had he lived a couple of years longer, he would have shared the Nobel Prize in Economics with Myron Scholes and Robert Merton for developing the model.

Goldman's genius in residence, Fischer served as a stop on the tour that we'd give to visiting clients, along with the coffee-tasting room. He loved paradoxes and provocations. I remember him asking visitors from a gold-mining company why they didn't just leave gold in the ground, where it was being perfectly stored, and sell or lease it in place, instead of going to all the trouble to dig it out, process it, move it, and bury it in secure holes elsewhere.

He had a good point in theory. But in the real world of metals sales, you couldn't just "assume" extraction. This was an expression of the kind of thinking some of us came to call "quant heaven." A lot of ideas worked on paper, in a frictionless world where there were no transaction costs, surprises, or geopolitics. In the real world, a theoretically advantageous transaction might entail numerous costly hedges or operational risks that would render the whole exercise impractical.

Mark wanted to hire technologists to sit on the trading floor and help design better tools for salespeople and traders, as well as new products and strategies for clients. He encouraged us to hire physicists, engineers, and other people with unconventional academic backgrounds to embed as strategists within trading units. Anybody can take a client out to lunch, but innovation driven by "strats" could help Goldman serve its clients in a differentiated way, by improving their performance. It turned out that a successful idea for making money bred a lot more long-term loyalty from clients than an expensive wine dinner.

Perhaps the most important person we hired under Mark's guidance was Armen Avanessians, an engineer who came to us from Bell Labs as our first currency strat. When Bennett Grau and I interviewed him for the position, we were both impressed. And Bennett was never impressed with anybody.

"You're a real rocket scientist!" Bennett exclaimed in admiration.

"Actually, I am not," Armen responded. "I design semiconductors. I don't deal with astronautics at all."

"Well, Mr. Fancy Pants," Bennett said, "we've got a very simple business here. What we've got to do is buy low and sell high. How can you help us?"

"Perhaps I could help you figure out when it's low and when it's high," Armen said.

An ethnic Armenian who was born in Forest Hills, Queens, soon after his parents fled Iran, Armen was one of my all-time greatest hires. It's hard to imagine a time when quantified risk management was not core to everything done by a trading firm or investment bank. But Armen's work building tools for our foreign exchange and commodities businesses was an early example of it. In those pre–Bloomberg terminal days, we didn't even have basic pricing tools. You called around for prices by phone or used a primitive mobile device with an antenna that provided quotes. In the mornings, Bennett and I used to ride the subway downtown together from the Upper West Side. We'd wait at the top of the stairs, where we had just enough reception to get a slow trickle of data, and then dash down to the platform when we heard the train coming.

Other tools we used were even more primitive. Our order book to keep track of client orders was literally that—a composition notebook where traders would enter trades in a ledger by hand. It often got lost. Once while we were discussing features for the new electronic version Armen was coding, the book went missing yet again. A salesman had seen someone take it into a toilet stall as reading material. He banged on the outside wall of the men's room for the guy to bring it back, which he did, not even slightly embarrassed.

Armen's solution to this analogue mess was a software program we called the Armenator, a rudimentary pricing tool for foreign exchange (or "forex") trading. The name caught on after Bill McMahon, one of the traders, said that it would terminate the controller who was feeding the trading desk bad numbers and bad advice. The Armenator helped to rationalize what we were doing. But that was just a warm-up exercise for Armen. He and his team were developing software we could use to price trades and assess the risk of all of our trading positions.

That program eventually developed into the Securities Database, or SecDB, which became the backbone of Goldman Sachs's risk-analytics platform. With it, you could see whether a new position added or subtracted risk in a large, complex portfolio of positions. Often the correlations across asset classes were the opposite of intuitive—an additional position in currency might mitigate risk in securities instead of adding to it. SecDB eventually allowed the firm to understand risk in an integrated way across all its businesses. It's one of the reasons that Goldman came through the 2008 global financial crisis without major losses. More than thirty years later, the core of it is still in use—something almost unheard of for a technology tool.

Mark added people and analytics to trade options and derivatives to every asset class traded at J. Aron. He took some of the most commercial people from the diminishing metals business and had them map out and create from scratch an energy-trading business that over time grew to be very lucrative and extensive. Eventually, the energy-trading business came to include physical assets—refineries, tankers, storage, and so on.

Marcy went part time after having her first child and left after her second one, so I was now in charge of the precious metals sales force, small as it was. On top of that, Mark tapped me to create a new sales force to execute forex business for clients—clients that we didn't yet have. Aron had a small currency business that arbitraged spot prices in the interbank market against currency futures on the International Monetary Market, on the model of our gold-arbitrage trading. Mark thought we could build a sales force to compete with banks for the business of corporations that wanted to hedge their foreign exchange exposure.

That sounded good, I said. Sales, which really meant figuring out how to relate to different kinds of people, came naturally to me. Of course, I knew nothing about the foreign exchange business. If I had, I might have quit before I started. I had no idea how far we had to go.

A seat at the table, age two.

With Mom and Dad and sister, Jacky, in our Bronx "backyard."

My sister, Jacky, took me places—here, Battery Park.

Police were a presence at my public high school in East New York, Brooklyn, though not always in such force or so prominent. Must have been a special day.

Bookish Lloyd in his Harvard dorm. This "candid" photo was taken by my roommate, David Grizzle, the yearbook photo editor.

My summer job at the Hotel Brickman in the Catskills. I was a lifeguard by day and nightclub server by evening.

My mom and dad at my college graduation. A proud day for them and a close call for me.

With Jacky, up for my graduation from Harvard Law School.

Two lawyers on a date. With Laura at the Franklin D. Roosevelt home and presidential library in Hyde Park, New York.

Dennis Suskind holding court. He handed out red suspenders to mock the investment bankers, but they didn't notice.

Executing gold orders for clients at J. Aron.

The coffee tasting room at J. Aron—not what Goldman Sachs bankers thought of as finance. They'd come to watch, like it was feeding time at the zoo.

The ever-intense Mark Winkelman telling a joke. His vision and ability righted the ship at J. Aron.

My brilliant partner Tim O'Neill, and me, behind the beard.

The foreign exchange corner of the J. Aron trading floor.

Jimmy Riley and Gary Cohn in the middle of much of the world's aluminum supply. Too much for the warehouses, the ingots we bought were stored out in the open on docks in Rotterdam.

My 1988 Goldman Sachs partner class. Pre-diversity.

The fixed-income trading floor at Goldman Sachs. The risk of data screens tumbling was an occupational hazard.

OPPORTUNITIES FOR DEVELOPMENT:

Better listening skills
More inclusive, less dominant in meetings
Can be overly harsh, adversarial, and intimidating
Tendency to micro manage
Inflexible, not open to other opinions
Needs to widen his group of trusted people
Needs to expand his external presence
Become more statesmanlike and positive
Willingness to occasionally lose a debate or argument
Sarcasm can be biting and sometimes inappropriate
Be viewed as more empathetic
Motivate more by influence and example than by fear
Broaden and deepen relationships with clients
More circumspect in how and where he criticizes others
Stronger presentation skills beyond Q and A
Exhibit more patience where appropriate
Consciously nurture the authority of his senior managers
Learn how to balance support with criticism
Understand better the impact of his current position
Expand presence outside the firm

Feedback from a 360 review in 2002 showing how badly I was misunderstood. The list of my good qualities is much shorter and less interesting.

CHAPTER 8

De-Vals and Re-Vals

Fear of failure weighs heavily on people—almost as much as fear of success.

Oblivious to the ramifications of the new initiative, I moved enthusiastically. I read everything I could about how the foreign exchange market functioned, and the math of it. Fortunately, there wasn't much to read.

A number of first-world countries still had currency controls and fixed or semifixed exchange rates. For those that allowed their currencies to float freely, spot forex prices were set by the market. But in the mid-eighties, and for a long time after, there remained various international mechanisms by which governments pledged to keep their currencies within a band of other currencies. Given different monetary policies, economic growth rates, and other structural factors, these bands could not always be held. There were constant and predictable devaluations and revaluations, which provided lucrative trading opportunities.

At that point, the European central banks were trying to control exchange rates under something called the European Exchange Rate Mechanism, or ERM. The ERM was supposed to serve as a kind of training wheels for an eventual common European currency, and it was already showing some of the problems that would later emerge with the euro. Weak and unstable currencies like the Italian lira were tied to strong and stable ones like the German mark. The ERM allowed trading within a range, but when a currency approached the bottom of the band, that country's central bank was supposed to intervene to support it by raising interest rates and perhaps by buying its own currency in the market. Betting with or against central banks (usually the latter) could be a way to make a lot of money. One such opportunity was the effective devaluation of the dollar as a result of the Plaza Accord in 1985. The most famous currency trade of that era occurred later, when George Soros "broke the Bank of England." Soros earned over $1 billion for his Quantum Fund by betting correctly that sterling would be devalued, despite the UK central bank's strenuous efforts to maintain its targeted exchange rate band against other European currencies.

It was also a good moment to be looking for opportunities as a service provider in foreign exchange. The 1980s were a period of rapid deregulation that led to globalization of markets and the expansion of cross-border trade and investment. Even major developed economies like Japan and the UK had protected capital markets. Goldman Sachs was only allowed to participate directly in the Japanese stock market starting in 1985 and in the UK stock market a year later. As those markets opened up—the watershed event was London's "Big Bang" in 1986—international capital flows expanded rapidly. With those flows came currency risk and the need for businesses and asset managers to deal with it.

Aron's legacy forex operation was a "riskless" arbitrage business. It consisted of taking prices that commercial banks were feeding into the interbank market and trying to capture price discrepancies against the IMM, or International Monetary Market exchange, which was a part of the Chicago Mercantile Exchange. The complexity we were able to take advantage of was that most currencies in the interbank market were quoted in foreign currency per dollar, while the IMM prices were priced in dollars per foreign currency, and to a forward or future delivery date. Today, a computer would conduct this arbitrage automatically and in microseconds. Forty years ago, it was done by traders with fast fingers, desktop calculators, and a phone on each ear.

Becoming a currency market maker created a much larger opportunity to profit. By offering a bid and an ask, our traders could capture the spread on ordinary currency transactions, not just the variance between the exchange rates in different markets. But this created a new problem I didn't know enough to anticipate. The convention in the interbank market was that you got prices from other banks only if you provided prices in return. We were not prepared to offer prices to other banks. As price takers and not price providers in the interbank market, we were appropriately labeled as customers of banks. But now we were going to other banks' corporate clients to compete for their business.

That put us in the lovely but unsustainable position of banks treating us like a customer while we were competing for their customer business with end users. For a while, we were able to build up a customer business under the radar. But as in riskless arbitrage, this was an advantage that couldn't last. After a while, we found that banks were not so eager to quote us prices; they'd do it when it suited them. More than one tried to exclude us from participating in the interbank market unless we stood ready to offer prices to other banks—which at that point we were not prepared to do. I naively thought it was our natural right to be treated well by banks.

To solve this problem, i.e., to become a "real" bank, we needed to achieve scale around forex transactions. But we were starting from zero, or something close to it.

AS A FIRST STEP, I TOOK STOCK OF MY "TEAM." THERE WERE A FEW folks hanging around the existing business whom I could put to work soliciting forex customers. But they were old school. Very old school. And because they knew a bit about the market structure I described, they were doubtful about our prospects for success. The big commercial banks had been in this business for a long time. The Bank of New

York had been making a market in foreign exchange since America was a country. How could we compete with them? the old hands asked. What advantage did we have that we could use to differentiate ourselves from the big commercial banks in the foreign currency business?

My answer was that we could compete with them by taking advantage of the brand, capabilities, and client base of Goldman Sachs. Part of the reason for the pessimism I heard from the existing team was that they were, at the core, J. Aron. Their business cards still said "J. Aron"; they still answered the phones "J. Aron"; they still booked transactions in the name of J. Aron. J. Aron couldn't do what was being asked of us. But Goldman could. Goldman had the brainpower and technical expertise to design new products for its clients. We could leverage Goldman's skill at analyzing markets, its intellectual and market savvy, and its reputation. The Goldman Sachs business card shifted the burden of proof the way a degree from Harvard did: People assumed you were smart and would add value unless and until you demonstrated otherwise. The Goldman Sachs name meant that potential clients would almost always take our call.

To pursue that strategy, I would have to recruit a strong new team—right from those banks we were about to start competing with. The status of Goldman Sachs was also critical for attracting high-quality people to a fledgling operation. I ended up hiring more than a dozen salespeople, most of whom knew something about foreign exchange but who were not so hidebound as to be overly pessimistic about our potential for success. I was fortunate that my first recruit was Jon Lopatin, who came from Bank of America. Jon knew the business and was smart and flexible. He and the other experienced hires I made never would have joined J. Aron. But they had faith in the brand of Goldman Sachs. Jon ended up as a Goldman Sachs partner.

Another key person was Tim O'Neill, my brilliant, tax law–loving friend from Donovan, Leisure. Tim had joined Goldman's tax department a year and a half after I'd joined J. Aron. Now, like me, he was finding tax law a little limiting and was interested in coming over to the commercial side. I went to his boss, who was, to put it mildly, apoplectic. Recruiting from inside the firm was strictly taboo. Tim's boss went to Mark Winkelman trying to get me fired. All I could say in my defense was that Tim was the one who initiated the move—trueish, but perhaps not the whole story. The tax department knew how smart Tim was and they didn't want to lose him.

And then there was Armen, who was eager to help build new products for customers as well as internal trading and risk-management tools. If I lacked the kind of precise mind needed to do what Tim did, there was no world in which I could ever do what Armen did. But I could do something they probably couldn't have done without me, which was to assemble and coordinate a lot of disparate pieces and people. We put our heads together to assess the potential market and the products and approaches we could develop for them. And that's where the innovation started to happen.

There were three kinds of possible customers for the expanded forex services we wanted to provide. The first were the traditional end users of the foreign exchange markets: companies that needed to hedge against foreign exchange fluctuations and transaction risk. The typical forex client at that time was a corporation that had to manage its overseas income and possibly hedge future flows or liabilities from the funding needs of its foreign subsidiaries. As markets opened up, those US-based corporations were getting involved in more complex cross-border activities. We thought they would respond to new products that could accomplish very specific objectives, such as currency options and derivatives tailored to M&A outcomes. Such products were more common in stock and government-bond markets. Applying the same logic to foreign exchange was an opportunity.

A second potential market was investors and asset managers who wanted to both hedge positions and speculate in currency movements. Now that markets like the UK and Japan were opening up, international capital flows were expanding rapidly. With all that new foreign investment came currency risk and opportunity for people managing funds. Here we could lean into Goldman's excellent, long-standing relationships with asset managers at mutual funds, university endowments, family offices, and sovereign wealth funds. Unlike corporations that wanted to reduce their exposure to currency risk, asset managers were seeking new kinds of exposure for gain. And their scale was potentially much bigger.

The third aspect of our strategy was helping clients in large strategic transactions that were separate from the regular day-to-day flow of business. In the 1980s, Goldman Sachs was frequently the number one firm in mergers and acquisitions and in IPOs, and there was a surge in such activities in other countries. At the largest scale, government-owned companies like British Gas and British Telecom were being privatized, i.e., sold to the public, including institutional investors from the US and other countries. Those investors needed to acquire British pounds to complete their purchases, and the timing of the currency purchase was critical to the performance of their investments.

For example, a US company might bid for a foreign company in that company's national currency. It could take many months for shareholders and regulators to give their approval and for the transaction to close. In that window, currency fluctuations could occur that would make the transaction much more expensive (or cheaper) in dollars. Swings of 10 percent or more were not uncommon. And if a transaction never closed, currency bought in anticipation could generate a large loss. Sophisticated hedging of currency risk was thus critical to M&A outcomes. In that kind of scenario, confidentiality was paramount, and currency strategy had to be embedded in the overall planning without involving banks that were not participating as M&A advisers. So it made sense for members of our group to join the Goldman M&A team, working "behind the wall" on transactions.

There was one other critical element to the strategy we developed, which was not a customer market per se but our effort to carve out a special role around research and analysis. It's one thing to be an effective executor of foreign exchange and potentially shave off some small execution costs for your clients. It's a whole order of magnitude more important to tell your clients whether, when, or how to take a position or to hedge. I knew that the reputation we created as good forecasters in the currency markets would be critical to our overall success.

And so we organized ourselves according to our strategy: a group that covered corporate clients; a group that covered asset managers; some folks dedicated to working behind the wall with investment banks on strategic transactions; and, finally, the analysts. The researchers and forecasters of currency movements who joined our team looked different from the foreign exchange groups at large commercial banks. At the core were David Morrison and Gavyn Davies, two Brits we recruited as a duo from a London-based advisory firm in 1986. Hiring these admired international economists, whose commentary was often quoted in the financial press and could move markets, gave our London-based sales force great credibility.

I felt a certain kinship with Morrison, who had a story parallel to mine. The son of a bus driver, David was raised in a tenement in a declining industrial town in the west of Scotland. Growing up without money left him (though not me) with a taste for the high life; he was known for his collection of Ferraris, as well as for his understanding of how macroeconomics drives long- and short-term currency movements. His reputation was enhanced by his impenetrable brogue. Unable to understand what he was saying, people assumed it was brilliant.

But David wrote without a brogue, and that was brilliant too. Every month, David and Gavyn would release their blue book, with research and analysis about the UK, and their green book, a tour of foreign exchange around the world. Unlike the tax advance sheets I dreaded getting when I practiced law, I loved when the blue and green books came and would carry the latest editions with me everywhere. David's skepticism about the viability of the ERM drove our emerging proprietary trading operation in London, which would soon become a huge profit center for Goldman. David believed that forcing economies to adjust to fixed currency rates was likely to create what economists call disequilibriums, such as unnecessarily high unemployment. In a steady stream of papers, comments, and appearances, he argued that fixed exchange rates couldn't hold. When Britain finally pulled out of the ERM in 1992, his view was richly vindicated.

As Goldman developed as a global firm, one of its greatest advantages was a culture that valued the talent and drive of people like Morrison and later Jim O'Neill, whom I recruited from UBS to replace David as chief international economist after David left to found his own firm. Jim was from Manchester, with a degree from the University of Sheffield. His career was another example of smarts and drive triumphing over class and connections—he subsequently became a minister in David Cameron's government and was admitted to the House of Lords as Baron O'Neill of Gatley. At UBS, he had a big reputation as an international economist.

At the eleventh hour, before he formally committed to Goldman, I was on a call with him from New York, and he was wavering. I told him I'd meet him for breakfast the next morning. Without stopping home, I went straight to the airport, flew overnight to London, and closed the deal by walking him over to our office to sign the paperwork. Perhaps I felt a special affinity for Jim because his Mancunian accent registered in London similarly to the way my Brooklyn accent did in certain circles in Manhattan.

Very few of the people Goldman hired would have been hired at the big merchant banks in London. City firms like Morgan Grenfell and Schroders hired young men from distinguished families with Oxbridge pedigrees—it was just a few years past the world of black umbrellas and bowler hats. Goldman, with its recent transfusion from J. Aron, looked for strivers who weren't wanted at those places—just as I hadn't been at the white-shoe law firms in New York. If they had attended Oxford or Cambridge, Goldman's new hires were likely to have gotten there as scholarship kids from state schools rather than as legacies from Eton or Harrow. In Japan, the other place we were setting up a significant hub for our expanding currency operation, we mostly hired bankers of Korean descent, whom we thought of as Japanese and the Japanese thought of as Korean, despite their families having lived in Japan for generations. They were versions of J. Aron's outerborough strivers with street smarts and something to prove. In those more class-bound and xenophobic societies, our ignorance of caste distinctions and appreciation of diversity conferred a significant advantage in the fight for real talent.

CHAPTER 9

Innovation

The necessity of breaking into a saturated market is the mother of financial innovation.

In our pursuit of new opportunities in foreign exchange, Tim O'Neill and I looked for analogues in the stock and government bond markets. There Goldman had the experience and the analytical team to create sophisticated products that accomplished more specific objectives but that could be complex to risk manage. For example, what if you wanted to buy a stock denominated in pounds and wanted to hedge out the currency risk? Before the late 1980s, the normal practice would have been to sell forward an amount of sterling equivalent to the current value of the stock. The client would offset a forex exposure by creating a short British pound forward contract. That would neutralize the risk, which would be good if the pound fell but would, of course, be regretted if the pound later rose.

That approach had significant limitations. The value of the underlying asset could fluctuate, and the number of pounds needed to remain fully hedged could be known only at the end of the hedge period. What you really wanted to hedge against was the value of the stock at an indefinite point in the future. An early product that Armen, Tim, and I helped to develop was the "quantity adjusting" option. Our "quantos" would automatically adjust the coverage of the option to the foreign currency value of the asset at the expiration of the option period. This was both more effectual and often less expensive than a traditional foreign currency option.

Or as another example, a client might want to hedge the currency risk of an acquisition in a foreign currency–denominated asset but need the option only if the underlying transaction were to go through as planned. We designed options that were contingent on the underlying transaction happening. Because there was usually a significant possibility of a deal falling through, a normal option would be more than what was needed, because the option would still have value even if the underlying transaction evaporated. So we designed a "contingent" option hedge that would disappear if the underlying transaction failed, even if the currency-option part of it was in the money. This contingent option hedge could be offered more cheaply while still satisfying the client's objective. There were many other such innovations during this period that helped establish our reputation for strategy and product development.

I'VE THOUGHT A LOT ABOUT THAT FUN AND FERTILE PERIOD IN MY early career, asking myself what made it possible. What were the factors that allowed innovation to flourish in the way it did at our J. Aron group in the late 1980s?

The political and economic moment was a crucial enabling condition. With globalization and the liberalization of markets, there were new opportunities for firms with international reach. New technologies were central too. When I went to Wall Street, Goldman Sachs still had huge, room-filling mainframe computers made by IBM or Burroughs. Mark Winkelman was advocating a move to what were then called microcomputers and today would themselves be preposterous antiques. But he couldn't get the firm to make the technology investment for the sake of J. Aron, where we were thought of as a lesser species. So Mark had the inspiration to withdraw from the big shared system and maintain our own separate hardware. Working for the first time with desktop PCs instead of mainframes and using new computer models, we could track prices dynamically and see risk holistically. Aron's move meant that there were fewer people to share the costs of the old mainframes, which drove up the allocation for the remaining users. By finding a way to shift overhead expenses for dated technology onto others at Goldman, Mark ultimately got the whole firm to change.

To take advantage of transformations in technology required a certain kind of mentality. If you were too steeped in the old world of finance, you might see the objections more clearly than the opportunity. A securities trader earning fixed commissions saw the downside of deregulation. Young outsiders like Tim, Armen, and I focused on the upside. We had less to lose and more to gain than our Goldman colleagues. We were in our early thirties, and it was an insurgent moment in finance generally, notable for the emergence of junk bonds and mortgage-backed securities. Our team was able to function as a kind of laboratory for new lines of business at Aron and provide a path out of the so-called innovator's dilemma that afflicts established businesses.

The foreign exchange business was my first opportunity to take a conventional, readily understandable treasury service and offer it to typical Goldman Sachs clients. Everything I had done previously at J. Aron in the metals business was esoteric (like metals hedging); was done with an unconventional client (Al Rajhi) or clients with specific connected businesses (gold-mining companies); or involved specialized procurement in a dedicated part of a company (say, platinum for catalytic converters in the automobile industry). Part of what was exciting about foreign exchange hedging was that we would get our feet in the door at Goldman by calling on relationships that our investment bankers had with their clients at the top levels of companies.

At least that's how I thought it would go. In practice, the investment banking division was somewhat helpful but not that committed. Every organization has its hierarchy of status and prestige. Investment bankers are at the top of the heap at Goldman Sachs, which for decades had been the leading adviser on corporate dealmaking and financial decision-making. They're always prepared, highly polished, and invariably impressive. A couple hundred investment bankers at Goldman Sachs have peer-like relationships with top CEOs and CFOs, and the swagger to match. They behave like they're the best in the world—and they're often right.

Inside the organization, we were trying to develop a business relevant to executives operating below the strategic level of big companies. The skepticism we felt from the investment banking side wasn't just a matter of arrogance or a superior air. Goldman bankers had an understandable fear that the little-known new arrivals from J. Aron would wreck their hard-won relationships. But beyond that, there were limits on how helpful Goldman investment bankers could be, because while most large companies engaged in forex activity, it was normally the treasurer or assistant treasurer, not their C-suite superiors, who managed their companies' short-term liquidity. We were able to get a bit more help and more appropriate introductions from Goldman money-market salespeople with contacts at that level as well as from the people we were hiring laterally from commercial banks.

Most people at Goldman responded positively to my curiosity about their parts of the business and my enthusiasm for collaborating with them. But I sometimes had to use sticks as well as carrots. I remember one investment banker whose help I wanted with introductions and who wouldn't call me back. After three tries, I phoned his boss to complain—people at Goldman were supposed to operate as a team. A short time later, the banker was on the phone cursing at me. At Goldman, not supporting a colleague was regarded as a cardinal sin. How could I rat him out to his boss?

"I'm sorry I did that," I said. "Next time, return my call."

The new lines of foreign exchange business we were developing sometimes brought us into more explicit conflict with client-facing divisions at Goldman. It was a classic Thucydides Trap—established power threatened by rising power leads to conflict—but inside the same company. Within the fixed-income and capital-markets groups at

Goldman, for example, there was a substantial team that raised debt for its clients. A part of its business was to issue non-dollar debt for its corporate customers, often swapping that debt into dollars for them. But in those early days, Goldman would broker rather than "principal" the swap. It would collect an agent's fee rather than serve as the transactional counterparty. J. Aron would approach the same transaction from its recently developed principal background. To us, currency swaps and hedges were economically equivalent to forwards in the foreign exchange market. The only important difference was that swaps were for a longer term—the life of the bond.

The client base for both types of products overlapped substantially, and the factors that moved those markets also overlapped. The characteristics of non-dollar bonds made them look to us a whole lot like the forex business, and we viewed it as part of our natural expansion. I even came up with a slogan: Raisin' debt is our raison d'être. (Nobody liked it.) The Goldman groups perceived J. Aron as trying to muscle its way in, and they weren't entirely wrong. It was important for me professionally that an increasing part of my portfolio was in the fixed-income division, part of the "real" Goldman Sachs. Non-dollar bonds were a wedge into the non-Aron, regular business of Goldman, and we took advantage of the opportunity. This is when we started to hear that we were regarded as hegemonic (my word) or thuggish (their word). Goldman was a collegial place; the folks from J. Aron were hungrier and more aggressive. Some people at Goldman didn't take well to the rising power trying to take its place at the table.

We were also now calling on clients who wanted to take speculative positions in foreign currencies. But Goldman Sachs already had a futures services department that brokered futures of all kinds, including currencies, to clients. These were used to take risk in commodities, foreign exchange, and financial instruments, or to hedge unwanted risks. Should those clients call the old Goldman futures services department or the Aron forex trading desk? We were all essentially doing the same thing, whether trading in interest rates futures, currency futures, or shorter-duration foreign bonds. But in moving into this business, Aron was bumping into investment bankers and private wealth advisers at the "real" Goldman who owned those important client relationships. They accused us upstarts of un-Goldman-like behavior—calling customers behind their backs. To some of the genteel Goldman bankers, it was like Al Capone expanding into the South Side. Eventually, the conflict got bad enough that Bob Rubin had to broker a concordat, which we all signed in his office. Literally signed.

Everyone abided by the terms, but the sense that we were an invasive organism lingered. At 85 Broad, J. Aron had a separate elevator bank that went only to the lower floors we occupied. On "Black Monday," October 19, 1987, the stock market crashed and the Dow fell by 22.6 percent, the biggest percentage drop of all time. A few of us took the Goldman elevator for the upper floors to witness the bedlam where securities were traded. When the elevator doors opened, security shooed us away like unwelcome tourists.

Another problem was pushback from traders within Aron. On the Wall Street status ladder, sales ranked below trading. One options trader made that hierarchy clear by giving me the nickname Overhead. As in "Hey, Overhead, why are you costing us so much money?"

Happily, there was less friction around our work with asset managers, where Goldman's relationships were long term and deep. Asset managers were looking for advice and access to foreign markets, not to hedge but to acquire exposure. In this activity, and with their client base, Goldman Sachs was a natural and trusted provider, and often the appetite of such investors could dwarf the scale of more traditional corporate users of the markets. The portfolios that asset managers had to create and hedge were huge.

Clients of ours who managed international stock and bond portfolios from time to time wanted exposure to foreign currencies without necessarily buying the stocks and bonds of those countries. But currency risk was hard to obtain in dedicated stock and bond funds that didn't have mechanisms in place for holding foreign currency positions outright. To solve that problem, we created short-term money-market instruments, which we called Universal Commercial Paper, denominated in any foreign currency that a fund manager might want—Italian lira, Dutch guilders, Belgian francs, Hong Kong dollars, Australian dollars. They functioned like cash, but cash in a foreign currency. This had a nice symmetry: Commercial paper was Goldman Sachs's original business, going back to the 1870s. In the first weeks, we sold more than $1 billion worth of UCP. As a result, funds were able to hold currency as a distinct asset, not just as an adjunct to holding foreign stocks or bonds. Not everyone loved the idea. The central bank of Germany, concerned that we were creating "money" outside its regulatory purview, asked us to stop issuing commercial paper in deutsche marks. We yielded where necessary.

From a standing start, foreign exchange became an important and high-profile activity of the firm. In 1984, the year I began working on it, we made $10 million in profit on forex. The following year it doubled to $20 million. In 1986, *Euromoney*, a British magazine focused on international finance, published a poll that ranked Goldman Sachs as one of the top twenty bank foreign exchange teams. That was an extraordinary outcome given that we had been a nonplayer a few years earlier and still weren't functioning fully as market makers in currencies. Did we campaign for a spot in the rankings? You bet we did. We asked our clients to vote for us in the poll. Then we ordered hundreds of reprints of the article and handed them out as calling cards.

The other thing happening that would prove crucial to the future success of the firm was the rise of proprietary trading. Through the customer business and our analysts, we had our finger on the pulse of markets and were in a better position to trade currency and commodities than perhaps anyone else. But as an arbitrage business, J. Aron initially resisted taking risk with its own capital. Winkelman and Rubin thought that methodical risk-taking, drawing on our market insights, could be a large profit generator. They were right. Proprietary trading flourished first in London, where Mark hired Mike O'Brien to run a trading operation under the J. Aron banner. Fueled by their skill and insights from Morrison and Davies, the London traders flourished. By the end of the decade, foreign exchange would be providing the bulk of J. Aron's overall profits. Mike and his operation had a tremendous run, before they got clobbered by big losses in 1994.

IN FOREIGN EXCHANGE, WE LEARNED THAT THE ASSET MANAGERS seeking exposure had the ability to be much larger than corporate hedgers. Instead of just derisking their supply chain over a year or so, they were looking to add new types of assets to their massive portfolios. Goldman Sachs was an investment bank, and they were investors, so this was fundamentally in our wheelhouse. Given J. Aron's expertise, it made sense to extend the kind of product innovation we were driving in foreign exchange to commodities. But here the sell was going to be a good deal more difficult. Investors and asset managers were already involved in global equity and debt markets, where the relevance of currencies was obvious. Other than perhaps oil, the prevailing view was that commodities futures were for farmers.

As principals, we did some spectacular trades. One of our biggest stars was Gary Cohn, who came to work for J. Aron as a commodity trader. Gary, who suffered through school with undiagnosed dyslexia, is the classic case of someone who compensates for slow reading with fast math. He started arbitraging gold as a summer intern at a brokerage firm in Cleveland, using his own meager funds. Soon he had earned enough to buy his own seat on COMEX, where he traded commodity options and futures of all kinds. That trading brought him into contact with J. Aron traders, to whom he was often a counterparty. Recognizing how good he was, the head metals trader, Jim Riley, had the bright idea of recruiting him to work for us. At the end of his first year, we paid Gary a bonus, not realizing that it amounted to a fraction of what he'd been earning as an independent floor trader. Nevertheless, he stayed with us, and it all worked out in the long run.

Soon after he got to Goldman, Gary proposed a brilliant if slightly terrifying trade. As the Soviet Union collapsed, it was dumping massive quantities of processed aluminum onto the world market. This created a glut—there was much more aluminum than soda-can companies and auto manufacturers could absorb in the short term. As a result, refined aluminum was deep in contango, meaning that the futures price was significantly higher than the spot price. Even if nobody needed aluminum just then, buyers still wanted futures contracts for aluminum. By agreeing to buy it in the future, they were guaranteeing a high interest rate to the current holders. Even with the cost of storage, there was potentially a large profit to be made by holding the aluminum and hedging out other risks around currency and interest rates. This is what's called a cash-and-carry transaction. You buy the commodity on the spot market and sell it forward, locking in a return.

The catch was that you had to take delivery of physical aluminum. A lot of it. By buying spot and hedging it forward, we were, in effect, financing inventory, i.e., lending money, at a very high interest rate. But to earn that return, we had to be able to store the physical aluminum. When Gary brought the idea to Jimmy and me, I was a little skeptical. Owning physical commodities can involve all sorts of unforeseen consequences. At various times in the 1980s, when supply exceeded demand, J. Aron would step in and hold vast inventories of cocoa and coffee. As inventoried stocks kept building, the cocoa in the warehouses would become exposed to moisture, fungus, insects, and other critters. In another hard-to-forget episode, cattle stock we owned got stuck in four feet of snow in Colorado and couldn't get to green pasture. Through hard experience, we decided that it might be best to avoid taking delivery of commodities that could die on us, needed to be fed, or could be eaten by bugs.

Those aren't the only risks in arbitraging physical commodities. Crude oil might be worth more once refined into gasoline, even accounting for the cost of processing. But you can't profit from the conversion if you don't have the capacity to convert it. The same goes for a geographic differential. Natural gas might be worth more in one place than another, but only if you have the ability to move it. One of the biggest losses in our otherwise very profitable trading business occurred when natural gas was being extracted so quickly in Canada that the pipelines were at capacity and you couldn't transport any more of it to the US, where the price was higher. With the pipelines maxed out, the price of natural gas produced in Canada temporarily went to nearly zero. All you could do was flare it off. The best way to hedge against those kinds of risks is controlling the infrastructure you need to fulfill contracts.

There were also risks that went beyond financial harm. After the *Exxon Valdez* disaster in 1989, there was a smaller spill of oil owned by J. Aron in Narragansett Bay. I remember John Weinberg, the firm's legendary senior partner, making clear that he wanted no part of harming waterfowl or ruining beaches. A ship's owner and captain are the ones responsible in the case of an accident, and both paid fines under the Clean Water Act. In that case, the cleanup was relatively easy and inexpensive, and it never became an issue for Goldman. But the incident brought home that the greatest liability we faced with physical commodities was reputational. Financing and holding a huge share of the world's aluminum? What could possibly go wrong?

That's where Aron's global relationships and scale kicked in. The ability to source material, work out transportation, and arrange storage was a powerful differentiator for our firm. Gary had researched the storage problem thoroughly, so we told him to go ahead and start buying. Which he did, stockpiling the aluminum in a facility in Rotterdam. When the facility was at capacity, we piled the ingots outside. For more than two years, we built up an enormous mountain of processed aluminum. The glare off all that shiny metal was so strong that Dutch air traffic control asked us to put tarps over it so that it wouldn't blind pilots flying into Amsterdam's Schiphol Airport. When supply and demand came back into a more normal alignment, Gary's trade earned the firm hundreds of millions of dollars in profit.

Most traditional asset managers left that kind of dealing to the Gary Cohns of the world. They considered commodities to be a market for traders, not *investors*. They thought of commodities as a zero-sum game: For everyone who made a dollar, someone lost a dollar. Stocks were not a zero-sum game, because companies made profits, and growth and dividends and share buybacks all made for a positive overall expected return. Bonds paid interest, again, a positive expected return. But commodities by themselves earned no return. They cost money to store and secure. In the parlance of money managers, stocks and bonds were an accretive asset class—they grew over time. Commodities were a zero-sum game.

Or so it was thought.

In fact, commodities have a yield. There is always a cost to borrow or lend them, which is reflected in the futures market. Some commodities prices are typically in contango, like gold or Gary Cohn's aluminum mountain in Rotterdam. That premium of the futures price versus the spot price reflects an implied positive yield, which can be realized by selling the commodities forward. One of the first new products Tim and Armen developed to take advantage of this insight was a "Gold Bear Note," which also played on the end of the precious metals boom. If you thought gold was going to go down in value—as it tended to do in the mid-1980s—our note provided an effective way to make that bet. It was indexed to the price of gold, so the price would go below par if gold appreciated in value and higher than par if gold went down. Either way, the note paid a high rate of interest.

Energy commodities like oil often operate differently because they are typically in backwardation. Backwardation occurs when the futures prices are lower than the current spot prices. Commodities in backwardation also offer an implied yield, which can be realized by buying the commodity at a lower price in the future compared with the spot price. If the spot price remains unchanged by the end of the term, the difference between the futures price and the spot price becomes profit. However, there is risk involved if the price of oil moves up or down. The key idea is that if prices stay the same and the spot price doesn't change, you earn the discount. In this way, commodities in backwardation act as a growing asset, similar to a Treasury bill that increases in value as it matures and is redeemed at its face value. (The holder still faces the risk of currency value changes.)

Figuring that out was a big aha moment for us. That insight about commodities having a yield allowed us to go to the managers of long-term portfolios and recommend holding commodities. They were a great inflation hedge, a diversifier of risk, and an accretive, yield-generating asset class. We provided history and analytics in support of our theory. It was a major revelation to most, especially the last point about commodities being an accretive asset class. A wave of investment in commodity buy-and-hold strategies followed.

To gain traction for this opportunity, we had to meet some practical requirements that the prevailing commodities index, the Commodity Research Bureau Index (CRB), didn't satisfy. First, if investors wanted to invest in commodities as an asset class, they would need a convenient portfolio of commodities. That is, it had to be based on a basket. Second, that basket had to be rule-based and weighted, not *just* an arbitrary allocation like the CRB—one barrel of oil, one bushel of wheat, one ounce of gold, and so on. Third, it had to be investable, i.e., commodities for which there was a futures market or other financial proxy (like oil, as opposed to steel). Fourth, the value of the index had to grow by realizing the yield from "rolling over" the financial proxies for the commodities. Fifth and finally, there had to be transparency, i.e., a trustworthy source of price discovery for the basket of commodities.

These conditions were diligently checked by Tim O'Neill and Armen in creating the Goldman Sachs Commodities Index. The GSCI included only those commodities for which there was a public futures market. The index was weighted by the proportion each of those commodities had of total traded volume. The index "rolled over" at a prescribed time, and the yield was captured. That meant that the price of the index tended to rise over time, even if the prices of the underlying commodities remained flat.

An active futures contract was what would ensure liquidity and price transparency for buyers. So Tim spent a lot of time and effort convincing the Chicago Mercantile Exchange to support trading in a futures contract on the GSCI itself. A few years later, Harvard Business School published a case study about commodities futures that validated and endorsed our thesis. "The dynamics of the commodities futures marketplace are driven mostly by the actions of hedgers and speculators," it read. "Commodity futures, however, offer investors a chance to earn competitive returns, to protect their assets against inflation, and to diversify their portfolios for improved risk-return characteristics." That was sweet vindication for our idea.

What the GSCI did was enable a passive "long only" investment strategy in commodities that attracted capital from major institutions, especially those with a long horizon—Harvard Management was one of our first clients. The huge scale of these institutional investors meant that our clients were becoming a new and important sector of commodity demand, influencing markets in notable ways. Ultimately, Goldman essentially gave the GSCI to Standard & Poor's, to avoid any suggestion of a conflict of interest in the formulation and management of the index. It's still called the GSCI, though.

We accomplished a lot by bringing the esoteric products and investment opportunities of J. Aron's currency and commodities business to general asset managers whose focus had previously been limited to stocks and bonds. Foreign currencies became tradable in all sorts of ways that pushed economies around the world toward floating, i.e., genuine, exchange rates. The GSCI and a suite of investable products tied to it created a way for market participants to get exposure to commodities from a derivative rather than physical ownership, or by owning the shares of producers. They could benefit from owning a proxy for oil without worrying that if an oil tanker sprang a leak, they would be the ones in the headlines.

Our little group was getting credit for being aggressive innovators. I was getting a higher profile in the context of J. Aron businesses as a quick study who could work well with different kinds of people—but tough enough to run through the occasional stiff arm. The trading side of the business was doing very well, especially in proprietary trading out of London. But it was our sales and marketing efforts around currency and commodities that were driving the business and our external reputation. We weren't just taking market share from others; we were creating flows that otherwise wouldn't have existed. And we were contributing to the firm's reputation, not just living off it.

In a variety of ways, we were drawing our part of Goldman more deeply into becoming a global enterprise. But all this innovation and expansion at J. Aron contained the seed of something even more important for the firm—Goldman's transformation into a global firm comfortable taking greater risk with its own capital, and not just on behalf of clients.

CHAPTER 10

Howdy, Partner!

In moments of organizational-chart ambiguity, try simply acting like you're in charge anyway. If people listen, fine. If they don't, just shrug and move on. People usually respond to demonstrations of leadership more than to titles.

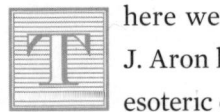here were two important transitions I was making in my J. Aron life in the latter part of the 1980s. One was from the esoteric commodities business to more "core" Goldman Sachs activities relevant to the traditional Goldman client base. The other, just as important, was from being a sales manager to being a trading and risk manager. It was traders and risk managers, in the context of the overall securities businesses, who were perceived to play the most consequential role in terms of P&L and protecting the firm.

One day Mark Winkelman called me into his office. He said that the trading side of metals and foreign exchange in New York would report to me going forward. This was a big deal. At Goldman, salespeople seldom crossed over and became traders. And at J. Aron, salespeople virtually never became heads of businesses that had trading elements. But there I was, or at least it seemed that way.

Upon announcement of my promotion, some of the senior traders, especially in the more elite "options" desk, protested. I didn't see or hear this directly. But shortly after the announcement, Mark told me that my new role was being rescinded. With regret, he said that his boss, Bob Rubin, after listening to complaints from a few traders, was acceding to their view that traders shouldn't report to someone who didn't grow up on the risk side of the business. One of the most vocal traders, I learned, was the guy who called me Overhead.

Rubin instructed Mark to back off from putting me in charge. A weak memo followed, implying that I would "participate" or "drive strategy" or some other weaselly walk-back of the original simple concept of my being in charge.

Fortunately, I didn't act disappointed. I acted as if I recognized that it was a natural and valid objection. This wasn't from a spirit of generosity or confidence or patience; I just didn't want to show that I was defeated or felt bad about it. As in other moments of organizational chart ambiguity, I simply acted like I was in charge anyway. If people listened, fine. If they didn't, I just shrugged and moved on and didn't get my back up. I gave a lot of instructions in the form of "advice." I remember asking one trader to do something, and he questioned whether he reported to me. I said I wasn't sure myself, but the risk was his. Over time, more senior management operated through me like I was in charge, and eventually practice became an official reality. There was no further memo.

Our business was expanding and so was my family. Our older son, Alex, was born in 1985. Our second son, Jonathan, was born January 1, 1988. Rachel would follow a few years later, in 1993. Like a lot of families raising kids in Manhattan apartments, Laura and I wanted somewhere we could take them on weekends. With both of us doing well at work, we decided on a modest starter house in the Hamptons. Buying it would max out our savings, and given the way we'd grown up, taking on debt and living close to the edge made us nervous.

Driving to the closing, anxiety attacked us both. The amount of our mortgage, the closing costs, the money in our checking account . . . The numbers didn't add up to the $350,000 price of the house. We kept going through the math, wondering how we could possibly have made such a large mistake. Only as we were pulling into the closing attorney's parking lot did it hit me: We'd forgotten to count the 10 percent deposit we'd put down a couple of months earlier. It's the feeling of chest-tightening panic, not the sense of relief, that has stayed with me.

GOLDMAN NORMALLY NAMED PARTNERS IN EVEN-NUMBERED YEARS, and the process was always consuming and distracting. (It was said to be every other year to allow time for healing of the inevitable rifts and hard feelings.) By 1988, no one from J. Aron had made partner beyond the six original J. Aron partners who became Goldman partners at the time of the 1981 acquisition. We Aron people were so out of the mainstream that I was mostly unaware of the partnership process. But by the approach of the 1988 election, I saw the possibility and my anxiety was high. As it was for Laura. To reduce the stress for her, I told her the white lie that the decision would be made at the end of the November fiscal year when in fact the announcement would come in mid-October. Meanwhile, I counted down the days.

Then one day the phone rang on the trading floor. "Lloyd, it's John Weinberg for you."

For a rare moment the desk went quiet.

"I would like to invite you to join the partnership," the firm's senior partner said.

It was John's practice to personally give the news to all the new partners. I remember his call as if it were yesterday. When I became CEO, I continued that practice, so important to the culture of the firm, of congratulating all the new partners personally, though as the firm grew in size, I split first-call responsibility with my COO. I always made sure that as part of the call, I said things that demonstrated awareness of the new partner's personal situation and his or her contribution to the firm. I knew that call would be remembered, so I worked my end accordingly. It was a joy to make those calls, especially in contrast with the consoling calls I had to make to the terrific professionals who came close to but just shy of making partner.

As soon as I got off the phone with John Weinberg, I called Laura, who was shocked and happy, as she wasn't expecting any news that day. I arranged to meet her for dinner at our favorite Chinese restaurant, Shun Lee West on Sixty-Fifth Street. But on the way out the door, I was collared and taken out for celebratory drinks by my colleagues in the forex department. I eventually made it to Laura at the restaurant, but wobbly and two hours late. Laura waited and didn't kill me, though I deserved it.

Four of us from J. Aron made partner in October 1988, among three dozen in total for the whole firm. Those biennial Goldman classes became informal peer groups, embedding friendships and rivalries, along with seeds of the firm's future story and the coming evolution of Wall Street. That class of '88 (all men!) included John Thornton and John Thain, key future leaders at Goldman, as well as other names that would figure prominently in the coming years: Robert Steel, Mark Schwartz, Christopher Flowers, Frank Brosens, and Gary Gensler, among others. Three others from J. Aron were part of the class: Steve Hendel and Steve Semlitz, the co-runners of the energy business, and Mike O'Brien, the foreign exchange trading leader in London. Gavyn Davies and David Morrison, technically part of the Goldman research department but very engaged with Aron, were made partners as well.

Though my job stayed the same, my status increased dramatically, inside and outside the firm. Inside, I now attended partners' meetings that discussed the whole firm. But I was still J. Aron, which was not the most prestigious part of it. Being a partner didn't make me feel quite like a full and equal citizen. The outside change was more immediately significant. People now knew better what to make of me. If I walked into a room, I didn't have to explain who I was anymore. I was a partner of Goldman Sachs.

The New York Times reported that the average Goldman partner had capital in the firm valued at $9 million. Maybe I would too someday, but my economic situation was not immediately improved. In fact, it worsened in the short term. I'd made $550,000 the previous year. But the way it worked at Goldman was that every partner received a "draw" of $200,000 and a share of partner profits. The draw was like a base salary. Your share of profits after taxes would feed into your "capital account," on which the firm paid you an 8 percent return.

However, my capital account started at zero. Like all new partners, I was expected to make an initial contribution to it out of my own resources. In my case, I was assured the amount would be relatively modest, because at that point in my life—and after buying the house in the Hamptons—I had very little in savings. I recall my initial capital contribution was only around $50,000, which came out of my pending 1988 bonus. Capital accounts could be drawn down if the firm had a very bad trading year, as happened in 1994. You could withdraw your capital only after you retired, and only then in stages. The only exceptions were that you could withdraw money to buy a house or make charitable donations. So while I began accumulating capital in my partnership account, I was now taking home much less in pay than I had in previous years.

Shortly after the call from John Weinberg, I was visited by his chief of staff, Jon Cohen, who served as a kind of minister of the interior—in the days when Goldman Sachs was a very private firm that didn't deal much with the exterior, such as the press. His job was to talk to me about expectations for partners of the firm. Of course, ethical standards were to be the highest, and he warned me against what we would today call "me too" behavior. From that point forward, the firm would prepare my tax returns. This wasn't just a perk. It was meant to ensure that all Goldman partners paid all their taxes on a conservative basis and that all information about firm investments stayed within the Goldman ecosystem.

In addition, the firm would help me set up a charitable foundation. I was expected to put money in, be philanthropic, and play a role serving local civic and educational institutions. Because of my interest in history, I lit on the New York Historical Society as a potentially good fit and later became a trustee there, as well as at Weill Cornell Medical School, and became an active fundraiser for scholarships at my alma mater, Harvard. Laura joined and eventually chaired the boards of the Ethical Culture Fieldston School and Barnard College, schools she had attended on scholarship.

As someone prone to anxiety, I now had the added worry that came with knowing general partners faced unlimited liability. That risk had become terrifyingly real for Goldman Sachs partners before my time, when the Penn Central Railroad went bankrupt in 1970. Creditors holding commercial paper issued by Goldman Sachs had sued the firm for more than the value of its total capital. The bankruptcy litigation dragged on for many years and was never far from the thoughts of the senior partners. With that episode in mind, I asked Cohen whether he thought it would be a good idea to put my home and other financial assets in my wife's name. He looked at me quizzically.

"Lloyd, I promise you that no partner has ever suffered liability beyond his capital account because of Goldman," he said. "But I can tell you that plenty of partners have suffered losses because they put assets in their spouse's name."

Finally, Cohen gave me some life advice. I was advised to conduct myself so that if I were to have an obituary of, say, nine paragraphs, no more than three of them would refer to Goldman. In other words, I was to contribute to the world separately from Goldman and was supposed to have a life after Goldman. The advice resonated, though I wasn't sure I would meet that test and am still not sure I will.

I understood, of course, that naming four of us who had grown up at J. Aron after the acquisition as partners was a statement about the growing role and importance of J. Aron at Goldman. Making us partners was the right thing to do on its own terms—we'd earned it. But it also sent a message that perhaps the acquisition hadn't been a mistake after all. Yet the divide was there. Even after nearly a decade and much financial success, J. Aron was still very separate. We were a distinct division; we occupied our own floors (though now in the same building); and we transacted commodities and derivatives in separate, J. Aron–designated entities. We still answered our phones "J. Aron" and referred to Goldman Sachs as "Goldman Sachs."

While our products and services increasingly touched traditional

Goldman businesses, they were still conceived of differently. Goldman Sachs charged fees in its investment banking business and earned brokerage fees in its equity business. J. Aron was a principal business. We now made most of our money buying from and selling to other principals, not by buying and selling on their behalf. This was another key distinction. While Goldman Sachs referred to its "clients," J. Aron had "counterparties." But over time, Goldman proper was evolving greater principal capabilities, while J. Aron was developing a client franchise and culture. The businesses were growing into each other, converging over time.

As a partner, I experienced more of the ways in which the cultures remained very different. Goldman is a competitive place with very competitive people. But it has always had a "we" culture rather than an "I" culture. It's anathema in the firm to behave competitively against your own colleagues—a good thought, even if it is sometimes optimistic in practice. For the first six years I was a partner, everyone in my class got paid exactly the same amount—a powerful statement about the culture of the firm. Every two years, our partnership percentage would be reset, and all of us became incredibly adept at multiplying any number by the .00346 or .00387 that would funnel into our capital accounts at year's end. We were like idiot savants—we might not have known our multiplication tables beyond twelve times twelve, but all of us could factor our potential share of any large number like the Dustin Hoffman character in *Rain Man*.

J. Aron was, by contrast, not a culture where commitment to team was paramount. Salaries and bonuses were far from equal, and people had less of a sense that the long-term health of the organization was synonymous with their own self-interest. But if Aron was more of a cowboy culture, the cowboys were driving the herd. By 1989, Aron contributed 30 percent of Goldman's $750 million in profits, while comprising only around 3 percent of its worldwide staff. In 1990, Aron generated 40 percent of Goldman's profits. At that point, even John L. Weinberg began to appear. On his first visit, he began his remarks to a group of us by saying, "I would have been here sooner, but I couldn't find anybody who knew which floor you were on."

The Goldman / Aron culture gap continued to play out against the increasing areas of intersection and overlap. The natural solution to internal conflict at Goldman was usually to rearrange businesses, complicate reporting lines, combine groups, and create co-head management structures—with a lot of quiet and sometimes not-so-quiet infighting and politics in the background. Sometimes it worked, sometimes it didn't.

It would take at least another decade for the Goldman / Aron dichotomy to fade away. Its persistence explains a lot about what happened in my life over the next several years.

CHAPTER 11

Paranoia Is a Job Requirement

Nothing gets me more rattled than everything going well.

Things were going very well for Goldman Sachs, for the J. Aron division, and for me at the firm. At the end of 1990, John Weinberg retired, and Bob Rubin and Steve Friedman became co-senior partners and cochairs of the management committee. That was all as anticipated. Less expected was when Rubin left two years later to become chair of President Clinton's newly created National Economic Council. Part of the idea of having co-heads was to create a balance between trading and investment banking. When Rubin left after such a short time in the job, there was no longer someone at the top of the firm with deep experience in trading. Steve Friedman chose not to elevate a co-head, leaving an imbalance that would have consequences.

Under Mark Winkelman's guidance, J. Aron had moved from arbitrage and risk avoidance to being a risk-based trading firm that was applying technology and quantitative analysis to foreign exchange, energy, metals, and fixed income. Aron was simultaneously becoming more of a client-focused business and more like a hedge fund.

The two went hand in hand. Being at the center of so much trading flow—and having top analysts like Morrison and Davies—gave us the confidence and credibility to expand our own proprietary trading. Proprietary trading benefited our client relationships because we were engaged in trading similar to theirs, and our market knowledge was much more extensive and on point. Proprietary trading didn't just make our advice more influential. It changed our relationship to clients, making us less a pure service provider and more of a peer. Taking large positions with Goldman's own principal gave our "macro" opinions about where rates, prices, and policies were headed more weight with clients and with markets. It was a kind of virtuous circle, where our views helped to influence markets in the direction of those views. At least sometimes, for a while, and up to a point—markets go where they want to go, not where you believe they should go.

Within the firm, J. Aron was driving unprecedented gains. It continued to contribute a third or more of even larger profits in 1991, 1992, and 1993. This was atypical of the industry. At most investment banks, currency and commodities trading contributed a smaller share of profits, closer to 20 percent.

The other driver of trading profits at Goldman in those years was the fixed-income division, jointly led by Mark Winkelman and Jon Corzine, a team of rivals. Fixed income on its own contributed $1 billion to Goldman's profits in 1993—more than the entire firm had ever earned just a few years earlier. That year, Goldman's pretax profits were an astonishing $2.3 billion. No Wall Street investment bank had ever had a year when it made that much money. The profits of those years funded rapid global expansion. Between 1990 and 1995, Goldman opened offices in Frankfurt, Mexico City, Vancouver, Seoul, Osaka, Taipei, Shanghai, and Beijing. The Cold War was over, and the era of globalization was underway, moving with astonishing speed. The size of Goldman's staff was multiplying along with the shiny new offices in exotic-sounding places.

It felt good to be a partner. I was able to focus on growing our businesses. I was traveling internationally, recruiting talent, working with clients, and expanding our revenue. I was already in charge of foreign exchange trading in the US and Asia and now began adding responsibility for bonds denominated in non-dollar currencies. When Dennis Suskind retired in 1990, Jimmy Riley replaced him as head of the worldwide metals business, reporting to me.

I brought a lot of intensity to my role. In those years, there were shortages of platinum-group metals that were needed to make catalytic converters, which the EPA required new cars to have in order to meet emissions standards under the Clean Air Act. Those elements—platinum, palladium, and rhodium—are mined in only a few remote locations, primarily in South Africa and the Russian Arctic. On the basis of weight, they were the most expensive metals in the world, the latter many times more valuable than gold (rhodium went to $7,000 an ounce in 1990, up from $1,200 the year before). Thanks to our long-term contracts, Aron was a critical supply conduit for auto manufacturers. General Motors named us Supplier of the Year four times in the 1990s for sourcing and hedging commodities. One year, they invited Jimmy and me to Detroit for a celebratory weekend that included driving all kinds of GM vehicles around a test track. Jimmy chose the Corvette. I went for the dump truck.

That was a rare domestic trip. More often, I was on planes to more distant places, including Malaysia, Hong Kong, Korea, and Brazil. Because we had young kids at home, I seldom tacked any leisure time onto my tightly packed meeting schedules. To this day, it's hard to remember whether I've been to certain countries or not, because all I would have seen there is hotels, offices, and taxis, which looked more or less the same everywhere I went.

Jimmy may have enjoyed some of these trips less than I did. I was obsessed with preparation and would badger him with questions and worries before every client meeting. He used to tell people that when he left on a work trip with me, he made sure he had a whole bottle of Tylenol.

I WAS IN OUR BACKYARD IN THE HAMPTONS WITH WEEKEND GUESTS when Laura called to me from inside the house.

"Lloyd, Robert Maxwell is on the phone for you."

I felt pretty pleased with myself. In 1991, Maxwell was one of the giants of global business and a press lord in the United Kingdom. He owned the popular tabloid the *Daily Mirror* and a variety of other businesses, including the publishing house Macmillan, various cable TV interests, and the Berlitz language schools. His personal story was the stuff of legend. Born into a poor Jewish family in Czechoslovakia, he escaped the Nazis as a young man and became a war hero fighting with the British. His reputation was far from spotless; British financial regulators had censured him decades earlier for "reckless and unjustified optimism." But that was in the distant past, and Maxwell was doing a lot of business through Goldman Sachs. He was even Goldman's landlord in London, where a senior partner in charge of the corporate trading desk, Eric Sheinberg, helped Maxwell syndicate loans and execute block trades. The firm also extended credit to Maxwell, based on his extensive assets.

And here the great man was calling me at home on the weekend to solicit my views about markets and currency trades. Maxwell transacted in the foreign exchange markets on behalf of his various business entities—something he was, naturally, authorized to do. For the foreign exchange transactions, he was referred to me. Given who he was, I dealt with him directly and was flattered by the engagement.

A few months after that call in the Hamptons, I was summoned to the phone again, this time with the news that Maxwell was missing from his yacht, which had been sailing off the coast of the Canary Islands in the Mediterranean. It's never been definitively established whether he jumped off the boat or had a heart attack and fell. But as the Maxwell story unspooled, it emerged that he had been committing financial fraud on a large scale. Maxwell was siphoning his company's pension funds to support an overleveraged and failing business empire. He died owing Goldman $62 million in unpaid loans and left the firm holding worthless shares in his primary media company, which was now bankrupt. He had stolen much more from his own workers.

And I had been one of the people he duped. While he had legitimate foreign exchange business to do, Maxwell was using Goldman—and me—to move money from where it belonged to where it didn't. In one or more trades that I facilitated, he had currency paid to Goldman from his publicly traded companies and then had the proceeds of trades wired to his private company. I had never even focused on the details of his settlement instructions. There was nothing inherently illegal or unethical about a client providing funds for a trade from one entity and having proceeds paid into another. But it should have raised a red flag.

When it all unraveled, I was interviewed by our internal Goldman Sachs chief counsel, Robert Katz, as well as our lawyers from Sullivan & Cromwell. Obviously, I wasn't malevolent, just another idiot taken in by Maxwell. The interview by our team was done in anticipation of the likelihood that I might be questioned by government officials in the US or UK. Luckily, I was never called to testify, because I would have made a horrible witness. I felt so guilty that if they'd asked me about the Lindbergh baby kidnapping, I would have confessed to it. I knew I wouldn't be fired or prosecuted, but at that time, looking naive and stupid to my partners was as great a punishment as I could have imagined.

The transactions I'd been involved in weren't even a footnote in the huge report on the Maxwell affair that UK Department of Trade and Industry eventually issued. Goldman ended up paying a small fine to the British authorities and a very large settlement—$254 million—to the pension funds looted by Maxwell. While there was no admission of wrongdoing, it was reputationally damaging to the firm and could have spelled the end of Goldman's aspirations in the UK and Europe. For a firm trying to break into Britain's financial establishment, it was a significant setback.

Like other partners, I had to cover my share of the costs. The $254 million bill didn't go to the partners at the time of the settlement, in 1994. It went to the smaller number who had been partners between 1989 and 1991, when Maxwell was actively doing business with Goldman. Because the partnership was reorganized every two years, that meant that many former or "limited" partners, who had retired after the years covered by the settlement, had to write checks to the firm. Many of the limited partners thought it was unfair that they had to contribute to settling claims arising from transactions they'd had nothing to do with, at a firm where they no longer worked.

Occasional squabbling between classes was one of the consequences of remaining a private partnership—an issue that had arisen before my time with the Penn Central bankruptcy in the early 1970s. The financial upside to a partnership was great, but the liability was unlimited. The Maxwell episode brought home for me and partners of my generation that anyone at the firm could do something at any time that meant you could lose not only your job but also your home and all of your other financial assets.

I got an education with respect to Maxwell—an education that almost killed me. I learned that problems could come from any direction, or out of nowhere, and that it paid to be paranoid about what could go wrong. I also came to see that my rising status and growing success at the firm created a susceptibility to being used. It's always nice to have the powerful and important flatter you. But for the first time in my career, I was in a position to do things for them, to affirm or decline a growing variety of transactions.

That is, I was now someone worth manipulating. The real danger wasn't that important people would sweet-talk me into doing stupid things. It was that I would delude myself about my own importance and fail to apply the requisite suspicion about their motives. My power required a certain kind of reserve in dealing with people, especially those whose approval I sought. The temptation was always to say yes to someone who was a personal friend, a celebrity, or a more successful or influential businessperson—in short, anyone you instinctively wanted to please and impress. Especially when dealing with someone I was flattered to be dealing with, I had to cultivate a self-protective cynicism.

A BIGGER PROBLEM AT GOLDMAN WAS THE PSYCHOLOGICAL IMPACT OF A long run of gains and the lack of risk controls in our principal trading accounts. John L. Weinberg used to say that success causes some people to grow and others to swell. The traders in the proprietary trading group based in London definitely swelled. If ever there was a group that needed close supervision and a system of risk controls, they were it.

At the end of 1993, the firm was still riding favorable market conditions. We were in a bull market in bonds driven by interest rates falling for more than a decade. Older bonds carrying higher interest rates are more valuable than newly issued debt with a lower yield. In other words, if you bought bonds, you got used to their mostly going up in value. The one-way bet on that trend had been paying off for more than a decade—and, with some significant interruptions, would continue to do so for two decades more.

With that wind at our backs, it's fair to say that we were suffering from overconfidence, collectively and individually. A distinct culture within a culture had emerged on the second floor of Goldman's London office, where the fixed-income and currency departments were housed. Conspicuous displays of wealth, which always cut against the grain at Goldman, were becoming more common. Nonpartner traders whose salary and bonuses came in the form of fully liquid take-home pay, not an accumulating capital account, were buying luxury penthouses and chartering planes for their ski vacations. A trader would get a bonus check and buy a Ferrari. They seemed almost like children to me. In Britain, company-provided cars weren't fully taxed as income, so it was standard for companies to lease cars for their employees. Newly hired traders would negotiate for fancier and fancier cars—you couldn't pay them enough to get them to stop talking about it. I remember one lateral hire going five rounds with me on the class of BMW he wanted. I eventually relented.

Bolstered by a long winning streak, Mike O'Brien, a member of my 1988 partner class who ran the currency trading desk in London, would exhort traders to "bet the ranch." Those trading under him had wide latitude to take large positions with the firm's capital. If you wanted to take an unusually large position, you just phoned your manager and asked. The answer was seldom no. It was as if every trader had an American Express card with no credit limit. In this environment, risk-taking by even a single trader out of hundreds could become a huge problem.

And how was the firm tracking risk overall? It wasn't—or not adequately. Equities, fixed income, and J. Aron—meaning currencies and commodities—were the three trading divisions. Each of these divisions had its own dedicated sales, trading, technology, and risk-management systems. Think of it as similar to the way infantry, artillery, and armored units operate in the US Army. These units are organized to be largely self-sufficient and to have their own support around intelligence, logistics, reconnaissance, and so on. When it works well, this kind of diffused authority allows for tactical flexibility and focused accountability. When it doesn't, business units can suffer from severe failures that go undetected for too long and affect the firm as a whole.

J. Aron and equities used different risk-management systems. J. Aron used the Armenator, which—not to get too technical—was a simulation-based system. We ran ten years of historical returns and reported the worst, the fifth-worst, and the tenth-worst returns as our "risk." Fixed income based its system on the Black–Litterman model (the fascinating Fischer Black again). It was linear, which means that it projected forward a range of possible outcomes. There are advantages and disadvantages to both methods. A historical model is by definition limited by what has happened in the past. A linear model can lead to a significant understating of risk if you are writing out-of-the-money options. Under many circumstances, though, options don't behave in a linear fashion.

There was no firm-wide committee to allocate or manage risk overall. We didn't have SecDB yet. Value-at-risk systems that could track risk levels on a daily basis were just starting to emerge and weren't much used. Despite the collective liability imposed by the unlimited partnership, a great deal of deference was given to the heads of divisions. I had the impression that people felt it would be impolite to poke your nose into whatever they were doing in other areas. Given that Steve Friedman's background was in investment banking, risk supervision in J. Aron and fixed income essentially ended with Mark Winkelman and Jon Corzine. They had deep experience. But everyone needs a manager, and they didn't have one experienced in trading after Bob Rubin left at the end of 1992.

Making matters worse, traders who had been very successful were granted latitude to trade across asset classes and weren't limited to their areas of expertise. It seems crazy in hindsight, but people were accorded deference simply because of their apparent success. The theory was that they were "macro" traders, and that their positions came out of their views of currencies, interest rates, and government policies, which affected all markets. So proprietary traders in London were taking positions not just on foreign exchange, where they'd been so successful, but on debt and equities as well. Too much value was being attached to their prior success based on a limited track record. In reality, they were young guys with a few years of good results, not Warren Buffett with decades of market-beating performance.

Compensation practices further incentivized risk-taking, creating a kind of moral hazard. If you were a partner, you had a powerful incentive to calibrate risk and protect the firm, which also meant protecting yourself. As the Maxwell episode demonstrated, losses as well as gains would be shared by all of us. But if you weren't a partner—and most of the traders weren't—you had an asymmetrical upside. In a year when you lost money for the firm, or didn't make much, you would still earn your salary and likely a modest bonus. In a year when you took more risk and made outsize gains, you could earn more than many Goldman Sachs partners did. And at any point, you could simply walk away. In those pre-IPO days, compensation was entirely in cash; if traders went to a competitor, there was no unvested stock that they had to leave behind. Through this whole period, competitors who envied our trading success were aggressively courting our most profitable traders. As a group, their loyalty tended to be highly conditional. In my experience, the traders who were the hardest to manage and most demanding ended up defecting anyway and left a mess behind when they did.

What went wrong in 1994 was a bet that interest rates would continue to fall and the failure to adjust course quickly when the market did what it wanted to do. In the US, signs of incipient inflation prompted Alan Greenspan, the chairman of the Fed, to begin hiking rates for the first time in five years. A quarter-point increase in February was followed by six more increases over the next year, which raised the federal funds rate from 3 percent to 6 percent at the end of the tightening cycle. The Morrison and Davies view had been that the UK and other European central banks shouldn't raise rates, which would increase unemployment and have other negative effects on consumers. But the central banks disagreed and raised interest rates anyway.

That shift in the market caught our traders flat-footed. They were holding US Treasuries, securitized mortgages, and other fixed-income assets that were now declining in value on a daily basis. Currency trades were based on future interest rates, and wrong bets on where rates were headed produced large losses in forex as well as in fixed income.

For years, everything had seemed to be going right in our trading businesses. Now everything was going wrong at the same time.

CHAPTER 12

My First "Crisis of the Century"

The cost of a trading blowup is not just the loss on the position but the way that the aftermath makes you risk-averse and less able to take advantage of new opportunities. That excessive caution can turn out to be even more expensive.

The 1994 losses were the first existential threat I experienced at Goldman. In some ways, what happened in 1994 was worse than what happened during the global financial crisis in 2008, because in 1994, Goldman was really on its own. Other firms sustained losses with the shift in markets, but not of the same magnitude. The experience challenged my view of the firm's culture as an unshakable Rock of Gibraltar.

Mike O'Brien's traders had succeeded in forecasting where interest rates were going when they were dropping for a long period. But once rates started moving in the other direction, those traders were no longer so smart. They argued that it was a temporary adjustment: Rates would perhaps increase slightly and then remain stable. Instead, rates rose faster than anticipated and continued to do so. And instead of taking more modest losses, traders wanted to show their nerve by holding on to their positions, or even doubling down on them. It was a very macho world, and hanging tough was seen as virtuous.

Loss aversion is a natural cognitive bias. Correcting for it and adjusting quickly to new realities is part of what makes a superior trader. Managing traders, I observed that what distinguished the best ones wasn't that they were necessarily right more often than others. They simply adjusted more quickly. They made more money when they were right and lost less money when they were wrong. They internalized the observation often attributed to John Maynard Keynes that the market can stay irrational longer than you can stay solvent.

The dynamic of loss aversion led to major trading losses for the firm in 1994. One hundred million a month in losses turned into $200 million a month by the fall of 1994. Traders soon gave back most of what they'd earned for the firm in 1993—$800 million in the London office alone. The grinding effect of losing money every day upset everyone at the firm. Steve Friedman, for whatever reason, couldn't make it stop and didn't order Corzine and Winkelman to make it stop. With salaries and bonuses for staff pointed drastically lower, people started to leave for competitors. Deutsche Bank alone poached fifty employees from Goldman.

Goldman was on its own not just in the size of its trading losses but in being a partnership—the last major one on Wall Street. Like the Maxwell episode, which was finally winding down in 1994, the trading disaster made clear what it meant to have most of your net worth tied up in that structure. The losses were personal to everyone, and our capital accounts would reflect them. That year, I lost about a quarter of what I'd built up in six years as a partner.

For a couple of partners who joined the partnership laterally and off cycle at the end of 1993, the effect of 1994 would be that they would have negative balances in their capital accounts. Hideo Ishihara, one of our first Japanese partners, joined Goldman after he missed out on getting the top job at a Japanese bank. Prior to coming to Goldman, he had never earned a Wall Street–level salary. Having earned very little in his first year, he now faced the prospect of losing the savings he had put into his capital account. It played out well for Hideo over time, but it must have been quite bewildering in the moment. The same thing happened to Sharmin Mossavar-Rahmani, who was recruited as an off-cycle partner in 1993. Sharmin was hired from First Boston to work in fixed income for our asset management business. In 1994, she must have doubted the wisdom of that move. Today Sharmin is chief investment officer for Goldman's wealth management division, the person private clients regularly hear from with the firm's views about markets in relation to the economy. She is one of only a handful of partners remaining from before the 1999 IPO.

IN SEPTEMBER, IN THE MIDST OF THE MOUNTING LOSSES, STEVE FRIEDman announced to the management committee that he would be leaving as CEO. He was worn out by the job and had been having heart palpitations—he thought the stress would kill him if he stayed. Earlier in the year, he had discussed his plan to retire with Bob Katz, our general counsel, and no one else. A lot of people at the firm were dismayed not just that Friedman was leaving at that perilous moment but also by the way he handled it. Steve hadn't wanted a co-head, and he hadn't paved the way for a succession. A lot of partners still held his departure at an inopportune moment against him many years later. I would point out, though, that at an even more dangerous moment when the firm needed him, Steve redeemed himself. At the height of the 2008 financial crisis, he was on the Goldman board. When the head of the board's risk committee left to run the insolvent insurance giant AIG under government supervision, Steve stepped up to take a job that no one else on the board was qualified for and no one else wanted.

Steve's departure opened the floodgates, giving license for other partners to leave. Soon they began announcing their departures. Moses K. Tsang, who headed the Hong Kong office, quit. So did Henry James, not the novelist but the president of Goldman Sachs in Japan. With the large losses we were facing, these were rational financial decisions for individual partners. A partner who retired or "went limited" was no longer personally liable for future losses. It also meant he could withdraw his accumulated capital over a period of five years. And that capital would instantly be safer. Limited partner capital functioned more like senior debt. It was paid first, at a fixed interest rate, out of pretax profits. Once you became a limited partner, it didn't matter to you financially if the firm made a lot of money. But with every departure, the firm's primary capital would diminish, making it weaker and less resilient. It was a vicious cycle where partners jumped into lifeboats because other partners were jumping into lifeboats and they were panicked about missing the last one.

The departures were incredibly upsetting to everyone who stayed. It wasn't just that the firm was losing senior talent; it was that every departure signaled a lack of confidence in the firm. *What do all these people know that I don't know?* We'd had a long run of good years. The previous eight of them had been *really* good years. All it took was one bad—okay, genuinely terrible—year to send people running for the tall grass. The departures cut against the ethic of the firm, which was to support the partnership through thick and thin.

It was an embarrassing moment for the vaunted Goldman culture. John L. Weinberg, who was personally affronted by Steve Friedman's peremptory departure, just as he had been about Robert Rubin's unexpected retirement at the end of 1992, came back from his own retirement to rally the troops in New York and London. He talked about how the firm had gotten through tough times in the past and how it had emerged better and stronger. But the fact that people needed to be reminded to be loyal to the partnership in a difficult moment was more than a little disconcerting.

At the same time, there were some unexpected, moving displays of loyalty. The partner in charge of J. Aron's coffee business, Howard Katz, had previously told me that he was planning to retire. We were winding down that part of the commodities business, so his retirement actually made sense for the firm. But that fall Howard came to me and said that under the circumstances, he felt he had to postpone his retirement for a year or two. He didn't want to look like he was abandoning ship and joining the exodus. Like others who stayed, he was rewarded for the decision. As it had during previous crises, the firm did indeed bounce back stronger.

But for what felt like an excruciatingly long time, there wasn't anyone in a position to stop the hemorrhaging. There wasn't even a clear management structure in place. Most companies have a CEO. At Goldman, it could be one senior partner, two senior partners, a chair and vice-chair, or some other variation. The management committee was left with the urgent problem not only of who should succeed Friedman but of what the management structure should be. Despite his role in the trading losses, Steve wanted Jon Corzine to replace him as senior partner. He also recommended that Corzine be offset in some way by Hank Paulson, who had come up on the banking side—the classic balance.

There was a tradition at Goldman of often appointing co-heads, both at the top of the firm and at key division and business levels. That's something that isn't as common at other firms but that serves an important function in training highly ambitious and competitive people to work with one another as equals. When it works well, one plus one adds up to three. When it doesn't, one plus one can be zero, or worse. However, after much discussion, the management committee agreed on appointing Corzine as chairman with Paulson as vice-chairman. Not making Paulson coequal with Corzine probably sowed the seeds of their future conflict. Because of the circumstances, it was far more rushed and less thought out than the typical Goldman succession. The management committee had to skip over the normal vetting and selection process. It was a little like Joe Biden stepping aside and handing his presidential nomination to Kamala Harris. And it worked out about as well.

Departures by those who had been passed over followed. Mark Winkelman, who had been my rabbi at J. Aron and was a rival to Corzine, simply walked out the door. A *Wall Street Journal* story the next day quoted him saying he was looking forward to spending more time with his family and called his departure a "particularly chilling blow" to Corzine. It was certainly a blow to me. I'd spent years cultivating the brilliant but aloof Winkelman and was now going to be working for Jon Corzine, someone who never got along with him, perhaps as a consequence of their professional rivalry and very different personalities.

Corzine, who had come up through fixed income with Winkelman, was his temperamental opposite—an easygoing Midwesterner raised on a family farm in downstate Illinois, where he'd been the quarterback of his high school football team. He had a salt-and-pepper beard, wore sweater-vests, and had approximately a million friends. The bond business in which he'd grown up was, after all, a relationship business. Corzine was easy to get along with, but because I'd worked in Winkelman's world, I wasn't one of his people. Paulson, an investment banker based in Chicago, was just a reputation to me: a driven and highly capable but often inarticulate Christian Scientist who drank milk and loved bird-watching. In the sometimes tribal politics of Goldman Sachs, my J. Aron tribe was in exile, or at least in a kind of disfavor.

Corzine's appointment was of a piece with what would become a significant trend on Wall Street in the late 1980s and '90s: the rise of the bond trader. If you go back to the 1970s, bonds had a lower status than equities on Wall Street. Trading them was thought to require less smarts and sophistication. You didn't have to really judge the future prospects for companies; you only had to gauge whether they were going to repay the money they borrowed on time. Lacking the polish and finesse of investment bankers, who court CEOs and fall into the CEO role more easily themselves, bond traders weren't necessarily well-rounded thinkers. But everywhere on Wall Street, they were ascending to the tops of firms, because the fixed-income business was driving huge profits.

There was a macro explanation for this trend. With fiscal deficits mounting during the Reagan years, the US Treasury issued government bonds in unprecedented quantity. The Federal Reserve's policy interest rate spiked above 19 percent in 1981 and then began a long slide to nearly zero after the global financial crisis. Declining interest rates fueled a thirty-year bull market in government debt, creating an enormous tailwind for bonds. A version of the same phenomenon was occurring with debt issued by European countries and Japan, which rose in price as yields declined.

And it wasn't just government bonds. There was an explosion in what were then called junk bonds, or high-yield debt. That boom was personified by Michael Milken at Drexel Burnham Lambert, before he went to prison for insider trading. There was also the development of trading in mortgage-backed securities. Those phenomena made the bond trader a figure in popular culture. They also propelled bond traders to the tops of the leading Wall Street firms. In addition to Corzine, the generation that rose with the bond market included John Gutfreund at Salomon Brothers, John Mack at Morgan Stanley, Stan O'Neal at Merrill Lynch, and Dick Fuld at Lehman Brothers. The last three would be in place for all or part of the financial crisis, which revealed, among other things, the limitations of old-line bond traders as the leaders of firms.

DECISIONS ABOUT WHETHER TO SIGN THE NEW PARTNERSHIP AGREEment had to be made by November 30, 1994, the end of the fiscal year. The departures were mounting, and many partners were dithering about what to do. "Get into the boat or get out," Corzine demanded in conversation after conversation.

That final weekend, on the Saturday after Thanksgiving, Goldman was holding its annual partners' dinner dance. All of the firm's New York–based partners and their spouses would gather at some elegant spot like the New York Public Library or the Rainbow Room. It was an event I usually looked forward to. But this year's dinner, held under the suspended whale at the Museum of Natural History, was going to be a grim affair—and a lot smaller than usual, given that around 50 partners out of 162 had already announced their departures and wouldn't be attending. The head of investment banking services,

Chuck Davis, agonized until the very last minute and then quit on the last day of the fiscal year, just before the big dinner. He said he waited so that he could be more effective in trying to convince other partners to stay! Especially for me, who after six years had fully absorbed the ethos of the partnership, it was pretty damn demoralizing.

The departures in 1994 were a strong indication that Goldman needed to take seriously the option of becoming a public company—something that had been discussed and rejected many times over the previous years. Being an unlimited liability partnership just created too much risk and vulnerability when times were hard. A crisis was so threatening to the general partners that it created powerful pressure to leave, just to protect the wealth they'd built up over the years. In those circumstances, the firm couldn't maintain a healthy capital base. The same logic had driven the other big Wall Street firms to convert themselves to public companies. We needed a more stable and ever larger capital base to compete with them. The 1994 losses made this problem fully apparent. But shaky as it felt at that moment, the belief in the partnership culture ran deep at Goldman, and the resistance to going public remained intense.

Nineteen ninety-four was a partnership year. So while trying to preserve capital, we had to figure out how to make the partnership work for a new class that was about to join. It was decided that the members of the new class, our largest ever, with fifty-eight new partners, were all going to receive $500,000 bonuses for their prepartnership year, much lower than most had been earning previously. Some people, for whom 1994 wasn't a bad year, were especially shocked. But shouldering the burden collectively was appropriate after a rare year when Goldman had effectively lost money, after paying its limited partners and other debt holders. To make up for lower cash compensation than the new partners would have expected in their first year, the management committee decided to award them a larger partnership percentage, thirty-two basis points instead of the twenty-five that new partners expected. The increment continued for later years. When the IPO eventually happened, the numbers of shares partners received were affected by their partnership percentage. So the 1994 partners did well as a result of taking a one-year hit on their compensation.

All the departures in 1994 had the effect of elevating the prominence of my class, the class of 1988. Two of the most important members were John Thain and John Thornton. Thain replaced Corzine as CFO and was made head of a new risk committee. Thornton, who launched Goldman's European M&A business in the early 1980s, was made co-CEO of Goldman Sachs International. Steve Hendel and I were appointed as co-heads to succeed Winkelman in his role managing J. Aron. We split the portfolio. Steve would be in charge of energy trading, which was expanding to include natural gas and renewables. I would be in charge of everything else—currency, commodities, and metals. In Steve's and my case, these battlefield promotions were given with a lack of enthusiasm and a lot of limitations. We were co-heads of a division, but with a very short leash. Those of us at Aron, who were still sometimes regarded as second-class citizens, were tainted by the losses. Even someone as naturally optimistic as me had to feel apprehensive about the firm's future.

Especially with so many unexpected departures, my new status should have qualified me for a seat on the management committee. But there was clearly still some ambivalence about me (and Steve). That was reflected in the management committee's decision to grant us observer status, like Washington, DC's delegate in Congress. Even as observers, Steve and I were invited to *take turns* coming to the management committee meetings. I don't remember there being any precedent for that strange idea. As I had when my responsibilities for managing traders were withdrawn, I didn't make a fuss about it. I just waited it out. And before long, I was going to all the management committee meetings as a regular member. Whether there was ever a memo confirming my upgraded status, I can't recall.

CHAPTER 13

How I Earned My Reputation for Being Difficult

If I knew I was going to go so high in the firm, I would have been a lot nicer to the people I dealt with along the way. It would have saved a lot of time I had to spend making up with them later.

After a series of layoffs and cutbacks in operations, the firm began to stabilize in 1995. Profits returned—not to 1993 levels, but they were again looking healthy. Morale was improving. Before long, some of those partners who had joined the panicked exodus asked to come back—and almost all were refused.

When it came to trading risk, the pendulum swung too far in the opposite direction. It was understandable, of course, that the firm wanted to batten down the hatches, apply risk limits at various levels, and put all our trading under a formal risk committee that John Thain was now heading, and on which I had a seat. But when previously there had been excessive risk-taking, there was now excessive caution. Where there had been inadequate supervision of trading, there was now too much micromanagement and second-guessing. Where there had been too few controls, there were now too many.

This issue played out in the risk committee, which met every

Wednesday morning at 7:30 a.m. That was a little rough. When I was a lawyer, we rolled into work at 10:00 a.m. At Goldman, my responsibilities spanned all the world's time zones, so I saw no reason why I should have to get to the office by 7:30 a.m., if the night before I'd had a long client dinner followed by calls with Tokyo and Hong Kong. The early hour might have contributed to my surly mood. I felt that the language Thain and others used showed contempt for traders, the vast majority of whom had nothing to do with the problems of 1994. People who looked smart when they were making money became idiots when they lost money. The closest thing to approval I ever got from Thain was his once saying in a large group meeting that a suggestion of mine wasn't the dumbest idea he had ever heard. "Thanks for the compliment," I shot back, "but my own bar is higher than that."

Thain was my boss. He was good at his job, and I should have made it easier for him to manage me. Some of it was that old chip on my shoulder. But I also knew that the firm had to get its trading mojo back, and that wasn't going to happen by condescending to traders and making them afraid to lose money. Ironically, the issue wasn't traders straining at the new constraints put on them, though the constraints were very real. It was that trading morale was low, and people became very risk averse. Traders singed by losses were now overcompensating—they were shrinking from any and all risk, like J. Aron in the pre-Winkelman riskless arbitrage days. The pullback was necessary, but as markets tend to do, it went to an extreme. If you feel you're not allowed to lose money, you can't make money.

I remember one strategy meeting in 1995 when the people in the room shot down one trading idea after another. *We're talking ourselves out of everything*, I said. I walked out and placed a big bet myself—my first for Goldman—on the dollar rising against the yen. After the 1994 debacle, I felt that in my new role, leadership required me to set an example.

I had come up through sales, not trading, but I continued to take positions to encourage (shame?) the professional traders to get going again. And it turned out I wasn't bad at it. I took more sizable positions on the dollar rising against the yen, and they continued to pay off over several years as the dollar rose from its low of 81 yen to the dollar in 1995 to a high of 146 a few years later.

Useful and largely profitable though it was, there was probably some collateral damage to my trading. When I lost money, it pained the traders under me, of course, because they were part of the same P&L. And when I made money, it was even more painful, because they were shown up. I continued to run risk positions for several more years, simply making my P&L less visible. By that point, I had accomplished my primary objective of getting others to take more risk. It was time to abandon my secondary objective—showing off. Besides, others were better at it.

But once I got the bug, I never entirely shook it. Today you can usually find me at my desk around the stock market open and close, trading for my own account. I do this less for the money I make than for the fun (and intermittent pain) of it.

AFTER 1994, I STILL FELT LIKE SOMETHING OF AN OUTSIDER AT GOLDman. But it began to dawn on me that I could go further up the ladder. When Mark Winkelman was running J. Aron, there was a ceiling on how high I could rise. After Mark left, I had more room to ascend. In 1995 and 1996, I was doing something I had never imagined: running a division of the firm, with increasing authority over more and more of it. Mike O'Brien, blamed for the trading losses in London, stayed on awhile. But he never returned to his previous role, which meant I was now in charge of forex trading in London as well as in New York and elsewhere. In a funny way, it was my first whiff of real ambition at Goldman proper. Running Goldman, though, was never in my head at that stage. For one thing, John Thain and John Thornton were the leading figures in my partnership class, and everyone thought they would take over at some point in the future, presumably after Corzine and after Paulson.

It was also unthinkable at that point that someone from J. Aron would ever become senior partner. Aron was thought of as being overly aggressive. I disagreed—I thought we were entrepreneurial and performance driven. But there was no question that we were now encroaching on traditional Goldman activities, especially in the fragments of fixed-income activities we were adding. To the fixed-income division, those of us on the Aron side were seen as invaders with hegemonic intent. And as co-head of J. Aron, a lot of that reputation rubbed off on me.

The initial point of overlap with fixed income was around the interest-rate swaps business. Think of swaps as the market where companies optimize their cash flows by managing their interest-rate and currency exposures. Companies can swap one kind of cash flow for another—fixed-rate debt for floating-rate debt, or dollar-denominated revenues for yen-denominated revenues.

Goldman had someone who was in charge of interest-rate swaps—Mark Schwartz, a fellow member of the partnership class of 1988 and an important and well-liked partner at the firm. As head of global debt capital markets, Mark led Goldman's business intermediating swaps, which were usually long dated. This was a fee-based business. Aron's angle was different—we were focused on serving as a principal counterparty for shorter-dated interest-rate and currency swaps. This was a more profitable activity but inherently riskier. As the swaps market became more institutionalized, Mark's team started to act as principal, and the Aron team started to write contracts for longer-dated swaps. In other words, our two swaps businesses were converging, and it made less and less sense to manage them separately. In typical Goldman fashion, Corzine made swaps a joint venture between Goldman Sachs fixed income and J. Aron.

Mark and I continued to compete, but pleasantly. (Ten years after he retired from the firm, I persuaded him to come back in 2012 as a firm vice-chairman to run Goldman's overall business in Asia.) When Mark made predictions of how much business he would bring to our joint venture, I bet him that he wouldn't hit his mark. The stakes were that the loser of the bet would have to shave his beard (they were very popular at Goldman in the Corzine era). Mark missed his number. But he was so skinny, I didn't have the heart to insist he make good on the bet. Without the beard, he'd be like the Invisible Man with his bandages removed—nothing left to see but a pair of glasses.

Aron's expansion into fixed income became inevitable with the deregulation of international markets and the pending integration of European currencies. Currencies were J. Aron's core business. In helping clients hedge long-term foreign exchange risk, and placing currency futures bets ourselves through swaps and derivatives, we were effectively taking positions on future interest rates, which drive exchange rates. That meant trading bonds and other debt instruments directly.

Our trading in non-dollar bonds and swaps led to clashes between me and the co-heads of fixed income, Mike Mortara and Rick Garonzik, both of whom saw me muscling into their turf. Garonzik was a mild-mannered figure based in London whom I didn't speak to very often. Mortara was the dominant personality of the duo. He was the most important of the traders whom Bob Rubin and Steve Friedman had hired from Salomon Brothers to buck up Goldman's fixed-income business several years earlier. He helped to invent the mortgage securities business at Salomon in the 1980s and was the epitome of the gruff, testosterone-driven culture depicted in Michael Lewis's book *Liar's Poker*. Mortara was large and lived large (and died young, at fifty-one). His house was in an uncommutable part of Connecticut, and he took a helicopter to work, dispensing big tips to drivers and doormen along the way.

I wasn't impressed with a lot of the people in the fixed-income division Garonzik and Mortara had inherited from Corzine. The bond business was becoming much more sophisticated in those years because of new instruments and methods of analysis. Corzine grew up in the old school. On the government bond trading floor, you'd hear his voice coming out of the squawk box, exhorting his traders to "shoot 'em in" when he saw a buying opportunity. The old-school bond salespeople hustled to move product. Tom Wolfe got at that culture pretty well with the character Sherman McCoy in his novel *The Bonfire of the Vanities*. Back then, a bond salesman worked to get people to like him enough to buy whatever company's bonds he was selling. That business rewarded affability more than smarts or innovation. The new breed of bond trader was epitomized by Jacob Goldfield, a brilliant and eccentric Harvard grad who had studied physics and econometrics. He'd dropped out of law school to go into fixed-income trading, where he was a favorite of Bob Rubin. Jacob and his peers used statistical analysis to find arbitrage opportunities across the yield curve and credit curve and different kinds of debt instruments. Though I'd been a salesman and not a quant, I related much more to the quants and the analytical thinkers.

The truth is that we needed both types, and Mortara, who worked under Corzine, bridged the divide. He was good at keeping the old-school members of the team on the reservation while making the quanty ones feel special. Corzine, affable as he was himself, sometimes had a weakness for people who had affability and not much else going for them. He would often promote people he loved, even if they weren't likely to take us to the next level. Mortara, following Corzine, also tended to promote people he loved. I tended to fall in love with people who deserved promoting.

IN EARLY 1997, CORZINE DECIDED TO SOLVE THE PROBLEM OF OVERLAP around all of our trading businesses by fully merging J. Aron and the Goldman fixed-income division. I suggested calling it Fixed Income, Currency, and Commodities (FICC). This felt like the last step in the merger process that had begun with the acquisition of Aron in 1981. Jon put Mortara, Garonzik, and me jointly in charge of FICC.

That decision had a big effect on my position at the firm. J. Aron was much smaller, with six partners versus fixed income's thirty-seven partners. Some thought it a hostile takeover by our smaller group. Some of the reaction was to what people saw as my gang of tough and streety currency and commodity people. It didn't help that Corzine used to call me "Shiite," which I assumed he meant affectionately.

In retrospect, I can see that the reputation I developed for being tough wasn't merely a function of my expanding role. I was not, and am not, a naturally deferential person. Even on the management committee, I never held back my opinions. If I felt condescended to, which I often did, I would use humor to slash back at the offender. In a large meeting, I might talk over someone I disagreed with or ask too many questions too quickly. I was told I should listen to the answer before interrupting. *I am listening*, I said. *I just hear faster than you talk.*

Around that time, Goldman started doing 360-degree performance reviews, which solicited feedback not just from your boss but from subordinates and peers as well. My 360 reviews were generally very positive but always had the same criticisms: I didn't listen well. I was intimidating. I was too harsh. Of course, I was sure that wasn't true and for a long time proved the point by choosing not to hear the criticism. How could they misunderstand me that way?

But I do have a healthy awareness of how others see me, something that goes back to my teenage years. The truth was that I often did see this kind of tense reaction on other people's faces. After you hear the same thing over and over again from everyone who works with you, you start to recognize that there might be some scintilla of truth to it. I was getting in my own way and had to change—at least, I needed to try. My wife is more athletic than I am and was always after me to take tennis lessons. She wanted me to be able to hit balls with her. I knew I'd never be a good tennis player, so I resisted taking lessons.

"Of course it's beyond hope that lessons will make you good," Laura said to me one day. "But you can always be better."

That idea stuck with me. *I might not be able to make you good*, I used to half-joke to people who reported to me, *but I can make you better.* I applied that to myself. I didn't become a different person overnight. It wasn't like I flipped a switch one day, but I made a conscious effort to improve. I figured out that I would create less friction if I directed my cutting humor at myself instead of others. So I became easier to get along with, without necessarily becoming easy to get along with. Not perfect—but better. Anyone who knows me will tell you that there have been plenty of relapses.

A manager's most important job is to get the best out of his or her reports while assessing whether to replace any of them with someone else who might have even more to give. The book on a lot of failed managers who can't create good team culture is that they can deal only with smart people or "don't suffer fools." I've always hated that expression. If you are the smartest person in the room, *everyone* around you is dumb by comparison. If you can't work with someone who isn't as smart as you, you should assume it's your problem to fix, not theirs.

I came to appreciate the way in which the normal, hierarchical org chart is inverted. Who really works for whom? If you want to keep growing and rising in an organization, you need the support of your subordinates, not their grudging cooperation. If the people below you aren't happy, you live in a world of monosyllabic answers and rote execution—they'll make you work for everything. I think I was able to rise at Goldman Sachs because I got better at managing down, not managing up.

Managing down means recognizing an implied contract. People who work for you should get the credit, and you as their boss should take whatever blame gets meted out. There's an old aphorism that the captain can do every job on the ship—probably no longer true in a nuclear navy. It certainly wasn't true in my world of complex finance and global markets. I had been in sales, and I'd dabbled in trading and had a good and evolving sense for risk management. I was a quick learner. But I didn't have the quantitative training to be a great trader in the modern era. I needed the people who did have that background to give me their best, and to make it easy for me to understand their specialties. If they were going to do that, they had to know that I'd appreciate their good work and return the favor.

CHAPTER 14

Lloyd of London

You can take the boy out of Brooklyn...

I'd been back and forth to London many times before, during, and after the 1994 crisis. But in my new position as co-head of FICC, Jon Corzine thought it made sense for me to be based there. Full European currency integration, slated for New Year's Day 1999, was creating tons of new opportunity. Even though the UK wasn't giving up its separate currency, much of the activity around European financial integration was centered in London. Jon may also have thought I could shake up what had become, post-1994, a somewhat staid and cautious UK operation, even though I wouldn't be the most senior person there and wouldn't have formal management responsibilities over the UK office or other European operations. I suspected, though, that the main reason Jon wanted to send me to London was to get me away from Mike Mortara, with whom I was constantly battling.

At the end of a client weekend at a resort in South Carolina, where spouses were included, Jon took Laura and me out for a long after-dinner drink to try to persuade us to move to London. When he had broached the topic with me previously, I had been less than enthusiastic. For one thing, I would just be doing the same job as co-head of FICC from a different geographic base, which would create a higher degree of difficulty. His reasons didn't seem strong enough to rearrange my life and the lives of my family. We had three young kids who were all settled in their schools. My oldest, Alex, was going into sixth grade, and Laura felt the next year would be an important social year—the year of the bar mitzvahs. However, I didn't feel I could go to the mat over the issue. I had pushed many people to uproot their families for work, and now I was being asked to move myself. And not to Moscow or Mexico City but to London, where they spoke a variety of English.

It was hard to turn Corzine down, partly because he worked so hard and was so committed to the firm. As he was talking about how important this would be for my career, Jon said that in the new globalized world we were living in, no one would rise to a high level in the firm without working overseas. That seemed pretty compelling. Globalization was in the air, and Goldman was obviously becoming more and more an international firm, with partners coming from our new offices around the world. London was on its way to becoming not just a European financial hub but the key international hub.

In fact, Corzine's forecast did not turn out to be true. The CEO who followed him, Hank Paulson, and the CEO who followed me, David Solomon, are among those who came to run the firm without ever being based abroad. But Jon was absolutely right about the value of working in a foreign country, in terms of how it widens your perspective and helps you understand what it means to be a global company.

As Jon went on about how great our lives would be in London, I could sense Laura starting to soften—from absolutely no to just plain no. The waiters were putting up the chairs, and we had been the last people in the restaurant for a long time. Well past midnight, we went back to the hotel, where a car was waiting to take Jon to the airport for another work trip. No one could question his commitment. He would be sleeping on a plane that night.

Back at our hotel, Laura agreed to move to support my career—for a year. She wasn't thrilled about it. Shortly thereafter, we made a trip to London to find a house and schools for the kids. In all of that we were helped by our close friends Tom and Jill Marino, who had moved to London a couple of years earlier for his job at Lehman Brothers. Our two older kids were the same ages as theirs, and we'd gotten to know each other at playdates. We were thrilled when Tom and Jill found us a house on their block—a house they moved into after our tour in London was over.

We had agreed to move at the end of the summer. Laura pushed our departure so late into August that we dropped Alex off for his first day of school on the way in from Heathrow. Upon arrival, we were greeted by a shipping container's worth of boxes filled with everything we'd have needed if we were spending the year camping off the grid, including cans of tuna fish, jars of peanut butter, and six hundred rolls of American toilet paper. Laura had heard that they didn't have nice toilet paper in England.

It was an adjustment for us as a family. Instead of living in a single-floor apartment, we were in a narrow town house in Kensington, which had developed into an expat neighborhood. We discovered this several weeks later on Halloween. It seemed the entire city converged on our block because the Americans handed out candy. Unprepared, we exhausted our supply after an hour and had to turn off the lights and pretend we weren't home.

Laura dealt with the jet-lagged kids, schools, unpacking, getting a car with right-side steering, stocking the fridge, and learning how to use appliances that I recognized from my childhood in the 1950s. I went straight to the office to hide from the chaos. When I got a desperate call from Laura, threatening first suicide and then murder, I asked our London administrator for help getting us moved in. She sent over a team of four junior analysts, who put their Ivy League and Oxbridge degrees to use unpacking boxes.

After a couple of days there, I got the punishment I deserved. I was up on the top floor when the phone rang downstairs. Laura wasn't home, so I ran to answer it. The new carpet on the narrow stairs was slippery. I fell down one flight, bounced off the wall like a character in a cartoon, and fell down another flight. I crawled to the phone. It was Laura, who had gone shopping for more supplies. She was calling to tell me that Princess Diana had been killed in Paris, a tragedy I think about when I feel the lingering effects of my torn rotator cuff.

Our two sons found places at the American School in London. Our three-year-old daughter went to the London Acorn School, where at holiday time she played the Virgin Mary in the school's Christmas pageant. She was asking our nanny, who was from Costa Rica, a lot of questions about Baby Jesus that her Jewish mother couldn't answer. Nearly every weekend, we left to explore somewhere new in Britain or Europe—the Cotswolds, Edinburgh, Bruges, Normandy, Barcelona—often right after I returned on Friday afternoon from a business trip. This was part of my penance for moving the family to London, but I usually loved the excursions, once we got to wherever we were going.

AT THE OFFICE, THE AFTEREFFECTS OF 1994 LINGERED LIKE A MUSTY smell. The London partnership was dominated by investment bankers who still had an attitude stemming from the trading losses three years before. The bankers were patronizing to the traders. Even though a lot of those partners were senior to me, I challenged them as a voluble champion of trading. There's often a gap in presentation skills that makes traders seem weak in comparison to bankers, who are more honed and polished. Many brilliant traders are underestimated. Many less-than-brilliant bankers are overestimated. As I formed my opinions about the UK-based traders, I continued to wrestle with Mortara long-distance. If I switched a trader's seat in London, the trader would get a call from him in New York telling him to move his seat back.

The residual mood of risk aversion was such that many of the London-based traders were still shying away from even the most obvious arbitrage opportunities. At the start of 1999, the ECU—an accounting currency that was a basket of other European currencies—was going to be converted into the euro, which would actually replace many of those European currencies. They weren't quite the same thing, because the ECU included sterling and certain smaller currencies that weren't going to be included in the euro. The ECU was trading at such a huge spread in relation to the euro that it cried out to be arbitraged. But the currency traders were afraid to take more than a modest position. They were spooked.

For better or for worse, I have no poker face. This has the virtue of saving time—everyone always knows what I think. I wasn't successful at hiding my low opinion of some of the more rigid fixed-income people or of the investment bankers who held sway in London. A number of the senior partners there seemed pretentious to me. Even the Americans were sending their boys to Eton. They didn't like trading or traders and were still punishing them for the role of others in the 1994 debacle. I let them know what I thought about that pretty directly. I was sticking up for the traders, for the J. Aron contingent, and for myself.

What really brought trading back after 1994 was the rise of the quants. In the late 1990s, fixed-income trading was being driven by people with backgrounds like Armen's and Jacob Goldfield's—people trained in physics, mathematics, and engineering, who were comfortable with quadratic equations featuring the Greek alphabet. They were evolving the business away from a simple suite of products to more complex instruments, including mortgage-backed securities, swaps, and other derivatives. Another way of describing the shift that took place in the 1990s is that we went from narrative-based trading—trades you could explain with a story about a company, a country, or a policy—to purely quantitative trading that used mathematical models and large datasets. Thanks to the way the pendulum swings in financial markets, this kind of trading was already sowing the seeds of the next financial crisis, which would come in 1998. But unlike in 1994, the 1998 crisis didn't single out Goldman.

WHEN I WORKED IN GOLDMAN'S NEW YORK OFFICE, IT WAS EASY TO think that I had a global perspective. After all, there were lots of international staff, and I was constantly traveling to far-flung places. But trying to understand Goldman from New York turned out to be a bit like trying to understand war from books, without ever experiencing the horror of it (not that I have—I learned that from books). When you work abroad for Goldman, you see that the US office is very provincial compared with the rest of the world. In London, the professional staff is genuinely international. The office tended to organize itself into national pods, with clusters from France, Sweden, and many others. It reminded me of Disney's "It's a Small World" ride. It made London feel like the center of the world.

Living there, I understood why people sometimes said—in those pre-Brexit days—that London and not New York should be Goldman's global headquarters. With the coming of the euro and the expansion of the EU after the fall of the Berlin Wall, a unified, democratic Europe was poised to become a new superpower, matching the US in population, GDP, and cultural influence. London was the most natural place for the nations of the EU (eventually twenty-seven of them) to do business with one another—German nationals were there selling German bonds to German portfolio managers. Everyone spoke their home language—and English, the lingua franca of finance. Goldman saw the top British, German, and Swiss merchant banks, which were consolidating their European operations in the UK, as our most important global competitors.

Later I had a taste of some of the frustrations that would push the UK toward its self-destructive rejection of the EU. Visits to Brussels were field trips into a bureaucratic labyrinth. Every committee had members from each of the member states, and it sometimes felt like you had to visit as many different offices in the same government building to discuss issues around financial regulation. It was the standardization around more mundane regulations, like work rules, that stuck in people's craws. I remember a trip to Ireland when our driver announced he had to clock out en route to a meeting and had another car meet us. He'd started with us early in the day and was barred by some formula from working more than eleven consecutive hours—driving one more mile would make him a criminal.

Throughout much of its history, the UK's geographical advantage was the moat of the English Channel, which separated it from the rest of the continent. Today its big geographical advantage is its time zone. Greenwich Mean Time—GMT—makes London a natural place to be the center of global finance. Business hours in London start in the Tokyo afternoon and run through the entire morning in New York. New York and Tokyo business hours do not overlap with each other. Managing and trading on a British or Continental European time zone fundamentally makes more sense.

Even as a global firm, Goldman remained New York–centric in its practices. The New York workday dictates when everyone else has to be available, creating unnatural rhythms for the rest of the world. On the other side of an ocean, time zones and time zone management become huge challenges. Goldman had most of its senior people in New York, so each global business (and the firm as a whole) was usually run by a partner based on East Coast time. Global calls and meetings would be scheduled without much regard for the inconvenience to people based overseas. For example, monthly partner meetings, in the pre-IPO days, would be scheduled for 4:15 p.m., after the 4:00 p.m. NYSE close. That was 9:15 p.m. in London and 4:00 or 5:00 a.m. in Tokyo. Sometimes when I was in London, I would be on a conference call that would start in my evening, and someone on the line from New York would suggest taking an hour's break. Well, at 11:00 p.m. in London, I wasn't about to take a break and resume at midnight. Time zone issues are a small thing for folks in New York, who tend to call the shots, but a big one for those overseas.

Huge burdens fall on spouses at a place like Goldman Sachs. And thirty years ago, the spouse was almost always the wife. Having to uproot to London reminded me that it was Laura who made my career possible, and that she'd sacrificed her own to do so. Laura had worked at a corporate law firm and in the office of the Corporation Counsel, New York City's law firm. She worked until Rachel, our third kid, was born—at which point she decided to give up practicing law. After that, Laura did important nonprofit work and served on educational boards while managing all of our lives.

Her family management responsibilities really amped up in London, where doing everything was harder—arranging for schools, learning to drive on the wrong side of the road, planning our weekend excursions, and taking the boys to baseball practice (yes, baseball) at a field adjacent to Wormwood Scrubs, the notorious London prison. On top of that, Laura went with me to work dinners as we tried to make new friends and cement business relationships. It made me aware all over again of how lucky I was in my family and domestic situation.

Laura was a good soldier through all of it, but I knew she couldn't wait to get home. Was never unpacking her suitcase a hint about how she felt? She held me to our original deal. About a minute after the bell rang on the last day of school, she moved back to New York with the kids. We repacked the many boxes and moved out of our Kensington town house, bequeathing 520 rolls of top-quality American toilet paper to the next occupants. With six more months in London ahead of me, I moved into a dark and depressing service flat, where I spent as little time as possible. By the time my assignment was completed, I was desperate to get home.

A couple of years later, we were at a Goldman Sachs event, a buzzy cocktail party with a lot of people from New York and London. Through the hum of conversation, I overheard Laura telling someone that she really liked being in London and that the year abroad had been great for our family. And then it seemed the room went totally silent as she declared, "I just wish we'd stayed longer!"

CHAPTER 15

To IPO or Not to IPO

When Goldman Sachs went public, someone who was the 150th luckiest person in the world was totally distressed that he wasn't the 125th luckiest person in the world.

The question of whether to become a public company had long been contentious within the firm. Arguing in favor was the reality of a changing financial services industry to which a nineteenth-century partnership structure was increasingly unsuited. Arguing against was the pull of history, tradition, and culture—a fear that the secret sauce of the partnership would be lost.

Goldman considered going public many times. The first was in the late 1960s, when Sidney Weinberg thought it might be a good idea and sent his deputy Gus Levy to canvass the partners. Sidney Weinberg started at Goldman as an assistant to the janitor at sixteen and spent three decades as a senior partner. If anyone would have been in a position to bring about structural change, it was him. But a core value of the partnership was that you needed a consensus around big decisions. When Levy reported that the idea lacked support among the partners, Weinberg dropped it.

In 1970, Donaldson, Lufkin & Jenrette became the first investment bank to be listed on the New York Stock Exchange, soon to be followed by Merrill Lynch & Co. in 1971. At Goldman, the management committee decided to dissolve the partnership and incorporate as a prelude to a public offering. They went so far as having new business cards printed up before reversing themselves. There was still little appetite for the change among the wider body of Goldman Sachs partners.

Over the next few decades, nearly every other major Wall Street firm floated shares on the NYSE. That included Goldman's traditional rivals Salomon Brothers (1981), Bear Stearns (1985), and Morgan Stanley (1986). The reasons those firms chose to go public were apparent. One was the problem of unlimited liability, which Goldman Sachs partners referred to by the shorthand "Penn Central" and "Maxwell." But the more important rationale was offensive, not defensive. As they grew, Wall Street firms needed a source of capital more permanent than the wealth of their partners, which generally left when the partners retired or died. Publicly traded stock gave those banks a ready way to increase their capital base as they grew. It allowed them to finance M&A deals and to move into new areas like proprietary trading and principal investments. As listed companies, they were in a better position to extend credit to clients and to invest in technology. At Goldman, by contrast, the capital could essentially walk out the door, as a lot of it did in 1994. That put us at a serious disadvantage.

Without a publicly traded stock, Goldman had to raise capital on the private market. Following another decision not to go public in 1986, we took a $500 million investment from the Japanese bank Sumitomo, in exchange for a 12.5 percent equity stake. There were several more equity infusions, including another major one from the Bishop Estate, an enormous Hawaiian educational trust, in 1992. But that capital was inherently much more expensive, because those private investors were buying in closer to book value, not at the value that shares would have had, which for a Wall Street firm in those days could be anywhere from 2x to more than 4x book value. Stock was especially important as currency for mergers and acquisitions, which our competitors were all pursuing in the 1990s. Goldman couldn't readily make a large acquisition.

Through that period, Goldman managed to remain the top destination for the most capable aspirants. Our salaries were competitive, but without the ability to offer equity, we were at an increasing disadvantage in recruiting and retention. Morgan Stanley might give new hires $100,000 worth of stock options or restricted stock, some or all of which they would forfeit if they left before four years. Employees got the advantage of being able to defer the tax on that income. If they opted to go elsewhere before their shares vested, Morgan Stanley got those shares back and could use them for something else. If, by contrast, Goldman wanted to hire someone away from Morgan Stanley, we'd have to pay them a signing bonus to make up for the value of the shares they were giving up. Every time we poached someone, we were effectively subsidizing our competitors by paying out the value of their unvested stock options. If we paid someone a $100,000 end-of-the-year bonus, they could leave with it the next day. As a retention incentive, Goldman could only dangle the possibility of partnership, which just a small fraction of our employees would ever attain.

ONCE I BECAME A PARTNER, I DEVELOPED A BETTER APPRECIATION FOR the powerful arguments against going public. The larger objections flowed from the deep culture of the Goldman Sachs partnership and the values it embodied: client focus, collaboration, collective participation in decision-making, financial privacy, and optimizing for the long term. These were the qualities that made the firm different and special. They were what made us the top choice for MBAs and graduates in finance. They're the reason that people who have worked at multiple Wall Street firms still identify themselves as alumni of Goldman Sachs.

There were also straightforward financial arguments against going public. In a partnership, profits "pass through" to the partners, who pay tax on them as individuals. The profits are taxed only once. Incorporating, you pay corporate tax on profits, and then pay tax again as individuals when the corporation distributes its after-tax earnings. The profits are taxed twice. And while that drawback didn't outweigh the benefits for our Wall Street competitors, there was reason to think Goldman would receive a lower valuation in the public markets than they had. Merrill Lynch, Morgan Stanley, and Dean Witter derived much more of their revenue from commissions on trading. They had enormous consumer-facing businesses including credit cards and asset management for individuals. Those businesses tended to produce steady, growing earnings, which the stock market liked. As compared with its competitors, Goldman was more profitable, but our earnings were more volatile. We earned more of our revenues from investment banking, which ebbed and flowed with the business cycle, and from trading, which was inherently much less consistent. The market awarded a lower valuation to firms with more volatile earnings. As a partnership, we could ignore that bias in the market. Short-term variability didn't matter to us. If the firm made more money over time, the partners were better off.

There were also burdens associated with being a public company that we were happy to avoid. SEC filings and compliance and having to deal with public shareholders and analysts all consume time and energy and cost money. Executives at public companies put tremendous effort into preparing for quarterly earnings calls. And then there are the activists: You need to own only a single share of stock to attend the annual shareholders meeting and raise any kind of wacky complaint. The gadflies I later had to deal with as CEO included rejected job applicants, socialist nuns, and Evelyn Davis, who was relentless, especially if you failed to subscribe to her expensive and worthless newsletter. Employee distraction is also a hazard at public companies. When you're private, the value of the company is always moving, but you're not aware of it hour to hour because there's no share price to check. When you're public, it's hard not to be taking in the fluctuating share price all day as a minute-by-minute mark-to-market of your performance and net worth.

Many highly successful companies, such as Mars, Koch Industries, and Fidelity, resist going public for these and other reasons. Some, like Dell, Hilton, and X (Twitter), have gone from public to private. In

2023, there were only around 3,700 publicly traded companies left in the United States, down from over 8,000 in 1996.

When the partners gathered, these arguments pro and con were sometimes debated openly. Other times, they just hung in the background, aspects of the Big Unsettled Question shadowing the partnership. If we did decide to go public, it wouldn't be as simple as just pulling a switch. Everyone knew the execution of an IPO would present issues that could be wrenching to the firm. There were questions of fairness and the ethos of the firm, which was where the issue could become emotional.

Obviously, none of the current partners were founders—we were merely the current partners. So why should we be the ones to reap a onetime financial reward? The limited partners still had equity, but it functioned more like preferred stock, and their relative payout would be much less. More recently named partners, who had had less time to build up equity, would take out much less than partners a few years ahead of them. The longer-lived partners closest to retirement would get the most. But even the newest and youngest would receive enormous payouts relative to someone who might have contributed to building the firm for thirty-five years and retired four years earlier. How would that be fair? Well, it wouldn't. There was an implicit randomness to who would benefit from an IPO executed at any point in time.

Goldman Sachs went back to 1869. People had put their lives into it for generations, always focusing on the long-term interests of the firm. When we needed to make a large capital expenditure around a new office, a building, or a piece of technology, the more senior partners didn't react by saying, *I'll be paying for this but not benefiting from it, because I'm retiring in a few years.* They thought: *Is this in the interest of Goldman Sachs as an institution? If so, we should do it.* The mere question of an IPO forced people to consider their self-interest and focus on the many ways it could diverge from the overall interests of the firm.

The implication that they were thinking about their financial self-interest in a division of spoils made everyone uncomfortable. Every

Goldman Sachs partner was already rich by most standards. Most partners weren't working solely to maximize their net worth. If that was your primary goal, you would leave and launch a hedge fund or a private equity firm or an advisory boutique, where you could make much more money—albeit with more risk. People didn't like the implication that their work was motivated only by their financial compensation. Some didn't even want to think about how a windfall would change their lives. Even highly paid traders and bankers are uncomfortable talking about money when it concerns them personally.

Just over the horizon was the question of what would happen to all of us after receiving a huge, unanticipated gift. One of the TV shows I loved watching as a kid was *The Millionaire*, a CBS drama that ran for many seasons. In each episode, the mysterious billionaire benefactor John Beresford Tipton gave a random person a check for a million dollars, the equivalent of more than $10 million today. Tax-free! You saw Tipton only in shadow or from behind. He would hand the envelope to his loyal executive assistant, Michael Anthony. "Our next millionaire, Mike," Tipton would say, chuckling. The one condition of the gift was that you couldn't tell anybody, except your spouse. If you did, you forfeited the money.

Tipton's fascination was with "the mystery of man." All his beneficiaries' lives were transformed, some for the better, some for the worse. One recipient turned down the money. It was a fictional drama, of course, but it explored the ways that windfalls can change people, while reminding viewers that money isn't the most important thing in life.

THE FIRST ATTEMPT TO GO PUBLIC AFTER I JOINED THE PARTNERSHIP was in late 1993. Steve Friedman, who became the sole senior partner after Bob Rubin left, was readying another proposal when the trading losses of 1994 prompted him to table it. You couldn't very well go public on the back of your worst year in recent history.

Once he stabilized the firm after Steve's departure and the 1994 exodus, Jon Corzine decided to give it another go in 1995. Corzine had been among the minority of partners favoring an IPO back in 1986, and now he was in a position to formally recommend it from the top. Hank Paulson, who was the firm's number two, publicly endorsed the recommendation. But where Jon was strongly in favor, Hank privately expressed opposition, as did a number of the investment banking partners close to him. The topic was so sensitive that it could be hard to know what people really thought. The politic thing to do was shake your head gravely and say that you were concerned and doubtful about the idea. No one wanted to advocate openly for something that was so powerfully in their own financial self-interest. The politically correct posture for those in favor was to appear troubled, deferential, and conflicted. Even as the IPO took on a kind of inevitability, each of us wanted our partners to appreciate that *we* weren't one of the ones pushing for it.

Before Corzine became senior partner, the management committee ran the firm. But just as I was easing my way onto it, he decided to get rid of it. Corzine replaced the then-eleven-person management committee with a six-person executive committee, which functioned as the politburo. In addition to Corzine and Paulson, it included Roy Zuckerberg and David Silfen, who co-headed equities, Bob Hurst, a senior banker, and Jon Thain. John Thornton joined a year later, when Silfen retired. Paulson chaired a new eighteen-member operating committee—i.e., the junior politburo—to which I was appointed. Corzine chaired a new partnership committee, also with eighteen members, that dealt with issues around electing new partners, reviewing performance, and so on.

Majorities at both the operating and partnership committees were against the IPO. Despite their opposition, Corzine presented the proposal to the full partnership in January 1996 at a meeting held at the Arrowwood conference center, an off-site facility we used in Rye, New York. He hoped to get approval from the partners that weekend. But when he made his presentation on Friday, the response was strongly negative. The partnership agreement stipulated that the decision required a vote of the full partnership. On Saturday, when a vote would have taken place, Corzine was faced with a solid block of the most junior partners, who had only had one year to build up equity in the firm and would be walking away with much less than the more senior partners—the old structural problem. In the face of opposition, Jon threw in the towel.

"There will be no IPO," he said. "The IPO is off the table. It's over." The partners gave him a standing ovation.

Instead, the firm addressed some of the long-standing disadvantages of the partnership without eliminating it. Partners' capital would now be locked up longer term—some of it for up to eight years after retirement. Corzine started calling himself the CEO instead of senior partner, which rubbed some people the wrong way. And Goldman filed paperwork to become a limited liability corporation. That meant that while the partners' capital accounts were still on the hook for any losses, we no longer faced the risk of losing personal assets held outside Goldman in the event of a catastrophic loss or liability. We slept a little easier knowing that with an LLC, our homes weren't at risk. Finally, the firm created the more industry-standard title of managing director. All of the 190 partners were now "participating" MDs. The other 220 managing directors were not partners. But to the outside world, there was no apparent difference. Their business cards looked the same. It did mean we had to hold that year's dinner dance at the Javits Center, the largest venue in New York City and nobody's favorite.

Those changes removed some of the arguments in favor of an IPO. But even with an LLC, the vast majority of the wealth of the partners was still tied up in the firm and fully at risk. And it still was not permanent capital. Through 1996 and 1997, the issue never went away. In general, investment bankers tended to be more against an IPO, because they were less attuned to the problems of managing risk and a large balance sheet, and more conscious of the cultural benefits of the partnership. Those on the trading side usually had the opposite perspective because they wanted to expand risk-based trading and grow the business more quickly. The retired limited partners, whose capital would likely be paid out at a modest premium to book value in an IPO, tended to be against it, as did the newest partners, who hadn't built up as much equity. People who had been partners for some time and would be paid out more handsomely tended to be in favor. That's not to say that people lined up according to their self-interest. All the partners would benefit personally from an IPO. But everyone would not benefit equally.

Strong results in 1995, 1996, and 1997 made their own argument for going public, because those rising earnings would drive the valuation of an IPO. But when Corzine proposed it again at the end of 1997, there was still enormous resistance. In my opinion, there was a lot of disingenuousness in the opposition. If you were making an argument that going public was a necessity, it was easy for people to conflate your concern for the firm with a selfish interest in getting rich off it. Some estimates were that an IPO would leave partners with an average paper wealth of $100 million or more. No one liked the look of wanting $100 million. Whereas if you argued for staying private, it looked like selfless citizenship.

TO HELP RESOLVE THE ISSUE, PAULSON ANNOUNCED THE FORMATION OF a committee on strategy, a subcommittee of the operating committee that he chaired and to which I was appointed. The eight members would represent the various Goldman divisions. The motto was "Structure follows strategy." The mandate was to take a longer-term perspective and think through what formal structure—including but not limited to an IPO—would make the most sense for the firm. We were supposed to issue recommendations to the executive committee, which would then take them to the full partnership at a two-day off-site scheduled for June.

The strategy committee's meetings, intense and sometimes contentious, continued through the spring of 1998, when I was living in England. That meant that I was zipping back to New York every week on the Concorde, which reduced the flying time to three hours. I had such high status on British Airways that they gave me a nonadvertised very-frequent flyer card beyond gold or platinum—it was plaid. The company's most senior person at Heathrow Airport would come to meet me personally at the gate, until I figured out what was going on and asked them to please discontinue the practice.

It was an amazing experience, one you can no longer have, to leave London at 5:00 p.m. and arrive in New York at 3:30 p.m.—a three-and-a-half-hour flight with a five-hour time difference. Flying at Mach 2 at fifty thousand feet, you could see the curvature of the Earth out the window. You were also aware of the plane's fragility. Once, the pilot came into the cabin, lifted a panel in the floor of the aisle next to my seat, and went to work on some mechanical problem with a giant wrench. On another flight I won't forget, the plane went into what felt like a nosedive. Sitting in front of me was the pope of the Coptic Orthodox Church, in full regalia, with his crook. Would this strange vision be the last thing I saw before we plunged into the Atlantic? The headline might read COPTIC POPE, OTHERS... Apparently, the dip was just a glitch caused by uneven consumption of the plane's special fuel. By the way, I seldom took the Concorde back to London, where the five-hour time difference worked against you. You wanted an overnight flight that was longer rather than shorter so you could sleep.

The strategy committee embraced the idea of expansion through acquisitions, especially in Europe and Japan. But the majority opinion was still against going public. I drove the final section of the strategy committee report, which reviewed the pros and cons of an IPO. Noting the 1994 partner exodus, the report pointed out:

> Our current partnership structure creates economic incentives for this type of behavior. That is, partners who have built up a significant amount of net worth within the firm and have a negative outlook for the firm have an incentive to retire in order to "lock in" the value of their capital account and insulate it from potential future losses. In a public structure, the impact of a negative outlook (if it is shared by the market) on net worth is immediately recognized and therefore does not create an incentive to retire.

This stated the problem gently, but the point was clear. My overwhelming worry was that the firm might not be in a position to survive the next major crisis if we remained a partnership. And those once-in-a-century crises, it seemed, were happening more and more often.

WHAT REALLY SHIFTED THE THIRTY-YEAR DEBATE ABOUT GOING PUBLIC was the slow erosion and eventual repeal of the Glass–Steagall Act of 1933. As Glass–Steagall receded, a wave of consolidation swept through Wall Street. Commercial banks were now permitted to compete with investment banks as brokers and advisers. They were making acquisitions that would empower them to challenge us on our home turf. In 1997, Morgan Stanley acquired the retail brokerage Dean Witter. Citigroup was in the process of acquiring Salomon Smith Barney, which had itself absorbed Travelers Insurance. Merrill Lynch acquired Mercury Asset Management, the largest investment manager in the UK. And in Europe, the Swiss bank UBS acquired S.G. Warburg. As profitable as it was, Goldman was smaller than these new "universal" banks.

In our M&A practice, we increasingly had to lend money to acquirers to get their business as an adviser. We needed to make bigger and bigger capital commitments to support our franchise. But unlike the behemoths, we didn't have a large enough balance sheet to finance most of the M&A deals we advised on. A Morgan Stanley or a Merrill had more than twice our capital. The universal banks could advise on M&A deals and finance them too. In other words, the big banks were moving onto our turf, but as a partnership, we couldn't move onto theirs. We were losing business to fuller-service competitors. Without structural change, Goldman couldn't expect to remain number one in global M&A for long. More than anything else, it was the intensifying need to offer capital commitments that made it untenable to be private with impermanent capital.

The weight of opinion among senior leaders at the firm seemed to be shifting as we talked through the strategy questions with the rest of the operating committee, the partnership committee, and the executive committee. But as the debate swirled, with an unusual number of leaks to the press, Corzine and Paulson were having a harder and harder time getting along. Jon saw himself as a CEO who ran what would soon be a publicly traded company. The executive committee and other partners saw him as a senior partner who needed to fully involve them in making major decisions. Faced with the demise of Glass–Steagall, Jon had held preliminary talks about a merger with the CEOs of J.P. Morgan, Chase Manhattan, US Trust, and Mellon Bank. The executive committee thought he had gone off the reservation in exploring these possibilities without their authorization. At the root of Paulson's opposition to the IPO was that he didn't trust Corzine, thought he wasn't disciplined enough about taking risk, and didn't want to give him more power.

At some point during the spring of 1998, Hank decided he could no longer work with Jon if Jon remained the sole CEO. He wanted equal billing. Three of the other four members of the executive committee—Thain, Thornton, and Hurst—agreed with him and insisted that Jon share responsibilities with Hank. The premier had lost power within the politburo. After Thain, who had been Corzine's protégé, delivered the news, Corzine reluctantly accepted the new reality. He announced that Paulson would now become cochairman and co-CEO, returning to the familiar paired management structure. A complicated succession struggle was underway. But with the prospect of an impending IPO decision, the press didn't focus on the management change. They never understood the depth of the conflict between the two top leaders of the firm.

Because of the media attention around the IPO, we surreptitiously moved our June partners' meeting from Arrowwood to the Palisades Conference Center, north of the city. Media camera crews showed up at Arrowwood and either stood in the rain outside or tried to breach the gate. Those who slipped through found themselves peeping on an accounting seminar. Half an hour away, the firm's 190 partners were holding a two-day meeting with very high stakes.

On the first day, we sat through various presentations about the mechanics of the IPO. Corzine read aloud from a letter that John Weinberg and his former co-senior partner, John Whitehead, had written to the partners making their final case against it. With his family's long-standing connection to the firm, Weinberg felt that the firm wasn't the partners' to sell. Whitehead was equally forceful but somewhat appeased when the firm committed to put $200 million into a new Goldman Sachs Foundation and made him the head of it. In that setting, even Corzine took pains to be fair and appear as if he weren't quite sure about the decision himself. The mood was such that even if, like me, you were convinced of the need to move ahead with an IPO, you wanted to play up your ambivalence and act like you weren't fully decided.

The second day, Saturday, was a kind of town meeting. It went on for more than six hours, and it seemed that nearly every partner spoke. The argument boiled down to "capital" versus "culture." When I got my turn, I said that I thought it wasn't a question of whether going public was desirable. It was necessary because of the downside risks of remaining private—the next crisis like 1994 would kill us. I said that when I was starting out at Goldman, I didn't use my first paycheck to buy a house or a car. The thing I did with my first dollars was to buy an insurance policy to protect my family against unforeseen circumstances. The risks we were taking now were foreseeable.

A few people really played up their opposition. *Please don't do this*, some of them begged. I remember Phil Murphy, a partner who was subsequently elected and reelected as governor of New Jersey, giving one of the most rousing orations. *Ain't no mountain high enough*, he proclaimed, pumping his clenched fist in a "power to the people" salute.

I mean, *c'mon*. I couldn't help feeling that a lot of my fellow partners were at that point being not just melodramatic but hypocritical. The IPO had become inevitable for business reasons, and it was going to be extremely lucrative to them as well. They were objecting to the IPO secure in an awareness that the executive committee was in favor and was poised to proceed. At the end of the meeting, we all filled out a confidential survey. It revealed that the partners favored going public by a margin of three to one, the opposite of how it had appeared in the room.

On Monday, June 15, 1998, the executive committee announced that Goldman Sachs was planning an IPO in the fall. The senior investment banking partners spent much of July on a road show to make the pitch to institutional and large private investors. In early August, the full partnership approved an offering in a formal vote—the first one it had ever taken in its 129-year history.

AT THE TIME OF THE JUNE DECISION, MARKET CONDITIONS LOOKED close to ideal. An Asian financial crisis, which had roiled US and European markets in the fall of 1997 and spring of 1998, had seemingly worked its way through the system. Stock valuations were robust, with the Dow setting new daily records above 9,000. Comparable listed firms like Morgan Stanley Dean Witter were trading at around 4x their book value. Goldman would be discounted to some degree because of the volatility of our trading earnings. But analysts still pointed to a valuation in the range of $30 billion.

By late August, the stock market was down more than 10 percent from its peak earlier in the summer, and people were getting nervous. The focus of worry was Russia, which was poised to devalue its currency and default on debt held by investment banks and hedge funds, and on loans from the International Monetary Fund. I'd gotten a sense of the stress when I traveled there a few months earlier as part of Goldman's effort to expand its presence. We hosted a fancy dinner for a group of oligarchs and flew in former president George H. W. Bush as a guest speaker. The vodka toasts to US-Russia relations were underway when pagers started to beep and buzz. Without ceremony, the oligarchs all rose as one and exited before dinner was even served. Boris Yeltsin was summoning them to the Kremlin—presumably to help him try to shore up government finances. I was left to have a quiet evening with former president Bush, who talked up his oldest son, George W., as a presidential prospect.

When Russia announced its default on August 17, it prompted a "flight to quality"—a dumping of risky assets of all kinds in favor of US Treasury bonds and other low-risk securities. Goldman's own losses on Russian debt and correlated positions were substantial, hundreds of millions of dollars. On August 31, the Dow fell 512 points, its biggest drop since the 1987 crash. A drop in the stock market, even a big one, didn't mean that we'd need to postpone the IPO. But watching Wall Street firms listed on the NYSE lose half their value in a short time was sobering. Instead of $30 billion, the IPO might value the company at something more like $15 billion.

The instability got worse in September. Now the chief problem was Long-Term Capital Management, another instructive story about the failures of risk management. LTCM was a quantitative hedge fund that John Meriwether, a former Salomon Brothers bond trader, founded with Myron Scholes and Robert Merton, the two Nobel Prize winners who had been Fischer Black's partners in developing the formula for pricing options. LTCM was Wall Street's version of *The Best and the Brightest*. The episode demonstrated the way that the most brilliant financial minds of their generation had become arrogant and prone to shared blind spots and delusions.

LTCM had several highly profitable years making what are called relative value or convergence trades. These are trades based on the assumption that correlated securities, such as five-year and ten-year Treasury notes or French bonds and Italian bonds, might deviate from but would eventually revert to their long-term historical relationships. Because these paired positions were diversified across asset classes, LTCM was meant to be well insulated against risk. That theoretically low risk was the justification for LTCM's leveraging itself at more than thirty to one. After returning a substantial share of its "excess" capital to its investors earlier in the year, the fund held just $3 billion in capital against more than $100 billion in swaps and derivative positions.

The hidden flaw in LTCM's model was that making huge leveraged bets on those patterns affected them, just as taking many bets on one side of a football game changes the bookies' odds. As an example, for sixty years, the S&P 500 went down on average on Mondays and went up more on Wednesdays than on any other day of the week. There was money to be made by consistently buying the index on Monday and selling it on Wednesday. But then word spread, and an academic paper was published. Once everyone knew about the pattern, the pattern vanished. LTCM's leveraged bets were much too large for the markets it was investing in. The profit went out of its trades by virtue of its making them at scale. Quantitative traders at other firms were observing the same patterns and piling into the same trades. As those trades got more crowded, the opportunity effectively disappeared.

Worse, LTCM's bets were correlated to one another in a way the great minds hadn't anticipated. That made it vulnerable to an exogenous shock like the Russian default. In August and September 1998, all markets reacted to Russia in a similar way: by bidding up safer, more liquid assets and bidding down riskier, less liquid ones. Instead of converging, the spreads between the matched pairs were all growing wider. LTCM had assumed a high degree of liquidity. But now there were no buyers for its riskier positions.

Given its leverage, LTCM was faced with a crisis not just of liquidity but of possible insolvency. That wasn't just a problem for its investors. The Federal Reserve was concerned that a default by LTCM could create a chain reaction that would freeze the global financial system. It was a preview of the "too big to fail" phenomenon that would become familiar to everyone a decade later. Global finance was intertwined in ways that meant LTCM's poor decisions could drag its counterparties and lenders down with it.

There was no political appetite for using government funds to bail out a private hedge fund. As an alternative, the Federal Reserve Bank of New York encouraged the private sector to act collectively. It wanted the big banks that were counterparties to LTCM's trades to buy its positions. But because of LTCM's secrecy, and the lack of market liquidity, it was hard to say what LTCM's positions might be worth. On September 24, a consortium of private financial institutions agreed to buy LTCM's assets for $3.5 billion. All of the big banks participated, with the exception of Bear Stearns (costing them goodwill they would need during the financial crisis a decade later). Goldman put in $300 million, more as a matter of civic duty than self-interested risk-taking.

It was simply something we had to do. But the high-pressure negotiations further strained Corzine and Paulson's troubled relationship. Hank felt that Jon was once again dealing behind his back. What's more, we and other trading firms were facing big losses of our own because of positions smaller than but similar to LTCM's. Our losses weren't on par with those of 1994, thank goodness. But they were concerning nonetheless.

On September 29, Corzine and Paulson called off the IPO. Though pulling it had more to do with market conditions than with any missteps by Corzine, it precipitated a palace coup. In December, Hank forced the issue by saying that it had to be him or Jon running the firm. That made Thain and Thornton the decisive figures, and they both sided with Hank, giving him a majority inside the politburo. It fell to Thain to deliver the news to Jon that he was out. It was agreed that Corzine could stay on as co–senior partner until the IPO was completed, but he was no longer going to be co-CEO.

This kind of thing didn't happen at Goldman Sachs—except it did. It was a shame that things worked out the way they did. Jon was not suited to be CEO, and Hank was much better positioned to take us through the IPO and run the firm afterward. But whatever else you say about Corzine, he worked tirelessly for the firm, and everything he did was in the firm's interests as he saw them. I was sad to see him leave the way he did, but he didn't do so badly in the aftermath, becoming a senator from and then governor of New Jersey. Unfortunately, his high tolerance for risk caught up with him in his postgovernment life as CEO of the commodities brokerage MF Global.

Around this time, John Thornton, with whom I'd never had much interaction, started sending me voicemails with his views on different issues, inviting me out to lunch, and asking about my opinions on a host of firmwide matters. I was flattered by his newfound interest in me, but it seemed... calculated. I pictured Paulson, Thain, and Thornton meeting and dividing the responsibility for pacifying the colonels who might feel loyalty to the previous regime. I imagined someone saying, "Thornton, you make sure Lloyd is okay." After a coup, you want to make sure that the troops stay in their barracks.

It wasn't clear how the change would affect my career. Once again, as happened after Mark Winkelman left, the leader I had worked for and done my best to cultivate was unexpectedly gone. At that point, I had a friendly but not a close relationship with Hank. Thain's and Thornton's roles in the coup made it evident to all that they were Hank's eventual heirs apparent. As they were about my age and partners from my class, there was no path for me to rise higher in the firm. I was fine with that. I was content running FICC. I enjoyed the content of my job and was helping to drive trading profits for the firm.

BEFORE GOLDMAN SACHS COULD SUCCESSFULLY CONCLUDE ITS IPO, IT had to resolve a host of philosophical and practical issues. There were contentious discussions about how to allocate shares among different classes of current partners. Should the distribution of shares be more of a reward for past service (which would argue for giving the older partners more) or an incentive for the future (which would argue for giving more to the younger partners, whose service lay ahead)? The outcome needed to strike a balance between the contributions of those who had been partners for many years and those who had been named more recently, including the class that almost didn't happen, the class of 1998. Hank advocated for a relatively flat distribution of shares, where allocations for senior partners weren't drastically higher than those for junior partners, in keeping with Goldman Sachs's culture. He also supported generous treatment for retired partners who still had funds in their capital accounts, agreeing to a payout in shares at 1.5x the firm's book value.

We would have liked to put in place a vesting period and noncompete agreements for partners, but that proved to be impractical.

In order to be subject to advantageous capital gains tax treatment (21.1 percent tax, due whenever you sold) rather than ordinary income tax treatment (39.6 percent, due immediately), the shares had to be exchanged only for our partnership interests and not related to future employment. We had a letter from the IRS approving the plan as a tax-free exchange, but any deviation from it could call the tax treatment into question.

The firm also had to address how both partners and nonpartners would be compensated following the IPO. After the IPO, "partners" would technically no longer be partners but employees, just like the rank and file. The payment for their future services would be ordinary income, just like everyone else's. That meant we could attach vesting and noncompete requirements. So we had to figure out how we would pay all our employees, partners included, for their work. How much should people be paid in cash and how much in stock, and what should the vesting terms and noncompete considerations be? Naturally, a five-year vesting period would have far more retention impact on a nonpartner than on a partner, who would receive a significant distribution of shares.

The offering prospectus also had to detail new governance structures. Prior to the IPO, Goldman Sachs had been run by a small group of partners, with decisions often made through a more informal, consensus-driven approach. Now the firm had to meet the requirements of being a publicly traded company, which included a new board of directors with independent members. This shift was necessary to align with the expectations of investors and regulatory bodies, but it also required careful consideration of how much influence the existing partners should retain. We had to balance the need for strong corporate governance with preservation of the culture that had made us so successful as a private partnership. As a condition of receiving their shares, partners and managing directors entered into a shareholder agreement to vote as a bloc with management. Initially, and for many years, effective control of the company stayed with management. But that control would dissipate over time as partners sold off their shares.

Getting all of this settled and right was of paramount importance. The execution of the IPO had to be flawless, because taking companies public was our business. We had to demonstrate the skills we were selling to clients by executing it without a glitch—especially after calling it off the first time. Among other things, that meant calculating the size of the offering and the share price so that it would rise on the first day. The offering was priced at $53—squarely in the valuation range we had contemplated a year earlier. Demand was strong, and the stock closed on its first day, May 4, 1999, at just over $70. If you'd been through the internal deliberations, there was a certain irony to all of it. Many of the Goldman executives smiling ear to ear as they rang the opening bell on the balcony at the New York Stock Exchange were the ones who at various points had spoken most vociferously against the IPO.

The successful completion of the IPO meant that partners at Goldman were now all much richer—the average value of GS stock received by a partner was $84 million at the closing price. Those at the very top, Paulson and the departing Corzine, had stock worth more than $200 million each. My 2,385,170 shares were worth $168 million at the end of day one. Twenty-five years later the stock was trading ten times its IPO offering price. Its performance has far outstripped that of the five other biggest US banks.

Did that wealth make everyone happy? Certainly not in the way you might think. People who were getting a massive windfall could still be bent out of shape that others were getting a bigger windfall. I think the envy and competition speak to a truth about human nature rather than anything specific to Goldman Sachs, or to Wall Street, or to the kinds of people who tend to go into finance. Watching people I knew react to this bonanza was like watching all the episodes of *The Millionaire* at once—a kind of natural experiment in sociology, psychology, and human behavior.

The story of the IPO partners has played out over the intervening quarter century. As in 1994, a lot of partners retired, but not suddenly, and not out of fear of losing what they had. Now they were leaving because they had much more money than they'd thought they would. In general, the new wealth lowered people's thresholds for annoyance and their tolerance for the parts of their jobs they didn't like. If you're rising in your career, and your manager aggravates you, you're likely to sulk for a while and try to work it out. But if someone hands you $84 million and your manager is driving you nuts, you're more likely to say, *Life is too short*. Pre-IPO partners didn't have to take any crap from me or any other boss. The bar for leaving got lower and it shortened partner lifespans.

Did the IPO windfall make *me* happy? I liked living well, of course, but I already had more than I'd ever expected in life. What mattered to me far beyond the incremental wealth was my sense of being a part of a respected, established institution. After my childhood in Brooklyn, I had found comfort and an increasing sense of belonging at Harvard, Harvard Law School, a prestigious law firm, and eventually Goldman Sachs. Growing up with a chip on my shoulder, I wanted to solve it, not carry it. I valued teamwork and the crucial role Goldman Sachs played in the financial system, business, and the world. For the same reason, I never had the desire to strike out on my own. It wasn't about the wealth I could accumulate—it was about the connection to an important institution that made me feel anchored. Following the IPO, I was happy—but mainly because the firm was in a better position and my role in it was growing.

SOMEONE COULD WRITE A FASCINATING BOOK ABOUT WHAT THE 221 Goldman partners did after the IPO. Corzine wasn't the only one to go into politics. Phil Murphy later followed him to become governor of New Jersey. Malcolm Turnbull, an Australian partner, became leader of his country's Liberal Party and eventually prime minister. Paulson became Treasury secretary in 2006 and played a truly heroic role in preventing the global financial crisis from turning into a second Great Depression. Hank, who grew up on a farm and always lived modestly, planned to give nearly all of his money away to support environmental protection. He bought a pristine eleven-thousand-acre barrier island off the coast of Georgia to turn it into a wildfowl sanctuary and legally protect it from any future development. Steve Mnuchin, who worked in mortgage securities, eventually became US Treasury secretary as well.

Others pursued personal passions and interests. Eric Grubman went to work for the NFL. David Baum became a golf writer. Lee Vance published well-regarded novels and became a helicopter pilot. He left a year after the IPO. Lee said he had always planned to leave when he was worth $50 million. It was his stroke of luck that the IPO bounced his net worth from $45 million to $100 million and he departed Goldman with far more than he was planning to.

Gregory Zehner became a pastor and wrote a book about Christianity. Jon Lopatin, whom I'd recruited for my forex sales venture, trained as a rabbi at the Jewish Theological Seminary. There were several new college professors. In the UK, Gavyn Davies became Lord Davies, chairman of the BBC. Others chaired universities, started nonprofit organizations, or ran existing ones, including the Nature Conservancy and the Clinton Global Initiative. Not surprisingly, lots of hedge funds, private equity funds, and investment banking boutiques were founded by partner leavers who took the money and ran. But a solid core of the partnership stayed with the firm.

That included me and most of my crew. We just kept plugging away. By now I was back from London, reunited with my family, and no longer dealing with 10:00 p.m. conference calls. I liked my job.

The irony was that while the partners were free to follow their bliss, nonpartners were locked up by their IPO awards, which vested over five years. Part of our decision-making around the public offering was to be very generous with the nonpartners, who weren't formally owed anything and who at many other firms wouldn't have received any extra compensation in an IPO. At Goldman, all full-time employees down to the assistant level received significant grants of restricted stock. We were especially generous with the couple of dozen people who had missed making partner in 1998 but would have been likely candidates in 2000—they each got stock grants worth $12 million at the end of the first day's trading. Two years later, we were thinking about how to manage some of them out—Goldman Sachs is not about attaching people to the firm forever. But it felt like a moral obligation to keep senior employees for the length of their initial vesting, which meant that the normal culling was suspended. A lot of partners whom we would have liked to have stay left, and a number of nonpartners who should have left stayed. That made management at the firm more challenging for a time.

I SPENT THIRTY-SIX YEARS AT GOLDMAN SACHS—HALF WHEN IT WAS A partnership, half when it was a public company. So I'm in a good position to compare the before and after. The IPO undoubtedly had an effect on the culture at Goldman, but it was less than I thought it would be. In the most important ways, the partnership culture and the quality of the people stayed consistent and strong. Through the early years of the twenty-first century, Goldman remained the top destination in finance. We maintained the title of "partner" even though we were no longer a partnership. The title came with outsize compensation and other perks and still carried high prestige in the financial community. The network among current and former partners remained vibrant. The process of electing partners continued to be competitive, tense, and highly consequential. After I was named CEO in 2006, maintaining that partnership culture became a central preoccupation of mine.

Looking back on the IPO from the perspective of twenty-five years later, the firm is different in many ways. But going public wrought less change on Goldman than did transformations underway in the economy, politics, and the regulatory environment. It was globalization and the end of Glass–Steagall that created the need to increase our head count and the size of our balance sheet. Going from 10,000 to 45,000 employees created a different feel at the firm. But that was something that had to happen for us to remain competitive in the arena we chose to be in.

It's impossible to separate those changes brought about by the IPO from others driven by growth, globalization, technology, and other transformations in a rapidly evolving industry. In my opinion, the biggest differences were positive ones. The IPO put Goldman in a position to grow and compete internationally. It also changed the firm's relationship to the public. Because all sorts of information now had to be disclosed publicly, corporate communications became an important new discipline. We went from being a private partnership that simply said "No comment" to being a company that thought about its image and engaged with the media—if not always successfully. Another irony is that Goldman provided more information to the public than we previously had, but less information to partners below the senior management level, because partners were free to buy and sell Goldman's stock and having material nonpublic information would restrict them.

Without an IPO, Goldman might have vanished in the global financial crisis of 2008. Or it might have evolved before then in a different direction, perhaps shrinking into a small advisory boutique, like Lazard Frères, which was the last Wall Street partnership to become a public company, in 2005. There's nothing wrong with being a boutique. But the partners of Goldman had pointed us in a different direction many decades earlier. They wanted to build a powerful and influential firm that mattered to the world. Given our ambitions, becoming a public company was the only choice we had.

CHAPTER 16

The Unforeseen

If you were so smart to have predicted what was going to happen, please tell me what's going to happen next.

fter the IPO, I thought that there would be a bigger price to pay in terms of the firm's culture—I was afraid that we'd lose a lot of the secret sauce. That we didn't owed a lot to the habits of partnership, transmitted across generations. And to the reality that, at that point, current and former partners still owned the firm, or at least around 85 percent of it. Only 15 percent of the shares had been sold to the public. It would take years of partners and former partners reducing their stakes to eventually vest majority control in outside owners.

With Hank in charge, important memos were signed "Hank, John and John," indicating that he, Thornton, and Thain were standing behind major decisions. But beyond that triumvirate, Hank was eager to expand the circle of participation. One of his first moves as a public company CEO was to dissolve the six-person executive committee and reconstitute the management committee as the forum for high-level discussion inside the firm. It swelled to twenty-nine people, which was a lot. But convening that larger group of partners underscored his commitment to relying on a kind of cabinet government, not just a small clique of insiders, to help him run Goldman.

The growing size of that group reflected that Goldman is a complex firm operating around the world in a complex industry. Anything that goes significantly wrong anywhere affects us and a large number of our clients. Often, Goldman got blamed for whatever the problem in financial markets was, and we would have to deal with a media clamor. Our weekly management committee meeting became the place to which everything important, especially problems, got elevated. Later, after I became CEO, I found that my sleep benefited from hearing from the major business runners every week at that two-hour Monday-morning meeting—the good, the bad, and the ugly. Airing all the risks and problems we faced provided a kind of reassurance. I never felt as on top of things as I did the moment that meeting ended. The next day, things could be very different.

Even though being a partner no longer had the same personal financial risks and rewards, Hank maintained the terminology of the partnership and the process of elections every two years. The partnership committee still spent months "cross-ruffing" candidates, a term from bridge that we used to describe our highly evolved way of considering new partners. If there were forty-five candidates up for consideration in the FICC, senior partners in FICC would stack-rank them. But then, as a kind of quality control, we'd appoint high-caliber partners from another division—say, investment banking—to produce their own ranking, based on not-for-attribution interviews with all the partners in FICC. The outside reviewers would compare their results with those of the inside reviewers, and unresolved differences would be brought back to the senior leadership of the firm. Cross-ruffing made partnership election significantly more complicated, because candidates were never officially informed that they were under consideration and the reviews had to be conducted with discretion. But the value of that labor-intensive process went beyond making the selection more objective. It meant that the partners got to know one another across divisions and through the years, even as the firm grew ever larger.

Perhaps most important was the attitude Hank projected. He continued to behave more like a senior partner than a CEO. Because he was without guile and didn't need to vent his own ego, Hank was able to draw out the best that people had to offer. He never competed with those below him, he never felt the need to impress them, and he never tried to prove how smart he was. He was willing to get advice from whatever quarter it came—the status of the person didn't matter to him. He evaluated what he heard, from wherever he heard it.

I learned a lot from Hank over the years, but at first, I was as much a teacher to him as he was to me. As someone who had come up through investment banking, he needed a better understanding of the trading side of the firm, which in the late nineties overtook investment banking as the largest contributor to our P&L and has provided the lion's share of the firm's profits and growth ever since. Hank wanted to find someone on the front line of the trading business in whom he could place his confidence. Through a series of conversations and visits to the J. Aron trading floor, that someone became me. The fact that I grew up in Aron and didn't owe my position to Corzine made me unusual. That I was an unaligned trading leader was no doubt a plus for Hank. When he came down to the fifth floor for tutorials, I found him to be a terrific listener, always wanting to understand what was going on and eager to be helpful.

For a time after the IPO, I was running FICC by myself. Hank had solved the problem of my feuding with Mike Mortara by putting Mortara in charge of GS Ventures, Goldman's newly created e-commerce incubator and venture capital fund. This was early in the dot-com frenzy, and we were getting caught up in it too. At the time, it seemed like a perfect assignment for Mortara. It looked less wonderful after the dot-com crash in March 2000, an event he survived by only a few months, sadly.

Hank thought I should have a partner in running FICC and appointed Jon Winkelried to be the co-head. That made sense. FICC was big and complicated, and I was relatively new to many of the activities that came with the old fixed-income division. Without Corzine, Winkelman, or Mortara around, it was important to bring up new management talent. And Winkelried, five years younger than me, was undeniably impressive. People viewed him as someone who could run the firm one day. Winks was a natural leader who seemed to be good at everything—a scratch golfer, an expert fly fisherman, and a contestant on the Western rodeo circuit from a ranch he owned in Colorado. His event was the cutting horse competition, a timed event where you have to separate a single cow from the rest of the herd. If you've never seen it, it's a lot harder than it sounds.

What did affect the firm's culture, far more than the IPO, was the explosion in scale driven domestically by banking deregulation and internationally by the forces of globalization. From 1998, the last full pre-IPO year, to 2006, our top-line revenue more than quadrupled, from $8.5 billion to $37.7 billion. Against the backdrop of that meteoric growth, we experienced in the space of just a few years the bursting of the dot-com bubble, the September 11 attacks, the accounting scandals at Enron and WorldCom, and the regulatory response to those scandals in the form of Sarbanes–Oxley. It was an intense, turbulent period in financial markets, with "once-in-a-lifetime" crises coming at us fast and furious.

Our global expansion was going full tilt. As we opened new foreign offices, a few people moved from New York to help build them, but more and more of the senior roles were filled by local lateral hires. In Japan, where there had once been no Japanese partners, the partners were soon all Japanese. The same was true in Germany and other countries where Goldman's presence was growing. Localizing those offices allowed us to expand more quickly. Being out front in those markets was worth the risks of overinvesting and expanding too quickly.

Our most consequential expansion was into China. We'd gotten permission to open offices in Beijing and Shanghai in 1994. That year, the People's Bank of China granted us a seat on the Shanghai Stock Exchange and a license to trade share issues reserved for foreign investors. Hank made dozens of trips there and helped us win the job of advising the government on the privatizations of China Telecom in 1997 and PetroChina in 2000. Goldman Sachs took no official position on the direction of history, but like a lot of people in that first post–Cold War decade, we saw financial and political liberalization breaking out everywhere we looked and liked what we saw.

It was Jim O'Neill, whom I recruited as our chief international economist, who coined the term *BRIC* to describe the most dynamic emerging-market economies—Brazil, Russia, India, and China. India was opening to foreign investment more slowly than China, but we saw the potential and diligently pursued opportunities to work with a local partner there. We also opened offices in São Paulo, Brazil, and Johannesburg in postapartheid South Africa. We were even returning to places like Russia, which we'd left briefly after the 1998 default, and Israel, which we'd also left after business dried up in the wake of 1998.

In Russia, people were happy to see us again—they barely noticed we'd been gone. Having chased commodity and foreign exchange business there since the late Cold War days, I was one of the few people around Goldman who had some experience with the place. The images in my head from that period were somber and gray. Now Russia was wild and in Technicolor. Everyone was happy to do business with us; the problem was with whom *we* could deal. Many of the oligarchs had acquired their fortunes by buying up privatized shares and consolidating industries by means that would be familiar to the heads of mob families. Everyone who was successful had strong political connections. One time we were en route to the house of an important businessman, got caught in terrible traffic, and called to apologize for being late. No problem, he said, he'd send someone to help us get through. Minutes later, we heard sirens behind us and saw cars giving way as a police van pulled up alongside our stopped vehicle. We got in, the sirens blared, and we cut our way through traffic to the destination. Could we deal with these people? Some yes, many not. Our decision-making was aided by profiles drawn up by our Business Investigations Group, part of our compliance unit. Drawing on their strong connections with intelligence and law enforcement agencies around the world, they sussed out who was and wasn't an appropriate business partner for the firm.

In Israel, which had developed a powerful start-up culture and a hot market, there was a certain amount of resentment that we'd changed our mind and were now changing it again. It was hard to break through the cold reception, but I got lucky. At Harvard, I'd been friendly with Lou Silver, a six-foot-eight basketball player who was in Winthrop House with me. Despite an opportunity to play professional basketball in the US, Lou had gone to Israel to play after graduation, and I wanted to catch up with him after many years. But with a full schedule, the best I could do was to tack him onto a lunch I had arranged with some of the country's highest-profile investors. I knew vaguely that Lou had had success as a player. Everyone else in the room knew him as the captain who led his team to ten Israeli league titles and two European Champions Cup titles. I had no idea how big a celebrity he was—the Michael Jordan of Israel! When he walked into the room, jaws dropped, and I was back in the fold.

IN OUR FIRST YEAR AS A PUBLIC COMPANY, BACKGROUND NOISE WAS provided by the dot-com frenzy, which was spurred both by the mass adoption of the internet and by low interest rates that lingered after the LTCM crisis in 1998. It was a classic bubble in many respects. At the core of it was something entirely real that eventually led to a loss of rational perspective. The 1990s saw the beginnings of an unprecedented transformation in information technology and communications. The rise of the personal computer and the World Wide Web changed every important industry. Venture capitalists were pouring money into start-up companies, which were being valued in unprecedented ways—on the basis of revenues or customers or, in the absence of either revenues or customers, on unproven business models and delirious fantasies.

Goldman led thirty-two IPOs for internet companies in 1999 alone. Those IPOs included many of the best companies that emerged in that era, including Yahoo!, eBay, and Red Hat Software. They also included many that turned out to be overhyped dogs, like Webvan, iVillage, eToys, and PlanetRx.com. Often those IPOs popped 200 or 300 percent from their offering prices, creating a frenzied demand for allocations of the IPO shares. Given the price jumps, we were sometimes accused of underpricing these offerings. Those companies were seriously overpriced relative to any notion of intrinsic value. As Warren Buffett likes to say, price is what you pay. Value is what you get. But we certainly believed the new dot-com companies had real worth.

When he was senior partner, Steve Friedman used to complain that by working solely as advisers to companies, we often lost sight of bigger opportunities in front of us. We were like coal miners who would sometimes break our drills on a diamond we'd accidentally come across in the coal seams. We'd throw the diamond away, replace the broken drill bit, and keep drilling for coal. After the IPO, we tried to keep some of those diamonds for ourselves. As a public company, Goldman had a much bigger balance sheet, which allowed us to expand our primary investing—buying stakes in promising companies for ourselves.

Through our principal investments area (later called the merchant banking division), we were functioning like a private equity firm, making our own large investments in many of the new dot-coms. We invested $100 million in Webvan, a business that promised grocery delivery in thirty minutes. The company didn't last much longer. It achieved a valuation of $6 billion in 2000 before achieving a valuation of zero in 2001. We made many terrific investments in this period, but the poor ones are much more memorable.

Contributing to the frenzied atmosphere was one of the best economies in memory. In 2000, the US was nine years into its longest peacetime expansion. Inflation, unemployment, and interest rates were low. For the first time in decades, the Treasury faced the problem not of a budget deficit but of budget surpluses. You'd think that would be an unalloyed good thing. But for a minute or two there were concerns that with the government issuing less new debt, the Treasury market would become less liquid, which could have other consequences. Our national debt is what other countries' currency reserves are made of. If they couldn't hold most of those reserves in the form of Treasury instruments, what would happen to the dollar as the world's reserve currency? The Treasury market also provides the curve against which corporate bonds and the credit of other governments are priced. If the US began paying down the national debt, what would credit spreads spread from? Those worries didn't last long. Soon enough, Congress passed the Bush tax cuts, and the government's borrowing began expanding again.

With hindsight, the shift of capital from established, large-cap companies to newly founded tech start-ups was wildly excessive. In 1990, the value of stocks traded on the tech-focused Nasdaq was 11 percent of the value of stocks traded on the New York Stock Exchange. By the end of the decade, the market cap of the stocks traded on Nasdaq was 80 percent of those traded on the NYSE. In 1999, the Nasdaq index rose 86 percent. This was the moment when CNBC emerged to provide constant market punditry. Day-trading, enabled by electronic trading platforms like Charles Schwab, became, for some, an obsession. People I barely knew from college would call me, hoping I could secure them an allocation of hot IPO shares that they could flip for an immediate profit. They were wasting their time—I couldn't and wouldn't.

Goldman and other Wall Street firms later came under regulatory scrutiny for conflicts of interest around the IPO market. The allegation was that analysts weren't independent—they were driven to say nice things about client companies by a desire to win investment banking mandates for their firms. Regrettably, there was truth to this. Goldman and others also got into trouble for allocating shares in hot IPOs to CEOs and corporate directors whose companies were clients of the firm. Those CEOs and directors were personal Goldman clients as well, but regulators saw a conflict of interest, because they were corporate fiduciaries, and the personal allocations could influence their decisions about where to take their future investment banking business. Goldman ended up paying a $110 million fine as part of global settlement with the SEC and New York attorney general Eliot Spitzer, informally known as "the Sheriff of Wall Street." Along with nine other banks, we agreed not to allocate IPO shares to anyone in a position to influence corporate banking decisions, and to take steps to keep our analysts' stock recommendations independent from influence on the banking side. Spitzer had his moment at our expense. He treated us like we were public enemy number one, before the world learned he was client number nine.

Given the tsunami of tech stocks hitting the market on Nasdaq, some of our partners worried that our capital markets business was at risk. Goldman was the go-to house that raised money for real businesses and established firms that made money, as opposed to the "new economy" companies that aimed to make money in the nebulous future. Without a large share of Nasdaq trading volumes, Goldman was in danger of missing the tech-underwriting wave and losing our dominant share in IPOs overall. In soliciting the mandate for a tech IPO, you had to convince the client that you'd be able to support the stock price after it was initially brought to market. Like other major investment banks, we were eager to add market-making capacity that would allow us to do that.

It was a little like the moment in 1981 when big Wall Street firms looked at the boom in precious metals and commodities and decided they needed to catch up. There were panic acquisitions happening. In June 2000, Merrill Lynch acquired Herzog Heine Geduld, a major market maker in Nasdaq stocks, for nearly $1 billion. The overheated atmosphere prompted Goldman to acquire Spear, Leeds & Kellogg, a Nasdaq-focused trading firm, for the much larger sum of $6.5 billion. It was by far the most expensive acquisition we ever did, driven by the desire to be at the red-hot center of tech stock trading. Spear, Leeds was the leading floor specialist on the NYSE, Nasdaq, and the American Stock Exchange, where it made markets in more than five hundred stocks. It had a profitable business in brokerage and clearing. It also had an early electronic trading platform, or "matching service" as people called it in those days. The acquisition was driven by the equities division, which reported to John Thain and John Thornton. It was far from my FICC bailiwick, but I was shocked by the deal. I thought we could build a version of what Spear, Leeds had on our own and produce a better outcome. I was aghast at how much we were spending for a not-very-special company. "There's no such thing as a bargain," Hank said.

Spear, Leeds certainly wasn't one. We got outtraded by the SLK partners. In some ways it was like the J. Aron purchase all over again, but at 50x the price and without the eventual silver lining of a cohort of terrific people who came with the deal and stayed. SLK had some smart, streety people too, but they weren't locked in and were made too rich by the sale to want to stay.

We completed the acquisition just in time for the bursting of the dot-com bubble. Between March 2000 and September 2002, the Nasdaq fell from a peak of 5,049 to a low of 1,140. (It wasn't until 2015 that it touched its 2000 peak again—or until 2018 if you adjust for inflation.) After the dot-com bubble burst, trading volumes declined drastically, and Spear, Leeds pretty much stopped making any money on trading commissions, which destroyed most of its value. Meanwhile, the floor-specialist business was going the way of my dad's old job of sorting the mail by hand at the post office. Goldman sold the remnants of that business in 2014 for $30 million. Our investment in SLK provided a steady source of write-downs of goodwill over the next several years.

The dot-com era is still the model that everyone uses as a reference point for speculative financial bubbles, alongside Dutch tulips in the 1630s, US stocks in the 1920s, and Tokyo real estate in the 1980s. Everyone sees bubbles for what they are—after they pop. *We knew what was happening all along*, they say. When people tell me that they knew about the thing that was coming, I say, *If you're so prescient, tell me what will happen next*. That usually shuts them up. They weren't actually right at the time. They just remember being right. Critics are always correct, because they don't have P&Ls to remind them how wrong they actually were.

In the run-up to the 2000 crash, certain stocks that were seen as representing the internet became completely unmoored from the idea of valuation based on earnings. We've seen that happen repeatedly around new technologies that excite people, including biotech, cryptocurrency, and electric vehicles. Typically, when the tides of overinvestment recede, many companies fail, but powerful winners emerge, such as Amazon amid the dot-com wreckage.

Is AI a bubble in the same way internet stocks were? As in 2000, the technological change driving the enthusiasm is absolutely real. But I suspect that much of the speculation will prove to be overblown—not necessarily about the potential of AI itself but about the companies thought to embody it and the amount of time it will take for AI to transform different sectors of the economy. That is only to say that there are likely to be big long-term winners, but that many of the emerging AI start-up companies and their enthusiastic investors will not be among them. Not every model will be valid. And with the valid models, not all will survive competition to become winners within the same market. Out of ten companies in a promising category, two or three might be the eventual champions.

WHAT CHANGED THE LEADERSHIP DYNAMIC AND EXPECTATIONS ABOUT an eventual succession at Goldman Sachs was September 11, 2001. The attacks posed an unanticipated test for everyone at a senior level at the firm. It was the rare crisis that no one blamed on us.

I was on the twenty-ninth floor of our office at 85 Broad leading a meeting on diversity at the firm when someone came in with a note saying that an airplane had flown into the World Trade Center. A couple of people left the room, but I continued the meeting until someone came with another note to inform me that a second plane had hit the towers. The session on diversity was done.

My memories from the rest of that day are a series of fragments and hazy images: people pulling shades down on the windows, as if there were a risk of snipers; security telling us all to evacuate the building; and hustling down the twenty-nine flights of stairs. Hundreds of people were standing outside our office, which was just a few blocks from the World Trade Center. It was what Pompeii might have looked like. The sky was black with soot and paper floating down from the sky.

Realizing that I was one of the most senior people in the office that day, I climbed back up the twenty-nine flights of stairs, accompanied by Ed Forst, Goldman's chief administrative officer. I stayed for a while trying to make calls that mostly didn't go through, and then followed instructions from security to evacuate, checking on every trading floor and finding pockets of people staring at TVs and computer screens. On the third floor, some J. Aron commodity traders had reconstituted a skeleton trading operation. Phones were mostly not working, but they were able to communicate intermittently with the London office, which was up and running. They said they were comfortable on the third floor, because if the worst happened, they were close enough to the ground to get out. Eventually, we ordered everyone to leave.

Sometime around midafternoon, I left 85 Broad Street and walked outside again into a choking haze. Following the urge to visit the scene of the crime, I moved toward the burning piles, where I gaped at the surreal, apocalyptic landscape. I wish I had given a thought to the carcinogenic air I was breathing in that day and in the weeks after. There's no way to know for certain, but I've long suspected that toxins I was inhaling contributed to my lymphoma diagnosis fourteen years later.

From there, I proceeded up Broadway and over to First Avenue. Covered in soot, I stopped into an open army surplus store, bought shorts and a T-shirt, and changed into them right there. Then I rolled up my soot-covered suit and threw it into a garbage can. Laura was trying to find me, but few calls were getting through. When we finally connected, I confirmed that she had picked up our daughter from school and that our boys made it home safely from their school in Riverdale. Our friend Jill Marino was desperately trying to locate her husband, Tom, at Lehman Brothers, which was headquartered in the World Financial Center, right across West Street from the towers. Part of the South Tower fell into his building, but he had gotten out and was okay. Had he stayed in his office, he wouldn't have been. Cell phone service was down until late afternoon, and it was impossible to reach anyone.

Through the horrific and traumatic days that followed, I found it emotionally helpful to have a business responsibility to focus on. Thankfully, no one at Goldman Sachs was among the missing, though everyone had connections to people who were lost. One of our top traders, later the head of the trading division, Ashok Varadhan, called and spoke to his thirty-two-year-old brother, Gopal, who was an employee at Cantor Fitzgerald in the North Tower of the World Trade Center. Sadly, he didn't make it out. Hank was stuck in China and couldn't get back, as US airspace was shut down. John Rogers, who had served in the White House and State Department before joining Goldman, worked his contacts in Washington to get clearance for a plane to bring Hank back. It was several days before he was able to return.

I didn't think there was any way for me to get to the office the next day, so I didn't try. There was a police blockade of Lower Manhattan. National Guardsmen with rifles in hand were positioned at intersections, as if to repel an invasion, but really just to make people feel safer. It probably did the opposite. John Thain did manage to get through the roadblocks and go to the office. His driver was an ex–NYPD captain and put a siren light on top of his car so that it looked official. In those days before Hank returned, Thain really stepped up and took charge.

I was congratulating myself that after extraordinary effort, I got myself to our building on September 13. By the time I made my way to work, the kitchen staff had been there for hours and had prepared a breakfast buffet for the professionals who were straggling in. It was another reminder of the dedication of our support team. Everyone was improvising to keep our business functioning. Ed Forst, a wizard at logistics, leased a couple of ferries and organized service for our employees from Carl Schurz Park on the Upper East Side down and around the blockade to the foot of Wall Street. I'm not sure it was entirely legal, but no one stopped us. For the next couple of weeks, that's how I and hundreds of others got around the barricades and back home at the end of the day.

Naturally, we had business-continuity procedures. They envisioned that in case of a major disaster in New York, we would fly teams to London and work from there. Like all the best-laid plans of mice and men, we had failed to imagine a scenario where planes would be grounded for an extended period of time. The New York Stock Exchange remained closed because its central communications hub, under the World Trade Center, was destroyed. In a week, Verizon heroically got it open again.

In London, trading continued in energy and commodities. As during other world-shaking events, there was an initial spike in oil prices when people thought that a Middle East–sourced crisis would disrupt the supply. Then there was a big decline in energy prices when people took in the broader economic consequences of the attacks and foresaw a drop in demand.

Given the tremendous uncertainty, many firms and individuals needed to sell assets to raise liquidity. Potential buyers for those assets were scarce. With markets frozen, no one knew what the price of anything was. Goldman arranged the first major block trade, $2 billion for 135 million shares of Disney stock that the Bass brothers were selling to raise liquidity in the face of margin calls. That trade helped reopen the market. For weeks, the fires were still smoldering and a smoky haze filled the air. But slowly, markets resumed doing what markets do.

CHAPTER 17

Succession

Ask people on the front lines what they should do, and then tell them to do it. Often, it turns out they knew all along.

John Thornton's career at Goldman may have been a casualty of the Twin Towers. Thornton played a key role in developing our international investment banking business and had become a legend for how connected he was. It seemed like he could fly into a country and become an essential adviser to the government and its leading businesspeople in fifteen minutes. He knew everyone and sat on several important corporate boards. That was usually not allowed at Goldman, because it could discourage business from clients at competitive companies. But Thornton was an exception in many things. He had great charm, and everyone agreed that he was impressive—even if they weren't always sure why they were impressed. Some years later, Rupert Murdoch and I were cochairs of the Partnership for New York City, which is basically the chamber of commerce for New York City. Once, we were having a conversation in Rupert's office. *Can you explain John Thornton to me?* he asked. Thornton had been on the board of News Corp for several years, and he was asking me this—*now?*

Thornton was never a physical presence in the office. As Laura was moving back to New York with the kids at the end of our school year abroad, she got me as a birthday present a membership at a fancy gym opened by the owners of Annabel's, a fashionable London club. Thornton was also based in London in those days. You didn't see him in our headquarters in the City—he preferred to do business from a suite at The Berkeley hotel in Knightsbridge. Other than meetings he held there, I'd mostly see him whenever I'd make it to the gym, usually on a lounger, in a bathrobe, holding a phone to his ear—no doubt doing important business, but in a setting that would seem too stereotypical in a film script. I'd wave while huffing and puffing on my cardio machine and he'd nod back.

After 9/11, Thornton was nowhere to be found. We knew he spent at least part of that time in Washington, but he didn't try to get back to New York City in the subsequent days and weeks. For months, it seemed, he wasn't at Goldman. Eventually, he resurfaced in New York but didn't come to the office. Similar to his pattern in London, he did business from a suite at the Carlyle on the Upper East Side. When I or anyone else at the firm needed to meet with him, we'd have to trek up there. I understand his reluctance to visit our home office so close to the still-smoldering ruins of the World Trade Center, but Thornton was co-COO of the company, part of the trio that was supposed to be running the firm, and he needed to be present. His invisibility affected his internal reputation and Hank's perception of him. As adept as he was in many respects, he didn't show himself to be a leader. Soon Hank was confiding to a few of the other partners on the management committee that he wanted Thornton out.

The September 11 attacks drove other changes as well. Our vice-chairman, Bob Hurst, grew increasingly focused on his work with the United Services Group, the largest 9/11 charity organization. Hurst left in March 2002 to spend more time on those efforts and to join another former Goldman Sachs partner, Barry Volpert, who was launching his own private equity firm. Hank then created three new vice-chairmen, including me, Bob Steel, who had run the equities division, and Rob Kaplan, who had been a co-head of investment banking. Instead of Steel and me running our respective businesses, equities and FICC, day to day, we would now "oversee" all of the trading businesses together. Kaplan would do the same for banking and asset management. A younger generation of partners would be managing those divisions directly. At FICC, that was Jon Winkelried.

In the press, it was reported that Hank was putting some combination of the three of us—Steel, Kaplan, and me—in the running to lead the firm at some point, as either an alternative or successors to Thain and Thornton. I don't believe that was Hank's intention at the time. "Vice-chair" is a kind of kicked-upstairs, minister-without-portfolio title. It's what they call you when the focus turns to the next generation and they don't know what to do with you anymore. Typically, it's a signal that it's time to start thinking about your next job.

Hank says that moving the three of us out wasn't his objective, although for everyone who had previously held that title, it was a last stop before leaving the firm. That proved to be the case for Kaplan and Steel, though it was hardly the end of their careers. Both went on to do distinguished work in academia, government, and business. Rob Kaplan became a professor at Harvard Business School, then head of the Federal Reserve Bank of Dallas, and eventually came back to Goldman in a senior role. Bob Steel went on to a distinguished career as undersecretary of the Treasury for domestic finance, CEO of Wachovia, deputy mayor for economic development under New York City mayor Michael Bloomberg, and president of Perella Weinberg.

In any case, I didn't throw myself out the window or go on a hunger strike. Though I was possibly being put on a path to early retirement, I came to work to play and took seriously the concept of oversight. The silver lining was that I now had license to get involved in equities, the only major part of our trading businesses that I hadn't been supervising.

MONTHS LATER, HANK ASKED ME TO FOCUS DIRECTLY ON FIXING THE equities division. My first question to him: Why weren't Thain and Thornton doing it? Modernizing a major division should have been a job for Hank's designated successors, the co-COOs. In an earlier era,

Bob Rubin and Steve Friedman had been asked by John Weinberg to do something similar for fixed income and had carried it off with great success. The answer was that the two Johns didn't want to take on the work—or, more likely, the risk of failing at it. They were looking at their watches, impatient to step into the CEO role. But Hank was not so impatient to give it up. He didn't like that they were waiting for him to finish so they could take over, or the sense of entitlement they radiated. There was a feeling that Thain and Thornton acted like "the owner's sons," as John McNulty, the co-head of investment management, once said to me.

My arrival on the scene at the equities division was scary to people. Behind my back, one of the division heads called me Keyser Söze, after the terrifying villain played by Kevin Spacey in *The Usual Suspects*. From the way some people responded, you would have thought it was the Huns entering Europe. But I understood why people were alarmed. I thought the division was really bloated. And everyone knew I thought that and expected some jobs to be consolidated or cut.

The division's traditional, plain-vanilla business was marketing our stock research views to large, institutional asset managers and executing their stock trades. There were also some heavily risk-based activities in equities like block trading and risk arbitrage, Bob Rubin's old department. But those were isolated pockets. As with commodities and fixed income in the old days, most of the equities division didn't actually seek risk on equities, other than short-term risk from market-making activities.

In some cases, traders didn't even expect to make a profit. Goldman was underwriting IPOs on a near daily basis. We pitched the IPO business to potential clients by promising that we'd support the market in their shares in the aftermath of the IPO, which meant trying to limit wild price fluctuations. Improving our ability to do that was the main reason we'd acquired Spear, Leeds. Equities trading was therefore primarily a facilitation business—it was viewed as a cost of obtaining fees from the IPOs. The equities traders thought of their P&L

as the net of the fees and commissions we brought in, less trading losses. In other words, they were trying to not lose as much money trading a newly public company's shares as we made in fees from that company's IPO.

It was apparent to me that equities needed to evolve in the way fixed income had, becoming more analytical and quantitatively driven. These were expert traders—it was within their competency to buy low and sell high, to be right more often than they were wrong, and to express those views more aggressively. As with the FICC businesses, we needed to become more sophisticated traders to serve our increasingly sophisticated clients. Hedge funds were becoming a more and more significant part of Goldman's business. If we wanted to be more important to them, we had to approach the stock market the way they did.

The client-facing part of the equity business was inefficient and strangely organized. We employed pure research analysts along with people in the hybrid roles of "research salesperson" and "sales trader." The division staffed itself that way to correspond to the way major fund managers like Fidelity and Vanguard were organized. The research analysts issued company reports and offered high-level advice on industries and stocks. The research salespeople would present and market that research to the fund's portfolio managers, who, if they wanted to act on that advice, would give orders to their own trading desks. The sales traders would cultivate those execution specialists at the fund companies, hoping to get their business for Goldman Sachs.

What's more, we had teams with those overlapping roles all around the world—in New York, Europe, and Japan—covering clients twenty-four hours a day. There was a Japan auto industry desk in New York and a US auto industry desk in Tokyo. Everything was multiplied by the industry, the time zone, and the function. I learned that we had more than eighty specialists speaking daily to many fewer people within Fidelity. For Fidelity and other major customers that bought and sold equities around the world and around the clock, our structure meant a confusing bombardment of calls rather than a coherent system of coverage. Why couldn't one salesman read the research, convey it to a Fidelity portfolio manager, and ask the execution desk for the order? That's the way we used to do things at J. Aron.

There were very smart people managing this coverage and they knew the system didn't make any sense. As I learned about it from them, I used a management technique I had figured out while running FICC. I'd ask the people in the division, "Does the way we're doing this make sense to you?"

"No, it doesn't," they'd say. "We should do it this way instead." And then they'd describe a more rational system.

"Okay," I'd say. "Do that."

And then they'd do it. And I would get excessive credit for being a good manager. More often than not, the people closest to a business are the ones who know best how to fix it. They just don't do it until someone gives the order. People get stuck in a trap where they just keep doing the same thing because, well, *we've done it that way since Sidney Weinberg was running the firm.* Or maybe they didn't think about fixing a flawed system at all. Things remained the way they had been out of sheer inertia, even though people knew it was ridiculous. It turned into a pointed joke I'd make: *Tell me what you should do, because then I'm going to tell you to do it.*

Sometimes people leading a department would even get dejected after implementing a change because they had originated the good idea and felt they didn't get enough credit for it. *Yeah, it was your idea—but you didn't do it until I told you to. Let that be a lesson to you!*

In theory, I was "overseeing" equities, not "running" equities. At some point, I made some recommendations that may have come across as instructions. I remember one of the department heads in equities asking me, "Do I report to you? Do I have to listen to you?" As I had back in the early days when given ambiguous authority over commodity traders, I said I wasn't sure myself, but it was his risk if it turned out that he did.

Soon we made a decision to merge equities with FICC, putting all of the firm's trading businesses in a single division. That made it easier to shift people and resources around within it. I moved several key people from FICC to help implement changes in equities. But given the dynamic, I made a point of not sending in Gary Cohn, the brilliant, dyslexic commodities trader, right away. I thought Gary, who had worked closely with me and was seen as a kind of protégé of mine, would ultimately be the best person to run the combined FICC and equities division. But I also knew that he was impatient and gruff and would break a lot of eggs. To make things 20 percent better, I didn't want to risk making them 80 percent worse. I had a feeling that if I brought in Gary at the outset, a lot of people in equities would have run for the hills.

Instead I put in a few strong managers who were easier to get along with. I brought Gary in later, once the ground was softened up. After his arrival, we merged the research-sales and sales-trading functions and told the traders that they were there to make money separate and apart from IPO and brokerage fees. In equities, the P&L went up and the head count went down.

THE UNSTOPPABLE FORCE OF JOHN THORNTON'S AMBITION RAN HEADlong into the immovable object of Hank Paulson, who was doing the CEO job happily and successfully. The problem wasn't that Thornton didn't work hard. He would fly to Asia for lunch and fly back the next day—he would do anything to drive business. But he wasn't close to many other partners. After he and Thain carved up the world and divided the business units of the firm, Thornton seemed to lose interest in those falling under his domain. Despite the title of co-COO, he didn't engage in the operating part. No one really understood why he didn't put in more effort; he seemed to want to be the executive chairman of Goldman Sachs without climbing the rungs along the way. Meanwhile, investment banking profits were plunging, from $1.7 billion in 2000 to $376 million in 2002.

This wasn't Thornton's fault, or not primarily his fault. The dotcom crash was followed at the end of 2001 by the collapse of two companies, Enron and WorldCom, which shook confidence in markets and seriously dampened M&A activity. Enron was an energy supplier and trading company that over just a few years became a dominant player in the energy futures markets. It was the bane of my existence, because it was purportedly making huge profits in energy and commodities, much larger than the profits we were making, and we couldn't figure out how they were doing it. They were selling long-dated contracts in power and other commodities without there being, to my understanding, any apparent source for the other side of the transactions. How could they continually add illiquid, one-way risk without any apparent hedging of that risk? It didn't make sense. Enron seemed to be accumulating larger and larger unhedgeable positions and booking enormous profits on its unrealized gains. Goldman was also a major provider of long-term power contracts, but there was a huge gap between us. We were limited by what we could hedge.

Enron also seemed to be innovating in new products the way my team at J. Aron had in the late eighties and early nineties. For instance, they figured out how to trade digital bandwidth as a commodity. I remember Bob Hurst, when he was running investment banking and had Enron as one of his clients, saying to me, "Why aren't you doing what they're doing?" We couldn't even imitate them, which made us look really stupid. Enron disclosed at one point that it had as many as a thousand people trading bandwidth, which in those days meant the cable or fiber being laid underground for the delivery of high-speed internet, phone, and TV. But bandwidth wasn't like oil that you consumed; the marginal cost of delivering service from fiber that was already in the ground was close to zero. We couldn't figure out how to make money trading it, or how Enron was doing it.

As we later learned, Enron was an enormous fraud. It did not, in fact, have an innovative way to hedge its long-term risks. It was accumulating unhedged, long-dated risk that it marked at levels it could not trade out at. When the company filed for bankruptcy in December 2001, it was the biggest in US history—but only until WorldCom filed for bankruptcy seven months later. For us, Enron's apparent success before its collapse had meant tough questioning and a nagging worry that they had figured out something we hadn't. We survived it and, when we looked back, had a good laugh about it.

For others, the consequences of those accounting frauds were much more serious. Mike Armstrong, the CEO of AT&T, laid off twenty thousand workers and ultimately lost his job because he couldn't compete with WorldCom and Qwest, another fraud-riven company that was offering telecom services for close to nothing while hiding its losses. When what they claimed to be doing was revealed to be impossible, WorldCom went bust and Qwest vanished in a merger. That was cold comfort for Armstrong and all the other people at AT&T who got killed because they couldn't compete with fraudulent businesses. Once you're dead, you don't come back to life after everyone comes to their senses.

When Enron collapsed at the end of 2001, it took with it Arthur Andersen, one of the Big Five accounting firms, which had somehow missed its hiding billions in debt and other forms of financial chicanery. In response, Congress passed the Sarbanes–Oxley Act. Some parts of that bill were necessary, and some were excessive in ways that vastly and unnecessarily expanded the costs and administrative burdens of operating public companies.

In my life, I've learned that I shouldn't shop at the grocery store when I'm hungry and that I shouldn't make personnel decisions when I'm angry. In the same way, Congress probably shouldn't write enduring financial regulations in the immediate aftermath of financial scandals. Sarbanes–Oxley introduced some valuable changes, such as standardizing accounting definitions and making board audit committees more accountable. Less usefully, it fueled a bull market in compliance officers and class-action lawyers. The burdens it imposed increased the preference on the part of many entrepreneurs to stay private much longer. Those businesses sacrifice the many benefits of being public companies while the public loses visibility and the opportunity to invest in and influence them.

IN CONTRAST TO THORNTON, THAIN WAS AN EXCELLENT OPERATOR IN many respects. His liability was that he seemed stiff and robotic to people. He was not a great motivator or leader. It was known that he didn't enjoy working after 6:00 p.m. or on weekends, which cut against the work ethic of the firm. Thain had been anointed early in his career as a future CEO and had developed a sense of privilege that showed in the way he spent the firm's money. He insisted on flying private—even to Washington or Boston, where the shuttle was faster. In London, he rented a home that had been the US ambassador's interim residence while Winfield House, the official residence, was being renovated. Later, when he was CEO of Merrill Lynch, there was a scandal because Thain spent $1.2 million furnishing his office, including $88,000 on a rug and $35,000 for an antique commode that people thought was a toilet (it's actually a chest of drawers). Part of that sense of entitlement was to the CEO job at Goldman, which Thain, like Thornton, thought Paulson had promised to hand over within a couple of years after the IPO.

By early 2003, Thornton was ready to force the succession issue with Paulson. "Stay if that's what you'd like to do, Hank, but please tell me so I can make other plans," he told Paulson.

That initiated a chain reaction. Hank told Thornton that he should, in fact, make other plans, and he began the process of managing him out. With his strong connections in China, Hank helped get him a teaching position at Tsinghua University in Beijing, sometimes described as the MIT of China. Thornton didn't speak any Chinese, but he became the first American to be honored with a full professorship there.

At that point, it became apparent to me that I could be part of an eventual succession plan. After Thornton's departure was announced in March 2003, I took over his seat on the board of directors. John Thain, who was now sole president, COO, and heir apparent, didn't much appreciate that. Then Hank proposed making me copresident, which Thain appreciated even less. According to a *New York Times* story after the announcement in November 2003, I was now "the most likely candidate to succeed Mr. Paulson." The theory was that my part of the firm—trading—was driving the biggest profits.

Unhappy that Hank wasn't leaving on his timetable and that I was being given equal billing, Thain began looking for other opportunities. He was soon offered one he liked, as CEO of the New York Stock Exchange, where the previous CEO, Richard Grasso, was forced out over a $140 million pay package. When Thain told Hank he was leaving just before Christmas 2003, I don't think Hank was surprised. Thain's career had other significant chapters. He later became CEO of Merrill Lynch and engineered its acquisition by Bank of America during the global financial crisis.

I was genuinely surprised and disappointed by Thain's departure—I liked the idea of working with him as a copresident. But after he left, Hank appointed me as sole president and COO in early 2004. That put me in line to become Hank's successor as CEO—though it would be the board's decision. Reading the writing on the wall, Bob Steel announced—the same day Thain quit—that he was leaving to teach at the Harvard Kennedy School of Government.

Of the many nice notes I got about my promotion, one in particular meant a lot to me. John L. Weinberg wrote to say that reading my profile in *The Wall Street Journal* reminded him of the way his father, Sidney Weinberg, came up through the ranks in an earlier era.

With a bigger public role, I decided it was time to take some steps in personal improvement that I'd been putting off for a while. I'd quit smoking years before. Now I shaved my beard and lost some weight—ultimately 40 pounds. I put my size 44 suits in the back of the closet and bought some 42s, then 40s and 38s. But unlike Thain and Thornton, I wasn't in any hurry to take the next step. My expectation was that Hank was going to be around for many more years, quite possibly long enough that his eventual successor would come from a generation younger than mine.

CHAPTER 18

Is He Completely Housebroken?

I am good at taking down or bringing up tension in a room—sometimes intentionally.

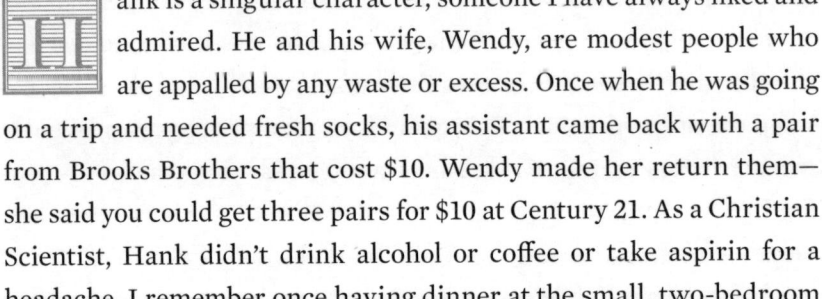ank is a singular character, someone I have always liked and admired. He and his wife, Wendy, are modest people who are appalled by any waste or excess. Once when he was going on a trip and needed fresh socks, his assistant came back with a pair from Brooks Brothers that cost $10. Wendy made her return them—she said you could get three pairs for $10 at Century 21. As a Christian Scientist, Hank didn't drink alcohol or coffee or take aspirin for a headache. I remember once having dinner at the small, two-bedroom apartment he and Wendy got above the Reebok Sports Club on the Upper West Side after he became CEO. Laura and I were there with another couple. Laura asked for a Diet Coke, and Wendy offered to go out to get it. (No need!) At dinner, we drank Hawaiian Punch.

The next time we had dinner there, Laura and I remembered to pregame in the car on the way over. We were laughing about acting like teenagers as we finished up our roadies on the sidewalk outside—when who should we run into but my colleague Scott Kapnick and his wife, Kathleen, drinking wine out of Solo cups. They were having dinner at the Paulsons' too. Scott, incidentally, was another Goldman partner who did spectacularly well after striking out on his own some years later. He built up HPS Investment Partners, an early player in the burgeoning private credit market. In 2024, he sold it to BlackRock for $12 billion.

Hank and I didn't share a lot of interests apart from Goldman Sachs, but we liked each other and worked extremely well together. With most senior people—and this is especially true if you're dealing with government officials—you have to convince them not only that your point of view is right but also that it is in their interest to invest the effort and take the risk to get something done. With Hank, you had to do only the first thing. Once he determined that something was right, he was on it. This quality was on vivid display during the global financial crisis, when Hank as Treasury secretary was always readier than anyone else in government to make and implement unpopular decisions to avoid economic catastrophe.

Hank is extremely smart—he was Phi Beta Kappa at Dartmouth—but no one would accuse him of eloquence. As CEO, he sometimes stumbled and said things that got him in hot water, like the time he was asked at a conference about staff cutbacks and said not to worry—20 percent of the people at Goldman Sachs did 80 percent of the real work. That really upset the staff—people at Goldman don't think of themselves as slackers. But Hank being Hank, he didn't make excuses or try to explain away what he'd said. He openly apologized for being insensitive and glib, in a voicemail he sent to twenty thousand employees. He then repeated the apology several times in person and in a heartfelt way. No one held it against him, because everyone understood that Hank doesn't have a bad bone in his body. It may also have helped that at Goldman, everybody thinks they're in the most productive 20 percent. At a partner off-site held shortly afterward, he was presented with a large plaster foot, because one of the feet he was born with was often in his mouth.

Because I was now Hank's most likely successor, the firm decided that it was time to help me smooth out some of my own rough edges.

It provided me with two coaches, one for media training, the other for management training. My media coach advised me to speak in complete sentences and paragraphs when I was being interviewed on camera. Well, I admire people who can do that, and it would have been good advice for people who are capable of expressing themselves that way. But it's not me—I couldn't do it. I talk in a stream of thoughts connected by dashes, ellipses, observations, and analogies that spontaneously occur to me. Sometimes that works to my disadvantage. But I found that trying to be someone other than who I was worked as badly on television as it tends to do in real life. The most useful bit of advice I took away from the media coach was that when speaking to large audiences, I should turn my head to the left as well as to the right. The habit of turning only one way was the legacy of a lifetime of lap swimming, where I always turn my head in the same direction to breathe. I found that with practice, I could turn in both directions. But it's not natural. I have to remind myself.

The more important advice about public speaking I picked up elsewhere. It's to leave people wanting more rather than less of you. How often do you listen to a talk and wish it had gone on for another five or ten minutes? Not so often, right? And when people tell me they get nervous speaking to large audiences, I have another line: When you're swimming, it doesn't matter whether the water is six feet deep or six hundred. So it shouldn't matter if you're speaking to six, sixty, or six hundred. It's the same stroke.

I liked the management training better because I got to talk about my favorite subject—me. When the coach did interviews with senior people around the firm, he heard the criticism I'd often received in 360-degree reviews: I could be impatient and harsh and was perceived to have a closed inner circle. Given the circumstances of my rise, with a series of rivals quitting or getting pushed out, many assumed that I just rolled over people. The management coach told me that without fully intending it, I could be intimidating. I was never a yeller, but I was too quick with a cutting remark. I was always that way, but the negative impact increased as I climbed the corporate ladder. Realizing the truth of this, I worked harder to direct my cutting humor toward myself.

Someone once said there was no one better than me at taking down or bringing up tension in a room. I tried to get better at regulating the thermostat intentionally, and over time, I found I could do that too. I also thought about how to be more open and available to people who were perceived as being on a different team, much as Hank had done for me. I did always have a close management group around me, but the membership wasn't fixed. I thought more about the value of moving people into and out of my circle. But there was one practice I continued to cultivate: I didn't promote my friends. I made friends with people who deserved promotions.

TO THIS DAY, I BELIEVE THAT COO MIGHT BE THE BEST JOB AT GOLDMAN Sachs. COO was an especially influential role during those years because of Hank's background as an investment banker. He spent most of his time externally, with a focus on our biggest clients and biggest deals. The CEO is the public face of the company—the one who gets subpoenaed. But as COO, I was on the board of directors and had visibility into and influence over all aspects of the firm without being as visible to the outside world. For someone like me who, despite appearances, has anxiety about being in the spotlight, it was an ideal position. Still, I had my share of client work and travel and leaned into the investment banking side of the house. Internationally, I focused on Germany, France, Spain, Italy, the Middle East, and Japan. Hank and I both did our stints in DC, walking the halls of Congress and meeting legislators and regulators, as well as their equivalents in many other countries where we did business.

Regulators tend to refrain from torturing the COO to the same extent as other top executives. Under Sarbanes–Oxley, the CEO and CFO have to personally sign a statement certifying the truth of the company's financial statements. The COO doesn't have to sign it. Later, after I became CEO, I was never fully comfortable with that responsibility.

Of course the CEO sets a tone when it comes to integrity and the buck stops with him or her. But how could you ever really know that numbers streaming in from all over the company were fully accurate, or that someone among forty thousand employees wasn't lying or cheating? You couldn't, which explains the insertion of a codicil "based on such officer's knowledge" in the final draft of the rules.

As COO, *operating* is your middle name, and that part of the role came naturally to me. I loved digging into the details, and I loved people who loved digging into details. My best management tool was always the P&L. Our trading units generated daily P&L reports, and I pored over them at the end of every day. Those reports helped me learn about all of our lines of business and revenue. When you read a daily P&L, you naturally have questions about things you don't understand or anomalies you notice. I'd see that a P&L that typically moved $1 million in a day instead moved $5 million and would ask for an explanation. Over time, I developed a grasp of more and more of the intricacies. I'd call someone and say, *Hey, we haven't spoken in a while. I was just going through the daily P&Ls, and I see a number that usually moves around 1 percent—today it moved by 9 percent. What happened?* A big fee came in from an investment banking assignment. *What did we do to earn it, and was the client happy with us?* It could be something good or something bad. In any case, we'd talk about it until I understood. It's like drilling test wells in a Texas oil field. Sometimes you strike oil, sometimes you don't. But continual sampling helps you draw conclusions about what's going on below the surface.

I learned that by making those calls, I was also demonstrating the depth of my interest in what people were doing and thereby helping to shape the impression they had of me. Word gets around quickly. The next day in the office, everybody would know that I called that guy up at home in the evening to ask him about whatever it was. People with operating roles at big companies often lament that they can't do everything or connect with everyone. You can't. But by digging in frequently when you can, you become known as the kind of person who is highly aware and cares about the minutiae. You'll be inside people's heads when they're making decisions, even if they're halfway around the world and you haven't spoken to them in a while.

You can also influence behavior by using P&Ls as a lever. When I wanted the equities division to start seeing stock trading as a profitable activity separate from the IPO fees, I had the trading P&L reported separately from the fees so they could no longer hide behind the IPO revenues. After that, I didn't have to say much—the visibility of the residual P&Ls was the best motivator. Generally speaking, when I wanted someone to take more risk, I'd lump P&Ls together so they could hide a bit more. When I thought there was a flaw in how something was working, I'd divide the P&Ls into smaller and smaller pieces until everything was isolated and everyone had to stand on his or her own.

I WAS WELL-KNOWN BY THE TRADING SIDE, LESS WELL BY INVESTMENT banking and asset management. As COO, I had opportunities to address the partners and the firm as a whole, and I took advantage of them. Beyond making new friends, I wanted to start to step back and explain how I viewed Goldman Sachs as a whole.

The agency parts of the business and the principal parts of the business—advising and brokering versus trading and investing—were a necessary but sometimes uncomfortable fit. Being an agent meant traditional investment banking activities on behalf of clients, which paid fees. Being a principal meant risking the firm's own capital for a return. We were always somewhat skittish about being a principal, not just because of the risk or volatility but because we were concerned that our clients would see us as competing with them. As a principal investor, you are at some level competing against your clients for investment opportunities.

In most years, Goldman was the number one adviser to private equity firms, while occasionally bidding against them in other situations. That could be awkward, to say the least. Plus, as the investment bank with the best corporate relationships and the best M&A franchise, we had a natural advantage in deal sourcing, which was also sometimes resented. We tried to reduce the awkwardness by partnering with our important private equity clients—but they complained anyway. In any case, we weren't going to walk away from being a principal, especially with many of our clients moving into some of our traditional advisory activities. Trading and investment now produced by far the largest share of our profit and growth. So we had to be both principal and adviser.

At other investment banks, the advisory and the principal sides of the business often couldn't stay together. Public firms didn't like the private equity business because of its inherent volatility and the stresses that created. In a public company, you will sacrifice profitability to reduce volatility in your earnings and support your stock price. At most banks, when merchant banking—the private equity division—lost money, whoever was running the bank got frustrated with that business. And when it made money, the people running the merchant banking business got frustrated with their parents and thought about striking out on their own. So the two sides alternately thought they were doing the other a favor. One by one, our competitors spun off or shrank their merchant banking divisions.

At Goldman, the partnership culture helped us resist doing that. Because Goldman partners and former partners still held the bulk of our equity, we didn't face the same market pressure to trade profitability for consistency of earnings. We didn't feel the same pressure to throw our private equity partners off the boat when they had a bad year. And because of their attachment to the partnership, they didn't feel the same urge to jump ship when they had a good year. Some left, of course, but even post-IPO, the partnership ethic held sway. Rich Friedman, one of the great partners of the firm, ran our internal merchant bank for decades. One of the few remaining pre-IPO partners, he has been at Goldman for more than forty years. Why did Rich stay? Because of Goldman's longer-term perspective and his attachment to the partnership. We understood the cyclical nature of the business and could stick with it through the down parts of the cycle. Our partners appreciated that the overall reputation of the firm supported their individual success.

Thinking like a partnership gave us a real advantage. But how could we ultimately compete with the much larger, universal banks like Citi, J.P. Morgan, and Bank of America? Not by taking them on in consumer-facing businesses like retail banking and credit cards; that wasn't in our DNA. And probably not by winning a bigger share of the pie. In the advisory and brokerage businesses that were the historical core of the firm, we were already number one and faced significant challenges. There are only so many companies in the world that are candidates for big-ticket mergers and acquisitions. Brokerage was becoming less profitable because of electronic trading and the end of fixed commissions. But there were other advisory roles that were natural to Goldman Sachs and that I felt confident we could grow, like asset management and private wealth management. Rather than overpaying for another acquisition—as we had for J. Aron and SLK—I believed that we could develop and expand those businesses organically.

However, the real opportunity, it seemed to me, lay in conceiving the totality of what we did as the work of a merchant bank. Goldman Sachs had a merchant banking division that made strategic investments in companies. But I was talking about something much more encompassing: integrating the three roles of advising, financing, and investing. Those three functions, which others thought were incompatible, actually belonged together. Financing a client's project shows confidence in the project. And there is no better way to demonstrate a belief in a client's venture than to go beyond lending and invest in it yourself.

That's what the classic merchant banks did. All through modern financial history, the great merchant banking firms, such as the House of Rothschild, played multiple, complementary roles. They were financiers, and people came to them for advice. They were also traders and investors. John Pierpont Morgan, the most important banker in US history, operated in this way. As a merchant banker, Morgan would invest alongside the clients he advised and finance their projects. Morgan was a hugely controversial figure in the late nineteenth century, largely because of his efforts to create industrial monopolies, which led to the rise of antitrust enforcement. But Morgan's role as a financier and investor was what enabled the construction of a network of national railroads, as well as the rise of the great industrial companies, such as U.S. Steel. When it came to his integrated approach to finance, Morgan served his clients well, and they loved him for it. I said we should be like J.P. Morgan—the man, not the bank.

All three of these functions and the ability to pull them together came more easily to Goldman Sachs than to our competitors. We could and should excel at all of them—there was no reason for us to be apologetic about it. More than that, I thought that engaging in advising, lending, and investing together was virtuous. By playing these multiple roles, an investment bank like Goldman became the practical embodiment of Adam Smith's invisible hand. We weren't just serving our clients better. We were playing a primary role in the allocation of capital, to the benefit of the economy and society. Being investors also gave us a certain confidence and swagger in dealing with our clients. Instead of being supplicants, always asking for their business, we were more like peers. Don't get me wrong—we were still the ones who picked up the check at dinner. But we dealt with them as equals, not humble servants.

The possibility of playing those multiple roles had ended with the Banking Act of 1933, known as Glass–Steagall. That law barred commercial banks from investment banking and underwriting and forced the House of Morgan to split into two separate firms—J.P. Morgan & Co., the commercial bank, and Morgan Stanley, the investment bank. Glass–Steagall hadn't restricted Goldman because we weren't a commercial bank. For more than sixty years, however, those restrictions shaped the competitive landscape in American finance. Now it was all changing. After Glass–Steagall was repealed in 1999, those functions were organically converging again. But the big commercial banks lacked the long-term perspective and collaborative culture needed to properly integrate them. At Goldman, I thought it was the moment to confidently embrace our unique ability to integrate the multiple roles of adviser, financier, and investor. We could deal with the problem of conflicts with our clients through transparency and sometimes simply by holding back on pursuing opportunities. Part of our reality was that relationships, internal and external, had to be carefully managed.

INVESTMENT BANKING INVOLVES CONSTANT COMMUNICATION. HANK, an investment banker by vocation, would call people up at any hour when he wanted to discuss things. Weekend? What's a weekend? With me, for some reason, Hank would rarely call outside of regular business hours and instead would leave voicemail messages. This was partly because one or both of us were usually traveling, but it went beyond that. Hank would call and leave me a voicemail message about something. Then I'd call back and leave him a voicemail. Sometimes we'd go back and forth eight or nine times in asynchronous conversation, never speaking directly. It was an odd form of dialogue, but that pattern held for years.

And then on the Sunday of Memorial Day Weekend 2006, while I was on the golf course in East Hampton, Laura called me on my cell phone.

"Hank's looking for you."

"Hank called the house?"

"Hank called the house."

So I knew this must be a big deal. And I had a guess what it was about.

Hank had told me—and the board—that he was being recruited for secretary of the Treasury but that he wasn't planning to take the job. He was reluctant for good reason. It was the middle of the second term of a president who was by that point pretty unpopular. Hank thought it would be hard to have an impact as the George W. Bush presidency was entering its final, lame-duck phase.

But Josh Bolten, the White House chief of staff, persevered in his recruitment of Hank. Josh was another Goldman alum (we were everywhere). Josh told Hank that the president could meet his terms around access to him and full authority over key issues like the economy and China. Hank left the conversation open and agreed to a meeting with Bush, who pressed him to accept. That was the end of Hank's stiff arm. It's difficult to turn down the president when he walks you through the Rose Garden and says, "Your country needs you."

When I called him back, Hank said he was taking the Treasury job and wanted me to be his successor at the firm. The ultimate decision would be the board's, of course, but he expected they would agree with him.

As I held the receiver and listened, I felt the weight of the moment. For me, a new opportunity always brings anxiety more than elation. Hank had often apologized to me in the past because he had no time frame for leaving his job. My response was always that he misunderstood me if he thought I was breathlessly waiting for him to go so that I could take over. I couldn't have been happier in my COO role and felt that if he stayed in his position forever, and I retired from the firm as his number two, I'd be perfectly content. The thought of being CEO activated my old impostor feelings and fears about a more public role. Even after twenty-four years in the firm, I still felt like the guy who got rejected at Goldman and entered through the back door at J. Aron. I hadn't gone through the Goldman trainee program or had anything like a typical career there. And I hardly looked like central casting's idea of a Wall Street honcho. Today I have mostly overcome it, but I was camera shy and inclined to avoid the limelight. What's more, the suddenness of Hank's departure meant that I was going to be pushed to the forefront without the normal transitional support from my predecessor. He wouldn't be there to take me around and assure everyone I was going to be great.

There are two kinds of succession planning, which are usually done in tandem. Long-term planning creates a framework for what will happen in the normal course of events. The second kind of planning is for succession if a sudden event whisks away the CEO. In the old cliché, you need a plan in case the person in charge gets hit by a bus. When Bush nominated Hank, it was the hit-by-a-bus scenario without any blood. Once formally nominated, he would be mostly walled off from Goldman.

Hank asked me to fly down to Washington with him on Tuesday morning for the Rose Garden announcement. He said the plane ride would give us time to talk about the transition. In that moment of self-absorption, I assumed he meant *my* transition to CEO. Of course, I wasn't the only one getting an important new job. What we talked about was *his* transition to Treasury secretary. Hank had accepted the job with the understanding that he would be the Bush administration's primary voice on economic policy. On the plane ride down, he was editing the president's draft announcement remarks and raising various issues with our Washington sage John Rogers about what elements of the agenda he would voice or manage.

Many of the partners at the firm, especially on the investment banking side, didn't know me well. I had been a trading guy, not an investment banker, and while trading was often dominant in the P&L, Goldman Sachs was culturally an investment banking firm. I had been on the board, but in board meetings I deferred to Hank as CEO and chairman and usually spoke only when asked. The outside board members, including John Browne, the CEO of British Petroleum, Jim Johnson, the former head of Fannie Mae, and John Bryan, former CEO of Sara Lee, didn't know me that well. In one form or another, some were asking, *Is he completely housebroken?* To those establishment CEOs, I may not have looked like the type of person who should be running the firm. As a piece in *The New York Times* put it, "Mr. Blankfein does not appear to have, at least not yet, the statesman-like aura that has been associated in the past with Goldman's leaders." Ouch.

I don't know that anyone opposed the idea of my getting the job, but there was a question of what the job should be. Word filtered back to me that there were some voices on the board arguing that they should put in a separate executive chair to provide "balance." At least one member of the board volunteered. I later learned that Hank fought that off. He took a sharp stand that I should have both titles, chairman and CEO, just as he had and the heads of most of the other major investment banks did. I also found out later that Steve Friedman, whom Hank had asked to return to the Goldman board the year before, was helpful to my cause. Hank tells the story that when he was puzzling over what to do about Thain and Thornton and wondering who should eventually succeed him, he had lunch with Friedman and discussed it.

"Well, if you had sole control of Goldman Sachs, and all your money and reputation tied up in it, who would you want to run the firm?" Steve asked him.

"Lloyd," he responded without hesitation.

"Well, that's your answer," Steve said.

On Friday, June 3, 2006, three days after the announcement of Hank's nomination, the board voted me in as chairman and CEO contingent on Hank being confirmed by the Senate a month later. The transition was not without complication. I was, for the time being, acting as CEO. Hank was effectively gone, but until he was confirmed by the Senate, he wasn't formally giving up the title. Before his hearings, he had to limit his communications with the firm to avoid potential conflicts. There were a lot of issues we couldn't discuss, both for the sake of propriety and because he was so focused on preparing for the hearings and his new job.

CHAPTER 19

A Modern Merchant Bank

What do you do when you have to manage a jungle full of eight-hundred-pound gorillas? You have to train eight-hundred-pound gorillas to stand aside, say "After you," and graciously let one another pass from time to time.

fter the announcement of Hank's nomination, we flew straight to Chicago for our biannual global partners' meeting. This was an elaborate, long-planned event with divisional dinners at iconic locations around the city, including at the Museum of Science and Industry, Wrigley Field, Orchestra Hall, and the Chicago Theater. It featured talks by Alan Greenspan, Warren Buffett, and the junior senator from Illinois, one Barack Obama. That event was also now going to be my debut appearance before the firm as its (still contingent) CEO. There was a lot swirling around in my head as the plane landed at O'Hare: whom I was going to appoint to key roles, what the fallout from those appointments might be, and how to characterize my concept of the job, the firm, and its future.

Hank opened the meeting with a moving testament to Goldman Sachs and its people, in the valedictory mode of a graduating senior giving advice to those following behind him. He said that Goldman needed to strengthen and protect its client franchise, its reputation, and its culture. "The firm is greater than any of us, and we need to put the firm first. We need to understand that we have one brand, one reputation," he said. "We rise and fall together."

I followed Hank and conveyed the firm's appreciation for him. My lengthier remarks came at the end of the meeting the next day. I focused on the distinctiveness of Goldman Sachs—what made us special and how we could take great advantage of it. It seemed to me that our core strength was culture—our ability to work collaboratively and to get people to think about the firm as a whole, not just as a collection of functions. We had an ability, rare at any organization, to get people to forbear when their own interests were in conflict with the highest benefit to the company as a whole. Some of that was accomplished with more subtle and subjective incentives. We didn't pay people as a percentage of their own P&Ls. We could compensate someone for walking away from a deal in the interest of the whole, as well as for bringing in business for other parts of the firm.

I had three main points on my agenda. The first was that instead of being sheepish about the inherent tensions among our businesses, we should be comfortable with the reality of our multifaceted role and sort through the inevitable conflicts openly. The reason we often found ourselves in the position of representing companies that competed with one another—multiple clients in the same industry—was that we were the best at what we did and always in demand. Successfully managing conflicts among our clients and our multiple roles would make us a stronger firm. I compared our strategic position to that of the historical merchant banks. Being bankers made us better investors. The fact that we were good investors made us better bankers and better financiers. No other investment bank had the balance sheet, the breadth, and the reputation to be able to carry off being a modern merchant bank.

The culmination of this idea, which happened from time to time, was when we played all three roles in the same transaction—what I called "the triple play," a situation in which we advised an M&A client on an acquisition, financed that acquisition, and invested in it ourselves. I saw those roles of advising, financing, and investing as mutually supportive and reinforcing—a virtuous cycle. The financing and advisory roles were obviously complementary. Naked advice is fine, but it's far more effective when you can help the client realize your advice with financing. Being an M&A adviser got us more lending business, which was often more lucrative than the M&A fees. And of course, being an investor and a partner is the best way of demonstrating your belief in the advice you're giving.

Those multiple roles inevitably involved conflicts. My view was that we had to confront those issues rather than flee from them. Conflicts are inherent in all service businesses where the client is relying on your advice and you get paid only if the client does something. Should a company buy another company? If it does, the investment banker gets paid. If it does nothing, there is no fee, only the possibility of future business down the road. For that reason, an investment banker's incentives always favor the client doing something rather than nothing. Even if all you do is advise companies, you're conflicted, because you get paid only when you do a deal. Goldman's record and reputation over 150 years, and the longevity of our investment banking relationships, were the best testaments to the quality and integrity of our advice.

My second point was about the opportunities we had for expanding globally. The US market was big, but China was projected to have an economy that would eventually exceed that of the US. It had little indigenous experience or talent in investment banking. That presented an enormous opportunity for us, but it was far from the only one. In my years as CEO, we opened offices in Mumbai, Dubai, Doha, Tel Aviv, Warsaw, and Amsterdam. As part of that process, we elected many more international partners and reduced somewhat the US dominance at the senior level. In some ways, doing that made the firm more challenging to manage, because it wasn't as homogeneous.

Some of this enthusiasm may now sound a little anachronistic. But I was coming into the job during a broad political consensus about the benefits of globalization. Thomas Friedman's *The World Is Flat* had been published the previous year, in 2005, and was named the

Financial Times and Goldman Sachs book of the year by a panel I co-chaired with the *Financial Times* editor, Lionel Barber. As the hopes around globalization have diminished, some of Friedman's views have come in for ridicule: It turns out that countries with McDonald's franchises do go to war with one another. But like Friedman, my colleagues and I saw a world marked by economic and political convergence—the single European currency, central banks managing economies cooperatively, the spread of democracy, and the eastward expansion of the EU and NATO. We were riding that wave of optimism, expanding in all the rising economic centers. I had a mantra for that: *Let's be Goldman Sachs in more places.*

The third part of my pitch was what I called our "Run Faster, Jump Higher" agenda. That was the slogan for an old sneaker brand called P.F. Flyers, a competitor to Converse and Keds in my childhood. We had some businesses that realistically couldn't grow very much because you couldn't create more opportunities. Mergers and acquisitions was limited by the pool of companies that existed in the world. But there were two parts of our business that were considerably under scale: asset management and private wealth management. We could grow those businesses by doing what we already did better, without the external world changing. In private wealth management, we advised and managed assets for the wealthiest families in the world, dominating the market among super-duper-ultra-high-net-worth individuals and families. But what about the people who were only very rich? Wealth was being created at a rapid rate in many places around the globe. Our position in the wealth-management market was highly prestigious, and the heads of that business saw it as a precious jewel—in my view a bit too precious. We left too much of the growth opportunity to the Swiss banks, and later to Morgan Stanley and others.

The rest of the meeting was wonderful, a big Goldman production at its best. Alan Greenspan spoke inscrutably about the economy, acknowledging that he was filibustering and not saying anything meaningful when it came to the topic of interest rates. Warren Buffett was interviewed by Charlie Rose over lunch and had us laughing most of the way through. He talked about his long career as an investor, beginning with his formative visit to Goldman Sachs at the age of ten, when his father brought him from Omaha to visit the 1939 World's Fair in New York. On that trip, his father, a stockbroker, took him to meet Sidney Weinberg. Buffett recalled how much it meant to him when the great Mr. Weinberg asked him what stocks he liked. Senator Obama spoke about meeting workers who had been laid off when a Maytag plant in western Illinois relocated to Mexico. After thirty years of work, they lost their union wages and health care benefits. The government was offering them retraining—to become nurses' aides, at less than half the pay and with a considerable affront to their dignity.

ONCE A YEAR, GOLDMAN HELD ONE OF ITS QUARTERLY BOARD MEETINGS in a foreign location to highlight that part of our expanding international footprint. As it happened, we had one coming up just a week after our Chicago meeting, in Beijing. Our ambitions there were very high. Goldman wanted to be the leading investment bank for Chinese companies, and the senior figures joining us for those events seemed open to our playing that kind of role. They included Wang Qishan, then mayor of Beijing and later the member of the Chinese Communist Party's Standing Committee who led President Xi's anticorruption drive. With Hank gone, the Goldman delegation was mine to lead.

John Rogers, who among his other talents is one of the world's greatest party planners, had orchestrated a truly spectacular series of events. We were to have dinner one night on the Great Wall, and another night in the Forbidden City, which was unprecedented. Before the twenty-course banquet, we were walking through the Forbidden City with our Chinese hosts and our directors. The Chinese leaders were walking in front. Still a contingent CEO, I was hanging back with my management team and our board members.

I was keeping stride and chatting, when, all of a sudden, I felt a swift kick in my butt. I turned around to see Ruth Simmons, then president of Brown University and one of our shrewdest independent directors, wagging her finger and looking at me sternly. She pointed to the Chinese officials walking ahead of us.

"You get up there with those guys," she ordered me.

My style of staying in my comfort zone and being self-deprecating wasn't going to cut it in this new role. The people in charge were now my peers. Like it or not, I needed to walk with them.

THE FIRST ORDER OF BUSINESS WAS TO NAME MY IMMEDIATE TEAM. MY own elevation was sudden, and so was the elevation of my replacements. This was not normal at Goldman, where most senior leadership transitions were socialized in advance. (It didn't happen with Corzine and Paulson—but look how that turned out.) To replace myself, I chose co-COOs, which was not atypical at Goldman. They were Gary Cohn and Jon Winkelried. Both were strong operators, and while both came out of FICC, their backgrounds were different. Gary, of course, was from J. Aron, and by this time he was our most prominent trading leader and risk manager. He had also spent four years working in London. Winkelried had come up under Jon Corzine in fixed income and worked in capital markets, which, because it raises financing for companies, was run as a joint venture with investment banking. Winkelried was viewed as a strong leader by both divisions.

I announced my recommendations to the board at our meeting in China, and they approved. Our senior executives were all in tow, and I thought the choices would be obvious and well received. But as I've often found with personnel decisions, what was obvious to me wasn't obvious to the people most affected. So there was more drama. To my surprise, the decision upset Tom Montag, then Winkelried's co-head of FICC and copresident of Goldman Sachs in Japan. He left China early, without saying goodbye. Tom was terrific and would have been great at the job, but in the context of his experience and the other candidates, it just wasn't his time. Feeling he'd been passed over, he eventually left Goldman for Bank of America, where he became president and COO. Some years after I retired, Montag returned to Goldman as a member of the board.

The second order of business was to "recruit" key people in the company who were closer to the firm's displaced executives than they were to me. After the meeting in Chicago, I shared a car to the airport with David Viniar, our CFO. John Thain had been Viniar's patron, and after Thain left, Viniar was expecting to leave. *Dave*, I said, *I really need you. I know you were close to Thain, but I'll treat you as part of my leadership team, on the same level with Gary and Jon.* Viniar remembers that I asked him to tell me honestly how he thought I should change. When he made some suggestions, I told him I thought he was right and that I was going to make an effort. That convinced him to stay. I'm not sure how much I really changed or whether he just got used to me. Along with Gary Cohn, David became a true, essential partner in the challenges that lay ahead.

I made similar pitches to our top lawyers, Greg Palm and Esta Stecher. Greg, who had coached me through the deposition I never had to give in the Robert Maxwell affair, was as awkward as he was brilliant. Growing up in Binghamton, New York, he never took a standardized test that he didn't get an 800 on. After MIT, Harvard Business School, and Harvard Law School, he was a Supreme Court clerk for Justice Lewis Powell and then a partner at Sullivan & Cromwell, before jumping the fence to Goldman Sachs. As general counsel, he was a member of the management committee. Anytime Greg made a presentation to the board, someone would advise me not to have him do it again. But whenever anyone engaged deeply with Greg on a substantive issue, they saw how valuable he was.

Esta, like David Viniar, thought of herself as a Thain person and wasn't sure about me. Thain had recruited her to run our tax practice from Sullivan & Cromwell, where she was a partner in the tax group. Over time, she had become a go-to person for critical projects and people issues at the firm. Her sound judgment and reputation for fairness made her the person to deal with sensitive issues involving the behavior of current and retired partners—for example, what the firm would and wouldn't allow them to do on the outside, to the extent it had control over their behavior. Esta took on the thorniest jobs. After the financial crisis, when Goldman Sachs converted to a bank holding company, she made it happen over a weekend. It might have taken someone else months. I knew I needed both Greg and Esta onside.

The other important person whose commitment I was unsure of, but whom I needed, was John Rogers. Rogers started working in the White House mailroom at eighteen, when he was a freshman at George Washington University. His first real job was running White House administration in Reagan's first term. That meant real power, allocating office space and perks that mattered to people, including time on the tennis court—something Jimmy Carter had, notoriously, done himself. John followed his mentor James Baker when Baker became Treasury secretary under Reagan and then secretary of state under the first President Bush. John was undersecretary in both departments, among the youngest people to have held either position. At Goldman Sachs, he became an indispensable political adviser and consigliere to four successive CEOs who couldn't have been more different from one another. As secretary to the board, he had a certain responsibility for my getting the hang of the job. I'd seen how good he was and wanted him to not just do his job but throw in with me. All it really took was for me to tell John honestly how much I needed him, and to reciprocate his natural loyalty.

Recruiting the people who already work for you isn't just an expression. The financial services industry was beset by a constant war for talent. The people I needed to manage were smart, accomplished, and constantly pursued by competitors. They often had opportunities to make more money, and I had to fight against the allure of the success that so many of our alumni had in the post-Goldman chapters of their careers. In my new role, I was managing thoroughbreds—expensive, very scarce talent in the context of a high-stakes business. A key person in risk management, the best investment banker, the best analyst—these people are so crucial to a firm's success that you'll do anything to keep them on your team.

A lot of guys favor sports metaphors. I'm not naturally one of them. But Goldman Sachs had a significant presence in the sports industry, assisting teams in selling, financing stadiums, and occasionally partnering. With the Yankees, we established a dedicated cable station, the YES Network, which generated substantial benefits for the Yankees and us. For a gathering of the NFL owners, I was asked to deliver a presentation on markets and the economy. Toward the end of my remarks, I pivoted to comparing my experience of managing top talent to theirs. *You have elite performers? I have elite performers. Your guys think they're the best in the world at what they do? My guys think that too—and many of them are right. Big egos? Check. Your guys get paid too much? So do mine. The occasional substance-abuse issue? That too. But there's one big difference*, I said. *Football players are under contract. Mine are at-will employees, and I have to re-recruit them every day.*

As I learned, paying people more money in the near term wasn't always the key issue. You had to treat people with respect and acknowledge their value to the firm. But more than anything else, most wanted to grow in their careers and be proud that they were accomplishing important things. To keep them, you had to offer them that opportunity. And depending on the career path and growth opportunity provided, a person could in a few years either be overcompensated at $500K or undercompensated at $5 million.

I WAS SOON FULLY IMMERSED IN THE PROBLEM OF WHAT IT MEANT FOR Goldman Sachs to be a modern merchant bank. Conflicts among our clients and the tensions among our own lines of businesses were a daily challenge. Goldman advised investors, but we were also an investor ourselves. When an opportunity for a transaction came along, the first order of business was to determine whether we were going to act as a principal, investing ourselves, or function as an adviser to a client. In those days, around 70 percent of our revenue was coming from trading and investing and around 15 percent each from asset management and investment banking fees. But our franchise, our reputation, and many of the opportunities in other spheres sprang from our success as an adviser, so we always favored that role, even if behaving as a principal might have been more lucrative. The investment banking role and relationships were foundational for us. If we had a chance to advise a client who wanted to buy a business, and we found it attractive enough to want to buy it ourselves, we would most often go with the advisory role.

Goldman had a whole department led by partners who helped sort out conflicts and make these decisions around business selection. The conflict-of-interest questions always came first. If there was a real conflict—say, the opportunity to represent a company trying to acquire a longtime client about which we had confidential information—we had to walk away from the opportunity. Sometimes the conflicts were subtle and took awhile for us to figure out. For instance, it might seem like an advantage to a seller we were representing if we could provide financing to the buyer. But we came to appreciate that we couldn't both represent a seller and finance a buyer in the same transaction. If market conditions changed and the value of the asset dropped, the buyer's interests and the interests of its lender could diverge. The seller and its adviser (us) would want the transaction to go forward, but the buyer and its lender (us) would want the transaction to fail.

Once we got past the question of conflicts, we got into the meat of the business-selection problem: Whom, if anyone, should we represent? Assuming we had the ability to represent a client, the next order of business would be to determine whether we would represent the seller or the buyer. You were more certain to earn a fee if you represented the seller, because the seller almost always sold. You never knew whether the buyer you represented, or another buyer represented by a competitor, would be successful. However, it was usually more lucrative to represent a successful buyer, because then you could lead the financing of the deal, which also generated a large pool of fees. The third order of business, if we decided to represent a buyer, was determining which of several potential buyers we should represent—there almost always were several. The decision would be a function of the firm's relationships and which potential acquirer had the most to gain—and therefore could pay the most and be the most likely to win.

Once a decision was made, I could usually count on an angry client whom we weren't able to represent calling to ream me out. *We'll never do business with you again!* In practice, "never" usually meant a few months. But those decisions also upset senior figures at the firm, which was much harder on me. Say a cable network is for sale and two competitors want to buy it. We can't represent both of them. A Goldman Sachs banker who spent years cultivating his client is livid at having to disappoint him. And perhaps our own in-house private equity partner sees the acquisition as a golden investment opportunity and wants us to acquire the company ourselves. Bear in mind that the people arguing for different outcomes are some of the smartest, most competitive people in the world. They're honed to be aggressive on behalf of their clients and will kill to win business, metaphorically speaking. They're pretty good at being aggressive on their own behalf as well. These are not people whose spouses send them back to the boss's office to be tougher when they don't get a promotion or a bonus commensurate with their sense of self-worth.

I always thought of this as the dance of the eight-hundred-pound gorillas. What do you do when you have to manage a jungle full of eight-hundred-pound gorillas? You try to train the eight-hundred-pound gorillas to stand aside, say "After you," and graciously let one another pass from time to time. You have to convince them that by making the company as a whole more successful, they can use the enhanced platform for their own personal glory. Rich Friedman, who ran the merchant bank, was an example of an eight-hundred-pound gorilla who appreciated my position. He would roar a bit and pound his chest, but he always understood decisions that went against him—and supported those decisions.

Having to resolve these internal conflicts wasn't a recipe for being universally liked. I wanted to be liked, but I cared more about being appreciated. There's a difference. I liked Corzine and Paulson. But I *appreciated* Hank. My goal wasn't to have partners or more junior people at the firm think I was funny or nice. My goal was to prove valuable to them in ways that would make a material difference in their careers and lives.

CHAPTER 20

The Partnership Culture

At Goldman, I was as much senior partner as CEO. The difference: more cajoling, socializing, and sharing information; less command, fewer lightning bolts from my fingertips.

As CEO, I wanted to have my cake and eat it too. That is, I wanted us to have the benefits of being a public company that could be global and at scale in terms of capital and people and second to none in what we could accomplish for our clients. But I also wanted us to be able to think and act like a private partnership and to retain our culture even as we grew into a vast global organization.

My fixation on revitalizing the old culture of the firm might have come initially as a surprise to people. I was still viewed by many as a J. Aron trading thug who had never gone through formal Goldman Sachs training or acculturation. Yet my proudest achievement at Goldman is to have maintained and even strengthened the partnership culture as the firm expanded in size and global influence as a public company. Twenty-five years after the IPO, that mentality is still, more than anything else, the special sauce at Goldman Sachs. My successor, David Solomon, shares my strong feelings about this and since becoming CEO has devoted a great deal of thought and energy to balancing Goldman's responsibilities to its shareholders with the ethic and legacy of its historical partnership.

What does it mean to be a partnership? A partnership is mutual agency. The partners are all owners of the business. As an owner, you feel entitled to get information, to know things beyond what's required to perform your narrow job. You expect to be consulted and contribute to a consensus. You have the long-term commitment of an owner, not the transient concern of a renter.

In a partnership, the head of the firm is the senior partner. The senior partner outranks the other partners, and the partnership agreement may give him certain powers and responsibilities. There is, of course, an org chart, and the buck likely stops with the senior partner as ultimate decider. But there is far more socializing of policies and plans, more consensus building than command. More rounds of listening to objections and contrary opinions and cajoling before a decision is made. There is always a sense that the senior partner governs by the consent of the governed, and that the subordinate partners think like fellow owners of the business.

It takes more time to treat your partners as owners. It takes time to inform people, entertain objections, and, sometimes, accede to contrary views. It means more iterations and slower decision-making. But the decisions are likely to be better, and the outcomes better accepted, because people were consulted and listened to, even if they didn't get their way in the end. Despite all that, Goldman could act faster than anyone when necessary, certainly in matters of risk-taking and risk management.

A classic corporation doesn't face the same challenges around decision-making. In a corporation, the CEO is a commander. Lightning bolts emit from his fingertips. There is a hierarchy of managers and subordinates. There's compartmentalization by division and function. If you have a senior job at Amazon working on expediting delivery, I doubt anyone asks for your opinion about cloud services. And you'd probably be considered a busybody if you offered one.

A partner, by contrast, has a higher expectation of getting information and having input across the range of a firm's business, not just of the part he works in. After all, a partner is a participant in the results of the whole company, not just his corner of it. Having broad information about the firm gives a partner a basis for opinions about the whole and the confidence to share his or her input.

How could I convey and transmit my commitment to Goldman's partnership culture, which had served the firm so well? To strengthen the feeling of co-ownership, I immediately began trying to revive the partnership committee. It had never gone away, but it had become a little sleepy, focused mainly on the biennial election of a new partner class. I wanted to do more to reward partners who did a good job keeping others informed and who focused on teaching young people and conveying Goldman's culture and values.

Much of what I did was through storytelling about my own career and exhortation about the benefits and responsibilities of partners. I did this at chairman's forums that we held around the world. The travel was often exhausting—a one-day side trip from Japan to Australia, where you land, shower at the airport, go straight to an office, and leave the country without so much as taking a walk around the block outside. I both dreaded those meetings and loved them. They were my best opportunity to impress on existing partners and managing directors what it means to act like an owner.

I usually started with a simple exhortation to care about and pay attention to everything happening at the firm. *We spend more of our waking day at work than at home. Our job is the source of our wealth and a big part of our identity. So we need to be conscious of what's happening at the whole firm, not just in our small corner of it. The firm has businesses all over the world. But it has only one reputation. A screwup in trading in New York affects our investment banking franchise in Japan and vice versa. At Goldman, every partner owns the consequences of everyone else's judgments, so we need to care about them, a lot.*

I reminded people that they can and should love their family more than anything. But the material success of their families depended on the reputation and success of the firm. So they should act accordingly. *If you saw anything that threatened your family, you would act on it immediately and ruthlessly—please bring that mentality to the job. If you hired a nanny who left one of your kids alone in a bathtub to take a phone call, you would fire her immediately, no questions asked. There shouldn't be any tolerance for bad behavior you observe at your company either, whether in your line of report or not.*

In a partnership, collective identity has to subsume individual identity. Partners have to sacrifice in the short term for the sake of the firm's platform. An important goal for me in managing such an accomplished group was to get them to subordinate their egos and restrain their selfish impulses for the good of the firm. If that meant making a sacrifice, it was only in the short term, because if we put the team and the firm first, it would make our platform more successful and influential. And we could then use that platform as individuals inside and outside the firm to advance our own agendas. Goldman Sachs on a résumé was viewed as valuable for high-level government jobs in the US and elsewhere. Goldman alumni went on to run important private equity and hedge funds. Every nonprofit in our host cities was thrilled to get Goldman partners and alumni as board members. And the prerequisite for all this individual success was putting the firm first.

In a partnership, status and compensation have to reflect those values. Goldman has never had an "eat what you kill" philosophy, because we always wanted people to maximize long-term benefit to the firm, not their personal book of business. When the market dipped and there were fewer M&A deals to be had, we still paid our investment bankers well—they didn't control the economy.

I thought that teaching partners to set a strong example began with giving them an appreciation of our influence. I told them that when I was a VP, I looked up to the partner in charge of my business, Mark Winkelman; that I was in awe of the partner in charge of my division, Bob Rubin; and that I was in complete terror the one time I had to meet with the head of the firm, John Weinberg. Over time, I ascended to each of those jobs, and I became each of those guys to everyone around me. I had to give myself a kick at each passage, because I never thought of myself in that next role—my head lagged the reality of my growing importance. I realize that younger people looked up to me, were awed or maybe even terrified of me, and I had to be disarming if I wanted to capture what they knew. And I had to act so as not to disappoint their high expectations of me. I tried to get my partners to understand this and to work genuinely to earn the respect that came with their positions.

As an exercise, I would ask a newly promoted partner, *Who had your job when you were early in your career? Do you recognize that you have become that person?* I blew a lot of minds that way, but I think I accelerated their acceptance of who they were and what that entailed.

As another exercise, I would ask a group of newly elected partners: *Do any of you ever go home and talk to your spouse or significant other about your boss?* Nervous laughter . . . Of course, everyone does that at some point, maybe all the time! I asked them to understand that the people who reported to *them* went home and spoke about *them*. *Of course that happens; you are important and so is their job. It is inevitable. When you think about it in that light, what do you want them to be saying? More than being liked, you should want to be* appreciated. You can like a clown, but you appreciate the person who invests in you and improves you, even if he's not much fun. A soldier doesn't want to be entertained by his commander. He wants to be well led, supported, and protected. Early in my Goldman career, the person who did that for me was Mark Winkelman—he was a valuable mentor and supporter, if not all that lovable.

A prerequisite for this leadership contract is mutual respect. You don't have to be reminded to respect your superior who is older and more experienced, but the contract has to apply in both directions. I reminded partners that their status didn't give them a higher IQ than their younger reports. For sure they had more experience, but were they smarter? The world gets more competitive every year; SAT scores tend to rise over time. Chances were that the résumés of the younger people at the firm were more impressive than their bosses' at the same age. For all the partner knew, one of his direct reports would have a career that went much further than his own.

Younger people aren't less worthy, they are just younger. Whenever I looked out at a sea of young analysts, I thought that in that group there were future heads of companies, possibly even future heads of state. They just haven't gotten there yet. I told each class of new recruits the same thing about their colleagues. They were about to embark on long careers, whether at Goldman or in another firm down the road. They were going to move through time as a cohort, and in twenty years they'd be running things. Even after thirty years, the impressions they had of one another, formed as analysts at Goldman, would stick. So keep that in mind and act accordingly, even with your peers!

People whose responsibilities are increasing need the support of their subordinates. On the org chart, they may work for you. But you are just as dependent on them. Maybe more so. Do they answer your questions narrowly and grudgingly, or do they enthusiastically fill you in about what's going on? Do they give you what it takes to make you an effective manager, or do they engage in passive resistance? The goal is not to be a buddy but to be appreciated as a good leader who respects the implied contract that leader and subordinate will fairly advance each other's interests at the firm.

Even though I loved (almost) all of my partners and colleagues, it was in the interest of the firm to be as clear-eyed as possible about people's strengths and weaknesses. There was always fairness, but management was also tough and effective when it came to culling underperformers. Fairness meant not using after-acquired information in evaluating people's decisions. What mattered was what was known, or could have been known, at the time. In the same vein, it was essential not to confuse wrong with stupid. Everyone is going to be wrong some percentage of the time. Only some of those mistakes are attributable to negligence or foolishness. A large part of the art of managing and assessing people is being conscious of the distinction and applying it when emotions are running high. I was recently reminded by twenty-year Goldman veteran Pablo Salame that when he was a youngish trading leader, he reported to me that his group suffered a huge loss, and he thought he would be fired or at least have his risk limit cut severely. After listening, I told him to get back to work, that it was a mere bump in the road and that I expected much greater failures from him in the future! Good judgment on my part—Pablo went on to become co-head of trading, vice-chair of the firm, and most recently co-CIO of the Citadel hedge fund.

Every year, we had an exercise of moving the bottom 5 percent of performers out. The reason for doing this was both that they weren't pulling their weight and to make room for new talent, including in the partnership. When people talked about how painful it was to let people go, I would sympathize but say that my obligation was to the living, not the dead. John L. Weinberg used to say that if you pruned someone from the worst-performing 5 percent, the chances were nineteen out of twenty that you'd replace that person with someone better.

Whenever I talked about the partnership, I said that we shouldn't overly romanticize the past in a way that would create impossible or unrealistic expectations. Partners in the past did not always behave in an exemplary way. We're human, and people flinch under pressure. Classes of partners fought. Corzine and Paulson visibly fought. Steve Friedman left when he was called upon to lead. Mark Winkelman left because he didn't get his next job, though at many other times he undoubtedly tried to persuade others to stay when they didn't get a job that they thought they had earned. In the 1994 crisis, a lot of partners who owed much to the firm walked out the door just when they should have doubled down.

HOW YOU TREAT ALUMNI IS ANOTHER ASPECT OF CULTURE AND ITS PERpetuation. Part of being a partner is to recognize and honor the contributions of predecessors. Those contributions form the bedrock of the firm's current influence and prestige. Retired partners and other alumni remain part of the vaunted Goldman network and are a source of business for the firm. Treating retirees well is motivating for current employees and beneficial to the recruiting process. If people see that there are lifelong benefits to affiliation with the firm, many will want to join and succeed in the firm to capture those benefits. During my first year, I set up an alumni office, modeled on a university alumni office. As part of that, we set up a website for retired partners to interact with one another, like on a Facebook page. And I made a point of inviting retired partners back to speak and of holding events for alumni in different areas. The network wasn't limited to former partners. We had an event for alumni of the firm who were running hedge funds, where I invited Goldman alum Jim Cramer to speak. (Before he became a personality on CNBC, Cramer ran his own hedge fund.) We held a separate event for Goldman Sachs alumni who were leaders of private equity firms. I organized another event for investment banking division personnel and alumni, which included a panel discussion composed of past and present heads of Goldman Sach's M&A business going back fifty years, to discuss its historical evolution.

Events like that served multiple purposes. I wanted younger partners to see that they had a continuing stake in the firm and its success, even after they left. Many of the former employees were or could be clients of the firm. Reminding people that Goldman Sachs gave them their start created a lot of goodwill. People at Goldman whom we invited saw how the alumni valued their relationship with the firm, and vice versa, almost like a university. It said to them that when they one day left the firm—which nearly everyone eventually does—they should depart on good terms and maintain good relations. For those thinking about joining the firm, either at the beginning of their careers or as lateral hires, the visibility of the Goldman network was a big selling point. That long connection of employees past, present, and future was something other firms simply couldn't offer.

It was especially important to me that we honored and took pride in our partner alumni. It wasn't always easy to do. When people left the firm—unless they were really retiring—it was either because the firm was done with them or because they felt there was a better opportunity elsewhere. Maybe they behaved poorly, maybe they left us in the lurch, or maybe they quit to compete against us. Sometimes it was a person I mentored, and his or her leaving broke my heart. I would walk out of the room, count to one hundred, and then come back and wish them well. Most of them would have other chapters in the business world, perhaps in highly influential roles and potentially as Goldman clients. We had to overcome grudges and recognize the value of goodwill in both directions. The Goldman alumni community is valuable not just in commercial terms but also for the aura it creates. Recruits are attracted to the firm because even if their tenure is short, they are acquiring a lifelong revenue enhancer and asset.

I made a point of going to the retired partners' dinners, and I enjoyed them. I was always amused at the way the history of the firm got played out. Old guys would hold court, admired by less old guys for contributions that younger partners didn't even understand. Some partners years out of the firm still were seething at former colleagues about some matter that everyone else had long since forgotten. But most people come back for the dinners because they still care a lot about the firm and how it regards them. That's culture in a nutshell.

Goldman's policy on nepotism plays a part in sustaining the culture as well. A lot of firms have policies against hiring relatives of employees. For the most part, those policies are sensible. But Goldman was founded as a family firm and retains some of its original sensibility despite its scale. It has benefited immensely from the intergenerational presence of Goldmans, Weinbergs, Mnuchins, and other families. Virtually every partner, it seems, has his or her kids work for the firm, at least for a summer and often in a two-year analyst position. While none of my three kids work at Goldman now, all have passed through on their way to other jobs and careers. Of course, it is tough for the kids of partners who work at Goldman Sachs—they face higher expectations. If they don't excel, they get managed out like anyone else. But having multiple generations of families with experience of the firm is another way to transmit a stake in its history and enhance the human dimension in a global institution.

Maintaining a culture is not easy. It can't be just in words; it has to be in actions. It's time-consuming to socialize plans with a broad community; it's frustrating to defer change until there is wider acceptance; it's painful to treat a departing partner graciously when his departure hurts the firm and helps the competition. But leadership has to see the big picture and have the discipline to maintain its most valuable yet intangible asset.

Running the firm like a partnership came with its own risks and costs. A partnership culture sometimes appears messy, the way democracy appears messy in comparison with an authoritarian system. Dictatorships can seem more efficient at decision-making. But a democratic system tends to work better over time, even if it has its own downside, which is that important decisions are sometime made more slowly, and that leaders are constrained in their authority. Jon Corzine's tenure as CEO was cut short in part because he began exploring a merger on his own initiative, without consulting the management committee ahead of time.

Size is often the enemy of initiative and flexibility. But with the right culture, size can be a boon, not a hindrance. Take the US, for example. The world's biggest economy is, in fact, the most flexible. It recovers from crises more quickly—even if it caused the crisis in the first place—and has consistently grown faster than all the other developed economies. That success flows from its fundamental culture and values that remain present despite its scale.

FINALLY, I ARRIVED WITH AN AGENDA AROUND RECRUITING AND DIVERsity. Once upon a time, when our clients and competitors were mostly white men, there was no obvious cost to our looking the same. But now that we were operating in so many different countries, markets, and economic sectors, it was simply a business necessity for us to have people with different identities, experiences, sensibilities, and perspectives. Emerging markets were growing faster than developed economies. Our goal was to be the employer of choice in every region of the world. In the global war for talent, we'd lose out to competitors if we weren't diverse enough.

A few years earlier, before I was COO, I had led a task force set up to address the lack of diversity at the firm, which was unfortunately typical of Wall Street. I put a lot of work into it and came away with a set of views about the problem and how best to address it. I presented our recommendations to the board. For Goldman especially, there was a type of diversity that was important beyond ethnic and gender diversity: diversity of national origin. Of twenty-nine people on the management committee when I became CEO, we had two people who weren't American—one Canadian and one white South African. To be a global firm, we needed more international partners and top leaders.

We regularly surveyed our employees and always learned a lot. The response rate was over 90 percent, which is unmatched, and I was pleased to see that we had job-satisfaction levels that were unheard of elsewhere. But people's perspectives on diversity were very, very different. Women thought our diversity efforts lacked sincerity and accountability. They felt the firm didn't appreciate different styles, that you had to participate in activities like golf to get ahead, and that being on the "mommy track" took your career off track. Many minorities felt they faced higher standards and fewer opportunities for advancement while being forced to serve as poster children for diversity. Non-US employees felt the firm was too US-centric and often exhibited a lack of sensitivity to other cultures. Many white men, by contrast, didn't see any problem at all. They tended to regard diversity as reverse discrimination and antimeritocratic.

The paradox was that Goldman's culture carried what the report I worked on called "antibodies" that resisted diversity efforts. Our belief in meritocracy meant that many people at the firm viewed any explicit affirmative action policies as anathema to excellence. Our elitism—that we wanted to hire the best people from the best schools—limited our vision of where excellence was to be found. And our American style of investment banking—brash people asserting strong opinions—cut against any other style that might be more effective in other cultures, such as in China and Japan, where more deference is expected. The firm's face-time culture, where junior people came early and stayed late to demonstrate commitment and ambition, made a healthy work-life balance difficult, something that had an outsize impact on women at the firm.

While I understood the case for affirmative action, it seemed to me the better way to advance the careers of women and minorities at the firm—and of non-US leaders as well—was by improving regular management practices and strengthening processes for everyone. Special programs we ran for minorities at the firm were often counterproductive. It tainted people to be in those programs, as if they were a kind of remedial education class. In practice, it was the programs and processes open to everyone, including ones around career development, performance management, and leadership succession planning, that did the best job of increasing diversity, without creating a stigma or objections around separate standards and unequal treatment. We'd gotten lax about some of those routine efforts. By making those processes better, we could advance diversity more effectively than by just pounding the table and demanding results. I was proud of that report and was now in a position to pursue the implementation of its conclusions from the CEO's seat.

MANY OF MY IDEAS ABOUT CULTURE, GLOBAL EXPANSION, AND DIVERsity came together around our philanthropy. Like other companies, we'd always participated in charitable giving. After making partner, one of the first steps I was instructed to take was to set up my own private foundation. At the time of the IPO, we'd set up the Goldman Sachs Foundation, chaired by John Whitehead, one of my predecessors. This was in line with how most companies do their giving. The CEO, or the top management team, decides whom to support.

My approach was to decentralize that decision-making and let partners decide how they wanted to direct their share of our giving.

That was the idea of GS Gives, a program that has now donated nearly $3 billion to more than ten thousand organizations in 140 countries. Every year, we would decide on an overall amount—depending on what the year had been like, it might be anywhere from $100 million to $500 million. Partners were allocated grants into a donor-advised fund in amounts roughly corresponding to their seniority. They could then use those funds for the causes and organizations that were most important to them. This wasn't additional salary, and there were restrictions, of course, on what causes partners could support with it, all of which had to be approved. In general, I wanted the money to go to needy people—you couldn't use your funds to get a wing of MoMA named after you.

The list of recipients always included antipoverty organizations, the scholarship funds of New York City private schools, and the city's major cultural institutions. Heads of major nonprofits like the United Way, Robin Hood, Save the Children, and the International Rescue Committee would come in to make pitches. Part of what I loved about GS Gives was the way it encouraged partners to solicit one another and work together to support favorite causes. At the end of the year, you'd see them huddling in one another's offices, putting together resources to support one another's pet projects. Our partners in Tokyo built an orphanage. Partners in NYC raised $20 million to help build a charter school in Harlem, part of the Harlem Children's Zone program developed by Geoffrey Canada. Beyond edifices, GS Gives was another way we built firm culture.

The younger generation at the firm expressed in many ways that they were there not just to make money but because they believed in the firm's role in society and the economy. Supporting small businesses and ambitious outsiders was central to their sense of mission and morale. I wanted our philanthropy to go beyond writing checks for good causes, and to do things that underscored the transformational power of markets and of capitalism.

Toward the end of my first year as CEO, we initiated a major philanthropic initiative, 10,000 Women, which was focused on the developing world. It was soon joined by another project, 10,000 Small Businesses, which was focused on the United States. Those programs were designed with the goal of increasing economic opportunity by providing women entrepreneurs and small business owners with things that Goldman and its employees were well positioned to provide—business education, mentorship, strategic advice, and access to investment capital.

Both programs began with mini MBA courses for entrepreneurs, few of whom were likely to see the inside of Harvard Business School. To qualify, they had to have real businesses and at least four full-time employees. We developed the curriculum in partnership with Babson College, a business school in Wellesley, Massachusetts, and delivered it through community colleges around the country—and around the world in the case of 10,000 Women.

After graduation, entrepreneurs worked with mentors from Goldman Sachs to develop their business plans. Then we helped them find capital, partnering with community development banks in the US, and with the International Finance Corporation, an arm of the World Bank, for 10,000 Women. The IFC ultimately set up a $1.4 billion lending facility that allowed the program to expand its reach—to date, 164,000 women in fifty-five countries have received over $4.5 billion in loans. The success of 10,000 Small Businesses led us to expand it with a fund for rural areas and to launch a parallel program in the UK. After more than fifteen years, both programs are still thriving and expanding.

Once, when I was in Saudi Arabia, I made a side trip to Jeddah to speak at Dar Al-Hekma, a women's college. The trip involved a very early departure from Riyadh, we got going late, and it's fair to say I was ambivalent about the whole idea.

I walked into the room of around a hundred women, all wearing traditional abayas and head coverings, and made my remarks. Then the questions came.

"How do you think about the trade-off between holding more capital and lower returns?"

"What is the future of the asset-based securities market given new securitization rules?"

"What risk-management assumptions failed in the global financial crisis?"

The technicality of the questions coming from a group of shrouded women was remarkable. For me, the takeaway was how widely distributed talent and interest in finance and economic issues were around the world. I only wish opportunity were as well distributed. If I'd met with the same group in New York, I might have hired a few of them on the spot.

I can't tell you how often someone has come up to me at an event to tell me that they, a family member, or a close friend benefited from the curriculum and training we helped to develop. Once I visited former House speaker Nancy Pelosi, who brought up 10,000 Small Businesses to me because her daughter, under her married name, had gone through and appreciated the program. The stories of many of the graduates remain in my head: The "Demo Diva" in New Orleans, who deployed hot-pink excavators to tear down houses ruined by Hurricane Katrina. Or the ex-con who had built a good business delivering cold products to New York City bodegas. He didn't have the analytic tools to figure out whether it made sense for him to invest in his own refrigerated delivery trucks. Through the program, we helped him to figure out how long it would take to recover his initial investment.

This wasn't the classic corporate charity, like writing checks to the United Way. These initiatives were places where Goldman people could apply their core skills and expertise on a human scale. People at the firm loved working on them, because it meant doing what they did for corporate clients, but for a person or a small group of people. It helped those at the firm, especially junior employees, understand the fundamental value of their activity to the economy and society at a scale that they could relate to. After all, what has done more for the world in terms of job and wealth creation and improving lives—the Ford Motor Company or the Ford Foundation? Microsoft or the Gates

Foundation? The transformative role of capitalism and our contribution to it were clear to me—Goldman led the IPOs for both Ford and Microsoft. But I wanted them to be clear to our people as well.

We devoted considerable resources to these efforts—initially $100 million to fund 10,000 Women. (I said I would have preferred $10,000 to fund 100 million women.) The 10,000 Small Businesses program cost significantly more, with $200 million coming from the Goldman Sachs Foundation and more lent to the graduates by community development banks. But it was money well spent. Studies of the two programs showed that they meaningfully increased both revenue growth and job creation for participants.

Michael Bloomberg loved the programs and signed on as cochair of the 10,000 Small Businesses advisory council, along with me and Warren Buffett. Buffett, who never gave commencement speeches, spoke at several of our graduation ceremonies around the country. Graduates—who worked long hours in their businesses and took our classes over evenings and weekends—brought their families to the ceremonies. People would be in tears at those events, me included. The small business program restored everyone's faith in the American dream. You saw up close how success was still possible for people starting from the bottom. By doing on a small scale what Goldman did for big companies, that philanthropy made the impact of our corporate work more vivid and comprehensible.

For the most part, the younger generation at Goldman believed, as I do, that democratic capitalism is the best way to advance the environmental and social goals we care about. So supporting big businesses like Tesla that really could change the world was also central to cultivating a sense of mission and morale. Gary Cohn, who spent a lot of time getting to know Elon Musk and understanding his business, was eager for us to underwrite Tesla's 2010 IPO. But to Gary's surprise, the commitments committee, led by a senior investment banking partner, voted to turn it down—he didn't think Musk could produce enough cars to succeed. Gary came to me and asked what to do. After hearing him out, I decided in favor of Gary. It was exceptional to overrule the commitments committee, and after I did, I'm afraid my relationship with the chair of that committee was never the same.

But it was the right decision. After leading Tesla's IPO in 2010, Goldman continued to support the company through its ups and downs, underwriting two convertible bond offerings and a high-yield bond offering in 2017. Given the capability and resilience of its founder, Tesla would no doubt have survived and succeeded without Goldman's help. But we were proud to have supported a company that accelerated the transition to electric vehicles by a decade or more. Our only mistake in that case was failing to invest more in the company ourselves.

AS I THINK BACK ON MY FIRST COUPLE OF YEARS AS CEO, I SYMPATHIZE with Lyndon Johnson (not to suggest any equivalence of our jobs). Despite becoming president unexpectedly, Johnson developed a powerful domestic agenda, known as the Great Society, for which he received a resounding mandate in the landslide election of 1964. But before he got far in implementing it, the Vietnam War took over his presidency. The Gulf of Tonkin incident in August 1964 signaled the beginning of a spiraling escalation. In the end, Vietnam overwhelmed everything else and defined his presidency. Johnson's handling of it became his most significant legacy.

If circumstances hadn't forced me to become a wartime CEO, my tenure would have looked very different than it ultimately did. I had a clear vision of the firm, which was less about transformation than it was about conceptually and practically bringing together Goldman's disparate roles and activities. I wanted to strengthen our distinctive culture and expand our work in many arenas and regions. I got a decent start on all that before we got interrupted by an economic crisis bigger than any of us had experienced or could even have imagined. If my agenda was Goldman Sachs's Great Society, the global financial crisis risked becoming my Vietnam.

CHAPTER 21

The Storm Before the Storm

I'm like a flight attendant during turbulence. Smile like you're enjoying yourself. If you look afraid, the passengers will freak out.

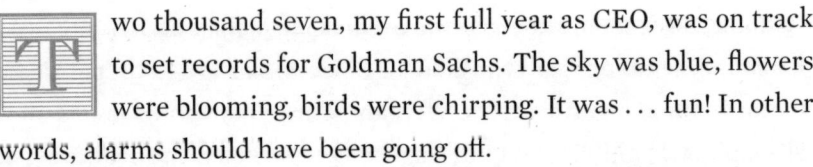 wo thousand seven, my first full year as CEO, was on track to set records for Goldman Sachs. The sky was blue, flowers were blooming, birds were chirping. It was . . . fun! In other words, alarms should have been going off.

One night that summer, I was sitting in a movie theater with Laura half watching the latest *Die Hard* sequel. I was surreptitiously looking at my BlackBerry, glancing over the daily P&Ls that started showing up in my email around 6:00 p.m. And because I was stuck in the same seat in the dark for a couple of hours, I was digging into them a little more deeply than usual. What jumped out was the day's decline in one of the hedge funds we managed. The asset value of that fund usually moved hundredths of a percent in the course of a day. But that day, even though the overall market hadn't dropped, it was down by 6 percent. This is the scene in the movie—not necessarily the one I was watching—where the sky darkens, the birds fly away, and the horses start whinnying. It was, for me and for Goldman, the overture to the global financial crisis.

As soon as the movie ended, I called Gary Cohn and then David

Viniar. The Global Equity Opportunities Fund was part of Goldman Sachs Asset Management (GSAM) and so not part of Goldman's balance sheet or P&L. GSAM's portfolio managers operated semi-independently—it was almost like a separate firm, with its own infrastructure, compliance, and risk-management systems. While it reported to me, as did every part of Goldman, my involvement in GSAM's investment decisions was usually minimal, unless there was a problem that could have implications for the reputation of the firm. This looked like that kind of situation. Goldman Sachs couldn't escape responsibility for a significant decline in the value of one of its funds—losing investors' money felt worse to me than losing our own.

Similar to GSAM's larger Global Alpha fund and another fund focused on North America, Global Equity Opportunities was a quant fund. These funds all used computer algorithms to suss out mispricing and relative-value gaps—a kind of arbitrage. After I spoke to Gary and David, it became clear that the value of the fund was being affected by the recent turbulence in the subprime mortgage market. As its name suggests, the Global Equity Opportunities Fund was focused on international stocks, and it didn't hold any mortgage-backed securities directly. But at that point, rising default rates on subprime mortgages were triggering all sorts of unusual behavior in assets that weren't supposed to be correlated to them. Because of the "crowded trade" phenomenon, herd behavior was accelerating price declines in a lot of less-liquid assets. Many quant funds, not just ours, had similar positions. And now that those positions looked riskier, those funds were all trying to unwind their positions at the same time. A market-wide "flight to quality" was exacerbating the downward price moves.

Gary and David agreed that the market was likely overreacting; the assets on GEO's books were largely sound and continued to hold value. The problem was that our quant funds were both very large—around $10 billion of capital—and highly leveraged, at something like twenty to one. Selling down the large positions they held at an illiquid moment would move the market in whatever was being sold. If selling a position moved the market down by 5 percent, the 20x leverage meant you would lose 100 percent of the capital associated with the position. In other words, when you sold an asset and realized the loss, the proceeds would have vaporized. As we well understood, it would be a losing battle to try to raise capital by selling huge, highly leveraged positions in such a skittish market. While I was in bed that night, my anxiety and imagination ran amok as I conjured scenarios in which GSAM's highly leveraged funds could contribute to a market meltdown.

I'm not sure the people managing the GSAM funds had the same level of worry. They knew that their performance was sharply down, of course. But like our London-based traders in 1994, they thought it was a temporary anomaly. If they just held on, their positions would revert to the historical mean. There are few more frustrating conversations than the ones that happen at moments like this between quants and more traditional traders like Gary and me. The quants tell you what should happen based on statistics. The traders know what can happen in markets, based on hard experience.

Gary, David, and I gathered in my office the next day along with members of our risk-management team. Some of the positions in the funds were huge—200x the average daily trading volume in, say, Israeli shekels. The obvious way of deleveraging a fund, by selling assets, would be, as noted, a losing battle. We quickly concluded that the only way to take down the leverage was to put money into the fund in order to handle redemptions and ride out the market weakness. Otherwise, while we were high-fiving our way through a record year at the parent company, investments in those GSAM quant funds would potentially get wiped out. Additional capital would allow the fund to wait for markets to settle down and for its positions to recover enough that we could have an orderly liquidation at better prices.

Putting more money in would be a highly unconventional thing to do. Buying into those weakening positions was not a way we ordinarily would have wanted to risk our own capital. And there was another obstacle. Viniar was concerned that if the firm was perceived as injecting cash into a fund's balance sheet to protect Goldman's overall reputation, the ratings agencies would infer that Goldman was taking full responsibility for those hedge funds and would no longer regard them as separate from our own balance sheet. Doing that could add a massive quantity of assets against hardly any additional capital—raising the leverage ratio of the whole firm. That would make us appear far riskier and less creditworthy.

But the funds were meaningfully undervalued. If a third party came to us and said, "Here's a portfolio that looks like GEO," I asked, would we buy it at the current marked price? Everyone agreed that we would. It was undeniable that part of our motivation for investing in the fund was to protect the outside investors and our firm's reputation. But that couldn't be our only motivation. We needed to demonstrate that there was a sound investment motive behind the decision—namely that it was a distress moment and that we expected to profit when markets stabilized.

So we came up with a clever solution. We would invest $2 billion of our own liquid capital and raise an additional $1 billion from independent investors who would be motivated solely by seeking profit. The large combined investment would help to deleverage the fund and allow it to stop selling assets into a panicked market. We expected that doing so would produce a good return for all concerned when markets eventually stabilized. The thesis was compelling enough that investors including Eli Broad; Perry Capital, a hedge fund run by former Goldman trader Richard Perry; and CV Starr, a financial vehicle run by former AIG insurance chief Hank Greenberg, all came in with us on the new investment, agreeing to a six-month lockup and no management fee.

It was a smart and original step to take, but we weren't out of the woods. Even after we increased the capital buffer, it was possible that the market panic would continue and—following the attributed-to-Keynes quote—the increased capital buffer would quickly erode.

A much better movie than the third *Die Hard* sequel, *Apollo 13* tells the story of how NASA engineers scrambled to rescue three astronauts on a damaged spacecraft after an accidental explosion on board. Mission Control in Houston improvises a Rube Goldberg device to filter out poisonous carbon dioxide gas before it kills the astronauts. As the air in the space capsule worsens, the NASA people are all staring at the rising needle of the CO_2 monitor. Unless the needle levels off and starts to drop, the astronauts will slowly suffocate.

As we deployed our solution, Gary, David, and I had our eyes glued to our own version of that needle—the fund's net asset value. After we announced the investment, it kept dropping. We spent the week watching it and worrying. For the first time in twenty years, I wanted a cigarette.

We went about our normal jobs and tried to get the fund managers to sell bits and pieces of their positions where they could, always eyeing the needle. The fund lost almost a third of its value that third week of August. But just as the tension was becoming critical, on Friday, the needle changed direction. The relief came over me like a wave. I would experience many moments of intense stress and relief over the coming years, but that was around a system-wide crisis affecting and attributed to a wide swath of financial institutions. In that GEO–Global Alpha crisis, it was just Goldman Sachs, out there alone. I vowed never to allow that kind of leverage again.

The weekend was upon us. I now felt comfortable enough to join my family in the Hamptons. I usually drove to our weekend house, but Gary had bought a block of helicopter tickets and offered a ride to me and Robin Vince, then head of operations at Goldman and formerly head of our risk-management team (he's now CEO of BNY Mellon). No start to a weekend ever felt better. Later, weekends would be a time of particular stress and dread, because that was when a series of critical problems had to be worked through before the market opening in Tokyo on Sunday night. When our wives met the three of us at the East Hampton airport to drive us home, I felt like I was returning from a war. I'm not sure what Gary and Robin did, but I mostly drank my dinner that night.

After about six months, the new $3 billion investment had produced an annualized return of around 20 percent and we were able to liquidate the fund. The original investors ended up with losses, but it was nothing like the total wipeout that occurred at a couple of Bear Stearns hedge funds that went bankrupt in a very public way. Ours had been a very Goldman response: clever and client friendly, and potentially at our own expense—but worth the risk to protect our relationships and reputation.

That was the beginning of a larger story that in many ways is still unfolding. No one alive on Wall Street had ever experienced anything as calamitous and dramatic as the global financial crisis of 2007–8. The panic triggered the longest and deepest economic contraction since the Great Depression and reversed a decades-long trend of market integration and globalization. The causes and consequences of the financial crisis will be discussed and debated for generations to come. But almost two decades later, we are living in the world that the crisis made—an era of intense polarization, distrust of institutions and authority, rising inequality, class conflict, populist movements, and authoritarian government. I would love to have the perspective of a remote observer and recorder of events. Unfortunately, I was right in the middle of it.

AT GOLDMAN, THERE WERE REALLY TWO FINANCIAL CRISES. THE FIRST was the existential crisis, when everyone on Wall Street was worried about going out of business, and several storied firms vanished as independent entities. The second was a reputational crisis that followed for us specifically, once it became clear that we not only weren't going out of business but had emerged in good shape relative to our competitors. In many ways, the reputational crisis was the more painful phase—a continual onslaught from government and the press that, as opposed to risk management in dangerous markets, we were not experienced at handling. People's reaction to our making money when others were losing money went from amazed admiration to angry indictment. The response went from an awed *"How did you do it?"* to an aghast *"How did you do it!"*

The crisis started in the securitized mortgage market. Home mortgages first began to be securitized—sold by the original lenders, sliced, diced, bundled, and resold—in the 1970s. The securitization market took off in earnest in 1983 when Fannie Mae, the government-backed mortgage insurer, introduced the first collateralized mortgage obligations. CMOs and CDOs—collateralized debt obligations—were derivative securities based on the income stream from implicitly government-backed home loans. By 2000, the global trade in US mortgage-backed securities had become a ginormous, multitrillion-dollar market. If you want the simplest explanation, the global financial crisis happened because, beginning in the early years of the new millennium, low-for-too-long interest rates fueled a credit bubble and drove real estate prices to excess. Excessive leverage joined forces with declining lending standards to magnify risk. The interconnectedness of financial institutions—their daily lending, borrowing, and transacting with one another—meant that a panic could rampage through the system like wildfire. As a result, the kind of default that in earlier days might have been contained within individual institutions instead threatened a devastating chain reaction.

Why was Goldman Sachs in a different situation from others on Wall Street when enormous losses began to unsettle markets in 2007 and eventually to upend entire firms in 2008? The main reason was our superior risk management. At its core was a rigorous commitment to marking all of our positions to market on a daily basis. Other firms carried a significant portion of their assets on their books at their original cost or marked to some midpoint between bid and offer where they couldn't be sold. At Goldman, the daily marks were put on not by traders but by dedicated risk-control personnel, whose compensation and status at the firm were on par with that of the traders. When the controllers came up with marks that were in conflict with what traders thought they should be on illiquid securities, management always sided with the control people. However, we offered traders a simple way to challenge a mark. *You think the mark is wrong? Go out and sell some of your position and show us that you're right.* Sometimes the traders did that, but most often, the controllers' conservative marks held.

Our mark-to-market theology meant that David Viniar, who as CFO was at the top of our risk-control apparatus, became conscious of declines in the mortgage-backed securities market much earlier than his peers at other firms. In December 2006, long before declining lending standards and rising default rates were on many people's horizons, David summoned all of our traders involved in the mortgage market to a meeting. He told them that the firm as a whole needed to get "close to home" on mortgage risk.

David continued to repeat that mantra. "Close to home" meant not having aggregate positions across the firm that would accumulate to large longs or shorts. We had no overall view about which way the market would go. And the uncertainties of the moment suggested that it was not the time for heroics in either direction. By the end of January 2007, Goldman Sachs was effectively neutral on the mortgage market. At that point, there was little comprehension even among the most sophisticated thinkers in finance about the way defaults on subprime loans could affect AAA-rated mortgage securities, and credit markets generally. In a May 2007 speech, Federal Reserve chairman Ben Bernanke said, "We do not expect significant spillovers from the subprime market to the rest of the economy." A few months later, Secretary Paulson said that the subprime problem was "largely contained." At the firm level, Goldman didn't have any different or more dire prediction. We were just being careful about managing risk.

Views about the mortgage market on the trading floor and in other parts of the firm were all over the map—and in some cases diametrically opposed to each other. There was a mortgage-derivative group within Goldman Sachs led by a very successful trader named Josh Birnbaum. Birnbaum made a strong argument that mortgage defaults would rise and begged to take an even larger short position. And he turned out to be completely right. But simultaneously, there were traders within the area responsible for holding, packaging, and selling mortgages who followed Bernanke and Paulson in believing that the issue was localized and restricted to certain kinds of mortgages. They wanted to build a bigger long position, at least in AAA-rated mortgages. Who was correct? I had no view, and frankly, it wouldn't have mattered much if I had.

I did have a view about the right way to manage traders. I believed in letting different traders pursue their own strategies and not telling them what to do, so long as the firm's overall risk was comprehended and contained. If, as a trading manager, you grab the steering wheel, the trader may feel absolved of responsibility; the position effectively becomes the manager's, not the trader's. Our job at the top of the firm was to limit the overall risk in any one direction—managing Goldman's amalgamated position so that it stayed within a band around neutral. Usually, the band was pretty wide. But at that time, for mortgage risk, we purposely narrowed it. Birnbaum was welcome to go short, and he made large profits doing so. But the length of his leash was determined by what was happening elsewhere in the firm. He was constrained so as not to get much shorter than others were long, and vice versa. Through 2007 and 2008, the firm was within a couple hundred million dollars of flat in its gains and losses on mortgage-backed securities.

Lacking our culture around risk control, including our commitment to mark-to-market accounting, Merrill Lynch, Citigroup, UBS, Bear Stearns, and Morgan Stanley, among others, kept buying more mortgage risk at a discount through the summer of 2007. In some cases, theoretically off-balance sheet structured investment vehicles, which were invented at Citigroup, made their exposure even less visible to the people at the tops of those firms. Their collective losses would ultimately reach into the hundreds of billions.

At Goldman, one of the ways that we hedged our mortgage risk was buying credit default swaps, instruments that function as insurance against the failure of a security or a firm. At an early stage, CDS insurance against highly rated mortgage-backed securities was incredibly inexpensive. "Super senior" CDOs were regarded as safer than mere AAA. The risk of their default was viewed as being so low as to be effectively nonexistent.

At Goldman, we were deservedly famous (or notorious) for taking big, bold bets in markets when we felt we understood the risks. But my temperament was that of a worrier, not a warrior. Maybe owing to what I had lived through in 1994 and 1998, I was always focused on remote or "tail" risks and insisted on our hedging against them. Buying a lottery ticket may be a bad bet, but it's not existential. Going short a lottery ticket could be. As I liked to say, it's not that anything can happen. It's that given enough time, everything *will* happen. There are limits to what you can plausibly protect yourself against, of course. I used to say that I'd write all the insurance anyone wanted against nuclear war, but only because no one would be around to collect, and I wouldn't be around to pay. When it came to remote but imaginable possibilities, we were happy to buy insurance from other firms that thought they were earning free money.

We bought much of that coverage from the insurance giant AIG. Given that AIG was the primary issuer of CDSs on mortgages, we recognized that as defaults increased, we were building up a great deal of exposure to AIG—not an obvious problem, as AIG itself was that increasing rarity, an AAA company. It was uncommon, to say the least, for a broker-dealer with a single-A credit rating to have the temerity to ask for a collateral agreement with an AAA-rated insurer. But we did just that, and got it. Almost immediately, we found ourselves in a dispute with them about the value of some of the subprime securities they had insured and therefore about the amount of collateral or margin they needed to post with us. Where we religiously marked to market, we thought they were practicing mark-to-make-believe. The dispute went back and forth. I'd tell Gary Cohn to call Steven Bensinger, AIG's CFO, and I'd hover while Gary pushed him. AIG increased its collateral somewhat, but by less than we thought it should. Given the way markets were moving, by the time they paid us, they owed us more. They were perpetually short and disputing our marks. Our answer was the same one we'd give our own traders arguing with our risk controllers: *Go out and sell some at the price you think it's worth, and then we'll use your mark. Call them again, Gary!*

Were they dumb or in distress? Unable to secure what we regarded as sufficient collateral in a timely manner, we bought credit protection against AIG itself from multiple European and domestic banks—in effect, insurance on our mortgage insurer. Even though AIG was one of only half a dozen American companies with a AAA credit rating, we wanted to be fully hedged against the possibility of their nonpayment. Because of AIG's high credit rating, we once again paid very little to insure against the risk of their default. We bought CDS insurance on AIG for as little as nine basis points, or less than a dollar for $1,000 of coverage.

August 9, 2007, was a watershed moment. That was the day when the biggest French bank, BNP Paribas, froze three of its investment funds, saying it had no way to value CDO positions in illiquid markets. The whole world was heavily invested in American mortgages. Now an enormous European bank was blocking withdrawals—the surest way to precipitate a bank run, although we weren't there yet.

At that point, the situation looked to most observers like something no worse than a liquidity crisis, which central banks know how to cope with. The European Central Bank responded by making more money available for banks to borrow. But after Countrywide Financial, the largest US mortgage lender, found itself unable to roll over its overnight funding, its stock began to drop precipitously. On August 17, the Fed responded by cutting its discount rate, the rate at which it lends to banks, by half a percentage point.

BEFORE HE MADE IT RAIN FOR FORTY DAYS AND FORTY NIGHTS, GOD told Noah to build an ark. But what about all the people with whom God didn't share his plans? For the first day or two, they probably thought they were just having some bad weather. Better take an umbrella. Might have to cancel the picnic.

In the early stages of the crisis, everyone assumed that the problem would stay confined to subprime, a small sector of the overall mortgage market. Then it began to spread to a much bigger part of the market—conforming mortgages insured by Fannie Mae and Freddie Mac. With real estate prices falling in an unexpected way all around the country, a lot of those loans were underwater. A growing percentage of borrowers with high credit scores were late or in default. Triple-A-rated CDO tranches weren't looking so AAA after all.

As market anxiety grew, I began to realize that the crisis, however it played out, was likely to define my tenure leading Goldman Sachs. The modern merchant bank agenda I had described in Chicago the summer before would have to wait. My job now was protecting the firm and dealing with the fallout from what was happening in the markets. It was up to me to reassure our anxious staff. In the back-to-school atmosphere after Labor Day weekend, I sensed that everyone at the firm was feeling nervous.

I focused intently on communicating—openly, honestly, and frequently. I increased the number of town hall meetings we held and spent as much time as I could answering questions. My best tool for communicating firm-wide, as odd as it may sound today, was voicemail. Voicemail conveys much more than typed words in an email—there is tone and emotion. I would record and send out lengthy voice messages, sometimes to just our six hundred managing directors but increasingly to our entire global staff. Ordinarily, my voice messages would be fairly impersonal—routine announcements about top-level staffing changes, discussions of our quarterly earnings, or observations from my constant travels and meetings with clients, all with the requisite cheerleading. In the fall of 2007, that changed. I began sending much more personal, unscripted messages much more often. You could hear the vacillation between worry and optimism in my voice when I announced our Q3 results on what happened to be my fifty-third birthday.

9/20/2007: *This is the longest quarter that—personally—I've ever slogged through. Long, exhausting, emotional quarter. I swear it feels like a year. . . . It's a very nervous time and, you know, we'll get through that. . . . We got caught in this market just like everybody got caught. And you can't get caught without getting clipped. But you'll see from some of the results here—in certain surprising areas where everyone knows people would have done very poorly in this kind of environment—we were able to reduce risk because the word went out that we needed to reduce risk. People didn't fight and they worked to get that done. And people put on hedges and were very nimble. . . . Another thing is people worked hard. People were killing themselves. I know that people from junior people to the most senior people in the firm gave up nights and gave up weekends. . . . I would say that in a moment of extreme crisis and stress, only people's best sides came out. I'm always proud of this firm, and to be involved as long as I have with you, but never, never more so than in this period of difficulty and stress—which we didn't handle so badly, as you'll see.*

Our quarterly results remained strong: $2.85 billion in earnings on $12.33 billion in revenue. (And they stayed that way through our fourth quarter and into 2008.) Goldman avoided the losses happening everywhere else by hewing to Viniar's motto of "close to home." We didn't want to miss a distressed buying opportunity. But I remained highly conscious of balancing our long positions on the mortgage market with our short positions, not letting our risk go too far in either direction.

Markets settled a bit, a calm before the storm. Then, near the end of October 2007, Merrill Lynch announced a $7.9 billion mortgage-related loss, the largest write-down ever recorded on Wall Street. Merrill was a big packager of CDOs, and it kept a lot of them on its own balance sheet. Stan O'Neal, Merrill's CEO, was out of a job. Then on November 4, Citigroup announced that it would beat Merrill's record with an $11 billion write-down. Chuck Prince, Citi's CEO, was gone as well.

Speaking at the Merrill Lynch Banking & Financial Services Conference, a regular event for Wall Street CEOs to address the analyst community, I was asked if I expected significant write-downs at Goldman Sachs.

"No," I said. That one-word answer sent our stock shooting up.

On the last day of our fiscal year, November 30, before our fourth-quarter results were tallied and reported, I shared another voice message:

> 11/30/2007: *Through the third quarter, the firm experienced strong performance, and I'm confident that our results for the full year will reflect the tremendous hard work and talent of our people. But the operating environment for much of this quarter is an important reminder that cycles are a natural part of life in our industry. For many of you, particularly our more junior people, this may be the first time you are experiencing a significant correction in the equity markets or shift in the credit cycle. While I am not predicting that next year will be characterized by similar difficult conditions, all of us need to recognize that economic growth isn't linear. If not next year, then sometime in the future, we will contend inevitably with tough markets and a slowing global economy on a sustained basis. In up or down markets, we should all keep our sense of perspective. A focus on the needs of our clients and the stewardship of our reputation should be our priority at the firm. This mentality keeps us grounded when sentiment is unusually high or unusually low.*

A couple of weeks later, we announced our fourth-quarter and total earnings for 2007 (our fiscal year used to run December 1– November 30). It was the firm's strongest year on record—earnings of $11.6 billion on $46 billion of revenue. That represented a 22 percent increase over our revenue in 2006. The contrast with our peers in the industry couldn't have been starker. We won multiple awards from trade publications and were named one of the 100 Best Companies to Work For by *Fortune*.

> 12/18/2007: *In the course of a year, it seems as if we experienced almost a complete business cycle. The available credit, easy investment terms, and undisturbed economic growth that characterized the first half of 2007 have given way to constrained funding, periods of extreme volatility, and heightened economic uncertainty. At each turn, our people—across every part of the firm—have responded to help differentiate Goldman Sachs in the eyes of our clients. By any objective measure, we have had an outstanding year.*
>
> *Every one of you is at Goldman Sachs because of your talent and skills. But we shouldn't forget how random life can be. For many people around the world, access to education, opportunity, and the support of family and community may be lacking. For many, these are very trying times.*

MORE DECEPTIVE CALM, AND THEN ANOTHER STORM. I WAS IN A HOTEL room in Boston, where I was speaking to a local business group, when I caught wind of Bear Stearns's impending bankruptcy. It was both shocking and the basic story of the crisis. Bear was the smallest of the major investment banks. It borrowed too much—its leverage was thirty-three to one. It borrowed too short term, relying heavily on repo loans. And it invested too much of what it borrowed into speculative mortgage securities that were now illiquid. As the housing market declined and borrowers began defaulting on their mortgages, those investments became unpriceable, toxic assets.

Investment banks financed a major part of their operations in the repo markets. *Repo* is short for *repurchase agreement*—it's a kind of short-term collateralized loan where the borrower commits to buying back the collateral at a higher price. The repurchase price embeds an interest rate. As confidence in Bear's viability waned, interbank lenders demanded more and higher-quality collateral to roll over the loans it depended on to finance its operations. Eventually, even more collateral couldn't satisfy interbank lenders. Given Bear's obvious vulnerability, they weren't willing to provide credit on any terms. In the event of a failure, no one wanted to be responsible for seizing and liquidating collateral assets.

By the second week of March 2008, Bear was essentially cut off from any form of borrowing. It was clear to the market and to regulators that the firm would very soon lack sufficient liquidity to cover its ongoing obligations. On Thursday, March 13, Bear's remaining capital was down to $2 billion. Barring outside intervention, it would have to file for bankruptcy the next day. If it was going to continue operating, the Fed would have to do something to help, immediately. With Paulson's backing, it did, invoking a clause in the Federal Reserve Act, section 13(3), to justify a $13 billion emergency loan. The loan was intended to keep Bear alive through the weekend.

Alone among the major firms, Bear had declined to participate in the collective private-sector rescue of LTCM in 1998. Some of the people who had worked their way through that crisis found a certain poetic justice in its situation. But everyone recognized how threatening Bear's looming collapse was for the whole industry. Had Bear been allowed to fail, its repo lenders would have had to dump as much as $80 billion of its CDOs and other asset-backed securities into a market that was already experiencing serious liquidity issues. That would have triggered further markdowns in the value of assets on the books of other institutions. The problem wasn't that Bear, the country's seventeenth-largest financial institution, was too big to fail. It was that it was so interconnected that its failure would have been messy and dangerous. A Bear default would have disrupted banks and financial institutions around the world that were larger and even more systemically important.

Paulson and Tim Geithner, the chair of the Federal Reserve Bank of New York, pushed for a sale of the firm to J.P. Morgan, whose CEO,

Jamie Dimon, was willing to make a deal. J.P. Morgan was Bear's clearing bank, so it had a pretty good idea what the underlying reality was. Dimon agreed to buy the firm for a pittance—$2 a share. Paulson and Geithner insisted on a very low price to deal with the problem of "moral hazard," the tendency of implicit insurance to encourage irresponsible behavior. To close the deal, the New York Fed agreed to guarantee that J.P. Morgan would not lose more than $1 billion on $30 billion of Bear's most toxic assets.

That commitment wasn't a government rescue of Bear's shareholders or executives, or at least not much of one. The firm was gone, and its shareholders and management were poised to take a near-total loss on their equity holdings—Bear had traded at $165 a share a year earlier and $93 just a few weeks earlier. The purchase price was eventually raised to $10 per to encourage Bear's shareholders to approve the deal. Even at that price, Bear's fate was close to a worst-case scenario for the management and shareholders of a financial institution. It *was* a bailout for Bear's creditors, who were everywhere. It's worth pointing out that the Fed did not ultimately absorb any costs related to its guarantee—there was value in the toxic assets, when markets eventually returned to something resembling normal. But taxpayers were on the hook for potential losses up to $29 billion, and in the public mind, egged on by some of the more demagogic voices in Congress, this was a government bailout, plain and simple. Following the announcement, there was a furious political reaction against putting more public funds at risk to save bankers from the consequences of their own mistakes. Jim Bunning, a Republican senator from Kentucky who had been a famous baseball pitcher, denounced the rescue as "socialism."

> 3/18/2008: *Since Friday, with the developments surrounding Bear Stearns, broader concerns about liquidity pressures have increased significantly. While we don't minimize the stresses on the financial system right now, the firm's capital and funding positions have never been stronger. We have had no real issues with counterparties. In fact, money has come into the firm in recent*

> days as clients look for quality and stability. I'm sure there are many lessons to be drawn about the collapse of Bear Stearns. But one is paramount in my mind, and that is the fragility of confidence. Whenever a client solicits our advice, asks for our help to execute a transaction, or engages us to manage his or her assets, it is confidence in Goldman Sachs that prompts that client to pick up the phone or accept a meeting. In this environment, it is easy to lose one's perspective or focus. Our job is to keep our focus on the needs of our clients. None of us can say what the rest of the year will look like. At least in the shorter term, we can expect volatile and dislocated markets. And in that sense, we will experience our fair share of challenges. At the same time, I believe our relative strength puts us in a position to seize market opportunities likely to emerge in the next several months.

The Bear rescue again brought a feeling of relief that didn't last long. With the approach of summer, there were unpleasant surprises every day. The sense of doom was fueled by CNBC, which was on in every office, muted. On the top right of the screen, you'd see the cratering stock price of whichever company was in the eye of the storm. Sometimes it would be Goldman's share price. I couldn't help but be fixated on it too. I found the charts and quotes auguring doom so distracting that at some point I just turned off the TV in my office.

In fact, while market professionals cared about a company's stock price as an indicator of its health, the barometer they focused on more was its credit spread—its cost of borrowing in relation to the reference of safety, the ten-year Treasury note. Companies weren't out seeking credit every day, so you determined that credit spreads were widening or narrowing by watching prices on CDSs written on the company. If insurance against its failure got more expensive, a company's credit was worsening. You could survive a low stock price. You couldn't survive a collapse of your credit. But CDSs were hardly a perfect barometer. They were thinly traded and manipulable, which added to the market stress and volatility.

Credit spreads continued to widen, not just for Bear but for other Wall Street firms, in a way that suggested a classic panic—fear that becomes a self-fulfilling prophecy. Ben Bernanke's complacency of a year earlier evaporated. In July, there was a literal bank run at IndyMac, a California thrift that specialized in issuing subprime mortgages. Depositors were lined up outside the bank's branches, like a warm-weather reenactment of *It's a Wonderful Life* with Encino standing in for Pottersville. In September, there was a modified run at Washington Mutual, a much larger thrift with similar issues. Deposits at those banks were guaranteed by the FDIC, but only up to $100,000.

The fast-moving storm headed next toward Fannie Mae and Freddie Mac, the New Deal–era government-sponsored entities (GSEs) that underwrote the lion's share of all residential mortgages. Fannie and Freddie existed to provide homeowners with long, fixed-rate mortgages. They were single-handedly propping up the mortgage markets and incurring huge losses against far too little capital. Given their imminent failure and the likely consequences for millions of homeowners, Paulson asked Congress for emergency powers to stabilize them—essentially authorizing the funding to nationalize them, if necessary. "If you've got a bazooka, and people know you've got it, you may not have to take it out," Hank said in his congressional testimony. Several weeks later, he fired the bazooka—the government took both GSEs into government conservatorship.

It wasn't just financial firms that were under stress. That summer, the whole economy was hurting. Unemployment was rising rapidly, gas prices topped $4 a gallon, and auto sales were down sharply. A record share of mortgages—one in eleven—was past due or in default. Goldman was in a queasy position, a well-maintained house in a scary neighborhood. As our second quarter ended, I was proud to announce that we were continuing to do well, with a profit of $2.1 billion on $9.4 billion in revenue. But I was feeling increasingly anxious.

> 6/17/2008: *It would be easy to be overconfident when you consider our relative performance. It would also be foolish. Looking*

> at the economic and market picture today, it is impossible to predict the extent or severity of the challenges we will face in the months ahead. Current dislocations may linger. New ones may emerge. We remain focused on finding an appropriate balance between internal priorities and external opportunities. While we are conservatively managing our capital and liquidity and structuring various business to meet longer-term realities, we are also aggressively seeking new ways to assist our clients.

By that point, I'd been running the firm for two years, with the unfolding crisis the dominant reality of my tenure. Goldman's position seemed exceptional. We were mostly hedged against the mortgage market, we held strong cash reserves, and we were continuing to make profits quarter by quarter. Did that mean we were safe?

Not at all. In a tsunami, it wouldn't matter if the person on the beach was a young child who couldn't swim or an Olympic gold medalist. Both would drown. It's the same in a major crisis, when even the strong performers can be overwhelmed by events. And in a financial crisis, the perception of vulnerability can quickly become the reality.

CHAPTER 22

Don't Get Dead

Goldman Sachs is much easier to manage in bad times than in good times. In flush times, everyone believes he was the principal driver of the firm's success and wants to be compensated accordingly. In difficult times, people are nervous, maybe even scared. We all know we must pitch in and are embarrassed to act selfishly.

fter the demise of Bear Stearns, the market's focus turned to Lehman Brothers. With plenty of illiquid, toxic assets on its books, Lehman, like Bear, lacked sufficient good collateral to maintain easy access to credit markets. As the summer wore on, the situation grew increasingly desperate. Lehman was much bigger than Bear, and the risks of a failure correspondingly larger. But the furious reaction to the Bear rescue meant that the New York Fed and Treasury could not, or would not, simply step in.

If Lehman was, as it insisted, merely facing a liquidity crisis amid badly strained market conditions, it was a matter of providing breathing room. The simplest solution would be to find a healthy buyer with a bigger balance sheet. Dick Fuld, Lehman's grim-faced CEO, recognized the need to bring in fresh capital. But he obstinately refused to accept offers at prices below his unrealistic view of what the firm was worth in that distressed moment. Talks with the Korea Development

Bank and with Warren Buffett went nowhere—Fuld was asking too much, valuing his possibly insolvent firm too highly. It was hard to tell just how bad the situation was, because Fuld also resisted writing down illiquid assets held on Lehman's books even to the extent that other firms had. Instead of facing reality, he complained bitterly about short sellers driving the price of his stock down. It was $80 in June; by late September it was less than $10.

The clock was running out and Paulson and Geithner were trying to walk a fine line. They wanted the country's top bankers to find a solution that would prevent Lehman from failing. If successful, this would be a reprise of the Fed's successful intervention with LTCM in 1998, when all of the other biggest banks (with the exception of Bear Stearns) put money in to buy LTCM's distressed portfolio. Over time, assets reverted to the mean, and there were ultimately no losses to the banks that bought the distressed assets. No taxpayer dollars were implicated in the LTCM rescue. This time, however, it was far from clear that collective action by the private sector could arrest the contagion. Banks were all under varying degrees of strain. And it was difficult to get a read on how big Lehman's hole really was.

It was an incredibly stressful time in markets and at our offices. But the familiar functions of my job were much as before. I continued to meet with clients and make public appearances. At the end of the day on Friday, September 12, I attended an event promoting volunteerism at the giant Hilton Hotel in Midtown. Then-Senator Hillary Clinton was a speaker and so was I. I was excited to talk about the rollout of our 10,000 Women program. In the greenroom, where I was waiting, the senator asked if she could speak before me so she could get to a dinner on time. *Sure*, I said, *no problem*.

Then, a little before five, my phone buzzed. I was needed urgently at the New York Federal Reserve, along with all the other big-bank CEOs. I had a pretty good idea what might be on the agenda—getting the banks together to save Lehman. There were also growing worries about AIG, which was far larger than Lehman. I apologized to Hillary—would she mind if I spoke first after all, so I could get down to the emergency meeting at 33 Liberty by 6:00 p.m.? *You go right ahead,* she said.

I gave my speech, skipped the questions, and took off. My driver pulled straight into the Fed's basement parking garage, avoiding the reporters who were standing in the rain outside the front entrance, trying to figure out what the hell was happening. New York Fed staff ushered me into a windowless conference room on the ground floor.

Over the next half hour or so, in walked the heads of what, at a previous gathering, I had called the fourteen families: Merrill Lynch CEO John Thain, Morgan Stanley CEO John Mack, Citigroup CEO Vikram Pandit, J.P. Morgan CEO Jamie Dimon, and others, accompanied by their CFOs. Also present were the US heads of some leading foreign financial institutions, including Barclays, UBS, and Deutsche Bank. The US government didn't regulate their parent companies but did have authority over their US branches. Dick Fuld and his team from Lehman were in the Fed building, but elsewhere—in the infirmary (symbolism duly noted). The rest of us sat there and made small talk amid the tension.

After about forty-five more minutes, Paulson, Geithner, and SEC chairman Christopher Cox strode into the room. Paulson opened the meeting by saying that there were two potential buyers for Lehman—Bank of America and Barclays, the British bank. That these acquisition conversations were even happening was Hank's doing. But neither potential acquirer was willing to take on the full risk of a merger. And this time, he said, there would be no government money or guarantee. There was neither the political will nor the legal authority for another bailout.

Geithner then summarized the grim reality of Lehman's balance sheet and told us that it was our job to come up with a plan to keep it out of bankruptcy. He wanted us to solve the problem by Sunday, so that we could announce what we were doing before Asian markets reopened on Sunday night. SEC chairman Cox didn't contribute anything meaningful. Though often present, the impeccably dressed former congressman from California was mostly a bystander.

All of us grasped the stakes. If Lehman failed, the private sector didn't act, and the government didn't step in, the only question was who would be next. Lehman's declining position was already threatening the credit of other, more solvent institutions. The failure of one major institution with highly leveraged obligations could set off a chain reaction through the interbank lending market. Its default could trigger the default of others. When market confidence is lost, the distinction between insolvent institutions like Lehman and solvent ones like Goldman can evaporate overnight. Customers tap their credit lines. Counterparties withhold payments. Lenders demand collateral. Clearing institutions can refuse to take your name. If no one will extend a company credit, it ceases to operate, despite what might appear to be a healthy balance sheet.

Moreover, market participants who wanted to hedge against or profit from a market collapse would short the stocks or bet on credit spreads widening for the next-most-vulnerable banks up the food chain.

If anyone still lacked motivation, being locked in a room by the Treasury secretary and the chairman of the New York Fed created powerful pressure. Paulson was artful in applying muscle. He didn't have the authority to order us to act—any of us could have walked out at any time. But he said that he and Geithner would remember who was helpful and who wasn't. I smiled, remembering Hank's nickname as an offensive lineman at Dartmouth: the Hammer.

I was back at nine o'clock on Saturday morning with a bigger team that included Greg Palm, our chief counsel. We were divided into task forces, one to explore the scenario of a Lehman bankruptcy, another to evaluate what spinning off Lehman's assets into a "bad bank" might look like. With our leading position in M&A and finance, Goldman was probably more knowledgeable about the reality of Lehman's situation than anyone else in the room. That's why Tim and Hank assigned us, along with J.P. Morgan, to report back on Lehman's assets.

What we learned that day provided the opposite of reassurance. Lehman's assets—not just mortgages but outstanding loans and loan commitments as well as real estate and other securities—were consistently marked higher than the same or similar positions we held. By any realistic measure, Lehman was not just illiquid but actually insolvent, with assets worth less than its liabilities. Under those circumstances, Paulson and Geithner believed they lacked the legal authority to intervene. The Fed could use its emergency powers to lend under section 13(3) only if it determined the borrower had satisfactory collateral. It had made that determination with Bear Stearns—perhaps a stretch it was willing to make when the company at risk was smaller and the crisis seemed more containable. But now, both the politics and the reality of Lehman's finances pointed in the opposite direction.

Especially the politics. In the aftermath of these events, there would be a lot of second-guessing about what the Treasury and the New York Fed could have and should have done. But at the time—and until more lessons were learned—the politics simply would not have permitted another bank bailout.

Paulson and Geithner pulled some of us out of the room and asked us individually what we thought. I told them I thought the banks in the room would come together to collectively acquire those toxic assets in a bad bank if they leaned on us to do so. The number thrown around to finance the bad bank came to $1 billion per institution. I said I'd go along, but I was basically against it. With so much suspicion of everyone else's balance sheet, it seemed like a poor idea to drain a billion dollars of capital each from some barely healthy banks to rescue the one that was sickest, probably already fatally so. Doing so would leave the system more vulnerable to a run. And how could the strongest among us—which Goldman pretty clearly was—remain strong if we were seen as responsible for bailing out our weaker competitors? Merrill Lynch would be next in line, and it was much larger than Lehman. Also, although I didn't really articulate this until after that weekend, the downside to forestalling a calamitous event is that you never live through and learn from it. Regrettably, something would have to blow up for us to fully appreciate the consequences of a blowup. Painful though it would be, I thought we should brace ourselves and accept a Lehman bankruptcy, rather than have the same conversation in a few days about an even larger institution when the system was further drained.

I don't know what the other CEOs were thinking, but in public most were willing to go in whatever direction Paulson and Geithner were leaning. By the end of the day, a plan emerged to split Lehman, putting the toxic assets into one bank and the healthy assets into another. The bad bank would be financed by the companies in the room and US branches of a few additional foreign banks that hadn't made the meeting. We would collectively put up the money for a fund that would hold and eventually unwind Lehman's hard-to-value assets, including mortgage-backed securities and CDOs. That would have been a hard enough pill to swallow. But it was the selling of the "good" bank that proved to be the bigger problem. Bank of America, led by Ken Lewis, was no longer interested in acquiring it, at least not without a government guarantee of the kind Jamie Dimon had secured with Bear Stearns. The good news was that there was still a buyer in the wings. Bob Diamond, the American who headed Barclays, was present that weekend and stood ready to do the deal.

We were back at the Fed early on Sunday. But that afternoon, the news came that the Barclays deal was not to be. The British financial authorities said they would block the merger—if Bank of America didn't want Lehman, they weren't going to trust what was under the hood. Hank and Tim were out of options. There was no other plan. We CEOs began once again to focus on our own institutions, to prepare for the turmoil ahead.

In the wee hours of Monday morning, before the market open, Lehman filed for bankruptcy—the largest one in US history. Everyone saw the pictures of employees streaming out of its headquarters in Midtown holding boxes filled with their family pictures and personal effects. Lehman Brothers was an even older firm than Goldman Sachs. On September 15, 2008, it failed and was gone after 158 years in business because people lost confidence, and it didn't make a deal when it could have. Dick Fuld kept holding out for a higher price or better terms from potential acquirers. A lot of great firms have as part of their history surviving huge losses and near-death experiences. Fuld broke the basic rule of running any institution: Eliminate the biggest existential risks at any cost. The first requirement of business is to stay in business. You can recover from losses and live to fight another day. You can't recover from being dead.

ON MONDAY MORNING, WE DROVE PAST THE HORDE OF CAMERAS, PRO-testers, and gawkers gathered at the entrance to the New York Fed and into the underground parking garage. I assembled there with the rest of our team before heading up to the boardroom. We hadn't gotten much sleep and were about to go into a fourth consecutive day of meetings, likely to continue into the evening.

"I don't think I can take another day of this," one of our team members complained.

"For crying out loud, you're getting out of a Mercedes in the basement of the New York Fed. You're not getting out of a Higgins boat on Omaha Beach! Get a grip!"

It was a performance for the team. But I was speaking to myself as well.

The collapse of Lehman Brothers began a week that felt like a year yet also went by in a dizzying flash. Those of us who favored letting Lehman go, including Ben Bernanke, saw quickly how big the price was. The results were near catastrophic, and the shock waves just kept coming. The stock market fell 5 percent that day, with all the major financial firms dropping by double digits. The most immediate consequence of the default was that a huge money-market fund that held a small portion of its assets in Lehman's commercial paper "broke the buck." That meant that a dollar held in the fund was worth less than a dollar—something that isn't supposed to ever happen. Not surprising, that news triggered a run by people desperate to get their uninsured deposits out. Unable to meet redemption requests, the fund froze withdrawals and then quickly began liquidating. Even "as good as cash" now seemed unsafe.

After Lehman, the next most vulnerable investment bank was Merrill Lynch. After Merrill, it was Morgan Stanley. And if Morgan Stanley, then potentially Goldman Sachs, despite our healthy balance sheet and lack of material net subprime exposure. It was like living in a five-story building with the waters rising. Bear Stearns was on the first floor and Lehman was on the second. Merrill Lynch was on the third floor. Morgan Stanley was on the fourth. Goldman was on the fifth floor, the highest one. But if you dropped a pebble out the window, you heard the splash a little too soon.

The only good news on Monday was that Merrill Lynch, widely regarded as the next domino after Lehman, had found a buyer: Bank of America, which agreed to acquire it for $50 billion, or $29 per share. The acquisition explained why Ken Lewis had pulled back from acquiring Lehman. He naturally preferred the more solid Merrill. The most disturbing news that day—and there was plenty of it—was that AIG was on the verge of default, with no acquirer or government rescue in view. Its shares plummeted to less than $5, from what had been a peak of nearly $150.

Lehman was much larger than Bear Stearns. AIG was *much* larger than Lehman, and as an insurer of many businesses, it extended deeply into the real, i.e., nonfinancial, economy. Among its main business lines, AIG also managed pensions and wrote life insurance policies for millions of Americans. It had a *trillion*-dollar balance sheet. Even more than Lehman's, its collapse would spread contagion to its creditors and potentially lead to the entire financial system freezing up. The government couldn't let AIG fail—could it?

We had a team at the Fed working, at Geithner's request, alongside bankers from J.P. Morgan to look at whether we could jointly arrange a loan to AIG large enough to address its problems. And this while we were pressuring them to send us more collateral! On Tuesday, we reported back that we simply couldn't provide a big enough loan. The hole in AIG's balance sheet was much larger than anyone thought.

Meanwhile, on the thirtieth floor at the top of our headquarters at 85 Broad, we were setting up deal teams in the conference rooms where we'd meet with clients, this time to run through scenarios for ourselves. Goldman was the top M&A firm and excelled at contingency planning. I wanted to consider every possible merger contingency, however far-fetched—I said we should be ready to merge with Starbucks if we needed to. We had teams looking at potential mergers with every other financial institution, including the healthier-seeming British banks. Chris Cole, one of our top M&A bankers, who specialized in financial institutions, organized the war rooms. The conference rooms were filled with pizza boxes and Chinese takeout containers. Some people slept at the office, or barely slept at all for nights on end.

In a way, the most important team was the one I asked Tim O'Neill and Armen Avanessians to lead: Fortress Goldman. If we didn't do a strategic transaction with anybody and went it alone—in a difficult-to-imagine circumstance where we paid out everything we owed, no one paid what they owed us, and no new funding came from any source—how long could we hold out? What would our liquidity look like under circumstances ranging up to that unlikely worst-case scenario? This was our own internal stress test.

Armen and Tim were focused on what we called the BONY box—a throwback to the days when Goldman, as a private partnership, stashed bearer bonds in a literal safe-deposit box at the Bank of New York. By 2008, the BONY box was a lot more high-tech, but the principle was the same: liquid assets you could repo for cash right now. We still had a substantial cushion, but it was eroding. Short-term financing, which a vast swath of corporate America relies on to keep operating, was quickly drying up.

> 9/16/2008: *I know the events of the last few weeks and months have been unsettling. And as you would expect, our levels of capital and liquidity are higher than we would typically maintain.... Like all periods of uncertainty and market stress, this one will come to an end. But because no one knows when that will happen, our collective responsibility is to manage the firm conservatively, communicate issues and problems up and down the*

organization, and remain focused on opportunities. As I mentioned yesterday, all of us share in the responsibility to help bring normalcy back to the markets. In every area of the firm, in every Goldman Sachs office around the world, we need every person to be totally focused, to be looking around corners, to be serving clients, and to escalate potential issues before they arise.

That week, I started holding daily 4:15 p.m. conference calls with our board after the New York stock market close. I thought that not knowing the real state of affairs was even scarier than the reality, and that a daily update might help. I told the board that the calls were optional but would be a good way to keep up with what was going on, share any good ideas, raise questions, and vent anxieties. Everyone on the board joined. Those daily calls, which continued over the next several weeks, showed me once again how essential it is to have channels for constant communication in a crisis. They also demonstrated the value of having a board composed of people with crisis-management experience, who didn't freak out in a perilous moment.

> 9/17/2008: This is Lloyd on Wednesday evening in New York. As you are all aware, markets—particularly in the financial sector—continued to deteriorate today. Given relatively solid earnings and our strong liquidity profile, the pressure on our stock price appears to be driven less by specific fundamental concerns and more by anxiety about credit markets. Another factor may be an attempt by short sellers to take advantage of the broader situation. I want to assure you that we are well positioned to weather the challenges facing the firm and the industry. Our funding position has never been stronger, and our risk management—which relies on diversification and ongoing measurement of all exposures—is making adjustments on a real-time basis. Today we had several conversations with regulators at the Federal Reserve, US Treasury, and SEC, and of course we have been keeping our board of directors informed throughout this period. I know that all of us

> are working our way through a very stressful set of events. But it's important to remember that so are many of our clients. They are looking to you for reassurance and thoughtful judgment. This is a defining time for financial markets—and with it comes the opportunity for us to truly distinguish ourselves.

People were passing around rumors, speculating about what could happen. In one of the worst moments, some people raised concerns about Goldman's credit. This may have come from our competitors—some of the rumors cited Deutsche Bank or J.P. Morgan. It wouldn't have been rational for anyone to do that, because at that point, we were all dominoes. If one of our competitors went up in flames, any satisfaction would be fleeting, because the fire would spread to the neighboring buildings.

But sometimes overly enthusiastic junior people do stupid things. I remember once getting a call from Donald Trump, who in a very nice way complained that one of our traders had told a broker that Goldman Sachs wouldn't buy the paper debt of the Trump Organization. If that was true, it was a breach. It's one thing to not take a particular offer. It's quite another to say that we wouldn't take the name at all—that is, trust his company's credit. I said I'd look into it, and after calls to various people involved, I determined that it was true. I reprimanded the offender, who knew he had made a mistake. Then I called Trump to apologize. I said that I was embarrassed and that it wouldn't happen again. He didn't pound me, and that was it—he was gracious about it.

What the episode shows is that you can never be sure what's going on in the trenches. So while I never believed that senior people at other firms were intentionally disparaging us, I thought it was possible that junior people might be. I asked my counterparts at the big commercial banks to caution their people and said that I was doing the same. I then wired some of our liquidity as deposits into several of those banks to demonstrate, and not just assert, that we still had plenty of it.

In the cafeteria, people would gather around TV screens and watch the latest horror on CNBC in a state of semiparalysis. I knew that wasn't helpful, so in town halls and smaller meetings of all kinds, I proposed a deal to the staff: You do your jobs as intensely as possible—call your clients and make yourselves more helpful to them than ever before. And in return, I will keep you fully informed. Even at the height of the crisis in 2008, I needed only around 2 percent of the company to work through the problems where we were our own client. I needed the other 98 percent doing their regular work. Our clients needed the support, and it was the best way to signal that we were in control of ourselves. That's how we would get through this and come out stronger.

I began to talk a lot about the previous crisis moments I had lived through, especially in 1994 and 1998. I told people that their reputations for the rest of their careers would be established by how they handled this moment. *And not just your reputation with others,* I said. *Your reputation with yourself—your own sense of confidence—will come from how you perform under the kind of pressure we're facing. When you look back at your career, you're going to think most about what kind of difference you made in challenging times like those we're in now, not the good times.*

ON WEDNESDAY, SEPTEMBER 17, THE NEW YORK FED ANNOUNCED THAT it would save AIG. In exchange for an $85 billion line of credit, the government would take possession of 79.9 percent of the firm. The CEO, Bob Willumstad, was out. In his place, Paulson appointed the former CEO of Allstate, Ed Liddy. This was good news for the world and a little inconvenient for us. Liddy was on our board and head of our audit committee. His appointment fueled more conspiracy thinking that the government was intervening to help Goldman Sachs. We had purchased credit protection on AIG from large European banks, so our true exposure was manageable. Our more immediate problem was that heading the audit committee was the most important and labor-intensive role on the board, and it was hard to see another board member wanting to step into it at that moment. Happily, Steve Friedman said he'd do it—an act of redemption, to my mind, for his precipitous departure as senior partner in 1994.

Despite the effective nationalization of AIG, markets were in full-blown panic the next day. Our own liquid capital in the BONY box, which stood at $120 billion at the beginning of the week, was now down to half that. A lot of counterparties weren't paying Goldman. And others were calling down credit lines and loan commitments.

At Morgan Stanley, one floor below us in that metaphorical five-story building, the linoleum on the floor was getting wet. I frequently found myself trying to buck up Morgan's CEO, John Mack. Mack was part of the generation of gregarious bond traders who rose to be heads of firms—including Dick Fuld at Lehman and Jon Corzine at Goldman Sachs—and was very well liked by people at Morgan Stanley. The traders used to applaud when he walked onto the trading floor. But that generation also had a tendency to mistake stubbornness for character, and their inflexibility was a big part of how they got into trouble. I wasn't so impressed with the way Mack accepted responsibility for the losses at Morgan Stanley and then blamed Zoe Cruz, his head of trading and the most senior woman on Wall Street, for losses on huge mortgage positions that no one in his role could have missed. *I take full responsibility—Zoe, you're fired.* But commiserating, I told him to hang in there. *We're very supportive of you,* I said. *Because if you go under, there will be immediate pressure on us.*

As the waters rose, the vultures circled. One of the calls I got that day was from the dealmaker Bruce Wasserstein. It was just a courtesy call, he said. Might he be of any assistance as an adviser? Did we have anything we wanted to sell? *Thank you very much,* I replied, *I appreciate you reaching out, but we're in full control and know how to do this stuff.* Bruce wanted to let me know that he might be calling members of my board, just to let them know he was there if they needed him. What a way to make a living, I thought. It was like the undertaker calling at your sickbed.

Then John Thain called from Merrill Lynch, freshly acquired by Bank of America. *Please take this the right way,* he said. *You know I love Goldman Sachs. My advice to you is to find a good buyer and merge the firm.* Well, that was particularly jarring, because Thain did love the firm and was sincerely trying to be helpful.

Whom could I call? I didn't want to leave any stone unturned. Maybe HSBC, which seemed to be conservatively managed. Its CEO, Stephen Green, at that point had a good reputation. (He was an ordained Church of England minister!) In our board strategy presentations, we had highlighted HSBC as a good complement without too many overlapping businesses and with a strategy focus on Asia that matched our own interest. When I called his home, his wife answered and said he was in the shower. Green called me back and said that with all that was going on, they couldn't consider it. I was embarrassed that I had been goaded into making such a dumb call.

The previous weekend had been the "Lehman weekend." I called the next one Wall Street's "existential weekend." We were facing a catastrophic failure, not of any one firm, or of several, but of the entire financial system. Not probable, but much too possible. Credit is sentiment. The withdrawal of confidence moves at the speed of fear. If you're scared that your counterparty is insolvent, even if it's a small chance, you're reluctant to pay them until they pay you first. Everyone wants to receive before they pay out. As a result, no one pays anyone. That's how a meltdown can happen. Once credit becomes frozen, it can unfreeze only when someone with a bigger balance sheet than the market shows up and assures everyone that they'll get paid. At that point, the only someone out there was the US government.

At the end of the week, there were three bits of news from Washington. Treasury announced its Troubled Asset Relief Program (TARP), which would be introduced as a bill in Congress. This would provide $700 billion, more than the entire annual defense budget, for the Treasury to purchase toxic assets at its sole discretion. It was a novel idea, but I didn't think it would work—it would simply take too long to set up and be too slow. At the SEC, Christopher Cox announced a temporary ban on short selling for 799 financial stocks.

Both announcements created a feeling of relief for some people. John Mack, especially, was an advocate for a short-selling ban, and after several conversations, I agreed to go along with it. But I knew it would be helpful only in the immediate moment. A short ban just makes everyone live in fear of the day it gets lifted. Those who might want to buy your stock will be reluctant, because with some people barred from selling, the quoted price is not the real, market-clearing price. If you really wanted to buy, it would be smarter to wait until after the short sellers were allowed back into the market. Ironically, a ban intended to stop short sellers also deters buyers.

One thing that did work that day was the Treasury stepping in with a new facility to temporarily guarantee money-market funds. If you already had $1 in a money market fund, the taxpayers would guarantee that you got $1 back.

> 9/19/2008: *This is Lloyd on Friday evening in New York. First, I want to thank all of you for your extraordinary efforts over the past week. It is my hope that for at least the next twenty-four hours, while global markets are closed, you will have a chance to get some rest. It has been a remarkable week. Even with twenty-five years in the industry, I would never have predicted we would be where we are at this moment. But my career at Goldman Sachs has prepared me to be ready for the unexpected, and I am grateful to be part of an organization that immediately assesses, adapts, and responds based upon strong analyses, good judgment, and unparalleled risk management. You are all to be commended. . . . I cannot predict what we will face in the days to come. I can say—with certainty—that we have the best team in any financial services organization to face the uncertainties, and I am confident that our efforts will strengthen our franchise and play an important role in stabilizing world markets. Thanks again for what you do for Goldman Sachs. Get some rest!*

No one got any rest. That weekend was a barrage of calls between officials at the New York Fed, officials at the Treasury, and the heads of all the major financial institutions. Between calls, Gary Cohn and I went room to room among the deal teams, trying to keep morale up and urge people along. Geithner and Paulson were now acting as matchmakers, trying to come up with mergers that could shore up the weaker firms, reassure markets, and bring back a sense of stability. There were great vulnerabilities on the part of the commercial banks, which had huge, direct exposure to the mortgage market. On the other hand, they had a much larger liquidity base in the form of deposits. The Fed and the Treasury wanted institutions with stronger balance sheets to combine with ones with weaker balance sheets. It was a kind of crazed speed dating for bankers. After the AIG plan was announced, Geithner thought it would make sense for Morgan Stanley to merge with J.P. Morgan, reuniting the old House of Morgan. He also wanted Goldman to merge with Citigroup.

Tim told me to call Vikram Pandit, the CEO of Citi, to discuss a merger. This was not a prospect that filled me with enthusiasm. At Goldman we knew a lot about other financial institutions, and our view was that Citi's net worth was negative by literally hundreds of billions of dollars due to leveraged mortgage exposure. (This was borne out by Citi eventually needing multiple rounds of government support.) What's more, Citigroup was ginormous, with around 350,000 employees. Would I now be running a firm ten times our size? Or the other way around? That was all TBD. Tim said Vikram would be expecting my call.

I checked in with the team on the thirtieth floor sorting through Citi's numbers. These were the kinds of deals that under normal circumstances could take months to work out. Now we were being asked to consummate them in hours.

When I reached him, Vikram professed to be surprised. "This is unexpected. I'm flattered that you would propose a merger with Citigroup."

"I'm not calling with a merger proposal to flatter you," I said. "I'm calling because the regulators told me to."

I called Geithner back and said Vikram was behaving as if the call were unexpected. Vikram was just playing dumb—they weren't any more enthusiastic about a shotgun marriage than we were. Then I went back into the room where bankers were analyzing a Citi merger and told them to put their pens down.

Tim's next proposal was for us to merge with Wachovia. I didn't take it as a suggestion—I took it as an order. *Wachovia deal team—go!*

It was Saturday and my birthday, and Laura and I were supposed to have dinner with a group of friends at Porter House in the Time Warner Center on Columbus Circle. I never made it there. Instead I spent the evening driving to Westchester County Airport to pick up Bob Steel, Wachovia's new CEO. At the height of the bubble in 2006, Wachovia had purchased Golden West Financial and its portfolio of mortgage-backed securities for $26 billion. Wachovia's massive losses, many of them flowing from that acquisition, had resulted in the ouster of its previous CEO. Newly installed in the job, Bob was flying in from an event at the Aspen Institute. Presumably he had gotten the same message I had from the New York Fed.

This was going to be a little awkward. Bob had previously been at Goldman for thirty years and had been considered a rival of mine. We had been made vice-chairs at the same time, he from equities, me from FICC. After he left Goldman, Steel's responsibilities were given to me. Paulson brought him into the Treasury as undersecretary and then asked him to become CEO of Wachovia in the middle of an emergency. Now Bob was going to be back at Goldman Sachs?

In the car back to the city, we discussed how Wachovia would function as a consumer division of Goldman. But the next morning, on Sunday, word from our deal team wasn't good. Steel had been there only a few months, and I think we may have had better information on the state of his balance sheet than he did. They were carrying mortgages on their books at par that were worth tens of billions less. The only way for us to do a deal would have been with some kind of government support. I knew that given Hank's prior history as Goldman's CEO, it was not likely that the government would provide us with any kind of financial backstop for the acquisition. Or for any acquisition, for that matter. After two years in the job, Paulson had only just secured a legal exemption to talk to us, his old firm, again.

But still we motored on with negotiations, as if a deal might happen. On Sunday morning, full deal teams from Goldman and Wachovia met at our office to iron out terms. Chris Cole, Goldman's top banker for financial institutions, led the team representing Goldman. Bob Steel, formerly of Goldman, brought in Wachovia's lead investment banker Peter Weinberg, also formerly of Goldman and lately the head of boutique firm Perella Weinberg. If it sounds a little inbred, that wasn't lost on us. We had gotten far enough to have drafted a press release announcing the merger when we received a call midday Sunday from one of Hank's deputies at Treasury who told us to put pens down. There would be no government support for any deal involving Goldman because the optics would be terrible. So there would be no deal. (A week later, regulators pushed Wachovia into the arms of Citi in a $1-per-share fire sale for which there was government support. To his credit, Steel managed to extricate the firm from that doomed transaction and secure a much better $7-per-share price from Wells Fargo with no government support.)

At one point on Sunday morning while all this was going on, I felt I needed a break. In the old days, I would have lit a cigarette. Instead I called Jeff Immelt, the CEO of General Electric and one of our most important clients. "I thought you might be at your desk too," I said.

"Yup."

It was nice to hear about someone else's problems for a change. GE financed itself through short-term commercial paper—another of those good ideas to save a few basis points of costs that turned into a dangerous idea when markets changed and the paper became more difficult to roll over. GE was an AAA-rated company and the largest borrower in the commercial-paper market. The government's program to guarantee commercial paper was implemented in large part with GE in mind. Ultimately, Paulson had to persuade Sheila Bair, the head of the FDIC, to include GE in its program to guarantee bank debt, on the theory that its finance arm, GE Capital, operated as a kind of bank. In that sense, GE was the only industrial company besides General Motors and Chrysler to receive government protection in the crisis.

WAS THE COLLAPSE OF GOLDMAN SACHS EVER A PROBABILITY? NO, BUT it was a possibility as part of a catastrophic system-wide failure. That weekend—and probably Sunday—was as close to the brink as we came. We still had about $60 billion in good liquidity. And we still had the capacity to raise capital quickly, even if the terms would have been unappealing. But almost no amount would have been enough for comfort at that moment.

Even if the chance of a catastrophic failure was only as high as 15 percent, that's a far greater risk than any responsible person would ever willingly take. A 15 percent risk is between one in seven and one in six. One in six is a turn at Russian roulette.

CHAPTER 23

How to Survive a Crisis

It has been said that because I'm good in crises, I go out of my way to create them. That's not always true.

There were, in fact, less drastic steps that could assure markets that Goldman was fundamentally secure. The first was to become a bank holding company. We'd discussed and debated this for years, most recently revisiting the idea after Bear Stearns collapsed in March. Our co–general counsel Esta Stecher was in charge of the thirtieth-floor team looking at that option over the weekend while the merge-a-rama was going on in other offices. Becoming a bank holding company would give us the Fed's confidence-inspiring imprimatur. It would also mean a much heavier hand of regulation and having to hold much more capital against our trading activity.

Over that weekend, Esta updated the application we'd prepared as a contingency in March. Once it was clear that Goldman wasn't merging with Citi or Wachovia or any other company, she and her team talked the matter through with the Fed. It was a mad dash. There was a ton of work to do to decide what parts of Goldman and what assets could and should be included in the regulated bank, as opposed to a nonbank affiliate; to connect our teams with their counterparts at the Fed; and to advise scores of other regulators, domestic and foreign. Yet after the Citi and Wachovia merger ideas fell apart, it became the inevitable remaining option. Following the takeovers of Bear Stearns and Merrill and the bankruptcy of Lehman, Morgan Stanley and Goldman Sachs were the remaining investment banks regulated by the SEC. That structure no longer made any sense.

The announcement had to happen by Sunday night. One of the Fed officials told Esta, "The application is approved. Where is it?" I decided we should go ahead and convene the board on another emergency conference call.

By turning into a bank holding company, we got direct access to the Fed borrowing window. Only banks had that. (We had previously had a "primary dealer credit facility" available, but using it would have required going through a bank, because we didn't link directly to the Fed.) One of the many projects that had to be accomplished over the existential weekend was working on those direct links. But the really important thing we got from the conversion was the Fed's implicit blessing. Because we met the Fed's regulatory threshold, which was presumed to be tougher, market participants were more inclined to accept that we were okay. If we weren't okay, and the Fed intended to let us fail, it wouldn't be bringing us in, would it?

> 9/21/2008: *This is Lloyd on Sunday evening in New York. . . . I am leaving you this message to advise that tonight we will announce that Goldman Sachs will become a bank holding company and will be regulated by the Federal Reserve Board.*

The second idea was to raise capital in the market from a confidence-inspiring figure. We thought immediately of Warren Buffett. I had always admired Buffett, not just as the twentieth century's greatest investor but as an explainer who helps people understand and appreciate finance without charts or graphs. He also had a long history with Goldman, starting with that trip to the World's Fair when he met the great Sidney Weinberg. The meeting made a lasting impression on the young Buffett (and probably on Sidney Weinberg as well).

Buffett is no fan of investment bankers, who he thinks add the unnecessary cost of their fees onto deals. But he makes an exception for his friend Byron Trott, who had been at Goldman for decades and was postponing his planned exit because of the extreme circumstances and his loyalty to the firm. On the morning of Tuesday, September 23, Trott called Buffett, who said that if we were looking for capital, he, Buffett, was interested. During that call, I was on my way down to Washington and got a message en route: CALL WARREN. As soon as I arrived at our DC office, I did.

Buffett does business in a way only he can pull off: a fair offer, no negotiation, that's it. With Warren, you get one shot. If he doesn't like your proposal, or you don't like his, it's over. He proposed putting $5 billion into the firm as preferred stock, which is really more like a loan, with a 10 percent dividend and ten-year warrants to buy an additional $5 billion of shares at the current price—$115. It was expensive capital, but reasonable under those market conditions. I started talking to him about how we would execute his investment and was about to go over some open questions.

Warren interrupted me. "That's all fine," he said. "I trust you. I'm taking my grandson to Dairy Queen."

"Maybe it's the lawyer in me," I said, "but I feel I should tell you some of the things I'm nervous about."

"You can worry for the both of us," he said. "You don't need to tell me."

"I'd feel better if you at least had someone talk to my CFO."

"Lloyd, for Berkshire, five billion dollars isn't even a couple of hurricanes on the East Coast," he said. "Let's just chat at the market close and establish the strike price for the warrants. And just one other condition. I don't want you, Viniar, Cohn, or Winkelried to sell any of your stock until I exercise my warrants."

"I'll get everyone to sign an agreement," I said.

"I don't need anything in writing—just your word."

Done. Elapsed time from Trott's call to consummation: five hours, during which Buffett was mostly engaged with his grandson, not Goldman. We spoke again at 4:00 p.m. to confirm before the announcement. The terms were attractive for Berkshire—a 10 percent yield and a ten-year option on the additional shares. As soon as we announced it, the stock price shot up into the $130s in after-hours trading.

> 9/23/2008: *This is Lloyd on Tuesday afternoon. I am currently in Washington, DC. . . . I am pleased to inform you that Berkshire Hathaway is to invest $5 billion in Goldman Sachs in the form of perpetual preferred stock by way of a private offering. I am also happy to advise that Goldman Sachs is raising at least $2.5 billion in common equity in a public offering. . . . This expression of confidence in Goldman Sachs by Warren Buffett, coupled with the support of other institutional investors, will further bolster our strong capitalization and our liquidity position and will enhance our ability to continue to take advantage of opportunities that exist in these difficult markets.*

I started hearing immediately from other investors, who called to say they would have given us capital for a lower price. *But with you, it's just money,* I said. No one other than Warren could have given us an equivalent confidence boost. Or, by doing a deal with us, enabled us to sell common equity to other investors at a higher price rather than a steep discount. Given the demand, we decided to double the amount of our planned offering to $5 billion, and eventually to $5.75 billion. We were able to do it at $123, rather than at a discount to our pre-Berkshire investment share price, which had fallen as low at $86 five days earlier. By the end of the day, the order book for our offering was so oversubscribed that we could have accepted $20 billion. For Goldman, at least, the capital markets were back open. The better terms on the common equity we raised offset the high cost of Berkshire's terms. The market, in effect, paid Buffett's premium. It was good value all around.

Buffett's support for Goldman and for me personally didn't end with his investment. He visited our trading floors and shook hands and took pictures with our people. Buffett had just bought Burlington Northern, so he asked a group of people what they thought of railroads. I interjected that some people think that on Wall Street, we use *railroad* as a verb.

Buffett made a presentation to the partners about his history with the firm, including a picture of the trade ticket from his purchase of Ford Motor Company stock at its 1956 IPO, which Goldman led. He delivered strong positive comments about Goldman at his 2010 shareholders' meeting in Omaha. I am not suggesting Buffett was intending to endorse us to the world or to take sides in any of the issues in which we found ourselves enveloped. Rather, he purposefully provided a big morale boost to the firm at a time when it was at its lowest. That was probably as valuable to us as his capital.

A couple of weeks later, Morgan Stanley reached a deal with Mitsubishi, a large Japanese bank, which agreed to invest $9 billion. But following the announcement, Morgan Stanley's stock continued to fall and Mitsubishi may have been disinclined to complete the deal at the agreed price. Paulson played a big role in getting them to close the deal, but I never asked how he did it. Because it was finalized on a holiday when banks were closed, the Japanese had to deliver a physical check. It wasn't one of those huge display checks that officials like to present on an easel at press conferences. It was a normal-sized check—for $9 billion.

BEFORE WE COULD BE EFFECTIVE HELPING OTHERS, WE EACH HAD TO get control of ourselves and stabilize the firm. This is like the instructions a flight attendant gives in an emergency: When the oxygen masks drop down, put yours on first before you help your kids with theirs. That flight attendant has to project calm to frightened passengers during turbulence—regardless of whether he or she really feels it. Through the whole period, I was meeting with clients and doing my best to be reassuring. Everything would be fine, I told them, and I believed it. And as we raised capital for ourselves, we did the same for many of our clients, including financial institutions that lacked our capital markets presence.

It has been said that because I'm good in crises, I go out of my way to create them. That's not quite the case, but I did have psychological mechanisms that helped me cope with that tremendous stress over a period of years. Sometimes I visualized myself engaged in some kind of medieval combat. Get up, face the enemy, fight till the sun goes down, return home exhausted, and dress my wounds. Repeat again and again, until one day I go out and there's no one left to face.... I've run out of enemies.

For whatever reason, I never had trouble falling asleep during the crisis. I would get home, open the door to the apartment, say hi to Laura, and leave a trail of clothes leading to my bed, where I'd fall face down, unconscious. I slept like a dead person. It was waking up and getting out of bed in the morning that was the challenge for me.

My lap swimming helped. I usually made time for it in the morning, when I had access to a pool, as I did in New York City and in many of the hotels where I stayed when I traveled. No sprints, just steady, repetitive strokes, zoning out as best I could. For self-hypnosis, I conjured another mental image. I tried to imagine myself as a cork, bobbing in a calm sea.

There were a few mantras I took to repeating:

No choice, no problem. When Laura asks me to choose between two nearly identical paint colors for a wall in our apartment, I freeze. In a major crisis, with nowhere to go but forward, I found decision-making much easier. It might be unpleasant, but it's not a hard choice between survival and ruin.

All you can do is the best you can do. If you leave everything on the field, with nothing left to give, then you never have to second-guess yourself.

If not me, then who? Might as well be me. Should you find yourself faced with monumental judgments at a critical moment, you might wish you were somewhere else, and that someone better suited was in your place. Well, guess what? They're not coming, but you are there. And who knows if someone else would be better anyway?

These were like swing thoughts that you tick through as you're lining up to hit your drive in golf: little sayings that keep the yips at bay and help you focus on what you're doing.

In a funny way, 2008 was the easiest time to manage people at the firm. Everyone was scared and not thinking so much of their self-interest. And even if they thought about it, they didn't have the nerve to lobby for it. Members of our senior executive team, including Gary Cohn, David Viniar, Greg Palm, Esta Stecher, John Rogers, Tim O'Neill, and a dozen others, were terrific, as were many more of the firm's rank and file. Some people who didn't look sturdy enough to walk up a flight of stairs performed magnificently. They went days without sleep and without complaint.

On the other hand, some guys who reveled in their toughness panicked. Jon Winkelried, our co-COO, was clearly struggling with the stress. Winks haunting the halls of the thirtieth floor with a ghostly pallor was making others even more worried. *I know it's a cliché,* I told him, *but I find if I take deep breaths, it helps.* To try to keep him productively occupied, I asked him to keep our overseas offices informed.

"I wish these windows opened," he apparently told Michael "Woody" Sherwood, the head of our European operations. "If they did, I'd jump."

That prompted a call to me from Woody. "It might be better if Winks didn't call us anymore," he said.

> 9/26/2008: This is Lloyd Blankfein on Friday evening. It has been quite a week. . . . I know some of you have general questions about our new structure, as well as specific questions about how these relate to your businesses. We have made it a priority to communicate with you as much as possible with relevant information and will continue to do that. But I want to remind you that none of these events or actions of the past week change the fundamentals of Goldman Sachs. In fact, it is the preservation of those things that most clearly define us—our culture, our people, and our strategy—which guides everything we do. . . . I hope you all get some rest this weekend.

On Monday, September 29, Congress rejected TARP, Treasury's plan for a $700 billion government fund to buy toxic assets. The Dow dropped 777 points and continued to swing wildly all that week.

> 10/02/2008: *This is Lloyd. Today I'm in California, meeting with several clients.... In the near term, much of the focus will be on the US Congress. The Senate passed the Emergency Economic Stabilization Act on Wednesday evening, and the House of Representatives is expected to vote on Friday. Until then, and probably for some time after, I anticipate that we will see continued volatility in global markets.*

A second plan—TARP II—was built around a capital infusion into the largest banks and financial institutions. The government would purchase preferred shares—essentially making loans to major financial institutions. Congress passed it the next day, October 3. But it didn't stem the panic, which was spreading brutally though European economies. On Friday, October 10, stock markets crashed across Europe and Asia. London, Paris, Frankfurt, and New York all dropped 10 percent within an hour of opening. It was the worst week for the S&P 500 since the crash of 1929. Our stock, which had traded in the mid-$200s a year earlier, fell to $86.

Barred from selling any stock because of the agreement with Buffett, Jon Winkelried put his Nantucket house on the market for $55 million. What kind of confidence signal was that? It obviously wasn't an opportune time for a real estate transaction, but it was indicative of his state of mind. "I have a fiduciary duty to my family," he said. Like Steve Friedman in 1994, Winks couldn't handle the pressure. He told me he wanted to leave the firm. *Don't leave now*, I told him. *That would look pretty bad. Just stop coming to the office and then leave when things settle down.* Steve Friedman recounted his own 1994 experience to Winks to try to settle him down, but it didn't help.

> 10/10/2008: *This is Lloyd on Friday afternoon in New York. As you know, we continue to deal with extreme market volatility. There have been steep declines in equity markets around the globe—especially in financials and in our own share price. Governments have intervened in the markets in the United States and Europe—including a globally coordinated central bank rate cut announced on Wednesday. Markets are at a point of fragility, but we are seeing strong action each day from governments, which are clearly committed to help stem this crisis. . . . It has been another challenging week. I want to thank you for all the work you have done to meet those challenges on behalf of our clients and the firm.*

On Sunday night, nine of us bank CEOs were summoned for another secretive meeting at the Treasury Department the next day. It was the weekend of the World Bank annual meetings, so most of us were in Washington anyway. Monday was Columbus Day, as we used to call it, and the banks were closed. No one knew what to expect as we were ushered into the ornate Victorian conference room behind the secretary's office. The heavy yellow curtains were drawn.

We were seated around a long table. Paulson began and explained that the Treasury was going to inject $125 billion into our institutions. Geithner spoke next and informed us of our prescribed amounts. Goldman was asked to take $10 billion. Sheila Bair, the chair of the FDIC, scowled at us bankers. Ben Bernanke was expressionless as usual and said little. (Fun fact: Bernanke and I were classmates and housemates in college. But it wasn't the time and he wasn't the guy to break into a chorus of "Fair Harvard.")

At that point, Goldman didn't need or want the capital. We'd gotten the Buffett infusion and raised $5 billion in common equity—and could have upsized that if we wanted to. Buffett later testified to the Financial Crisis Inquiry Commission that he wouldn't have invested in Goldman Sachs if he thought that we needed government money.

But we weren't being asked whether we needed it. They were going to announce the capital infusion that day, and no one was going to leave the building without signing a letter of intent to accept it. Dick Kovacevich of Wells Fargo, which was being given $25 billion, was the most resistant. Vikram Pandit of Citi, also the recipient of $25 billion, was the most enthusiastic. John Thain, whose Merrill Lynch was about to be acquired by Bank of America, took the occasion to ask about executive compensation. Ken Lewis, his soon-to-be boss, shut that topic down.

Ever the lawyer, I said that because this was a capital raise, I needed board approval.

Fine, Hank said, *go to another room and call your board. Take as long as you need. But no one's leaving the building until they sign the letter of intent.*

I did just that. I called John Rogers, who was secretary to the Goldman board, among his many other responsibilities, and asked him to convene the board on a conference call—and to make sure we had a quorum. *Look*, I said on the call an hour later, *I know I'm catching everyone flat-footed. We can weigh the pros and cons and talk about it as long as you want. But we're doing this, and I'd like your quick approval so I can leave the room where I'm being held hostage.* They all agreed.

Walking out of the Treasury after several hours was like stumbling out of a casino where it's all artificial lighting, no windows, and no clocks. I didn't know if it was going to be day or night. There was still some daylight, it turned out.

> 10/14/2008: *Today the United States Treasury announced several programs aimed at stabilizing financial institutions, unfreezing credit markets, and stimulating economic growth. You will learn more about the details of these programs in the next few days, but I want to highlight the cornerstone of the Treasury's plan: the Capital Purchase Program. Under this voluntary program, the US government will buy preferred stock in a broad number of financial institutions.... Goldman Sachs is one of nine major financial institutions to announce its participation in the program.*

HOW TO SURVIVE A CRISIS

ON THE THIRTY-NINTH DAY OF THE FORTY-DAY BIBLICAL FLOOD, IT WAS still raining, and it must have seemed like it would never end.

A SHORT TIME AFTER THE MEETING AT THE FED IN WASHINGTON, WE announced a 10 percent staff reduction to reduce costs in the face of the market weakness. Our stock was still dropping, to less than $50 in November, not because investors were still worried about solvency but because with the imposition of government controls, it looked to some like it would be hard for us to ever make money again. This was below Goldman Sachs's IPO price of $53 almost ten years earlier. I did my best to convince people that we'd entered an upside-down bubble, a wide pendulum swing in the opposite direction. Those able to think rationally about valuations reaped the benefit when the overwhelming force of mean reversion asserted itself.

It was getting close to November, and it was time for our normal year-end processes, like compensation. Under the circumstances, I wasn't going to take any bonus for the year. Our NEO team—the named executive officers—came to me and said they wanted to decline bonuses too. I argued with them. *It's a great gesture, and I appreciate it,* I said. But the world outside Goldman was focused on me, not them. It wouldn't comfort markets. Even though we were going to lose some money in the fourth quarter of 2008, we'd still made a sizable profit for the year—albeit a smaller one than our recent string of records. In the end I agreed, and we didn't pay bonuses to the senior officers. We paid bonuses to others at Goldman, much smaller than in other years, based on our diminished profitability. Many commentators thought it was a crime to pay anyone in banking anything ever again. It just wasn't practical to comply with that suggestion. We needed to keep our team intact.

> 11/16/2008: *There can be no doubt that these are difficult times for everyone—for every country, for every company, and for every*

> family. While reduced compensation will be in order this year, all of us who work at Goldman Sachs are very fortunate. In recognition of this, the senior management team proposed to our board that it not grant any discretionary bonus this year to me, Jon, Gary, Mike Evans, Michael Sherwood, John Weinberg, and David Viniar. We are pleased the board has fully endorsed this proposal.

Among those outraged that bankers were paying themselves anything was our incoming president, Barack Obama. At that point, we were symbols. There was a powerful narrative about reckless behavior on Wall Street, and the argument that Goldman was in a different position couldn't be won with facts.

But I can't hold a grudge, at least not for long. During the financial crisis, whenever someone was mean or hypercritical of us, I would cross them off my list. After two months, I had no one left to talk to, so I changed my policy. If anyone said mean things about us three times, I crossed them off. When again I had no one left, I decided not to keep a list.

Steve Friedman and Bob Rubin, co-senior partners who got along well.

Hank Paulson and Jon Corzine, co-senior partners who did not get along so well.

With Hank and John Thain, during John's and my very brief run as co-COOs and copresidents.

Hank and his sole president and COO, me.

Successive Goldman Sachs senior partners going back to John Whitehead, third from left, who joined the firm in 1947 and became co–senior partner with John Weinberg in 1976 after the sudden death of Gus Levy. Whitehead died in 2015, not long after this picture was taken.

The Blankfeins in Shanghai, after a Goldman Sachs board meeting. Left to right: Jonathan, Rachel, Laura, and Alex.

Warren Buffet's contribution to Goldman Sachs went beyond his small (for him) preferred stock investment. His presentation to our partner group and his walks around the trading floor provided a big morale boost during the global financial crisis.

Bank CEOs on one side, President Obama and his team on the other, working through issues in the Roosevelt Room during the global financial crisis.

A member of the Lloyd Blankfein fan club at an Occupy Wall Street protest.

Testifying before the Senate Permanent Subcommittee on Investigations, not as much fun as it looks. I was examined for hours on the stack of documents, which I wasn't given until I took my seat.

Another hearing on the mortgage crisis, featuring the major bank CEOs.

With Gary Cohn, who was president and COO for most of my tenure as CEO.

Laying sandbags ahead of Hurricane Sandy was another exercise in risk management.

Lower Manhattan skyline during the hurricane. Guess which is our building? One widely viewed tweet conveyed the photo with the caption: GOLDMAN TO GOD: NICE TRY.

Laura and me walking into the White House for a state dinner honoring Chinese Premier Hu Jintao. It was a long way from the Brooklyn projects.

Laughs with Cardinal Dolan, who I hosted for one of many Talks@GS, a regular interview series with a wide range of guests.

Working through chemo.

With David Solomon and Harvey Schwartz, my copresidents, co-COOs, and cocandidates to succeed me. The hairstyle was not a stated job requirement.

Feeling liberated after turning things over to David.

CHAPTER 24

How Did You Do It?

I was asked by CNBC if I was concerned about an angry mob storming my residence. No, I responded. I have a doorman.

No one sent out a memo announcing the end of the financial crisis—and markets remained extraordinarily volatile into the new year. But as 2009 began and Barack Obama was inaugurated, no other shoes dropped. In February, we successfully sold $2 billion in ten-year notes—our first credit offering since before the crisis. We represented Pfizer on its $68 billion acquisition of Wyeth and provided significant financing for the transaction. We advised on Genentech's $47 billion sale to Roche and Time Warner's $47 billion spin-off of Time Warner Cable. In the first quarter of 2009, the firm returned to profitability—it would be another record year. Slowly, our business seemed to be reestablishing some kind of normality.

As the acute danger subsided, Goldman was widely seen as a positive exception, a glowing example. The firm had managed its risk, hedged itself properly, and had not lost money while other firms lost tens of billions. If others had managed their risk the way we did, there would have been no banking crisis. There still would have been plenty of mortgage defaults, of course. But the losses wouldn't have upended secondary institutions that weren't mortgage lenders themselves. The crisis wouldn't have spread to Europe and beyond. We might have avoided the long recession with all of its awful effects on people.

Recessions have many causes. But a recession that is caused or accompanied by a banking crisis can be especially long and brutal. The reason for that is that government monetary policy works through the intermediate instrument of the private-sector banking system. The Fed can lower the cost of credit by taking rates down, but it doesn't directly lend to businesses or consumers. Banks do. If the banks are impaired, they accumulate capital to repair their balance sheets instead of lending. That makes the recovery slower and more difficult.

> 2/8/2009: *Over the course of the past several months, I have given much thought to what precipitated the financial crisis. I've had conversations with many of you about your perspectives, as well as with our board, investors, and clients. Many of the conversations revolved around the important lessons we should take away from this extraordinary period. . . . I do want to emphasize one point. As a firm, we certainly didn't get everything right. At the same time, our focus on risk management, our commitment to the rigors of mark to market accounting, and the importance we place on operations and technology are largely responsible for the continued strength of our franchise.*

In our 2008 annual report, released a few months later, I elaborated on my view:

> Risk management will come to define the events of 2008 and beyond. Our firm certainly didn't get everything right and there are some decisions we would prefer to take back, but how we dealt with potentially large exposures, our fair value accounting discipline and the independence of our risk management function were reinforcing for the firm in 2008.
>
> First, we sought to ensure that our exposures weren't outsized

in the first place, and worked to reduce such exposures whenever it was possible and made sense to do so.

Second, we have heard some argue that fair value accounting—which assigns current market values to financial assets and liabilities—is one of the major reasons for exacerbating the credit crisis. We see it differently. The proper valuation of assets and liabilities, of positions and commitments, is essential if risk is to be managed effectively.

For Goldman Sachs, the daily marking of positions to current market prices was a key contributor to our decision to reduce risk relatively early in markets and in instruments that were deteriorating. This process can be difficult, and sometimes painful, but we believe it is a discipline that should define financial institutions.

Lastly, we place great importance in the independence of risk and control functions. Just as important, risk managers have at least equal stature with their counterparts in producing divisions. If there is a question about a mark or a disagreement about a risk limit, the risk manager's view prevails.

The other crucial point, it seemed to me, was about culture and the legacy of the partnership. A sense of the firm's history and its continuities was uppermost in our thinking. I wasn't a founder of Goldman Sachs, obviously, or a creator of our culture. But I was an appreciator and maintainer of it. And in that, I was far from alone. With the exception of Jon Winkelried, no senior leader left during the crisis. And as I'd told everyone would happen, a new generation of senior leaders at the firm was forged in the crisis. That included David Solomon, Stephen Scherr, and Ashok Varadhan.

I was proud too of the role Goldman Sachs alumni played in solving the crisis. Paulson's role may never be properly appreciated. As bad as things got, the threat of systemic collapse was still the nuclear bomb that gets defused just in the nick of time in a James Bond movie. Because the bomb in those movies never goes off, the world never knows how close it came to Armageddon. Hank and Tim Geithner—who, contrary to legend, never worked for us—were surrounded by others who earned their stripes at Goldman: Bob Steel, Neel Kashkari, Dan Jester, Steven Shafran, and Kendrick Wilson. Ed Forst, formerly head of GSAM, helped Hank set up the Office of Financial Stability, tasked with overseeing the purchase of toxic assets under TARP II. Kashkari, a former Goldman technology banker who worked closely with Paulson at Treasury through the crisis, was put in charge of it. In the Bush White House, Chief of Staff Josh Bolten, yet another Goldman alum, was crucial in getting the president to support Paulson's recommendations. As the contagion spread, Italy's Central Bank governor and later prime minister Mario Draghi, a former Goldman managing director, played a pivotal role in ending the eurozone phase of the crisis. Another Goldman alum, Mark Carney, who became governor of Canada's central bank in the midst of the crisis, and later Prime Minister of Canada, was an important figure as well.

I often heard the term *Government Sachs* used as a pejorative—as if these former Goldman people, after they left, were somehow continuing to prioritize the interests of the firm. Nothing could have been further from the truth. Other firms hire *from* government to enhance their prestige and relationships. In Goldman's case, alumni for the most part join the government after leaving the firm, and they almost never return. It's not a revolving door. In my experience, everyone in government and at Goldman was exquisitely sensitive to the perception of special treatment and did everything to avoid there being any question about it. If anything, the connection meant that Goldman was excluded from the possibility of government guarantees of the kind that J.P. Morgan obtained for its purchase of Bear Stearns. I thought this was the moment when our commitment to public service mattered the most.

WE PAID THE GOVERNMENT BACK WITH SUBSTANTIAL INTEREST BY summer. As the urgency of the crisis diminished, at least in the United

States, the press was full of admiration for what we, alone among Wall Street firms, had done. The cover of *Bloomberg Markets* magazine: RESCUING GOLDMAN: LLOYD BLANKFEIN HAS SAVED HIS FIRM—FOR NOW. I was the *Financial Times* Person of the Year. It was recognition, the *FT* wrote, "that Mr. Blankfein and his bank have taken the leading place in the world of finance, while others have fallen by the wayside." I was in the *Time* 100, with a capsule written by the economic populist Robert Reich, who called me the "smiling Buddha sitting in the center of the simmering heap of Wall Street." On *Vanity Fair*'s New Establishment List, I leaped to number one, ahead of Steve Jobs, Jeff Bezos, and Warren Buffett. "It's hard to imagine another financial institution that has weathered the economic crisis quite the way Goldman Sachs has," the squib read.

You get the idea. Honestly, the praise just made me nervous. And for good reason. If the first half of 2009 was the "How did you do it?" period, we were about to transition to the *"How did you do it!"* phase of the crisis. Admiration was quickly curdling into hostility.

The epitome of the thinking in this period was a now-famous screed published in July 2009 in *Rolling Stone* that called Goldman Sachs a "giant vampire squid wrapped around the face of humanity." That article went on to blame Goldman for everything from the Great Depression in the 1930s to continuing high gas prices. At first, I thought it was so over the top that I didn't take it seriously. But it fed into all of the conspiracy theories that were swirling around.

I remember traveling to Paris around that time for my semiannual tour of French clients. I went to see Patrick Kron, the CEO of Alstom, an industrial manufacturer of trains and subway cars. "Welcome," he said, putting out his hand as I walked into his office. "The man who brought AIDS to the world!" He meant the financial crisis—had I really come to stand in for the whole catastrophe? I smiled and shook his hand. There was nothing to do but put on a happy face, show up at meetings, and carry on.

One sign of the turn was the interview I did with *The Sunday Times* of London that fall. I knew I was in trouble when the reporter sat down and began by asking me how much my necktie cost. It was an Hermès tie with bicycles on it—the kind John Baity had told me to wear back in my early days as a law associate. My daughter had given it to me as a birthday present.

The next day, I saw the British reporter in the waiting area outside my office, where he was interviewing some others at the firm. He said he had just a few more questions for me. Not breaking stride, I joked that I couldn't stop to talk to him because I was in a hurry, "off doing God's work." You could call it a Lloydian slip. I'd forgotten the advice from my handlers: *Remember, Lloyd, whatever you do, don't be yourself.*

In the piece, the reporter treated it as an ecclesiastical statement as opposed to a brush-off. When the story came out, that comment overshadowed everything else in his seven-thousand-word article, though there was plenty more: "Talking to him is like talking to a man who has greenbacks, not blood, running through his veins." There was plenty more where that came from. On its cover, *New York* magazine asked, IS GOLDMAN SACHS EVIL?

At least, I thought, *I'm getting higher name recognition with people who hate me.* It was tempting to fight back against attacks in the press, but I knew that it wouldn't help. I understood that the reporters had a job to do, and that the press's currency is to challenge and, if possible, bring down people in power. To defend yourself, don't argue. If you want to hurt a reporter, ignore him. If you really want to hurt him, indicate that you're unaware of his work. *Oh, are you still writing? I didn't know you were. You haven't written anything in a long time, have you?*

But by 2010, we were the scapegoat, to the point where it was painful to open up a newspaper. In the mob, the wiseguys get their wives to start the car in the morning. I had my wife go out and read the morning papers first, then tell me what was safe to read.

WHAT DID CRITICS THINK WE'D DONE WRONG? ONE LINE OF CRITICISM focused on repayments we'd received from the government as part of its bailout of AIG. There was a baseless suspicion that having so many highly placed alumni had somehow resulted in AIG being bailed out for the benefit of Goldman or gotten us some other kind of special treatment. Everyone was looking for a smoking gun indicating that Hank Paulson had saved AIG at our behest. Of course he hadn't. The reason to rescue AIG was the impact a default would have had on nearly every company in America. Goldman might even have been unique in not being materially at risk from an AIG default. Thanks to our aggressive collateral calls and CDS insurance, we were largely protected. In any case, we didn't lobby anyone.

There were good journalists who took the time to understand this. Andrew Ross Sorkin of *The New York Times* dug deeply into the matter. After reviewing emails and documents, he wrote, "The Fed believed Goldman was hedged the day it saved A.I.G." And was the Fed right? "By the calculations of the documents released Friday, Goldman had hedged its $2.5 billion exposure with somewhere from $2.375 billion to $2.5 billion on the other side, meaning it was pretty close to being fully hedged, with a little bit of wiggle room on either side of those numbers."

Another charge was that we'd designed mortgage products to fail. The accusation focused on a mortgage derivative product with the catchy name ABACUS 2007-AC1. We'd had put it together at the behest of John Paulson, a hedge fund investor who wanted to bet against the housing market. Paulson shorted ABACUS by entering into credit default swaps that would pay off if certain subprime securities failed. We found counterparties who wanted to go long those riskier mortgages. These were institutional buyers of that type of risk. When securities included in ABACUS did fail as a result of the subprime meltdown, Paulson made billions on his CDS and the counterparties that wrote insurance—the bond insurer ACA and two European investment firms—lost money.

In January 2010, I was called to testify at the first public hearing of the Financial Crisis Inquiry Commission, a panel appointed by Congress to investigate the causes of the financial crisis. I appeared along with Jamie Dimon, John Mack, and Brian Moynihan, the CEO of Bank of America. Phil Angelides, the former state treasurer of California, chaired the hearing and went after me straightaway. "It sounds to me like you're selling someone a car with faulty brakes and then buying an insurance policy on that car that pays you when it crashes," he said, referring to the ABACUS transaction.

I'm not sure Angelides quite understood how finance works. If you're a market maker, you often hold an interest in opposition to the performance of the securities you sell. But our goal wasn't to make a bet on the security ourselves. We were intermediating between sophisticated market professionals, one side that wanted to be long mortgage risk and another that wanted to be short. The security was not marketed to the public. Unless we did something to cause those mortgages to fail, which of course we didn't, we were simply a seller of a legitimate financial product that some investors wanted to bet on and others wanted to bet against. Goldman itself lost a significant sum on the deal because we were left with some of the ABACUS long.

In the punitive postcrisis atmosphere, however, that kind of intermediation looked more sinister. In mid-April 2010, the SEC voted 3–2 to bring a civil charge against us for misleading statements related to the ABACUS placement. The case focused on the actions of Fabrice Tourre, a twenty-eight-year-old French trader based in London who was accused of misleading ACA into thinking that John Paulson was long rather than short on the securities underlying ABACUS.

> 4/16/2010: *This is Lloyd on Friday evening in New York. As you know, today the US Securities and Exchange Commission brought a civil action against Goldman Sachs on a specific transaction. As we have made clear in our press releases and our internal announcements, these charges are completely unfounded, and we will vigorously contest them.*

"Fabulous Fab," as the media called him, had written a lot of braggy emails to his girlfriend, touting his supposed exploits. He facetiously boasted that he had sold complex mortgage derivatives to "widows and orphans that I ran into at the airport." Those emails fueled a full-blown media circus. Fabulous Fab was at the center of a media feeding frenzy—a new cover culprit for the *New York Post*. And a brief respite for me, as I appeared so often in caricature in that paper that I referred to it as "the Daily Tab-Lloyd."

> 4/25/2010: *This is Lloyd on Sunday. As many of you know, I will be testifying before the United States Permanent Subcommittee on Investigations, the PSI, on Tuesday in Washington, DC. David Viniar and others from Goldman Sachs will also be testifying. . . . Many of you have asked in earnest what you can do to be helpful. My answer is the same as it has been over the past week: Continue to stay focused on your area of responsibility, and especially on delivering the very best service to our clients. I appreciate your support for all of us, and we look forward to doing our very best to represent you well on Tuesday.*

I went to Washington that month to testify the way the ruler of Gaul went to Rome after Caesar's conquest—in chains in a cage. Seven of us from Goldman, including Fabulous Fab, were subpoenaed. The Senate Permanent Subcommittee on Investigations is best known as the vehicle Senator Joe McCarthy used to slander and browbeat alleged communists in the 1950s. With its broad mandate to "investigate inefficiency, mismanagement, and corruption in Government," the PSI still specializes in show trials. When it devoted a day to interrogating Goldman Sachs, the world was watching.

In the morning, the chairman, Carl Levin of Michigan, began the hearing by accusing Goldman of unethical behavior and dishonesty. "The firm's own documents show that while it was marketing risky mortgage-related securities, it was placing large bets against the U.S. mortgage market," he declared, glowering down from his elevated platform. "The firm has repeatedly denied making those large bets despite overwhelming evidence that they did so."

I finally came on at 7:00 p.m. and read my prepared statement. Code Pink protesters were seated behind me, wearing striped prison jumpsuits and waving signs saying SHAME. I'd always liked European history and couldn't help identifying with the French aristocrats being led to the guillotine (soon to be followed by the insufficiently radical leaders of the revolution themselves). A mass of news photographers was spread out on the floor between me and the senators, trying to catch any scowl or unflattering gesture. Goldman was meant to epitomize everything that was wrong with American finance, capitalism, and the economy. A decade or two earlier, if someone had told me I would one day become a symbol of the failures of market capitalism, I would have laughed out loud.

Senator Levin pressed his contention that we had taken a large short position on the mortgage market and tried to trick clients into taking the other side. He had big display charts showing our short positions and profits on them in isolation. I kept explaining, as Viniar had in the morning, that our goal was to limit our exposure in either direction. We had traders who were long and wanted to be longer and traders who were short and wanted to be shorter. We kept the firm as a whole "close to home." You couldn't look at our short bets against the mortgage market without looking at our offsetting long bets on the mortgage market. In issuing ABACUS and other mortgage derivatives, we were acting as an intermediary, not an adviser with a fiduciary obligation to clients.

Levin, of course, knew all of this. He was as smart as senators come. But facts weren't going to divert him from his political agenda. That agenda was to prepare the way for stringent new legislation restricting the financial sector. I would support much of that regulation, but I didn't think it should be predicated on a distorted account of Goldman's practices and role in the crisis. We went round and round, late into the evening.

After the hearing finally finished around 9:00 p.m., I went to the Capitol rotunda and did something like a dozen fifteen-minute interviews with different TV networks and financial broadcasters.

> 4/27/2010: This is Lloyd on Tuesday evening in Washington, DC. . . . As anticipated, the questioning during the hearing was rigorous, but we tried to remain focused on providing a complete context of our business, how we manage our risk, and the value we provide for our clients and to the broader system. In those instances where the subcommittee raised questions about ethics, we tried to convey the seriousness with which we adhere to the rules and regulations that govern our business, as well as the letter and spirit of our own business principles.

When that was done, it was time to drive back to New York City—it was too late for the shuttle or a train. I hadn't eaten all day and was feeling pretty miserable. When we stopped for gas on the Baltimore-Washington Parkway, I bought a hot dog that must been have been rotating in the display case for weeks.

"If you eat that, you're going to die," my driver said.

"Good," I said. "I really don't care at this point."

THROUGH THIS PERIOD, I WAS PERFORMING MY NORMAL DUTIES, LIKE managing the firm and our people; monitoring the balance sheet and risk; and pitching for business. But the moment was far from normal. The economy was recessionary and markets were skittish. The press was brutal and constant. Every major journal with a business section had reporters assigned to write about us almost daily. With all of that happening in the background, it became more important than ever for me to get on a horse and continually visit clients. I needed to get in front of them to defend our reputation, which was under constant assault.

The horse was a Gulfstream jet. Not Goldman's own but NetJets'. (We were the rare large company that didn't own our own plane.) The reader should not infer luxury. The privacy and flexibility afforded by private air travel translated into the reality of work the entire flight, airport showers, no downtime between meetings, and sometimes the disorienting experience of having breakfast, lunch, and dinner in three separate cities.

By this time I was nearly always accompanied by Russell Horwitz, a partner who ran the executive office with John Rogers and had previously worked on economic policy in the Clinton White House. Russell managed my briefing materials, shuffled memos requesting approvals for this and that, and brought up issues you wouldn't find in memos. He ferreted out information about what was going on at the firm that would have been hard for me to get on my own, and he conveyed it to me. Other partners regarded him as an honest broker and trustworthy confidential conduit.

CEOs of global firms travel a lot and at times run their firms from airplanes—no big deal. In those days, the toughest part of it for me was that planes didn't have internet access. Being out of touch for large blocks of time—as much as twelve or more hours on long flights to Asia—was a significant source of anxiety. People complain about being oppressed by the way that cell phones, texts, and email make them reachable 100 percent of the time. I had precisely the opposite feeling. For me, the biggest source of stress was being incommunicado while traveling—wondering if I was needed and couldn't be reached. What could happen in twelve hours in a risk-intensive business that's constantly getting bashed in the press? I dreaded the inevitable deluge of texts and emails that would flood in just as we were touching down. I find it liberating that planes now have internet. If the phone doesn't ring, it means there's no trouble looking for you.

Despite all of this stress—much of it inflicted on my travel companion, Russell—I don't know that we lost any business in that difficult period. Of course, you never hear the phone that doesn't ring, so you can't be sure. But our market shares stayed up.

BEFORE OCCUPY WALL STREET, THERE WAS OCCUPY LLOYD'S APARTment building. One evening, Laura and I were being dropped off at home after dinner. My driver got a call warning him that there was a larger-than-usual group of protesters outside the entrance on Central Park West. He suggested that we go through the garage.

Okay, I said, *let's go in through the garage.*

Laura turned to me and said, *We are not going in through the garage.* Unsaid, but hanging in the air, was a rebuke: *Man up!*

Thanks, Laura. She was right. I had plenty of occasion thereafter to reflect on being at the receiving end of so much public and political fury. Part of me thought, *Why us? We got things right, or at least righter than anyone else.* Well, the captain of a ship will be fired if the ship bumps into something, even if the captain isn't at fault—for example, if he was sleeping after working hours and another officer was on deck. It may be unfair to the individual captain, who didn't do anything wrong. But from the example, captains sleep less, and the world benefits from their insomnia. I consoled myself that there was a social good that flowed from my public flogging.

Laura and I managed to live close to normal lives, that is, as normal as life was inside the green zone around the American embassy in Kabul. There were the expected death threats, naturally. Goldman security didn't think our doorman was quite fierce enough, so they had a couple of off-duty cops sit in a car outside my apartment building when I was in New York City and trail me at a distance as I walked around town. (I live in an apartment building with many hedge fund managers, and I was amazed that I could have more enemies than they did.) Similarly, off-duty Southampton cops sat outside my Hamptons house 24-7, a discreet distance down the road from my driveway. Mail got to me days late as every letter and package sent to me was X-rayed. Such extreme precautions began in mid-2010 and lasted for about three years. When the cops stopped watching my house in the Hamptons, my neighbors were disappointed. The block was losing the free security service they had gotten used to.

Given my eventful tenure at Goldman, my skin was pretty thick. Laura's too. But not necessarily that of my kids, who suffered from seeing their father bashed in congressional hearings and in the press. Alex was working, but Jonathan was still in college. *Blankfein* is a pretty distinctive name; no way to hide from the connection. Rachel was in ninth grade. She attended the Fieldston School, which is probably the most progressive school in New York City. Progressive means that big contributors to the school were resented for having the capacity to contribute to the school. Rachel's fellow students were supportive of her, but a few of the teachers showed their biases. At least one made nasty comments about Wall Street and me in classes that Rachel and her friends were in. We complained to the administration, but nothing happened. And Laura was chair of the board! Needless to say, my grandkids go to a different school.

Goldman Sachs was easy quarry. Our people made too much money, our alumni popped up in high-profile positions, and as a wholesale firm we had no consumer business and hence no relationship with the broad public. Most people didn't have any idea what we did. While the world and most other firms were suffering, it looked like we'd sailed through the crisis with barely a scratch. That put a big, fat bull's-eye on our backs.

Firms that had gone under or lost billions of dollars were less useful as targets. The press and politicians sometimes seemed unable to decide whether the banks were stupid for getting caught by the mortgage-credit bubble or too clever by half for trying to profit by causing it. The banks that were big losers clearly were not at risk of being thought too clever, so that left stupid. But stupidity is not a crime; in fact, it can be a defense. Criminality requires intent, and intent means you knew what you were doing. That's why the claim that Goldman was deviously and deliberately shorting toxic securities was so important to Senator Levin's narrative. The fact that our gains and losses roughly netted out undermined that narrative.

In the end, Goldman agreed to pay a $550 million fine to settle the civil SEC charges. There's no choice in a situation like that. You can't litigate against your regulator. It's like the *Star Trek* episode where an alien occupies the bridge of the starship *Enterprise* and is going to turn off the life support system to the engine room unless the ship surrenders. Dealing with the government, you always settle in the end, even if you think you're right. The consequences of fighting are simply too great.

> 7/15/2010: *This is Lloyd on Thursday in Los Angeles, where I am meeting with clients. Today Goldman Sachs agreed to a settlement with the US Securities and Exchange Commission to resolve the SEC's pending case against the firm relating to disclosures in the ABACUS 2007-AC1 CDO transaction.... In connection with the settlement, the firm did not admit or deny any of the SEC's allegations. We acknowledged, however, that the marketing materials for the transaction mistakenly contained incomplete information concerning the role of Paulson & Co. We regret the mistake, and as part of the settlement, we have committed to the SEC to improve our procedures in this regard.*

WHILE DEALING WITH ALL OF THIS NEGATIVE PUBLICITY I WANTED TO avoid being so defensive that I couldn't think about the ways the firm might need to change. There were important lessons for us in the experience of the crisis. Even if I thought the way the media presented us was distorted, we needed to figure out how to respond substantively to events that had transformed our structure, harmed our reputation, and damaged our internal morale. In what ways could we hold ourselves responsible for inviting such unfair treatment, and how should we change our practices and policies in response?

After the Levin hearing, I named a new business standards committee, cochaired by Gerry Corrigan, a former president of the New York Fed, who joined Goldman Sachs in 1994 to chair our risk committee. The business standards committee was overseen by our board member Bill George, the former CEO of Medtronic. Bill, who a few years earlier published the book *True North*, was highly regarded for his clear thinking about business ethics and leadership. He was deeply engaged, and his contribution to the process was invaluable.

Among the outside luminaries we brought in to help were Arthur

Levitt, the former chair of the SEC, and, as outside counsel, Rodgin Cohen of Sullivan & Cromwell, who represented not only Goldman but also every other major firm on Wall Street—and the New York Fed for good measure. Internally, the committee included some of our other wisest and most trusted figures, John S. Weinberg, John Rogers, and Tim O'Neill. It also included some of our most important future leaders, among them Harvey Schwartz and David Solomon. It was viewed as a very important undertaking, like a constitutional convention, and, this being Goldman Sachs, partners who weren't asked to participate were suicidal. I asked the committee to look at all of the questions swirling around staff training, client relationships, conflicts of interest, and the creation of complex derivatives.

The report that the business standards committee issued seven months later in January 2011, and that we decided to release publicly, amounted to a road map for the firm's recovery and cultural renewal. It made thirty-nine separate recommendations dealing with aspects of client service, complex financial products, transparency, disclosure, employee training, and compensation. That we put our clients' interests first remained at the top of our business principles, which were first enshrined by John Whitehead when he was co-senior partner thirty years earlier. Those fourteen principles remained a kind of holy writ at the firm. But with the growing complexity of our business, we needed to be more explicit and consistent about the many roles we played: adviser, fiduciary, market participant, and underwriter. We needed to be clearer with ourselves and our clients about the capacity in which we were serving and the responsibilities we were assuming. The report called for plain-language explanations to our clients about our own activities.

The report recommended other changes as well. Our balance sheet should show our assets by business unit, as well as our liquidity. In place of our habitual secrecy and avoidance of press, we needed to communicate and disclose more information externally. For me, one of the lessons was that I needed to have a relationship with the public.

In the absence of that relationship, the press and the government were able to define me and put me in the position of having to overcome their version.

Part of the problem was that Goldman Sachs was an institutional firm with no consumer business. As an institutional firm, we wanted our clients forward and ourselves in the background. We never saw value in advertising or promoting ourselves to the public. That turned out to be a big mistake. "Consumers" have other names, like *citizens* and *taxpayers*. Goldman and I were largely unknown to them and not appreciated by them. So we were vulnerable to being defined by Senator Levin and *Rolling Stone*. (Today, would anyone miss that it's my joking style to say, "I'm off to do God's work?") Shame on me and Goldman. My advice to other CEOs: Create opportunities to show who you are and what you stand for. It's not very effective if you wait until there's a crisis to do that.

In terms of management structure, we decided to create a new, firm-wide client and business standards committee that would play a central role in the running of the firm, on par with the firm-wide risk committee. We decided that Gary Cohn should head the new committee, which we tasked with making decisions about reputational risk and client relationships, as well as about particular business practices. I undertook to communicate the message to senior leaders in part through our Chairman's Forum, half-day seminars I led with partners and managing directors. Over the next two years, I led two dozen of those sessions around the world.

The overall thrust running through the recommendations was that reputational risk and consequences needed to become central to our decision-making. "Goldman Sachs has one reputation," the report stated. "It can be affected by any number of decisions and activities across the firm. Every employee has an equal obligation to raise issues or concerns, no matter how small, to protect the firm's reputation. We must ensure that our focus on our reputation is as grounded, consistent, and pervasive as our focus on commercial success." Put another way, we needed to shift our decision-making approach from "Can we?" to "Should we?"

THE FINANCIAL CRISIS INQUIRY COMMISSION ALSO PUBLISHED ITS report in January 2011. The Senate PSI published its 639-page report in April. When it did, Levin said he was referring the testimony to the Department of Justice for possible criminal investigation. In addition to the charge of misleading clients, he claimed that I hadn't been truthful with the committee. Clearly, he was upset that my testimony didn't support his narrative.

A criminal investigation is another level of torment. Multiple times over the next year and a half, I was called in to testify under oath. FBI investigators would pick me up at the office and deliver me into the basement of the US Attorney's office in Lower Manhattan. I tried to engage without counsel, but the prosecutors insisted otherwise. When I hired Reid Weingarten, a renowned Washington criminal defense specialist, the government leaked it to the press, and the report drove our stock price down. People assumed that smoke equaled fire.

When things are going well, you might be lulled into thinking that who you have on your board is not that important beyond the prestige of the names. Boards mostly come into play when replacing a CEO. But during a crisis, who you have on your board becomes critical. Not necessarily their experience of a comparable crisis—in 2008, no one alive had lived through anything comparable to what we went through. What's most needed is calm, clarity, and practical judgment. Ruth Simmons, who was president of Brown, had a better sense than anyone else on our board about how to communicate beyond the business community. Bill George was wise about everything connected to ethics and corporate governance.

A strong board will have a thick skin and focus on what's in the best interests of the company. A weaker board, or weaker board members, can become overwhelmed by concern for their own reputations or potential liability. Our board was steadfast through the crisis, and I appreciated that support. On the one occasion when one of our board members raised the question of whether the board should have its own counsel, John Bryan, our lead director, shot him down. *We're not separating ourselves from management*, he said. I was lucky he did that. Bryan, who had served on the boards of banks and oil companies as well as universities, museums, and civic organizations in Chicago, had enough experience to know that retaining separate counsel would pit the board against the CEO. After all, the whole purpose of a second lawyer is to disagree with the first one. Had our board retained counsel and fixated on themselves, things could have gone south very quickly.

I was confident that I hadn't done anything wrong. But when the government is considering indicting you, it's a different level of stress, personal and intense, with no one in the boat with you. The dictum *Don't get dead* applies to people, not just to companies. I found that my daily zen moments were more important to me than ever. I continued to swim laps but now found my mind wandering into dark places. Sometimes, as an alternative, I worked out on an exercise bike, which I could ride while watching a movie and being distracted.

I KNEW THE CRISIS WAS FADING WHEN MY DOORMAN SAID, "YOU MUST be feeling pretty good, because the guy with the bullhorn in front of the building isn't there for you today."

Over a couple of years, it all got resolved, however painfully. My lawyer kept haranguing the Southern District to close a case that was based on nothing but a senator's petulance. During a bathroom break, a year into the torture, one of the FBI agents who had driven me to the interrogation sidled up to the next urinal. *We know there's nothing there*, he said. It made me feel a little better. (You could say I was doubly relieved.) Shortly thereafter, the assistant prosecutor in charge of the case left for private practice. My lawyer told me that indicated that the government wouldn't be filing any charges. His prediction proved correct. In August 2012, the Justice Department announced that it was dropping the inquiry.

Fabulous Fab declined to settle his civil suit. That case ultimately went to trial, and in 2013 a jury found him civilly liable for fraud and fined him $650,000. By that time, he was pursuing a PhD in economics at the University of Chicago. ACA, the bond insurer, sued us too, alleging that we hadn't informed them that John Paulson was betting against the ABACUS securities. We finally settled with them in 2016.

Finally, there was an investigation by the US Attorney's office in California into the role of banks in the residential mortgage-backed securities market. It drew in the Federal Housing Finance Agency's Office of the Inspector General and the Office of the Special Inspector General for the Troubled Asset Relief Program. Our 2016 settlement was part of an omnibus settlement with all the banks, which took in all the remaining state and federal claims. It cost us more than $5 billion. That included around $2 billion that we paid into a relief fund for distressed homeowners. For J.P. Morgan Chase, the bill was more than $13 billion.

Going into the crisis, I thought I was cynical about politics. It turned out that I wasn't cynical enough. We were easy targets for politicians and regulators. Of course, the official sector had a responsibility to identify flaws in the system and fix them. But on a couple of occasions, the government's "informal" actions went well beyond that.

In the middle of the legislative process that created the Dodd–Frank legislation, the terms of which would be highly consequential for us and our industry, Congressman Barney Frank, chair of the House Financial Services Committee, called me in with a specific request. He wanted Goldman to forbear from exercising our creditor rights against a media company controlled by the family of Percy Sutton, a prominent African American politician and civic leader in New York City. This had nothing to do with the legislation, other than that the Congressional Black Caucus wanted him to do it, and Frank wanted their votes. In another example, Sheila Bair, the chair of the FDIC, asked us to contribute $20 million as an investment in ShoreBank, a minority-operated community bank in Chicago. Neither were commercial decisions that we would otherwise have made, nor the kind of philanthropy that was compelling to us in that moment. But what choice did we have?

In novels and movies, gangsters extort legitimate businesses to give them as much as 30 percent of their earnings. But of course, as partners, the gangsters would then want the businesses to make money. The US government took 35 percent (then the corporate tax rate), while making it harder and harder for us to succeed.

In July 2010, President Obama signed the 2,200-page Dodd–Frank bill. I had mixed feelings about it. The basic thrust of limiting leverage to protect the system from the too-big-to-fail syndrome made sense. When presidential candidate Donald Trump said he wanted to repeal the law entirely in 2016, I publicly disagreed with him. But in many ways, all the postcrisis regulation, piled on top of the Sarbanes–Oxley Act, which followed the Enron and WorldCom debacles in 2002, simply made the environment in which we operated more rigid, complicated, and expensive.

Interpreting the Volcker Rule, designed to stop regulated banks from engaging in proprietary trading, made everyone's heads spin. You could be a principal so long as you didn't take proprietary risk—a contradiction in terms. The legislation somehow imported the question of motive, or state of mind, into the permissibility of trades. Was a trade meant to facilitate or hedge a customer transaction, or was it initiated to make money? What trader isn't trying to make money? Were we supposed to have psychologists on the trading floor? There were trades you could make if you were approached by a client but that you couldn't approach a client about making. From a practical perspective, many of the rules and distinctions seemed nutty.

A lot of what the regulators did after the crisis had the effect of not necessarily reducing risk but merely rearranging outcomes. With large investment banks like Goldman now fully regulated as commercial banks, unregulated firms that weren't covered gained advantage. Private equity firms like Blackstone and private credit lenders like

Apollo benefited through greater flexibility and much looser capital requirements and compliance burdens. They were able to poach a lot of talent from those of us that were now designated as SIFIs, systemically important financial institutions. Whenever a competitor hired one of our people, my standard line was that they thereby improved both of our firms. It brought up their average and brought up our average. That was glib, but unfortunately not always true. Of course, their recruiting advantage will last only until the next crisis, when the younger institutions will come under the yoke of regulation and the next generation of unregulated financial firms begins its rise.

After the crisis, I published a long piece in the *Financial Times* talking about risk and the danger of the pendulum swinging too far in the opposite direction.

"After the shocks of recent months and the associated economic pain, there is a natural and appropriate desire for wholesale reform of our regulatory regime," I wrote. "We should resist a response, however, that is solely designed around protecting us from the 100-year storm. Taking risk completely out of the system will be at the cost of economic growth. Similarly, if we abandon, as opposed to regulate, market mechanisms created decades ago, such as securitization and derivatives, we may end up constraining access to capital and the efficient hedging and distribution of risk, when we ultimately do come through this crisis."

It was understandable that people who lived through the financial crisis remained nervous and scared. It was a traumatic experience. But you can't run your life or business with the once-in-a-hundred-years event top of mind, or you'll miss ninety-nine years of opportunity and growth. It's a good thing people turned over so much after the crisis, because the turnover helps memories fade—not always a bad thing.

> 10/7/2011: *This is Lloyd. . . . Of course this is a discomfiting time for everyone. Many people around the world are disappointed and angry. They feel let down by their governments and the*

> managers of their economies. To our ears, some of the charges sound unfair or misplaced. But the economic frustration underlying those shouts and frustrations is real and warranted. So our focus must be on what we can do to help push the economy forward. We understand and take seriously our responsibilities to help companies expand and to help investors invest in stability and growth. While we are one of the most philanthropic companies, it's the regular business we do every day that directly and most effectively advances the economic interests of all of society.

In the postcrisis environment, a growing challenge was fighting off what I called the "ordinarification" of Goldman. Regulators wanted us to be more boring and reduce risk. But arguably, the reforms made the too-big-to-fail syndrome worse. They may have made the ten-year storm—say, the failure of a single institution—less dangerous. At the same time, they may have made the hundred-year storm—say, the failure of an entire exchange—more dangerous. As an example, thousands of bilateral credit contracts by SIFIs now need to go through a clearinghouse. That makes the system less vulnerable to the failure of any one of them. But if someday a clearinghouse fails, it will have all of those eggs in the same basket, and we might find ourselves regretting that high level of concentration. The next systemic event may be caused not by a credit issue but by a technology blowup. That technology problem could come from a hacker or other bad actor, or from a fat finger.

It's always the risks we can't anticipate that present the greatest dangers. When I heard people talk overenthusiastically about the market, I used to say, *Haven't felt this good since 1994.* Then I changed it to 1998. After the global financial crisis, it was 2007. It was a way of making the point that crises can sneak up on you, and that what will kill you is the thing you aren't considering and probably can't even imagine. But I can guarantee that once the unexpected happens, a thousand pundits on TV will brag that they predicted it.

After the crisis, I grew a beard again, which occasioned plenty of snarky commentary and personal speculation. I'd had one for a long time when I was younger, but when I hit fifty, it turned gray, and it made me look even older than I actually was. I'd walk into a room and pregnant women would get up and offer me their chairs. I thought the beard was not the best look for my rising status at Goldman. But then, after several years as CEO, I got tired of showing up at morning meetings with tiny pieces of tissue attached to my face. People welcomed the return of the beard—they saw less of me.

CHAPTER 25

Just a Few More Calamities

A past crisis never seems so bad in hindsight. It's over and done. What's the worst crisis you've ever faced? The current, unresolved one.

If you had asked people in the corporate world to name the five top global business leaders, Rajat Gupta would have been on everybody's list. Rajat was elected senior partner by his colleagues at McKinsey & Company three times, for a total of nine years. He was already a director of Procter & Gamble, American Airlines, and the Rockefeller Foundation, among other companies and institutions, when he was added to our board in 2006. I once attended a lavish event in Delhi at which *The Economic Times of India* named Gupta Global Indian of the Year. I've never seen anyone celebrated like that. It was a coronation.

And so it came as a huge shock in late 2010 when the Justice Department charged Gupta with insider trading. Rajat Gupta! According to the indictment, Gupta was the tipper and his friend Raj Rajaratnam, who ran a hedge fund called Galleon, was the tippee. A number of the tips Gupta passed on to Rajaratnam were confidential information gleaned from his service on Goldman's board, including advance notice of Goldman's quarterly earnings and of Warren Buffett's 2008 investment in the firm. Our emergency board call to approve the Buffett investment ended at 3:53 p.m. on September 23, 2008. Gupta called Raj Rajaratnam at 3:54 p.m. At 3:57 p.m., Galleon bought $25 million of Goldman stock, most of it intended for Rajaratnam's personal portfolio. That was all he could get his hands on three minutes before the market closed. It was a shocking betrayal.

I had to testify at both trials. In a weird way I was excited as I had been a member of the New York and California bars for over thirty years but had never given testimony or even appeared in court. Another check mark on the bucket list. In reality, though, I didn't have much to say. I was there on behalf of Goldman Sachs, the victim of an alleged crime, not as an alleged perpetrator. I answered questions about how our board meetings worked and the duty of confidentiality owed by directors. It seemed to be an open-and-shut case. There was a fuss in the media when I testified at the first trial, because I shook Raj Rajaratnam's hand coming in. It seemed like the human thing to do, and it was a spontaneous gesture—but apparently, it was a no-no.

In the second trial, Rajat Gupta's defense attorney kept me on the stand forever, making me answer the same questions again and again. *Yes, we discussed the Buffett investment at the board meeting. Yes, board discussions are confidential.* . . . After my second day of testimony, when I was told to be ready for a third day, I had a sidebar with the judge, Jed Rakoff. I told him that I couldn't come back the next day because my daughter was graduating from high school, and I had to attend.

"You might have to come in," he said.

"Your honor, I'd love to," I said. "But I'm much more afraid of my wife and daughter than I am of you."

We worked it out. I got away with an end-of-day appearance, after the graduation ceremony.

Rajat Gupta was convicted on four counts of securities fraud and served two years, the last six months at home with an ankle bracelet. Raj Rajaratnam served seven and a half years. The result was not surprising. Besides shaking my sense of trust generally, the episode underscored the curious phenomenon that Goldman, if it had any connection to a news story, was always put at the center of the media coverage. We had been just one of Gupta's victims—he was alleged to have disclosed inside information about Procter & Gamble as well. But the press treated us as if we were somehow responsible. Some sample headlines:

The Wall Street Journal:

> The Case Against Former Goldman Director Gupta

The Guardian:

> Former Goldman Sachs Director Rajat Gupta Guilty of Leaking Insider Secrets

The New York Times:

> Former Goldman Director Gupta's Last Days of Freedom

CNBC:

> Ex-Goldman Director Rajat Gupta Says He's Innocent

What the heck? Gupta ran McKinsey & Company, the world's largest consulting firm. On top of all his board directorships, he was an adviser to the prime minister of India and the Gates Foundation. He didn't belong to us. So why was he "Goldman's Gupta" when he got in trouble?

The experience confirmed what a Bloomberg reporter once told us. If Goldman Sachs appeared in a headline, the article got a multiple of the number of clicks it would get if it didn't mention us. A Goldman angle made any story much bigger news than it would otherwise be.

I EXPERIENCED THAT PHENOMENON AGAIN WHEN OCCUPY WALL STREET occupied Wall Street in September 2011. The movement was said to have been inspired by the Arab Spring and the protests against austerity in Spain and Greece. Also apparently by puppet theater. There were a lot of papier-mâché gargoyles and heads on sticks, many of them mine. It can be a little disconcerting to see people waving a giant photo blowup of your severed head with a bloody spike running through it. Outside my building, the occupiers handed out leaflets attacking me. That building, 15 Central Park West, had and has a lot of hedge fund activists and other financial types whose activities generated protests from time to time. So fortunately, the building staff and my neighbors were mostly sympathetic instead of being annoyed at me. I could tell that some of them were disappointed that the attention wasn't on them. A few times, I stopped to chat with the protesters. I don't think they had any idea that they were speaking to their number one target.

Occupy Wall Street was undeniably a new kind of protest, without leaders, spokespeople, or a list of demands. But it was hardly a mass movement. In New York, there were a thousand protesters the first day and never more than a couple of hundred "occupying" Zuccotti Park, a plaza in Lower Manhattan, just south of where the World Trade Center towers once stood. There were marches and small encampments in other cities. But it was the new phenomenon of social media that helped the self-identified anarchists who organized the events get so much coverage.

Soooo much coverage. In some ways, Occupy Wall Street satisfied the media's hunger for a left-wing counterpart to the Tea Party. *The New York Times* treated it as if the Great Uprising had come at last—it was like *Ten Days That Shook the World,* John Reed's soaring account of the Bolshevik Revolution of 1917, but with Wall Street CEOs in the place of the Romanovs. The *Times* ran hundreds of news stories and dozens of editorials. The coverage was breathless and promotional, like journalists were happy to be alive and witnessing a new age in American democracy. "The protesters, most of them young, are giving voice to a generation of lost opportunity," the *Times* intoned in a masthead editorial.

"Occupy Wall Street is starting to look like an important event that might even eventually be seen as a turning point," the left-wing columnist (and Nobel laureate!) Paul Krugman wrote.

Another over-the-top *New York Times* columnist compared Zuccotti Park to "Kent State, Tiananmen Square, and the Berlin Wall" and described it as an expression of Aristotle's concept of citizenship.

C'mon, guys. Because it was an unled movement whose most common features were drum circles and dreadlocks, it was hard to say just what the protest was trying to achieve. The press was too sympathetic to point out the obvious absurdity of anarchists trying to organize themselves. In reality, the occupiers tended to get endlessly hung up trying to decide on a process for deciding who could speak for them. Beyond that, there was the obvious contradiction of demanding that government take more control of the economy, while being opposed to government. Their demands—to the extent they had any—were to confiscate wealth and put rich people in jail. But most of them wanted to close down the jails.

After two months, the NYPD cleared out the encampment, ostensibly because of health concerns and the risk of fires. Protesters were allowed to return without overnight privileges, but by that point it was November, and the movement fizzled in the cold and damp. Without the cheerleading media coverage, it would have fizzled a lot sooner.

AFTER THE FINANCIAL CRISIS, WE WERE PAYING CLOSER ATTENTION TO communications, and I was appearing much more frequently in the media. But the credulous coverage around Occupy Wall Street made clear to me that we had a long way to go in explaining who we were and what we did. There was still a hangover from our days as a partnership, when our approach was "The less said the better." In 2012, to address our deficit around press and public relations, we hired Jake Siewert, Bill Clinton's former press secretary and an adviser to Treasury Secretary Tim Geithner, as head of corporate communications.

Jake was universally liked, and nothing ever seemed to ruffle him. That included his welcome present on his first day, a *New York Times* op-ed entitled "Why I Am Leaving Goldman Sachs" by a London-based futures salesperson named Greg Smith. I learned about it when I was awoken by Michael Daffy, a partner in our London office who assumed I had already read the newspaper by 5:30 a.m. In fact, I had never heard of Smith, who had spent twelve years at the firm without rising beyond the junior level of VP. When I asked, I was told he had been unhappy about his lack of advancement and compensation—which he apparently chose to respond to by publishing his piece.

Smith made the classic accusation—the firm had fallen off from its days of greatness because it was no longer focused solely on clients. We had betrayed our vaunted culture, etc., etc. One of the few specific charges he leveled was that he heard other professionals refer to their clients as "muppets," English slang for a foolish person. The piece was ridiculous on a number of levels, starting with Smith's phony more-in-sorrow than-in-anger tone and his boasts about "being selected as a Rhodes Scholar national finalist, [and] winning a bronze medal for table tennis at the Maccabiah Games in Israel, known as the Jewish Olympics." It was hard to see anyone taking this guy seriously.

But it wasn't just an op-ed: It was an ambush orchestrated for maximum effect. Smith's piece was accompanied by a news story on the front page of the business section that amplified and promoted it, and a follow-up story the following day. According to the *Times*, "Even bankers who disagreed with Mr. Smith's conclusions said the piece had struck a chord because it stirred up their own doubts, especially in the wake of the financial crisis." They did? No bankers at Goldman or elsewhere were quoted to that effect, even anonymously. There was, however, one professor at the University of Delaware who noted that Wall Street had changed in the 1980s with the rise of proprietary trading. That was a quarter century earlier.

But having an "insider" criticize the firm provided fresh fuel for round after round of stories, most of them consisting of victory laps by our critics. Matt Taibbi of "vampire squid" fame wrote on his blog that the piece was "historic" and "eloquent."

Obviously, people enjoyed watching us squirm. But even when Smith stretched his long op-ed into a short book, he wasn't able to come up with any meaningful examples to back up his accusations. It was just the same claim that we'd changed, that things had been better in the golden age, and a lot of moaning about people using salty language around the office. Like Senator Levin, Smith seemed to willfully misunderstand the different roles that investment banks play, with the full knowledge of their clients and customers.

Matt Levine, the brilliant financial columnist at Bloomberg, said that Smith's account rang false, because making money for clients and making money from clients are aspects of the same activity—trading.

"Greg Smith spent *twelve years* flogging equity derivatives to 'two of the largest hedge funds on the planet, five of the largest asset managers in the United States, and three of the most prominent sovereign wealth funds in the Middle East and Asia' and is just now discovering that they're designed to make money for his employer? I imagine his contacts at these hedge funds reading his op-ed today and being like 'holy shit, Goldman was trying to make money off of us?' Wait no I don't. I'm pretty sure they wanted to make money too."

Levine, who had previously worked at Goldman, noted that as a VP after twelve years at the firm, Smith's career was at a dead end. "Maybe if he'd gotten the Rhodes, or won a gold medal for regular tennis at the goyish Olympics, he'd have made MD and would still have a job," he wrote.

I HAVE A PRETTY THICK SKIN ABOUT CRITICISM AND UNDERSTAND THAT the media has an important job to do. But there was a common thread to these episodes: The press loved the clicks that went with any mention of Goldman. I was friendly with Arthur Sulzberger Jr., the publisher of *The New York Times*, despite the withering coverage his paper rained down on me and the firm. Occasionally, though, I got an opportunity to punch back. Almost every year, I appeared for a live interview with Andrew Ross Sorkin at the *New York Times* DealBook conference. This was a chance to speak to a broader audience in dialogue with a journalist whose work I genuinely respected.

At the 2014 conference, Andrew and I were having our usual spirited conversation. Goldman had recently comanaged the IPO of the Chinese e-commerce company Alibaba, and a controversial feature of it was supervoting shares that assured that the founder, Jack Ma, would maintain control.

"What do you think of companies," Sorkin asked me, which "have governance structures that effectively keep the founders in control and don't effectively allow the type of democracy that we've been talking about in the boardroom?"

"*The New York Times*?" I interrupted.

"*The New York Times* is one of them. . . . Touché," he stammered. "Let me go in a different direction for a second. Is Arthur still here?"

THE BIGGER GOLDMAN GOT, THE HARDER IT WAS TO BE ON TOP OF everything going on in the firm, especially in distant locales. No alarm bells went off for me when I was told that the nation of Malaysia wanted us to underwrite bond issues to support a new sovereign wealth fund, which we did in 2012 and 2013. I was confident that the firm's committees then in place would review the transactions to make sure they were appropriate.

Later, US government investigations concluded that the fund, 1MDb, was a vehicle for fraud. A young financier, Jho Low, who was a friend of the Malaysian prime minister Najib Razak, had no official role in the government of Malaysia. But it was Jho Low's scheme—one he used to siphon off $4.5 billion or so, much of which he spent buying a superyacht, a jet, and paintings by Van Gogh and Monet. He also paid for gambling sprees and nightclub parties with Paris Hilton and invested in films including *The Wolf of Wall Street*. Jho Low gave gifts worth millions of dollars, like artworks by Warhol and Basquiat, to his new celebrity friends. He was a generous guy—with stolen money.

When all of this came out, driven by coverage in *The Wall Street Journal*, there were street protests in Kuala Lumpur, and Najib, who reportedly also stole billions, lost an election. Jho Low fled to China and remains a fugitive, sometimes spotted in Macau or Myanmar. Two Goldman employees based in Southeast Asia, Tim Leissner and Roger Ng, were implicated in the scheme. Leissner, a partner in the firm, pleaded guilty in 2018 to conspiring to launder money and violate antibribery laws, and Ng was later tried and convicted.

As far as our internal compliance was concerned, I believed we'd had the right documentation and review processes for the transactions. But we clearly had at least two corrupt employees, and if such people are bent on evasion, they can be hard to detect and catch. It was difficult for us to even believe some of the eye-popping allegations from the indictments. Nevertheless, we had responsibility for the actions of those employees and our failure to prevent or uncover them. For that, the firm, after my tenure, paid a stiff price in terms of money and reputation. The settlements, with the US Justice Department and the Malaysian government, ran into the billions. Litigation with the Malaysian government continues to this day.

When the full story came to light, it left me shaken about our work in remote and corrupt countries. Goldman Sachs was good at managing financial risk—but how good were we at doing due diligence with politically powerful customers in countries with weak governance structures? Our people were dealing with the prime minister of a country in a transaction approved by its parliament as well as outside auditors and legal counsel. The 1MDb scandal made me think about how we managed people in far-flung places around the world. Leissner was seen as commercially effective and, like every other partner of the firm, was given a certain amount of leeway in which to operate. In a riskier country like Malaysia, we didn't take a broad enough view of what could go wrong. Like what if the most senior people in the government were crooks who intended to steal the proceeds? And what if one of our partners and another senior banker were crooked as well? In hindsight, the government identified red flags that I certainly didn't see at the time. There always are some, after you know things have gone wrong. As I sometimes put it, it's not what you look at that matters, it's what you see. Or what you fail to see.

IF OUR NOTORIETY MADE US AN ATTRACTIVE TARGET FOR THE PRESS, IT also gave us a platform few others in the business world enjoyed. When we commented about events, it would get a lot of attention. How should we use that position?

CEOs are often prodded to take stands on divisive political issues. Sometimes the pressure comes from employees and sometimes from clients or customers. Sometimes the CEO wants to influence the debate on an issue he feels strongly about. To me, this is dangerous territory and generally bad for business and the economy. My view is that we don't need to divide business into "red" companies and "blue" companies.

As a CEO, your prestige and influence are functions of your position. That influence is really an asset of the company and should be wielded with a fiduciary's mindset. I may be pro-choice, but it would have been a misappropriation of that asset for me to use the Goldman megaphone to make my views on the subject resonate more loudly.

However, there are cases where a CEO does have the right, and even an obligation, to promote a politically sensitive position. One category is where the issue falls within the recognized expertise of the business. On the question of whether fiscal spending should be cut or whether a short-term government shutdown or default would be just bad or really, really bad, a Goldman CEO not only is allowed to express a view but *should* express a view, because it is within the scope of Goldman's expertise.

Another category is where a CEO needs to act as a champion for employees, especially on issues where some outcomes might prevent them from performing to their full potential. I spoke up for marriage equality because without that, a same-sex partner could not easily get the same health care benefits and sometimes couldn't get a visa to accompany a spouse transferred to a foreign office, thereby causing the assignment to be rejected. I believed strongly, personally, in marriage equality. But I was public and aggressive in using my Goldman platform because it was an issue for Goldman employees, whom I was pledged to support.

Would that all issues were so clear-cut. A state's ban on abortion could create health issues for employees. What can and can't be taught in school may be an issue for employees who won't relocate to places where books are banned from the library or gay teachers have to hide their identity. At the same time, there are intense political divisions on such issues, and Goldman has employees on various sides of them. My framework doesn't resolve every issue easily, but it provides a way to think about the problem, bearing in mind that you have to choose your battles.

During the debate on marriage equality, I was cochair of the NYC Partnership, an organization of the CEOs of nearly three hundred companies headquartered in New York. In that role, I represented that organization's push for the New York legislature to pass marriage equality. In 2012, I was the Human Rights Campaign Fund's first national corporate spokesman for same-sex marriage, several years before the Supreme Court made it the law of the land with its 2015 *Obergefell* decision. A headline in *The New York Times* read BLANKFEIN TO SPEAK OUT FOR SAME-SEX MARRIAGE. I told Laura it was a typo.... I was speaking out for "some" sex marriage.

Joking aside, issues are different for different companies. I went on the road to promote marriage equality as an imperative for business. At a forum in Minneapolis, the CEO of a large consumer company came to me to say that he personally agreed with me, but he believed that taking a position would be negative for his business, because a significant share of their customer base was opposed. I agreed that it was sensible for him to leave the advocacy to others. Michael Jordan purportedly responded similarly when he was asked why he didn't comment more on social and political matters: "Republicans buy sneakers too."

Recently I've watched some bank CEOs take positions against financing coal-fired power plants or gun manufacturers. Or for DEI—and then against DEI. You might feel strongly about those issues. But half the country owns guns, and we still need to dig and burn coal. And some states have decided not to do business with those banks because of their public stances. The way to resolve political issues is through the political system, not through boycotts of businesses and retaliatory boycotts of boycotters. To quote *King Lear*, "that way madness lies."

CHAPTER 26

Notes on an Illness

Remarkably, when I was sick, I didn't change. I didn't get more spiritual; I didn't wish I had lived differently. I must be somewhat okay with my life.

Through the spring of 2015, I'd been coughing a lot, which, when it didn't go away, I attributed to allergies. By midsummer it had gone on too long, and I went to the doctor. That was an unusual step for me as I ignored most illnesses. I got perfect-attendance awards in grammar school and can't remember ever staying away from work or canceling a meeting or a trip because I was sick. My physician recommended Ricola, an herbal throat lozenge, and sent me on my way.

Other things were going on that in hindsight were symptoms, but at the time they just seemed like other things. Like I lost a lot of weight. I didn't connect that with a problem as I was always trying to lose weight, mostly without success. I just thought I had finally gotten good at it. I even started to give other people advice on how they could lose weight.

I was also tired a lot, but I was working hard and traveling and usually tired anyway. But the cough continued, and toward the end of the summer I went back to the doctor and he had me get an X-ray of my lungs. That always made me nervous as I had been a smoker in my younger days, but the X-ray read normal.

Still, I was coughing and feeling off. I was also frequently tripping while going up stairs. I thought I was clearing the riser, but I wasn't. Then one weekend in late August, I was golfing with some friends, and while I was usually a bad golfer, this time I was unusually bad. As we walked down the fairway together after our tee shots, I said to the others, *Why are you walking so fast? Slow down!* My friend Curtis Lane turned back to me and said, *We're not walking fast—you're walking slow!*

Back to the doctor. This time he prescribed a CAT scan, which I got just after Labor Day. The next morning at the office, my executive assistant, Julie Becht, called to me, "Dr. Blumenthal is on the phone." I got off my call and took his.

He said he wasn't exactly sure what it was, but the CAT scan showed a number of tumors, probably some kind of lymphoma. He wanted me to come to the hospital to meet with an oncologist.

I put down the phone. I wasn't panicked. In fact, in crisis moments, everything slows down for me and I get into the mental equivalent of an athletic crouch. Weirdly, I've always been a fatalist, and at every health exam I've ever had, I expected bad news. I was always pleasantly surprised when it didn't come. This time it came, and I wasn't shocked.

I called Laura. She was in a room full of people. I told her to step outside so she could speak in private. When she was alone, I told her what the doctor had told me, but before she could say anything back to me, Julie (who knew nothing about what was going on) shouted that a client I'd been trying to reach all day was calling in. I said to Laura, *Sorry, I have to call you back*, and disconnected, literally leaving her hanging. What a terrible thing to do to her. I guess I was more discombobulated than I thought.

Dr. Blumenthal sent me to John Leonard, a top specialist in blood cancers at NewYork-Presbyterian Hospital. I had been on the board of the associated medical school, Weill Cornell, for about fifteen years at that point. Memorial Sloan Kettering is the most famous New York City cancer hospital, but I am nothing if not loyal to my institutions. I'm glad that I was. I couldn't have had a better doctor than Dr. Leonard, whom I consider a friend today. He is a great oncologist by training and a great psychiatrist by dint of his life experience engaging with cancer patients.

Dr. Leonard said that it was undoubtedly a kind of lymphoma, but as there are more than seventy different types with widely divergent treatments and prognoses, I would have to wait for the biopsy and typing. It took a week to schedule the biopsy—a very nervous week. That was the first surgery I ever had under general anesthesia. I had the biopsy scheduled for the morning but then moved it to the afternoon so I could participate in a panel discussion at a *Wall Street Journal* conference.

IF YOU'RE GOING TO BE DIAGNOSED WITH A LIFE-THREATENING ILLness, you might not want to do it when you're leading a public company. A serious health risk to a CEO is a "material event," which could potentially move the share price. So when my doctor told me that I had a potentially fatal blood cancer, it was insider information. If I didn't want trouble from the SEC (that would be icing on the cake!), I shouldn't tell anyone, unless I was telling everyone at the same time. It was my own personal and unwanted restructuring deal, with life and death as the possible outcomes. So I kept my schedule and told no one other than John Rogers, our general counsel, Greg Palm, and Julie, who scheduled me. Poor Laura, who was with me the whole time, couldn't even share her anxiety with friends.

By the time I went to see Dr. Leonard for the biopsy results, I was really losing it. Losing more weight, losing my balance more. Laura and I went to the meeting accompanied by Michael Rendel, a terrific doctor and human being who ran Goldman's in-house clinic. Having

Rendel available to advise me and raise questions with my doctors was a huge benefit that I realize very few people have when dealing with serious illness.

The news was bad and good. And bad. And good. Dr. Leonard told me that the disease could kill me, but that it could also be cured. What I had was a common form of non-Hodgkin's lymphoma. It was "advanced stage" and highly aggressive. But that didn't matter so much, because if the chemo worked, it worked. Some lymphomas are very treatable—they're called indolent—but not fully curable. On the other hand, the very aggressiveness of my kind of lymphoma made it more responsive to the chemo, so it was curable—if the chemo worked. There was a real chance that it wouldn't work, which would mean resorting to plans B or C, which were unattractive and much lower in their effectiveness.

He presented my prognosis as optimistically as he could, but the good news seemed pretty marginal. My odds were better because I was not showing signs of physical deterioration—except that I was. The odds were better because I was under sixty—but unfortunately, I was just over sixty. If you gave me the benefit of the doubt, and my body didn't reject the chemo, I had something like a 70 percent chance of recovering. But without those dubious-seeming statistical advantages, it was more like fifty-fifty.

I asked when treatment would start. Right now, Dr. Leonard said. If you wait another week, you might not be walking.

I run a public company. I have to tell my board. I have to issue a press release. I was writing it in my head as I went upstairs, got admitted, and was administered a bone marrow test. I was told the test would be painful, but I was so busy on my phone that I didn't notice. I called John Rogers, who within a couple of hours convened a call for me to tell the firm's outside directors the news. And immediately after that, a call with our management committee, which John assembled on short notice in the usual conference room.

I told both groups that I expected to keep working during my treatment, and everyone was very supportive.

Then I started my first four-day round of chemo. While they were putting a line in my arm, I drafted a message to the whole firm and the public. I wrote that I had a highly treatable form of cancer.

When I showed it to Dr. Leonard to see if I'd gotten the facts right, he crossed out the word *treatable* and wrote in *curable*.

BECAUSE IT WAS A BLOOD CANCER, THERE WAS NO SURGICAL REMOVAL of tumors and no radiation to shrink them. Just chemo. But the course of the treatment was extensive. There were six three-week cycles. Each began with four days of continuous chemo infusion (ninety-six hours) in the hospital, followed by seventeen days for it to take effect. That would, hopefully, kill the cancer, but it would definitely kill my white blood cells and my immunity. The bags that fed into my bloodstream had to be changed several times over the four days as they emptied quarts of liquid. The nurse charged with changing them would do so while wearing a hazmat suit, lest a drop of the liquid touch her skin. Meanwhile, I was having gallons of the stuff pumped through my bloodstream for nearly six hundred total hours. I would walk around the hospital with the chemo bag and a pump mounted on a pole with wheels.

Four days and nights in the hospital out of every three weeks... That's a lot of laps around the fourteenth floor of NewYork Hospital, clutching my pole on rollers. When my friends and family weren't around, I was happy to chat with whoever was. Often it was visitors waiting outside the rooms of patients who were in worse shape than me, while doctors or nurses worked on their friend or family member. Sometimes the visitor was the parent of a kid sick with cancer. My overwhelming feeling speaking to those parents was how lucky I was that it was me that was sick and not one of my kids. I was so much better off than those parents were, even at my worst.

Unfortunately, the battery on the pump would last only about twenty minutes before needing a recharge, so I spent a lot of time pacing near a wall socket. Imagine, an electric car can drive three hundred miles on a single charge, but the hospital could not come up with a battery that would let me walk around for more than twenty minutes.

I felt constant anxiety every time I had a scan to determine whether the treatments were working. But on the whole, I handled the meds well. It was worse in the early rounds, better in the later rounds. I usually didn't feel that bad while I was getting the chemo. It was five days into the cycle, when I was back home, that the effects of the treatment would kick in. By the later rounds, the cumulative impact meant my immune resistance was low, and I had to be very careful about close contact with people. I would have blood transfusions and platelet transfusions frequently. But then my white blood cell count would go to zero, and they can't give you a transfusion for that. The drug they gave me to accelerate production of white blood cells was what I remember as the most painful part of the treatment. But the main effect of the treatment was weakness, not pain. The little hair I had fell out, which was barely noticed. I looked terrible for having lost a lot of weight, and when I looked in the mirror, I saw a ghost.

Managing my medications was its own job—different pills twice a day, once a day, every third day, and so on. Steroids required tapering down. Michael Rendel made me a color-coded spreadsheet telling me what pills to take, and what side effects to expect. Because I was getting so many infusions, the hospital installed something called a PICC line in my upper arm. That involved its own regimen of careful daily cleaning, a responsibility that fell to Laura. It couldn't get wet, and I tried a series of devices in the shower before a grizzled nursing veteran at the hospital told me to just cover my arm in Saran Wrap. That worked like a charm. I thought a lot about what this kind of treatment must be like for people without all the help, support, and financial resources I had. What if you didn't speak English fluently? What if you had a full-time job you had to maintain, without the flexibility I had? How could you track all the medications?

Laura was there much of the day, every day. She bought a new comforter, pillow, and six-hundred-thread-count Egyptian cotton sheets, and made my bed every day. My friends were terrific. I got DVDs of new movies from my friends David Geffen and David Zaslav. Others brought in food from great restaurants, and I ate with a rotating group of family or friends most nights I was in the hospital. I didn't lose my appetite—I never do. My metabolism must have been on overdrive, because despite eating multiple desserts, I didn't gain weight. Thanksgiving 2015 came during one of my four-day hospital stays. The hospital lent us a conference room. Laura decorated it appropriately, and my extended family and our friends the Marinos, over twenty of us in all, had a full Thanksgiving feast there, with the food brought in and me attached to the chemo bag and infusion pump held up by a pole.

My situation was very public, and I got hundreds, maybe even thousands, of supportive emails and texts. I felt like Tom Sawyer blushing at all the nice things said about him at his own supposed funeral. But it was terrible when friends and family had to leave and I was again alone in the room with the bright lights on and the monitor noises going all night, and my thoughts going back to dark places.

There were some positive, or at least comical, elements to having cancer, and I milked them. Things I didn't want to do I let other people do for me, even when I was feeling better. People at the firm were wonderful. When I was stuck in my hospital room during the part of the cycle when I was getting a chemo infusion, the office came to me. Gary Cohn was particularly attentive even as his workload increased due to his having to take on some of my commitments. My chief of staff, Russell Horwitz, would come to the hospital to work with me.

Laura was on duty around the clock, and I saw more of my kids than ever. Two of them were at school in Cambridge, Rachel at Harvard College and Jonathan in the JD/MBA program, and they came down regularly. Alex was in New York City, working in finance. Somehow, one or another of them was always available to walk me—slowly—around Central Park. For the moment, I was the focus of everyone's affection and attention, which was another unforeseen perk of having a serious illness. I loved their company, and it dawned on me how suddenly things had turned from my taking care of them to their taking care of me. I'd always known that day would come, as I had taken care of my parents as they aged. I just wasn't prepared for it to happen so soon. But as they say in *The Lion King*, "the circle of life..."

Some of that extra attention evaporated when Alex's wife, Cristina, gave birth in December to Laura's and my first grandchild, Nico, in a different wing of the same hospital. I lost the competition for attention and happily yielded.

Most of the time I looked worse than I felt. When I came in to work between hospital stays, Julie would clean all the surfaces in my office with the most stringent abrasives she could find, removing the veneer from all the furniture. She barred anyone who admitted to having ever coughed or sneezed. In group meetings, I would sit at one end of a long conference table with everyone else clustered at the other end, the same way Vladimir Putin conducted his meetings during the COVID-19 crisis. I stayed away from crowds, like my fortieth college reunion and a state dinner for Chinese President Xi Jinping at the White House.

Anyway, I survived and felt a tremendous sense of gratitude. I had enormous appreciation for the doctors and nursing staff. Dr. Leonard would come by at 7:00 a.m. and again at 7:00 p.m. I felt grateful to the pharma companies that had developed the meds that upped my odds of surviving.

Dr. Leonard had told me that 90 percent of recurrences happen in the first year, and I was counting the days. Six months after my treatment was finished, I was at home one night at our house in the Hamptons and felt my legs in agony. I lowered myself out of the bed and crawled to the bathroom. This was a fairly rare delayed reaction to the treatment that nobody had warned me about, and it was scary as hell. At Southampton Hospital they gave me a pair of crutches, and a day and half later, the pain was gone. Six months after that, I was on vacation with a group of friends in someone's damp vacation home in Ireland, when I couldn't stop coughing. Everyone else went out to play golf while I stayed home to die. In that case, my doctor thought I was sick from something else. The cancer never came back. Touch wood.

A couple of years after my recovery, I was sitting in a restaurant when a woman I didn't recognize came up and said hi, like she knew me. She said she and I had sat and spoken several times while she was visiting her son in a hospital room next to mine. He was a nineteen-year-old Boston College hockey player who suddenly discovered he had leukemia. I never heard the resolution of his case. I was afraid to ask, but I had to.

"How's your son?"

"See for yourself!"

I looked at her table, at a young man I would never have recognized. He didn't just look okay; he looked great. I was so happy for that family that Laura and I both started crying in the restaurant. His mother did too. A lot of bottled-up emotion got released in that moment.

HAVING CONFRONTED MORTALITY, MY PERSPECTIVE ON SOME THINGS changed. I worked through the idea that one day the world would go on without me. When that inevitably comes up again, I won't be starting from scratch. That is a good thing. On the other hand, there's always a bit of a cloud over my head. I used to ignore coughing or other aches and pains. Now, I revert immediately to the thought that they could be symptoms of something serious.

When you're sick, your thoughts wander in predictable directions. I remember discussing philanthropy with our Dutch country adviser, Victor Halberstadt, who quoted an aphorism: *It's better to give with a warm hand than a cold hand.* That struck me as obvious yet profound. You get more from giving stuff away when you're alive than when you're an estate.

But I don't think I really changed in a fundamental way. I wanted normality. I was sick and it could have been terminal, but I still stressed about the firm's problems and issues, which fabric to buy for new furniture in our home, or whether we had been overbilled on something. When I thought I might die youngish, I remember thinking that I wasn't going to get my money's worth on the tour of life, like it was a disappointing vacation. I wanted to complain to the Better Business Bureau. *I want to speak to your manager.* When I recovered, I felt like I'd been given a whole extra trip as compensation.

These days, I don't rue my birthdays. They make me feel like I'm getting my money's worth.

CHAPTER 27

Goodbye to All That

It's hard to know when to leave. When things are going poorly, you can't go. When they are going well, you don't want to go.

By 2018, I'd been CEO for twelve years, which is a very long time to run Goldman Sachs. In another era, John Weinberg was head of the then much smaller and largely domestic firm for fourteen years, nine of them with John Whitehead as his co-head. Before that, you had to go back to John's father, Sidney Weinberg, who became senior partner in 1930, to find someone who'd done the job for longer than I had. And Sidney Weinberg did it at a time when the size and scale of Goldman Sachs were a small fraction of the enterprise I was running. When I looked around at my peers, nearly all the other financial crisis–era CEOs in the US and Europe were gone, with the exception of Jamie Dimon at J.P. Morgan, God bless him. I used to joke that our succession planning was "What happens if I get hit by a bus?" Then it became "What happens if I don't get hit by a bus?"

More than two years after my illness was resolved, it no longer played such a large role in my outlook. But other things were weighing on me. How many more trips did I want to make to Singapore and Riyadh? When I was sick, I rolled dice in my head as I tried to come to grips with my odds as those odds changed over the course of treatment. Even after the results were going my way, I began to question whether I wanted to spend the rest of my life doing what I was doing, traveling overseas every three or four weeks, fighting with the press, struggling to satisfy regulators. That kind of experience does cause you to realize that we're all going to end up in the same place anyway.

But the bigger issue was the cascade of unpredictable blowups and crises. It nagged at me that every day I stayed, I ran the risk of getting dragged into another series of unfortunate events that could require me to stay five more years.

I knew that would be too long. The more introspective you are, the harder it is to stay in a job like that for an extended period of time. On Wall Street, there are people who started reading the financial pages in grade school. Many of them had no real outside interests and no identity beyond their jobs. Even after they leave, you'll still find them every year in Davos, keeping an oar in the water in whatever way they can. Being a one-dimensional person can be a big advantage in business, if it's the right dimension. Other choices don't distract you, because you don't see them. But that was never me. I hadn't set out to go into finance. When I had time to read books recreationally—usually on long flights back from foreign trips—they were mostly about history or science, not anything directly related to my job. I had other things I still wanted to learn and do.

Hank gave me some good advice when he left to become Treasury secretary. *Lloyd*, he said, *these jobs are hard to get, so don't be so quick to give yours up. Be sure that when you leave, you are certain about it.* I stayed until I was pretty definite that it was the right thing to do. The firm was in good shape. But the obligations were constant. You owe the firm 100 percent. That means that if there's a must-win pitch in Germany that your presence will increase the odds of winning, you get on a plane. If you don't want to do these things, you should give your job up to any one of the scores of competent people who'd be glad to take your place.

In that period, I found myself having the same kinds of conversations in my head that I had had with my college friends as a freshman. I had come full circle. What's the meaning of life? What should I do with the rest of mine? It couldn't be about one more weekend when I said goodbye to my family on a Saturday afternoon so I could travel for more than twenty hours to arrive in China for a meeting first thing on Monday. I knew I was nearing the end when I got picked up for an overseas trip and as we got close to the airport, I had the car turn around. I just didn't feel like going. I thought to myself, *I'd surely cancel the trip if I were sick. Isn't it better that I am* not *sick?*

Maybe it was coping with the aggravation of excessive regulation following the global financial crisis, or the media being so hostile to banking, or the rise of investor activism, or the nature of being a CEO in a highly scrutinized industry for more than twelve years. Whatever the combination of factors, it was apparent to me that a balance had changed: Previously I had to spend 20 percent of my time doing things I didn't like as the price for the 80 percent I loved. Now that statistic was upside down. The 80 percent was what I didn't like. Early in my career I had to work to make a living for my family. But that was no longer an incentive. In other contexts, when I had to deal with unpleasantness, I'd persevere with the mantra "No choice, no problem." But now I had choices, and thus I had problems.

And so I began a conversation with Goldman's lead director, Adebayo Ogunlesi. Bayo was a Supreme Court law clerk for Thurgood Marshall before going on to a distinguished career at Credit Suisse and founding a hugely successful infrastructure investment firm that he eventually sold to BlackRock. Bayo was supportive of my decision and helped me work out a timetable for the transition. I agreed to stay on as chair for a few additional months after resigning as CEO. Any more than that would have felt too much like looking over the shoulder of my successor.

A CORPORATE BOARD'S SENSE OF ITS RESPONSIBILITIES KICKS INTO overdrive when it's selecting a new CEO. Goldman had been public only since 1999, and the outside directors had never had a proper chance to pick one. When I was chosen in 2006, after Hank's sudden and surprising departure, there was very little board process. I could tell that the board welcomed the opportunity to do the most important thing that boards do.

I reviewed succession planning with the board every year, but the succession wasn't a foregone conclusion. Goldman Sachs is too complex to easily bring in someone from the outside. But there were several strong internal contenders, and they began to campaign in various ways. Each heir was never more than apparent.

Every board member had a lot of exposure to at least a half dozen credible candidates for leadership. Our quarterly board meetings would take place over two days. They would start immediately after lunch on the first day and end just before lunch on the second. On each of the two days, I would schedule for every board member a private lunch with one of our most senior executives, including my potential successors. All of them presented regularly to the board about their current and potential business plans. So when the time came to draw up a short list, the board knew all of the potential candidates well.

By the end of 2016, Gary Cohn had been president and COO for as long as I'd been chairman and CEO. We had had a terrific partnership, but ten years was a long time to be number two. The Trump administration was about to start and he was being recruited for a cabinet-level economic position. It was indicative of Gary's reputation that his services were sought despite his being a lifelong Democrat. At that point I was still in place, I hadn't spoken about leaving, and there was no assurance that the board would give him the CEO job when I retired. In any case, government service was the well-trodden next path for the most senior Goldman partners, and the timing was ripe. Gary left Goldman to become Trump's national economic adviser, where he partnered with Goldman alum Steven Mnuchin as Treasury secretary to run economic policy in the early part of the first Trump administration. It was the resumption of an earlier partnership between the two of them, who had both been members of my fixed income operating committee when I headed FICC in the late 1990s. Whatever one thinks of the Trump administration's policies in his first term, the strong economy before the COVID-19 pandemic was its greatest accomplishment, and Government Sachs had something to do with it.

Gary's departure left two principal contenders, Harvey Schwartz and David Solomon, whom I installed as copresidents and co-CEOs when Gary left. It was evident that the new CEO was going to be bald like me, but a lot... bigger. Harvey was six-four and had been a nightclub bouncer before he decided that what he really needed was a black belt in karate. David was also tall and athletic (and, though unbeknownst to me at the time, had a burgeoning hobby of DJing at dance parties).

I think the board's choice came down to type of experience. Goldman has had leaders like Gus Levy, Bob Rubin, Jon Corzine, and me, with backgrounds in trading. And it has had leaders like John Whitehead, John Weinberg, Steve Friedman, and Hank Paulson, who came out of the investment banking side of the firm. There was a semiconscious alternation going on. Harvey Schwartz came out of the trading side. He had done an excellent job as CFO after he replaced David Viniar, who had retired several years earlier. David Solomon was an investment banker and had run or co-run that division extremely well for a decade.

Goldman is fundamentally a service organization, and after a dozen-plus years of being led by a trading guy, it was time for someone from the banking side of the business to be in charge again. And so the board, with my encouragement, chose David Solomon.

As tends to happen in these situations, the runner-up left. A couple of years later, Harvey was named CEO of the Carlyle Group, the private equity firm. He has done a great job there, no surprise. Being a runner-up for leadership at Goldman has turned out to be a good thing for a lot of people.

I announced my retirement to the world in July 2018. By agreement with the board, I would pass my CEO title to David at the end of September, on the last day of the third quarter, but stay as chairman through the end of the year to help with David's transition. Then I would walk off into the sunset, retaining the honorary title *senior chairman*.

———

I GAVE A VALEDICTORY SPEECH AT THE ANNUAL RETIRED PARTNERS' dinner in mid-December, in the final weeks of my tenure.

"Now I'm about to join your ranks as a retired partner," I said. "Before I do, I'd like to get a few things straight.

"To those of you who made partner two years later than you should have, I'm sorry.

"To those who should have gotten the promotion your dumber co-head got, I'm sorry.

"To those who were paid too little for too long, I'm really sorry.

"And to those whose names I forgot when I ran into you in the elevator, I'm very sorry.

"Are we good now?"

———

YOUR LAST DAY IS A FRIDAY, AND ON MONDAY YOU WAKE UP TO QUIET. It's a very big change, and not an easy one to get used to. Some people handle it better than others. My longtime director Jim Johnson prepared me for this when he told me a story of his first day of retirement—made up, I'm sure—about his getting into the back seat of his car and it not moving, because there was no driver in the front.

Of course I miss my old job. Curiously, the times when I wish I were still there are the most difficult ones. I don't miss the normal, quiet days when things were going fine. I miss the challenge and excitement of a good crisis and the shared sense of commitment, working shoulder to shoulder with some of the smartest and most motivated people in the world. But that doesn't mean I regret leaving. There are more things that I'm not nostalgic for. I don't miss flying to industry gatherings in Singapore or Switzerland; or competing with other CEOs for the latest IPO pitch in China; or battling with regulators; or testifying in Congress about something that had gone wrong but could never have been anticipated. Those kinds of memories are the reason I have so far resisted the occasional urge to take another full-time position.

It's always hard to watch your successor make choices different from the ones you would have made. I tried to keep quiet. But I couldn't resist a quip when I was pushed to comment on CNBC. "My successor isn't that different from me. They just traded a JD for a DJ."

Growing up at the firm in the way I did, I continued to see calculated risk-taking and the partnership culture as the core of Goldman Sachs. David has done more to respond to the market's desire for smoother earnings. He has expanded Goldman's corporate cash-management business. He took most of the firm's investing off the balance sheet and into funds that generate fees rather than gains. He has perhaps thereby sacrificed some earnings potential for less earnings volatility, clearly a preference of public shareholders, who have awarded the firm a higher market multiple. I grew up as a partner in the private Goldman Sachs and am of that era. It has been said that Goldman always gets the right leadership for the times it is in. I can't argue with that.

What troubles me is the thought that as Goldman has gotten bigger and conformed more to market expectations, it has had to become a little less special. When you hear alumni grumble about how the place has changed, even though the share price is doing well, I think you're hearing expressions of that same feeling. And yet those same expressions were heard when I got the job, and probably when my predecessor got his. Sentimentalizing the past is a common affliction of mankind, but in truth the current generation is usually the greatest.

CHAPTER 28

Risk Is Risky

It's not that anything can happen; it's that eventually everything will happen.

ou've reached the part of the book where the author feels compelled to share some larger thoughts. I usually cruise though this part myself. Feel free to skip ahead to the epilogue.

But if you're still with me, I do want to say a few words about what I see as the great strength of the American economy: its remarkable resilience. It is amazing that the US remains the fastest growing of all the developed modern economies even as it is by far the biggest. Usually size works against adaptability. In our case, the opposite seems to be true—even when the US is ground zero for a global crisis, as it was in 2008. As in previous market downturns following the Russian default in 1998, the dot-com crash in 2000, and the global pandemic in 2020, we came back stronger and faster than anyone else. As Warren Buffett likes to say, never bet against the US economy. "For 240 years it's been a terrible mistake to bet against America," he wrote in his 2016 letter to his shareholders. It's time to update that. It's been a terrible mistake for *250* years.

If the US economy is the most successful in the world, the reasons are its culture around risk, resilience, and recovery, and its particular style of mildly fettered capitalism.

What does it mean to have an economy that can bounce back quickly from setbacks and crises? Our success flows in part from being an individualistic society that views risk-takers as admirable and is always inclined to give them another chance after they fail. In America, resilience is most prized, more than unearned or easily earned success. Steve Jobs wouldn't have been Steve Jobs if he hadn't been fired from Apple and come back. The same can be said for Jamie Dimon, who relaunched his career at Bank One after Sandy Weill fired him from Citigroup. In the US, you aren't limited to merely recovering your reputation. If you emerge well from a crisis, you can come out ahead. When I advise leaders who are getting overwhelmed by a problem or bad press, the first thing I say is, "Congratulations. You just satisfied the precondition for a fantastic display of resilience and character!"

Resilience also applies at the government level. There are inevitable moments when government has to intervene to prevent capitalism from destroying itself. What John Maynard Keynes called "animal spirits" can get out of hand, as happened in the run-up to the global financial crisis. Only the government has a balance sheet big enough to restore faith in the system when it periodically melts down.

After the global financial crisis, legislators clamored for new rules to make sure it would never happen again. That is a vain hope. Capitalism by its nature runs to excess and attempts to prevent the possibility of future financial crises are probably doomed to fail. When crises occur, my view is that government should step in to restore confidence, let the chips fall where they deserve to fall, and then get out of the way again.

Two out of three ain't bad, you might say. We recovered from the financial crisis better than other countries because, however messy it seemed at the time, the government did restore confidence and did let management and shareholders in failed financial institutions bear the consequences of their mistakes. Getting out of the way again is a little more complicated. Hungry to find, humiliate, and punish individual malefactors, the body politic demands that the system not go back to the way it was. That political dynamic can lead to rules that go too far in dampening the animal spirits that are so essential to innovation and growth. Trying to legislate against a once-in-a-century crisis risks causing slower growth for all the generations in between. The only way to get rid of the tail risk is to get rid of the whole tail—to ban risk-taking at scale and turn the entire economy into a T-bill.

In practice, we have our show trials, get them over relatively quickly, and get back to business. I remember sitting with John Rogers in Senator Chris Dodd's office after the crisis to discuss the eponymous legislation he was drafting. It was a friendly and constructive conversation, and we seemed to agree on almost everything. We got interrupted when Senator Dodd said he had to go to the floor for a vote. He returned to our meeting about ten minutes later. *What did you vote on?* I asked him. *Oh—a hundred-percent tax on bankers' bonuses*, he said. He'd voted in favor. It wasn't one of the topics that had come up when we were finding common ground.

But soon enough the finger-pointing winds down and the financial cycle revs up again. We get back on the road and start driving fast again. By contrast, Europe took more than a decade to recover from the last crisis, and in many respects the overhang is with it still.

SO MUCH OF RESILIENCE COMES FROM HAVING A BETTER UNDERSTANDing of risk, something our nature and emotions often work against. People are generally bad at thinking objectively and historically. We overvalue the present and recent past, thinking that the events we're living through are unique and unprecedented. They never really are. Of course, the worst crisis is always the one you're living through, because you don't know if or how it's going to be resolved. It's hard to be afraid of something that's resolved and on the shelf of history. The present, by contrast, is unresolved, with the potential to keep getting worse.

How often do I hear people say the country has never been through a more dangerous time? Nonsense—we had a civil war. Okay, that was a long time ago. But in my lifetime, I saw my parents transfixed, watching the television news during the Cuban Missile Crisis. We were enforcing a blockade around Cuba, forcing Soviet ships to turn around on the high seas, which is an act of war. (We called it a "quarantine" instead of a blockade.) It was the only time the US military has gone to DEFCON 2 status. DEFCON 1 is imminent or active nuclear war. President Kennedy went on television to prepare the country for just that possibility.

People say our society has never been more polarized. Nonsense again—my early memories also include the assassinations of JFK, Medgar Evers, RFK, and Martin Luther King Jr. When I was in high school, the National Guard was shooting kids protesting the Vietnam War on college campuses, at Kent State and Jackson State—the latter got more attention in the mostly Black neighborhood where I grew up. Kids were moving to Canada to avoid the draft. In 1968, revolution seemed to be breaking out everywhere in the world—there were barricades in the streets in Paris and tanks in the streets of Prague. I find it reassuring that we have navigated worse times than the ones we are in. If our parents and grandparents got through the Cold War, Vietnam, and the upheavals of the 1960s, there's no reason to be pessimistic about our ability to get through lesser dangers today.

Every so often, when a young person asks my advice on what to study in college as preparation for a career in finance, I always recommend history rather than math or economics. I say that because it is valuable to have a sense of what has happened before, a consciousness of historical cycles, and the ability to distinguish secular changes from the kind that tend to recede and recur. That kind of perspective helps you keep your head on when things go awry and keeps you from getting too cocky when things go well. Ultimately, an awareness of history makes you a better boss, a better leader, and a better risk manager. It makes you better able to practice resilience, knowing that things do recover.

WHEN SENTIMENT SHIFTS, IT NOT ONLY CHANGES PEOPLE'S MINDS BUT also changes their memories. When did we feel safer—on September 10, 2001, or on September 12? We felt safer on September 10, of course, because of our blissful ignorance. When were we actually safer? On September 12, of course, because we were fully attuned to the threat and on our toes.

After Hurricane Katrina and a series of other major storms in 2005, insurance premiums skyrocketed. But the risk of major storms hadn't increased in any appreciable way from one year to the next (although it has increased over a longer time frame because of climate change). People were just much more conscious of the risk and thus willing to pay more for coverage. Some of my wealthy friends are waiting for the next hurricane to buy beachfront property in the Hamptons. But when the next big storm comes, most of them will panic too. The future risk may not be any different, but it will feel a lot different in the aftermath of a bad event. Few people have cool enough heads to take on more risk when everyone and everything seems to be going the other way. Having a sense of the past helps to calibrate one's thinking about the future.

I like to remind people that risk is risky. It's an obvious truism at one level, but at another a crucial way of looking at the world. A firm like Goldman is fundamentally in the business of risk management. The challenge of risk management is that few people are capable of being objective or fully rational about risk.

When we were in risk-taking mode at Goldman, I was interested in people's predictions, although I always thought the future was basically unknowable. Most of the biggest changes of my lifetime, including the end of the Cold War, the rise of China, the arrival of the internet, and the rapid transformations wrought by AI, were not just unforeseen but largely unforeseeable until they were upon us. Predict the future? We can barely predict the present. Punditry is entertainment, and good punditry is good entertainment.

But when we were in risk-management mode at Goldman, I would have little interest in what people thought was going to happen. Rather, I wanted to know what could go wrong and what planning we had done to mitigate the consequences of each of those contingencies. If our planning was thorough and complete, when events went awry in any direction, we could react so swiftly that it would look to outsiders as if we had known ahead of time what was coming. In track-and-field events, athletes aren't allowed to anticipate the starting gun. You can be disqualified if you move off the starting block within a tenth of second *after* it's been fired. I used to say that was our goal: to react so quickly that people would think we knew what was going to happen before we heard about it.

Another way of putting this is that for purposes of risk management, you're not in the forecasting business. You're in the contingency planning business.

IF A PICTURE CAN BE A METAPHOR (IT CAN!), ONE PHOTO TAKEN DURING Hurricane Sandy in 2012 encapsulates Goldman's attitude toward risk, and the world's attitude toward Goldman. Our headquarters was opened in 2009 with expensive redundant systems. After all, we are located in a vulnerable spot between the site of the World Trade Center and the Hudson River. In case of a major weather threat, we kept thousands of sandbags in the basement and in nearby storage. When we received the forecast that Sandy was coming, we surrounded our building with a thick wall of sandbags. The storm caused severe and destructive flooding in New York City; cars floated by and all of lower Manhattan was without power—except for us. A picture taken that night from across the Hudson River shows a blackout except for 200 West Street, which had every light on per an automatic timer. The press took it as a taunt, and one caption transmitted with the photo was "Nice try, God."

AN ECONOMIC SYSTEM HAS TO BE STRUCTURED TO ACCOMPLISH TWO important goals: to create wealth and to distribute that wealth in a way consistent with a society's notion of fairness. Sometimes those two goals are at odds. Capitalism remains the best system ever devised for motivating individuals to engage in economically constructive behavior. But unregulated capitalism will create wealth mainly for the few. Socialism is fair on paper but disincentivizes the creation of wealth in the first place.

In a healthy capitalist system, large investment banks like Goldman Sachs function as modern-day manifestations of Adam Smith's "invisible hand," directing investment to where it is most needed and productive in the economy. Investment banks serve as sophisticated financial intermediaries that connect those in need of capital with those who have capital to invest. The investment bankers within investment banks form relationships with entrepreneurs, companies, governments, and other entities to help them raise funds by advising on and executing transactions such as issuing stocks or bonds.

In doing so, investment bankers determine the optimal mix of debt and equity, decide on the precise timing of the issuance, and structure the deal in a way that aligns with the needs of the client. This process is far more complex than simply matching borrowers and lenders. Borrowers may want to issue fixed-rate debt while investors want floating-rate debt. The borrower may need euros, but the liquid pool of capital may be dollar-based. A trusting relationship comes from understanding the client's long-term objectives and providing research-driven advice and execution. And because it has a reputation for serving good companies and weeding out unworthy ones (with some mistakes along the way), Goldman's involvement can be taken as a useful validation.

The sales and trading part of an investment bank performs the critical function of pricing, managing, and redistributing financial risks such as fluctuations in interest rates, commodity prices, credit defaults, or currency changes—that clients would rather not take. In those cases, the bank may take on these unwanted exposures. And because the specific risk profile that a client wants may not find an investor willing to take it on at the time or in the form that suits the client, the risk may need to be held by the bank for some time, until market preferences shift or the risk can be restructured. This might involve breaking up a large quantum of risk into smaller pieces or using derivatives to transform the nature of the risk. Traders and salespeople connect directly with institutional investors, asset managers, and hedge funds to facilitate the buying and selling of the financial instruments that have been created.

This dual role of both advising clients and actively participating in the market as a principal underscores the complexity of the bank's operations. Overall, by forming trusting relationships with capital consumers and capital providers, with risk-avoiders and risk-takers, and by managing positions that can't be bridged immediately, investment banks ensure that financial resources are allocated efficiently across the economy, contributing to both growth and stability.

Part of government's role is to set and enforce the rules restraining this activity. Only government can prevent bad competitive behavior and make sure no competitor wins to the point that it prevents further competition. But my experience is that government seldom succeeds in allocating capital in a way that best serves the economy. Would we want all transportation to be run by Amtrak? Logistics companies to be run like the post office? Housing to be run like the New York City Housing Authority projects where I grew up? Does anyone think NASA would be capable of moving as quickly as SpaceX or the other competitors in the new, privatized space race?

Just as important is the role firms like Goldman play in restructuring businesses that aren't working and recycling capital into more productive uses. Government isn't good at this. It faces a particular challenge when it comes to reallocating its investments, whether that means closing down scores of no-longer-needed nineteenth-century fire stations in New York City or repurposing unnecessary military bases in ways that can serve local economies. When it comes to ending what isn't working, the narrow interests of a few can block the imperatives of the many.

There are, of course, economic needs that only a robust public sector can satisfy. Government has an essential role to play in basic research, in stimulating early initiatives, and in promoting social objectives that the market doesn't provide for effectively. From rural electrification in the 1930s to the internet, which grew out of defense research in the 1980s, government has filled many gaps left by the free market. And of course, government has a central role to play in wealth redistribution through taxation and social benefits. The extreme inequality generated by free markets can be adjusted only through a progressive tax system and a safety net. That has to include a welfare system as well as income support and health care for retirees and disabled people.

ANYONE WHO WAS INVOLVED IN MARKETS OR POLICYMAKING IN THE 2000s and 2010s has to reexamine what they used to think about China and how we all got it at least somewhat wrong. At the DealBook conference in 2014, I predicted that that this could be "the Chinese century" to rival the American century. I was probably getting carried away and wouldn't be as sure today. I'm optimistic that over the long term, America will outperform China. But who knows—we have three quarters of the century left to go.

Like a lot of people, I believed China was evolving toward a more market-based capitalist system. There was plenty of reason to think so. Its unprecedented run of growth, beginning with Deng Xiaoping's Open Door Policy in 1978, turned a poor country into a middle-class one and seemed unstoppable. Liberalization of the society seemed to go hand in hand with liberalization of the economy, as it had in Russia in the period leading up to the fall of communism, glasnost, and perestroika moving in the same direction. China didn't have modern investment banking, and Goldman hoped to play a significant role, along with other US companies, in helping it build a robust financial and business sector with a degree of separation from the government.

But once again, the essential unpredictability of history asserted itself and the inevitable trend turned out to be less than inevitable. In 2018, Xi Jinping overturned the tradition of a ten-year term limit and essentially made himself into a new Chairman Mao. That the vote in the People's Congress was 2,958–2 (with three abstentions) told you all you needed to know. Today, China's economic system is firmly established as one of state capitalism, not market capitalism.

Is that system a genuine rival to ours? What I think today is that centralized decision-making and the repression of individuality can't work in the long term. There's too much rigidity in the system, and it becomes a serious liability. Leaders can't read the signals of change and so can't easily recognize and correct policy mistakes. For example, China was short on regional airports, so in 2012 it announced that it was going to build eighty-two new ones over the next five years. And amazingly, it built even more than that. But how many of those airports are in the right places?

Our market-based system, by contrast, reflects the input of millions of engaged decision-makers rather than the analysis of central planners. That doesn't mean that our decisions are always better, though I think they usually are. A more technocratic, less democratic regime might have wasted a trillion dollars constructing Al Gore's "information superhighway" instead of leaving it to the private sector to build out the internet. The fundamental advantage of a market-oriented system is that it identifies mistakes and forces change faster. In the US, if you develop housing or build a shopping center in the wrong place, people don't come. Fees don't get paid, the bank repossesses the land, and the land gets repurposed. In China, the mistake (and the blot on the balance sheet) stays there forever, or at least for a very long time.

Centrally planned, authoritarian systems are less likely to create and attract entrepreneurs, who by definition challenge convention. This point was highlighted for me in a surprising context. In a series of toasts at a dinner for business leaders in Beijing, I took my turn to flatter my hosts. "China will always be an economic powerhouse, because it can draw on the talents of 1.4 billion people." My Chinese counterpart one-upped me. "The US will always be great because it draws on the talent of 8 billion people, including many Chinese who go there to study and work." The Chinese recognize America's attractiveness to talented, striving immigrants; I hope we don't lose sight of that ourselves.

There is, of course, a kind of brutality to the American economic system. When businesses encounter hard times, we let them fire people, reallocate resources, and move on. The people get rehired into more viable enterprises, but only after they have suffered for a time a loss of salary and benefits. In many countries in Europe, you can't fire anybody. Workers are protected, but salaries are lower and opportunities fewer. Zombie companies persist, never growing. It's kinder in one way and crueler in another.

WHAT RISKS SHOULD WE WORRY MOST ABOUT TODAY? WHILE FLEXIbility and adaptability remain core advantages of the US economy, I'm troubled by the creeping ambiguity around the role of business. In my early days at Goldman Sachs, we were a partnership, accountable to one another. When we went public, we became—like the many companies we helped to take public over the years—accountable to shareholders. But there was still a clear goal of maximizing profits, subject to law, regulation, and ethics. In recent years, people have argued that a company is responsible not just to shareholders but to "stakeholders." Advocates of the stakeholder model of capitalism make the case for balancing profitability with a variety of social, environmental, and other concerns.

I dislike the language of stakeholding because of the way it muddies the waters around the respective responsibilities of government, corporations, and the nonprofit sector. Society can tax and regulate oil extraction and emissions in all sorts of ways to get less of them. But why should Exxon have to justify itself by building windmills? The fad for ESG investing, which puts the largest asset managers in the position of pushing for various kinds of policies, seems to me misguided. It asks finance to step in because politics isn't producing the desired outcomes. But certain goals can be accomplished only through politics, and putting them on business doesn't solve the problem.

The reverse is also true. Washington has been going through one of its periodic bouts of enthusiasm for industrial policy, which is premised on the idea that government should supplant some major market decisions. I've observed over the years that this seldom works. Government isn't good at picking winners, at the level either of companies or of whole industries.

At the same time, the pure free-trade model hasn't worked out so well in practice either. In my entry level economics class at Harvard, I learned that tariffs were always bad and that free trade enriched the world because every country could perform according to its relative advantage. In the years since the financial crisis, we've seen a political backlash to globalization, with populism and polarization fueled by the loss of well-paid industrial jobs and the hollowing out of the communities those jobs sustained.

It's not tenable, morally or politically, to say that all manufacturing should simply go to the lowest-cost producers, in countries without decent wages or basic labor and environmental protections. What's more, for national security reasons the United States can't abandon manufacturing. You can't scale up production in computer chips or cars on short notice. If the US doesn't retain the capacity to make certain strategic goods, it will be subject to the whims of the countries that do.

The relative advantage of some of our competitors is that they pay their workers a lot less and thereby have a relative advantage across the spectrum of labor-intensive industry and manufacturing. Americans don't want their workers to live like Vietnamese workers. If we want those jobs—if we want manufacturing to continue in the US—we have to make some imported goods more expensive. In my view, making up for differential labor costs is the primary justification for tariffs.

The risk of escalating trade wars is very real; it's something that we know can lead to a global depression, as it did in the 1930s. The math of tariffs does show how burdensome and counterproductive they can be. But so is a strike as part of a union/management negotiation. Such a job action hurts everyone, but it's necessary to move both sides to a "market clearing" settlement. Tariffs are sometimes unavoidable for the same reason. If you take them off the table, you can't negotiate effectively with other nations that retain them.

ANOTHER THING THAT KEEPS ME UP AT NIGHT IS THE INEVITABILITY of human error and the likelihood of unforeseen technology accidents. It's a funny truth that you can't hear an algorithm. In the old J. Aron trading room, there was a cacophony, but you could somehow hear through it. If a trader quoted the wrong price for gold—down when it should have been up—someone else would usually hear the mistake and catch it quickly. It's the same way that you can hear someone say your name across a noisy room. There was still an intuitive, human sense of trading activity. Today when someone deploys the wrong piece of software, there's no discordant sound as you bleed to death.

Everyone is appropriately afraid of a hack, but I have always thought the world would be more likely to end because of a "fat finger" mistake. During the so-called flash crash in 2010, the Dow briefly dropped 1,000 points for reasons that have never been adequately explained. Financial markets have experienced several other brushes with automated-trading catastrophe, in currencies, cryptocurrency, and stocks. At Goldman in 2015, we were testing some new software for automated trading when an engineer somehow managed to deploy a buggy program that began selling certain stocks in our portfolio for $1 per share. In minutes, we were down hundreds of millions of dollars. We had to go to the exchanges and ask them to reverse the accidental trades. In most, but not all, cases, they were willing to do so.

Technology is leverage, and leverage is a two-edged sword. A mistake in the past could never be that expensive. Prior to the nuclear age, a big industrial accident could kill hundreds or possibly thousands of people. The worst-ever industrial accident was the leak at a

Union Carbide pesticide plant in Bhopal, India, in 1984, which probably killed around eight thousand people and injured tens of thousands. In the nuclear age, the accidents at Chernobyl or Fukushima could have killed millions and displaced tens of millions more. If AI goes wrong, it has similarly catastrophic potential.

EPILOGUE

Life After Goldman

Motivation was easier to source when I had to make a living. Now I have to generate it another way. I didn't like serving my classmates breakfast in the food hall, but I knew why I was doing it.

I wasn't born to be a financier. I got to J. Aron, which became part of Goldman Sachs, on a fluke. I loved it, but I had other interests that I neglected. I always loved history, and I wanted to learn more about physics. I wanted to be a better student than I had been at Harvard, to do it right this time. For years, I could never follow up on those interests, other than by sporadic reading. Being able to pursue my curiosity freely over the last few years has felt like a luxury and a gift. In exploring new avenues, I often think of Jon Cohen's admonition to one day have an obituary that would describe a life beyond Goldman. Today I have one, even if a lot of it takes place inside my own head.

In the first few years after I left, I was genuinely torn about whether to take another job. Of my immediate six predecessors at Goldman Sachs, the only one who didn't go to Washington when he retired was John Weinberg, in 1990. So why didn't I pursue a government job like the others? One answer is that I'm a lifelong Democrat and I retired in the second half of the first Trump administration. I was glad that the Goldman alums—Gary Cohn, Steve Mnuchin, and Dina Powell—were there. But by the second half of that administration, there wasn't a place for another moderate globalist like me. A few friends flattered me by suggesting I run for mayor of New York City. I would love to be mayor, provided I didn't have to run for it.

The truth is I was feeling increasingly out of sync with the polarized political environment as a whole. Extremism on either side holds no appeal for me. Nothing important can get done without political compromise. Policies that are moderately left of center or moderately right of center have the best chance of providing stability. Policies driven by either party's extreme wing, on the other hand, are likely to be reversed when the political pendulum swings the other way. I don't think polarization created the problems in the system. I think the system itself drives polarization.

I started tweeting in 2017, when I was still in my Goldman job. It was fun to say what I thought! I tweaked the administration for pulling out of the Paris Climate Accords and criticized Trump for his support of white nationalists marauding in Charlottesville. I was getting close to violating my own advice about when a CEO should take sides on highly polarized issues—another sign that I was close to the end of my tenure.

> @Lloydblankfein Immigration is a complex issue but I wouldn't deport a kid who was brought here and only knows America. Congress must address. #DACA

When I weighed in, I tried to be somewhat circumspect. Still, these were personal opinions and probably more provocative than made sense for the head of a public company. After I left, I didn't have to be so cautious. Jack Dorsey, the founder of Twitter, sent me a plaque for my desk with something I tweeted when I announced that I was retiring: "Here's one thing I look forward to: unrestrained tweeting."

Now I could get into all the Twitter battles I wanted. It was fun to provoke New York City mayor Bill de Blasio and Senator Elizabeth Warren, and to poke my head into debates at Harvard Law School.

On the far left, Bernie Sanders's views are as unpalatable to me as extreme views on the Republican right. During his 2020 presidential campaign, Sanders put me on his "antiendorsements" list along with Jamie Dimon of J.P. Morgan and Bob Iger, the CEO of Disney. I figured Twitter might be a good place to respond in kind.

> @Lloydblankfein I don't know why Sen. Sanders picks on a retiree like me. I think he's always looked down on me because he grew up in a fancier Brooklyn neighborhood.

It's true—Sanders grew up in Midwood, which was a middle-class neighborhood, very different from East New York. Anyhow, he took the bait (or perhaps vice versa).

> @BernieSanders Actually my concern has to do with the fact that you had no problem getting bailed out by working Americans, while you've been picking on them by advocating for cutting Medicare, Medicaid, and Society Security.

> @Lloydblankfein Didn't know I was against all those necessary and well-established social programs. Actually, I think we have more in common than you think. . . . two self-made millionaires from Brooklyn who lean a bit to the left!

Twitter was sort of irresistible for me, given the opportunity to make points in a provocative, sometimes naughty way.

> @BernieSanders Lloyd Blankfein, the former CEO of Goldman Sachs, is correct that the money from stock buybacks "doesn't vanish." It increases the wealth of billionaires like him. Instead of making the very rich even richer, how about increasing wages for American workers. Is that a bad idea?

> @Lloydblankfein Never thought I'd hear Sen. Sanders criticize me for not paying higher wages at my old firm.

COVID-19 arrived just over a year after I left the job. Like a lot of people, I turned to social media to try to make up for the loss of contact with people outside my household.

> @Lloydblankfein Been quarantined with my wife for four weeks now. At this point I have more risk of getting killed by her than by a crummy virus.

> @Lloydblankfein I don't seem to be having much trouble getting people to "social distance" from me.

> @Lloydblankfein It's only now I appreciate how happy I was before Covid-19. I wish someone would have told me.

Ultimately, I stopped. Everyone on Twitter, it seemed to me, soon enough got canceled for some ill-judged or misinterpreted comment. As far as going back and forth with senators, I decided it was stupid to argue with folks who had subpoena power.

LAURA OFTEN REMINDS ME THAT OUR MARRIAGE VOWS DIDN'T INCLUDE lunch. But being at home in the daylight hours gives me the opportunity to pursue things simply because I'm interested in them. The bulk of my reading is history and biography. I suppose I'm a middle-aged male cliché, because I read a lot of military histories and biographies of the founding fathers. I like reading biographies because the subject who emerges as a hero on page five hundred is going through a crisis and trials on page two hundred, with no indication of how it will turn out. As a late bloomer, I appreciate the sense of persistent hope. The disappointments of the moment often yield to greatness down the line, and people's life stories prove it.

I read history because I enjoy it, but also because it has always provided a reference point for me in my career. Immersing yourself in history cuts against present-mindedness. History doesn't repeat in the same way, but in a line attributed to Mark Twain, it rhymes. History is just as important for business as for economics or high finance. In particular, business cycles recur. You have to know whether changes are secular or cyclical. And you have to respect a cycle. If you get killed in a tough cycle, you're still dead when it shifts back.

I've also become a dedicated amateur student of linguistics and physics, pursuing my curiosity by taking courses and reading books, sometimes the same ones more than once. Physics is hard! At some level, quantum mechanics is inconceivable and incomprehensible. I like that no one truly understands how or why the universe works—it takes the pressure off.

Not that I've walked away from finance. I continue to trade markets for my own account as a pastime, a lot, every day. I buy and sell equities, and to a lesser extent bonds, currencies, and commodities, because it's fun for me to make bets on the market. Another occupational hazard of a life spent in trading and finance is that I want to know the price of everything, all the time.

I enjoy trading in much the same way I like reading obituaries and the weddings section of the paper. Each investment engages me in a story, whether about a company, a country, or something going on in the world. I follow the opinions of various authorities and commentators and test them against my own. As an individual, it's not practical for me to do certain complicated trades, and while I generally make money at it, that's not the point.

I'm at a place in life where anything more that I earn will benefit someone I've never met—whether my future descendants or the unknown beneficiaries of charities I support. But if you grew up without money, it's hard to break out of the mindset of needing a regular source of income.

EVEN AS I PURSUE MY CURIOSITY IN NEW DIRECTIONS, I'M STILL FIXated on the firm where I spent nearly my whole career. What about Goldman has made it so durable and successful? Why do long-departed former staff still feel such a strong connection to it? It's part of Goldman's culture that people who worked there, even decades ago, still care about it—perhaps, if they're being honest, more than they do about the firms where they currently work. Goldman alumni have come to constitute a conscious diaspora in a way people who have spent careers at other Wall Street firms, even venerable ones like J.P. Morgan or Merrill or Lazard, just don't.

There's an invisible thread connecting Goldman partners—past, present, and future—that has no parallel at any other commercial organization I know of. We former leaders still care deeply about the place and sometimes find it hard to maintain an appropriate level of distance. It's not easy to watch from the outside an institution where you spent a whole career. For me, what happens at Goldman, and in the careers of people I worked with there, still stirs a full range of emotions—pride in accomplishment and sometimes anger about missteps. It's a connection that's impossible to really let go of, like your family, your old school, or your favorite hometown sports team. More than anything else, this book has been an attempt to share what I learned there and to explain why I feel that way about it.

Acknowledgments

First, I want to acknowledge the people who provided opportunities and supported me so that I could have a career that one day might be worth reading about. The list starts with my parents, my sister, and my friends—from the projects, college, law school, and during my false start as a lawyer at Donovan, Leisure.

And of course my colleagues and partners from J. Aron and Goldman Sachs. Early on I received support and encouragement from Dennis Suskind, Marci and Bennett Grau, Jimmy Riley, Mark Winkelman; later on from Steve Friedman, Jon Corzine, Hank Paulson, David Viniar, John Rogers, and Russell Horwitz. Tim O'Neill and Gary Cohn were important to me for almost the whole ride. There were dozens more I worked with over my thirty-six active years with the firm, and I'm afraid that if I named and recounted my debt to each of them, this section would be longer than the book.

My greatest thanks go to Laura and my kids, Alex, Jonathan, and Rachel, to whom this book is dedicated. Laura was an associate in a law firm herself and continued practicing as a litigator through the arrival of our third child. She understood and accommodated the stresses of my professional life, taking care of all of us while working and performing board responsibilities at several educational institutions. My kids have been a source of nothing but pride and pleasure. They were forgiving of my frequent absences, and supportive during my occasional pummelings in the press and during my bout with cancer. It could not have been easy for them, but they absorbed all of that and showed me only love and encouragement.

Second, I want to acknowledge the people without whose help this project would never have achieved liftoff. On my own, I wrote versions of the early chapters, and fragments of later ones. I also had a series of anecdotes from my career that I wanted to build lessons around. One day after writing for a few hours, I decided to take a break and put my pen down. Next thing I knew, four years had flown by. I assumed that would be it. At some point I mentioned my suspended project to my old Goldman colleague Jake Siewert, who encouraged me to go forward. He said I needed help (duh!) and offered to introduce me to his friend Jacob Weisberg, an accomplished journalist and the former editor of *Slate*. He thought Jacob could help with organization and writing and impose some discipline. Again, I got lucky. Jacob was the only person I considered to help me, and we worked well together. He's another of the great partners I have been blessed to have had. Most impressive, he is the first Rhodes Scholar I met who didn't let that slip out in the first ten minutes of a conversation—I only found out when I googled him weeks later. Jacob steered me to my extraordinary lawyer/agent Bob Barnett, and then to my publisher, Penguin Press, and to my superb editor, Scott Moyers. They were a great team and collectively made the job easy and fun. I wish I had met Jacob, Bob, and Scott a few years earlier—I'd be wrapping up volume II by now!

Finally, I am in the debt of a number of others who have helped with this project at various stages: my late and sorely missed assistant Julie Becht, and Gideon Leek, who helped with research, fact checking, and photo research. At Goldman, I had the support of the extraordinary archivists Melanie Edwards and Christina Boscarino, as well as Laura Ropas. At Penguin Press, I've benefited from the commitment of Gail Brussel, Matt Boyd, Mia Council, Elijah Matos, Jennifer Tait, Michael Brown, Helen Rouner, and Aly D'Amato.

Finally, I want to thank the friends and former colleagues who read drafts of chapters, gave feedback, and made corrections: Russell Horwitz (again), Tim O'Neill (again), Jake Siewert (again), Jimmy Riley (again), Armen Avanessians, Esta Stecher, and David Solomon, as well as Roy Geronemus, Lisa Cashin, the Lanes, and the Marinos. Blame me, not them, for the faults that remain. After you do, *I'll* blame them.

Image Credits

PAGE

1 *(top)*: Personal collection of Lloyd Blankfein.
  (bottom): Personal collection of Lloyd Blankfein.

2 *(top)*: Personal collection of Lloyd Blankfein.
  (middle): Personal collection of Lloyd Blankfein.
  (bottom): Personal collection of Lloyd Blankfein.

3 *(top)*: Personal collection of Lloyd Blankfein.
  (bottom): Personal collection of Lloyd Blankfein.

4 *(top)*: Personal collection of Lloyd Blankfein.
  (bottom): Personal collection of Lloyd Blankfein.

5 *(top)*: Courtesy of Goldman Sachs. All rights reserved.
  (bottom): Courtesy of Goldman Sachs. All rights reserved.

6 *(top)*: Courtesy of Goldman Sachs. All rights reserved.
  (middle): Courtesy of Goldman Sachs. All rights reserved.
  (bottom): Courtesy of Goldman Sachs. All rights reserved.

7 *(top)*: Courtesy of Goldman Sachs. All rights reserved.
  (bottom): Courtesy of Goldman Sachs. All rights reserved.

8 *(top)*: Courtesy of Goldman Sachs. All rights reserved.
  (bottom): Personal collection of Lloyd Blankfein.

9 *(top)*: Courtesy of Goldman Sachs. All rights reserved.
  (bottom): Courtesy of Goldman Sachs. All rights reserved.

IMAGE CREDITS

10 (*top*): Courtesy of Goldman Sachs. All rights reserved.
   (*middle*): Courtesy of Goldman Sachs. All rights reserved.
   (*bottom*): Courtesy of Goldman Sachs. All rights reserved.

11 (*top*): Courtesy of Goldman Sachs. All rights reserved.

12 (*middle*): Anthony Pleva/Alamy.
   (*bottom*): Brooks Kraft/Cordbis Historical via Getty Images.

13 (*top*): Scott J. Ferrell/CQ-Roll Call, Inc. via Getty Images.
   (*bottom*): Courtesy of Goldman Sachs. All rights reserved.

14 (*top*): Richard Levine/Alamy.
   (*bottom*): Courtesy of Goldman Sachs. All rights reserved.

15 (*top*): Brendan Smialowski/Getty Images News via Getty Images.

16 (*top*): Photo courtesy of CNBC.
   (*middle*): Courtesy of Goldman Sachs. All rights reserved.
   (*bottom*): Courtesy of Goldman Sachs. All rights reserved.

Index

ACLI International, Inc., 65, 68
Adams House, 31
affirmative action, 233–34
Afghanistan, Soviet invasion of, 60
African National Congress, 59
AI (artificial intelligence), 43–44, 115, 183, 348
AIG (American International Group)
    credit default insurance, 249–50
    liquidity crisis and bailout, 126, 261, 267–68, 271–72, 275, 296–97
Alibaba, 322
Ali, Muhammad, 46
Allstate Corporation, 271
Almaz, 60
Al Rajhi, 74–76, 84, 93
Alstom, 295
aluminum, 99–100, 101–2
Amazon, 183, 224
Angelides, Phil, 298
"animal spirits," 345–46
antiwar movement, 26–27, 239, 347
Apollo Global Management, 311–12
Apollo 13 (movie), 243–44
Apple, Inc., 345

Arab Spring, 318
arbitrage, 84–85, 138, 241
    bond markets, 70, 78
    gold, 55–68, 70–71, 74–76, 82
    interest rates, 62–63, 66
Armstrong, Mike, 195
Aron, Jack, 61–62
Arthur Andersen, 195
Asian financial crisis of 1997, x, 162
Aspen Institute, 276
Astoria Manor, 9
Atlantic Golf Club, 52
Atlantic, The, 29
AT&T, 195
Avanessians, Armen, 145
    financial crisis, 268–69
    hiring, 80–81
    risk management tools, 80–81, 87, 92, 94, 102, 103, 121–22

Babson College, 236
backwardation, 102–3
Bair, Sheila, 277–78, 287, 310–11
Baity, John, 42–43, 47, 54, 296
Baker, James, 218
Balducci's, 67

372 INDEX

bandwidth, 194
Banking Act of 1933. *See* Glass-Steagall Act of 1933
Bank of America, 86, 197, 205, 216–17
   financial crisis, 265, 267, 268, 273, 288, 298
   Merrill Lynch acquisition, 197, 267, 273, 288
Bank of England, 63, 84
Bank of New York, 85–86, 268–69, 272
Barber, Lionel, 214
Barclays, 262, 265
Barnard College, 46, 111
Bass brothers, 186
Battle of Waterloo, 7
Baum, David, 170
Beach Boys, 42
Beame, Abe, 36
Bear Stearns, 150, 248
   bankruptcy and bailout, 245, 254–58, 264, 267, 279
   J.P. Morgan acquisition, 255–56, 265, 294
   LTCM crisis, 165, 261
Becht, Julie, 328
Bell Labs, 80
Ben-Hur (movie), 54–55
Bensinger, Steven, 249–50
Berkowitz, David (Son of Sam), 36–37
Berlin Wall, 146
Bernanke, Ben, 247, 248, 258, 266, 287
Best and the Brightest, The (Halberstam), 163
Better Business Bureau, 336
Bezos, Jeff, 295
Bhopal disaster of 1984, 356–57
Biden, Joe, 128
Bidwell, Truman, 47–48
Big Bang (1986), 84
Birnbaum, Josh, 247–48
Bishop Estate, 150
Black, Fischer, 79–80, 121, 163
Black-Litterman model, 121
Black Monday (1987), x, 97, 163
BlackRock, 199, 339
Black-Scholes model, 79
Blackstone, 311–12

Blankfein, Alex, 15, 16, 30–31, 107, 142, 143, 144, 184, 303–4, 333–34
Blankfein, Blanche, 1–2, 3–4, 6, 8, 18, 20, 53
Blankfein, Cristina Ros, 334
Blankfein, Hannah, 3
Blankfein, Isaac, 2–3
Blankfein, Jonathan, 107, 144, 184, 303–4, 333
Blankfein, Laura Jacobs
   children and family life, 107–8, 142, 143, 147–48, 187–88, 303–4, 334, 362
   financial crisis, 276, 284
   Goldman Sachs and, 108, 109, 139, 302–4
   London move, 141–44, 187–88
   meeting and proposal, 45–47
   non-Hodgkin's lymphoma and, 328–30, 332–34, 335
   Paulsons and, 198–99, 207–8
   philanthropy, 110–11
   September 11 attacks (2001), 184, 187–88
   wedding, 71
Blankfein, Nico, 334
Blankfein, Rachel, 107, 144, 147, 184, 304, 316, 333
Blankfein, Saul, 2–3
Blankfein, Seymour, 1–6, 8, 23
   post office job, 5, 18, 44, 71
   son at Harvard, 16, 17–18, 20, 24
Blankfein, Sheldon, 3, 19–20
Bloomberg, 317, 321
Bloomberg Markets, 295
Bloomberg, Michael, 189, 238
B'nai Israel Synagogue, 8
BNP Paribas, 250
BNY Mellon, 244
Boca Raton, 25
Bolshevik Revolution, 318
Bolten, Josh, 208, 294
bond market crisis of 1994, x, 110, 123, 124–26, 134, 141
Bonfire of the Vanities, The (Wolfe), 137–38
Born in the USA (Springsteen), 60
Brennan, William, 28

Brexit, 146
BRICs (Brazil, Russia, India, and China), 177
Brickman Hotel, 27–28
British Airways, 157–58
British Gas, 88
British Petroleum, 209
British Telecom, 88
Broad, Eli, 243
Bronx High School of Science, 9
Brooklyn Technical High School, 9
Brooks Brothers, 198
Brosens, Frank, 109
Browne, John, 209
Brown University, 215–16
Brown v. Board of Education, 30
Bryan, John, 209, 309
Buffett, Warren, 122, 179
   Chicago meeting, 211, 214–15
   commencement speeches, 238
   financial crisis, 261, 295
      Goldman investment, 280–83, 287–88, 315–16
Bunning, Jim, 256–57
Burlington Northern Railroad, 282–83
Burroughs, 93
Bush, George H. W., 162, 218
Bush, George W., 162, 180, 207–8, 209, 294
Business Investigations Group, 177

Cameron, David, 90
Campisano, Mark, 28
Canada, Geoffrey, 235
Cantor Fitzgerald, 185
capital accounts, 110–12, 120, 125–26, 156, 166
capital gains, 75, 167
capitalism, 345, 350, 353, 354–55
Capital Purchase Program (CPP), 287–88
Capitol Records, 41–42
Capone, Al, 97
Carl Schurz Park, 185
Carlyle Group, 341
Carlyle Hotel, 188
Carney, Mark, 294
carrying cost ("contango"), 62, 100, 102

cash-and-carry trade, 75, 100
Catskills, 4, 27–28
Center for International Affairs, 26
Central Bank of the People's Republic of China (Beijing), 57, 67, 176
Central Bank of the Republic of China (Taiwan), 57, 67
Central Park, 303, 318, 333
CEO (chief executive officer) of Goldman, 211–326
   agenda, 212–15
   appointment, 207–16
   assembling a team, 216–19
   conflicts, 219–22
   criticism and negative publicity, 295–304, 318–22
   diversity efforts, 232–34
   financial crisis of 2008, 245–90
      aftermath, 291–314
      background and lead-up, 240–50
      bonuses, 289–90
      BONY box, 268–69, 272
      Buffett investment, 280–83, 287–88, 315–16
      business standards committee, 305–8
      Citi merger idea, 275–76, 279–80
      public announcements, 251–54, 256–57, 258–59, 268–70, 280, 282, 285–90, 292–93, 298, 299, 301
      public hearings, 287–88, 297–99, 308–9
      reputational crisis, 245–46
      SEC settlement, 304–5
      Securities Database (SecDB), 81
      TARP, 273–75, 286–89, 294, 310
      Wachovia merger idea, 276–77, 279–80
   Gupta scandal, 315–17
   Malaysia and 1MDB, 322–24
   Occupy Wall Street, 318–21
   partnership culture, 223–39
   political issues, 324–26
   retirement of, ix, 337–43
Chairman's Forum, 225, 307
Charles Schwab, 180
Charlottesville Unite the Right rally, 360
Chase Manhattan, 160

chemotherapy, 330–32
Chicago Mercantile Exchange, 52,
    84–85, 103–4
childhood, 1–15
China, 176–77, 215–16, 348, 352–54
China Telecom, 176–77
Christian Science, 129, 198
Citadel LLC, 229
Citibank, 63, 66
Citigroup, 205, 345
    financial crisis, 248, 252–53, 262,
        277, 288
    Goldman merger idea, 275–76, 279–80
    Salomon Smith Barney acquisition, 159
    Wachovia acquisition, 277
Civil War, 8, 347
Clean Air Act, 116
Clean Water Act, 101
climate change, 348, 360
Clinton, Bill, 114, 302, 320
Clinton Global Initiative, 170
Clinton, Hillary, 261
"close to home," 247, 252, 300
CNBC, 69, 180, 230, 257, 271, 291, 317, 343
Code Pink, 300
coffee business, 61–62, 65, 68–69, 100,
    127–28
cognitive biases, 125
Cohen, Jon, 110–11, 359
Cohen, Rodgin, 306
Cohn, Gary
    AIG and, 249–50
    as co-COO, 216, 217
    commodity trading, 99–100,
        101–2, 193
    departure of, 340–41
    FICC, 193, 340–41
    financial crisis, 272, 275, 281,
        285, 307
    global equity funds, 240–42,
        244–45
    hiring, 99–100
    Lloyd's illness and, 333
    as national economic adviser,
        340–41, 360
    Tesla and Musk, 238–39
Cold War, 347, 348

Cole, Chris, 268, 277
collateralized debt obligations (CDOs),
    246, 249, 251, 252–53, 255, 265
collateralized mortgage obligations
    (CMOs), 246
collective vs. individual identity, 226
COMEX, 55–56, 62, 67, 99
comic books, 7–8
commodity market, 62–69, 99–105
Commodity Research Bureau Index
    (CRB), 103
compensation
    Goldman Sachs, 109–10, 131–32, 151,
        167, 226, 289–90, 346
    J. Aron, 53, 72
    risk-taking and, 122–23
Concorde, 157–58
Coney Island, 12
conflicts of interest, 104, 180, 210, 212,
    213, 219–22
Congressional Black Caucus, 310
Continental Airlines, 28
"contingent" option hedge, 93
corporate taxes, 151–52, 311
Corrigan, Gerry, 305
Corzine, Jon
    bond market crisis of 1994, 125
    as CEO, 128–30, 136, 138, 141, 142, 216,
        222, 232, 272, 341
    departure of, 165–66, 169
    fixed-income division, 78, 115, 122, 129,
        137, 138–39, 216
    IPO, 154–56, 157, 160–61, 165, 168, 169
    Paulson relationship, 128, 160, 165, 229
    September 11 attacks (2001), 185
COVID-19 pandemic, 334, 341, 344, 362
Cox, Christopher, 262, 274
Cramer, Jim, 69, 230
credit derivative swaps (CDS), 248–50,
    257–58
Credit Suisse, 339
Cruz, Zoe, 272
Cuban Missile Crisis, 347
CV Starr, 243

Daffy, Michael, 320
Daily Mirror, 6, 117

Dairy Queen, 281
Dallas Federal Reserve, 189
Dar Al-Hekma, 236
Dartmouth College, 199, 263
Davies, Gavyn, 89–90, 98–99, 109, 115, 123, 170
Davis, Chuck, 131
Davis, Evelyn, 152
Davis Polk, 38
day-trading, 180
Dean Witter, 50, 57–58, 152. *See also* Morgan Stanley
  Morgan Stanley acquisition, 159, 162
de Blasio, Bill, 13, 361
DEI (diversity, equity, and inclusion), 326
Dell Technologies, 152–53
democracy, 214, 232, 319
Democratic Convention (1964), 3
Democratic Party, 6, 340, 359–60
Deng Xiaoping, 352
Department of Trade (UK), 118
deregulation, 40, 84, 94, 137, 176
Detmann, Johan, 58–59
Deutsche Bank, 125, 262, 270
deutsche marks, 98
devaluations (de-vals), 83, 84
Dewey, Ballantine, 48
Diamond, Bob, 265
Diana, Princess of Wales, 144
Dick Tracy (comic), 6
Die Hard (movies), 240, 243
Dimon, Jamie, 255–56, 262, 265, 298, 337, 345, 361
discrimination, 10–11, 38
Disney, 41–42, 146, 186, 361
Disney, Walt, 6
diversity efforts, 232–34, 326
Dodd, Chris, 346
Dodd-Frank Wall Street Reform and Consumer Protection Act of 2010, 310–11
Donaldson, Lufkin & Jenrette, 65, 68, 149–50
Donovan, Leisure, 38–48, 50
  departure, 50, 53–54
  hiring, 38–39

  recording industry cases, 41–44
Dorsey, Jack, 360–61
dot-com bubble, 66, 175, 176, 178–83, 193–94, 344
Draghi, Mario, 294
Drexel Burnham Lambert, 66, 130
Dutch tulip mania, 182

East New York, Brooklyn, 1–15, 16
eBay, 178
economic bubbles, 182
Economic Times of India, 315
ECU (European Currency Unit), 144–45
education, 8–10. *See also* Harvard College; Harvard Law School
Egan, Charles, 35
election of 1964, 239
election of 1968, 26
election of 2020, 361
election of 2024, 128
energy crisis of 1970s, 58, 64–65, 77
English Channel, 146–47
Enron, 176, 193–95, 311
EPA (Environmental Protection Agency), 116
ESG (environmental, social, and governance), 354–55
Eton, 7, 90, 145
eToys, 179
EU (European Union), 146–47, 214
euro currency, 84, 144–45, 146
Euromoney, 98
European Central Bank, 83–84, 123, 250
European Exchange Rate Mechanism (ERM), 83–84, 89–90
Evers, Medgar, 347
Exxon, 354
Exxon Valdez disaster, 101

Facebook, 15, 230
Fannie Mae, 209, 246, 251, 258
FBI (Federal Bureau of Investigation), 308, 309
FDIC (Federal Deposit Insurance Corporation), 258, 277–78, 287, 310–11

Federal Housing Finance Agency
    (FHFA), 310
Federal Reserve, 64, 123, 129–30, 164–65,
    247, 255–56
Federal Reserve Act, section 13(3),
    255, 264
Federal Reserve Bank of New York, 63, 306
financial crisis, 255–56, 261–65, 266,
    271–72, 274–75, 276
Federal Trade Commission, 35
Ferrari, 89, 120
Fidelity, 152, 191–92
Fieldston School, 46, 48, 110–11, 304
Financial Crisis Inquiry Commission,
    287–88, 297–99, 308–9
financial crisis of 2008, x–xi, 245–90
    aftermath, 291–314
    AIG liquidity crisis and bailout, 126,
        261, 267–68, 271–72, 275, 296–97
    background and lead-up, 240–50
    Bank of America acquisition of Merrill
        Lynch, 197, 267, 273, 288
    Bear Stearns bankruptcy, 254–58, 260
    Lehman Brothers collapse, 260–66
    resilience, 345–46
    TARP, 273–75, 286–89, 294, 310
Financial Times, 213–14, 295, 312
First Amendment, 46
Fixed Income, Currency, and
    Commodities (FICC), 138–39,
    141–42, 144–45, 166, 174, 175–76,
    189, 192–93, 216
fixed income trading, 70, 72, 78, 95–96,
    115–16, 121, 136–37, 144–45
flash crash of 2010, 356
Fletcher, Anne, 29
Flowers, Christopher, 109
Fly Club, 30–31
Forbidden City, 215
Forbidden City (Beijing), 215
Ford Foundation, 237
Ford, Gerald, 64
Ford Motor Company, 237, 238, 283
Ford Mustang, 42
foreign exchange markets (forex), 81,
    83–105, 116, 117–18, 120–21, 123,
    134–35, 144–45

foreign exchange risk, 84, 87–89, 92–93,
    97–98
Foreign Policy Association, 45–46, 71
Forst, Ed, 184, 185, 294
Fort Lauderdale, 24
Fortune, 254
Frank, Barney, 310
Freddie Mac, 251, 258
free trade, 355–56
Friedman, Rich, 204–5, 221
Friedman, Steve, 179
    bond market crisis of 1994, 122, 125–26
    CEO succession, 210
    as co-COO, 114, 126, 137, 189–90, 341
    departure of, 126–27, 128, 229, 286
    financial crisis, 126, 272
    IPO, 154
Friedman, Thomas, 213–14
Fuld, Dick, 130, 260–61, 262, 265–66, 272

Gaddhafi, Mu'ammar, 77
Galleon, 315–16
Gambril, Don, 22
Garonzik, Rick, 137–38
Gates Foundation, 237–38
gay marriage, 325–26
GE Capital, 278
Geffen, David, 333
Geithner, Tim, 255–56, 261–65, 267,
    275–76, 287–89, 294, 320
Genentech, 291
General Electric, 277–78
General Motors, 116, 278
General Post Office, 5, 18, 44, 71
Gensler, Gary, 109
George, Bill, 305, 308
George Gershwin Junior High School, 8
Georgetown Law School, 45–46
George Washington University, 218
German, Avner, 8–9
Geronemus, Roy, 21
Gettysburg Address, 6
Glass-Steagall Act of 1933, 159, 160, 171,
    206–7
Global Alpha Fund, 241–45
Global Equity Opportunities Fund,
    241–45

INDEX 377

global financial crisis of 2008. *See*
    financial crisis of 2008
globalization, 84, 93, 115, 142, 171, 176,
    213–14, 245, 355
Godfather, The (movie), 33
gold arbitrage, 55–68, 70–71, 74–76, 82
"Gold Bear Note," 102
Golden West Financial, 276
Goldfield, Jacob, 138, 145
Goldman Sachs. *See also specific persons*
    ABACUS 2007-AC1, 297–300, 305, 310
    alumni, 151, 226, 229–31, 293–94, 297,
        304, 343, 364
    as bank holding company, 218, 279–80
    board of directors, 167, 201, 215–16,
        226, 269–70, 308–9, 315–16
        CEO decision, 196–97, 201, 207, 208,
            209–10
        succession planning, 196–97, 339–40
    bonuses, 110, 112, 120, 131, 151,
        289–90, 346
    business-selection, 220–21
    business standards committee, 305–8
    CEO of. *See* CEO
    compensation, 109–10, 131–32, 151, 167,
        226, 289–90, 346
    COO appointment, 108, 197, 201–3, 208
    culture at, 68–70, 77–78, 111–13,
        120–21, 127, 171, 173, 176, 204,
        223–39, 293
    FICC, 138–39, 141–42, 144–45, 166, 174,
        175–76, 189, 192–93, 216
    fixed income trading, 70, 72, 78,
        95–96, 115–16, 121, 136–37, 144–45
    foreign exchange (forex), 81, 83–105,
        117–18, 120–21, 123, 134–35,
        144–45
    global expansion, 176–78, 213–14
    hierarchy of prestige, 72–73, 94–95, 97
    innovation, 92–105
    IPO of. *See* IPO of Goldman
    IPO underwriting, 178–79, 180–81,
        190–91, 238, 291
    J. Aron acquisition, 65–66, 68–71,
        78, 108
    London move, 141–48
    LTCM crisis, x, 163–65, 178, 261
    management committee, 132, 139, 155,
        173–75
    management structure, 128
    Maxwell affair, 117–20, 125, 217
    merging fixed-equities division,
        138–39, 192–93
    partnerships, 108–13, 115–16, 131–32,
        204, 223–39, 293
        exodus of 1994, 126–29, 130–32,
            158–59
    Penn Central bankruptcy, 111, 119, 150
    performance reviews, 139, 200
    philanthropy, 110–11, 234–39, 311
    profits, 65, 89, 112–13, 115, 151–52
    recruitment, 76, 86–87, 90, 150–51,
        217–19, 231, 232–33, 312
    risk committee, 126, 132, 133–34
    September 11 attacks (2001), 74,
        183–89
    Spear, Leeds acquisition, 66, 181–82,
        190–91
    stock price, 168, 181, 204, 257, 282,
        289, 343
    succession, 193–97, 339–40
Goldman Sachs Asset Management
    (GSAM), 241–45
Goldman Sachs Commodities Index
    (GSCI), 103–4
Goldman Sachs Foundation, 161,
    234–35, 238
gold standard, 64
Gone With the Wind (movie), 8
Gore, Al, 353
government-sponsored
    entities (GSEs), 258
Gracie Mansion, 13
Grasso, Richard, 197
Grau, Bennett, 54, 71, 80–81
Grau, Marcy, 54–56, 70, 71, 82
Great Depression, 3, 64, 169, 245, 295
Great Recession, 292–93
Great Society, 239
Great Wall of China, 215
Greece, austerity crisis, 318
Greenberg, Hank, 243
Greenspan, Alan, 123, 211, 214
Green, Stephen, 273

378   INDEX

Greenwich Mean Time (GMT), 147
Griffith, Melanie, 47
Grizzle, David, 21–22, 24, 27, 28–29, 32–33, 48, 50, 52
Grodin, Charles, 48
Gropius, Walter, 34–35
Grubman, Eric, 170
GS Gives, 235–36
GS Ventures, 175
Gulf of Tonkin incident, 26, 239
Gulfstream, 301–2
Gupta, Rajat, 315–17
Gutfreund, John, 130

Halberstadt, Victor, 335
Hallmark Cards, 35
Halloween, 143
Hamilton, George, 18
Hamptons, 107–8, 303, 334, 348
Harlem Children's Zone, 235
Harris, Kamala, 128
Harvard Business School, 68, 103–4, 189, 217, 236
Harvard Club, 17
Harvard College, 16–31, 69, 76, 333
    admission interview, 16–19
    arrival at, 18–20
    freshman year, 18–25
    scholarship fund, 48, 110–11
    senior year, 29
    sophomore year, 25–29
Harvard Crimson, 21, 69
Harvard, John, 19
Harvard Kennedy School of Government, 197
Harvard Lampoon, 21
Harvard Law School, 32–39, 69, 361
Harvard Shop, 23
Harvard Yard, 19, 20, 26, 34
Heartbreak Kid, The (movie), 48
Heathrow Airport, 158
hedging, 62, 64, 80, 82, 87, 92, 93, 96, 97, 103, 248–50, 297
hedge funds, 154, 162, 163, 164, 170, 191, 226
Hendel, Steve, 51–52, 109, 132
Hermès, 296

Herzog Heine Geduld, 181
Hilton Worldwide Holdings Inc., 152–53
Hoffman, Dustin, 112
Ho, Greg, 42, 53, 71
Holocaust, 4–5, 7
Horwitz, Russell, 302, 333
House Financial Services Committee, 310–11
Houseman, John, 33
House Un-American Activities Committee, 46
HPS Investment Partners, 199
HSBC, 273
Human Rights Campaign Fund, 325
Hunt brothers, 65
Hurricane Katrina, 237, 348
Hurricane Sandy, 349
Hurst, Bob, 155, 160, 188, 194
Hyde Park, 46

IBM, 93
Iger, Bob, 361
Immelt, Jeff, 277–78
immigration, 2, 3
IndyMac, 258
inflation, 56, 58, 64–65, 104, 123, 179
insider trading, 130, 315–17
interest rate risk, 122–23
interest rates, 123, 124–25, 129–30, 179
interest rate swaps, 136–37
Internal Revenue Code, 42
International Finance Corporation (IFC), 236
International Monetary Fund, 162
International Monetary Market (IMM), 82, 84–85
International Rescue Committee, 235
internet, 178, 183, 194, 302, 352, 353
investment banking, 50, 70, 72, 94–95
invisible hand, 206, 350
IPO (initial public offering) of Goldman, 149–72, 173
    arguments against, 150–54, 161–62
    first attempts, 154–56
    offering prospectus, 167–68
    Palisades Conference meeting, 160–62

partner shares, 131–32, 151, 153–54, 156–57, 166–68
strategy committee, 157–60
IRS (Internal Revenue Service), 41, 167
Ishihara, Hideo, 125–26
Israel, 178, 320
It's Academic (TV show), 10
It's a Wonderful Life (movie), 258
iVillage, 178

Jackson State killings, 347
Jacobs, Norman, 45–46, 71
James, Art, 10
James, Henry, 126–27
Japan, 84, 90–91, 130, 158, 176, 225, 234
J. Aron, 50–63. *See also specific persons*
  balanced books, 61–62
  bonuses, 72, 112
  coffee trading, 61–62, 65, 68–69, 100, 127–28
  commodity trading, 62–69, 99–105
  compensation, 53, 72
  culture at, 57, 66, 68–70, 77–78, 111–13, 120–21
  foreign exchange (forex), 81, 83–105
  gold arbitrage trading, 55–63, 64–65, 67–68, 74–76, 82
  Goldman acquisition, 54–55, 65–66, 68–71, 78, 108. *See also* Goldman Sachs
  Goldman postmerger, 77–82
  headhunters, 49–51
  job offer, 52–55
  merging fixed-equities division, 138–39, 192–93
  organization, 89, 94–95, 106–8
  partnerships, 108–13, 115–16, 135–36
  profits, 52, 63, 65, 66, 77, 78, 98–99, 110, 112–13, 115
  promotion to "options" desk, 106–7
  proprietary trading, 89, 98–99, 114–15, 120–21
  September 11 attacks (2001), 74, 183–89
  training, 55–57
Javits Center, 156
Jefferson High School, 9–10, 11, 13, 16, 54

Jester, Dan, 294
Jewish education, 8
Jewish Theological Seminary, 170
Jobs, Steve, 295, 345
Johnson, Jim, 209
Johnson, Lyndon, 239
Jordan, Michael, 178, 325–26
J.P. Morgan Chase
  Bear Stearns acquisition, 255–56, 265, 294
  financial crisis, 255–56, 262, 263, 267, 270, 310
  Goldman merger considerations, 160, 205
  House of Morgan and, 206, 275
  metals sales and arbitrage, 66
junk bonds, 94, 130
Justice Department, 308–10, 315–16

Kalb, Richard, 7
Kansas City, 28–29, 35–36
Kaplan, Rob, 188–89
Kapnick, Kathleen, 198–99
Kapnick, Scott, 198–99
Kashkari, Neel, 294
Katz, Howard, 127
Katz, Robert, 118, 126, 127–28
Kennedy, John F., 20, 347
Kennedy, Robert F., 347
Kent State shootings, 347
Keynes, John Maynard, 345
King Lear (Shakespeare), 326
King, Martin Luther, Jr., 11, 347
Kissinger, Henry, 26
Koch Industries, 152
Korea Development Bank, 260–61
Kovacevich, Dick, 288
Krellman, Lilly, 2, 3, 6, 21
Kron, Patrick, 295
Kruger Park, 59
Krugerrands, 57–59
Krugman, Paul, 319
Kuwait, 77

Lacoste, 23–24, 71
Laker, Freddie, 40
Lane, Curtis, 328

INDEX

lap swimming, 200, 284
Lazard Frères, 36, 172
Lazarsfeld, Robert, 20
LeFrak housing, 12
Lehman Brothers, 130
   collapse of, 260–66, 267, 273
   Marino at, 143, 184
Leiser, Ron, 12–13
Leissner, Tim, 323
Leonard, John, 328–30, 334–35
leverage, 163–65, 242–43
Leverett House, 25, 28
Levin, Carl, 299–300, 304, 305, 307,
   308, 321
Levine, Matt, 321
Levitt, Arthur, 305–6
Levy, Gus, 149, 341
Lewis, Ken, 265, 267, 288
Lewis, Michael, 137
LexisNexis, 44
Liar's Poker (Lewis), 137
Libya, bombing of 1986, 77
Liddy, Ed, 271–72
Lincoln, Abraham, 6
Linden Houses, 2, 6–7, 10–11, 13, 24
linguistics, 363
Lipset, Seymour Martin, 25
liquidity, 49, 103, 164–65, 186, 250, 255,
   256, 260, 275, 278, 282, 306
LLC (limited liability company), 156–57
"Lloydisms," xi
London, 141–48
London Acorn School, 144
Long-Term Capital Management
   (LTCM), x, 163–65, 178, 261
Lopatin, Jon, 86, 170
loss aversion, 124–25, 133
Low, Jho, 322–24

Maccabiah Games, 320
McCarthy, Eugene, 26
McCarthy, Joe, 46, 299
McDonald's, 214
McKim, Mead & White, 17
McKinsey & Company, 315, 317
Mack, John, 130, 262, 272, 274, 298
McMahon, Bill, 81

Macmillan Publishers, 117
McNamara, Robert, 78
McNulty, John, 190
macroeconomics, 89
"macro" opinions, 115, 129
"macro" traders, 122
Ma, Jack, 322
Malaysia, 322–24
Male Shop (Brooklyn), 19–20
M&As (mergers and acquisitions), 88,
   132, 150, 159–60, 205, 212–13, 214,
   226, 230, 268
Mansfield, Harvey, 26
Marino, Jill, 142–43, 333
Marino, Tom, 142–43, 184, 333
mark to market, 246–49
Marsella, Greg, 20
Marshall Scholars, 28
Marshall, Thurgood, 339
Mars, Incorporated, 152
Martindale-Hubble, 35
Marymount School, 52
Maxwell, Robert, 117–20, 125, 217
Maytag, 215
MBA programs, 33, 236
MCA Records, 41–42
Medtronic, 305
Mellon Bank, 160
Memorial Sloan Kettering, 329
mentors (mentorships), 67, 236
merchant banking, 146, 179, 204–6
Mercury Asset Management, 159
Meriwether, John, 163
Merrill Lynch Banking & Financial
   Services Conference, 253
Merrill Lynch & Co., 130
   Bank of America acquisition, 197, 267,
   273, 288
   financial crisis, 248, 252–53, 262, 264,
   267, 273, 288
   Herzog Heine Geduld acquisition, 181
   IPO, 149–50, 152
   Mercury acquisition, 159
Merton, Robert, 79, 163
military draft, 27, 347
Milken, Michael, 130
Millionaire, The (TV show), 154, 168

Mitsubishi, 283
Mnuchin, Steve, 170, 231, 340–41, 360
"mommy track," 233
money markets, 95, 97, 266, 274–75
Montag, Tom, 216–17
moral hazard, 122, 256
Morgan Grenfell and Schroders, 90
Morgan, John Pierpont, 205–6
Morgan Stanley, 50, 130
   compensation, 151
   Dean Witter acquisition, 159
   financial crisis, 248, 262, 267, 272, 283
   House of Morgan and, 206, 270
   IPO, 150, 152
Morocco, 40–41
Morrison, David, 89–90, 98–99, 109
Mortara, Mike, 137–38, 175
Moses Brown School, 20
Mossavar-Rahmani, Sharmin, 126
Moynihan, Brian, 298
Murdoch, Rupert, 187
Murphy, Eddie, 70–71
Murphy, Phil, 161, 169
Museum of Natural History, 130–31
Musk, Elon, 238–39
My Cousin Vinny (movie), 23

narrative-based trading, 145
NASA, 243–44, 351
Nasdaq, 66, 180, 181, 182
National Commercial Bank of Jeddah
   (NCB), 66–67
national debt, 129–30, 179–80
National Economic Council, 114, 340
National Guard, 185, 347
NATO (North Atlantic Treaty
   Organization), 214
natural gas, 100–101, 132
Nature Conservancy, 170
nepotism, 231
NetJets, 301–2
New Deal, 64, 258
News Corp., 187
New York (magazine), 69
New York City Department of
   Education, 20
New York City fiscal crisis, 44–45

New York City Housing Authority, 2,
   10–11, 351
New York City Law Department, 147
New York City Transit Authority, 25
New York Daily News, 6
New York Historical Society, 110
New York Police Department, 319
New York Post, 299
NewYork-Presbyterian Hospital, 328–29
New York Public Library, 8, 130
New York Stock Exchange (NYSE),
   149–50, 180, 197
New York Times, 37, 68, 69, 71, 109, 197,
   209, 297, 317, 325
   Occupy Wall Street and, 318–19
   "Why I Am Leaving Goldman Sachs"
   (Smith), 320–22
New York Times Spelling Bee, 6
New York World's Fair (1939),
   5–6, 215, 280
New York Yankees, 12, 219
NFL (National Football League), 170, 219
Ng, Roger, 323
9/11 attacks (2001), 74, 183–89, 348
Nixon, Richard, 27, 64
Nixon shock, 64
Nizer, Louis, 46
Nobel Prize, 79, 163
noncompete agreements, 166–67
non-Hodgkin's lymphoma, 327–36

Obama, Barack, 211, 215, 290, 291, 311
Obergefell v. Hodges, 325
O'Brien, Mike, 98–99, 109, 121,
   124–25, 135
Occupy Lloyd's apartment building, 302–4
Occupy Wall Street, 318–21
Office of Financial Stability, 294
Ogunlesi, Adebayo, 339
O'Hare Airport, 211
oil, 58, 99, 100–103
oil crisis of 1970s, 58, 64–65, 77
Olympics, 22, 60
O'Neal, Stan, 130, 252–53
O'Neill, Jim, 90, 177
O'Neill, Tim, 47, 86–87, 92, 103–4,
   268–69, 285, 306

382 INDEX

One L (Turow), 33–34
1MDb, 322–24
OPEC oil embargo of 1973, 77
Overfelt, Charlie, 28–29

Pale of Settlement, 3
Palisades Conference Center, 160–62
palladium, 60, 116
Palm, Greg, 217, 263, 285, 329
Palm, Julie, 329
Pandit, Vikram, 262, 275–76, 288
P&Ls (profit and loss), 27, 62, 106, 135, 175, 182, 190–91, 202, 203, 209, 212, 240, 241
Panic of 2008. *See* financial crisis of 2008
Paper Chase, The (movie), 33, 34
Paris Climate Accords, 360
Partnership for New York City, 187, 235, 325
Paulson, Hank
  background of, 129, 199
  as CEO, 142, 173–75, 193, 199
    succession, 189–90, 193–94, 196–97, 199–200, 207–12
  as co-CEO, 160
  Corzine relationship, 128, 160, 165, 229
  financial crisis, 169, 199, 247, 255–56, 258–59, 261–65, 275–78, 283, 287–89, 293–94, 297
  IPO, 155, 157–58, 160, 165–70
  September 11 attacks (2001), 185, 187, 189
  as Treasury secretary, 169–70, 207–10, 211–12, 247, 287–89, 338
  as vice-chairman, 128, 129, 155
Paulson, John, 297–300, 305, 310
Paulson, Wendy, 198–99
Paul, Weiss, 38–39
Pelosi, Nancy, 237
Penn Central bankruptcy, 111, 119, 150
People's Bank of China, 57, 67, 176
Perella Weinberg Partners, 189, 277
Peretz, Martin, 25–26
Perry Capital, 243
Perry, Richard, 243

PetroChina, 176–77
P.F. Flyers, 214
Pfizer, 291
philanthropy, 110–11, 234–39, 311, 335
Philipp Brothers (Phibro), 65, 68
Phillips, Nizer, Benjamin, Krim & Ballon, 46
physics, 145, 363
PlanetRx.com, 179
platinum, 60, 116
Poland, 2–3
politics (political issues), xi, 245, 310–11, 324–26, 347, 355, 360–62
PolyGram, 41–42
populism, 355
Powell, Dina, 360
Powell, Lewis, 217
precious metals, 55–68, 94
Prentiss, Paula, 18
Prince, Chuck, 253
private equity, 154, 170, 179, 188, 203–4, 221, 226, 230, 311–12
Procter & Gamble, 315
Pront, Richard, 67
proprietary trading, 89, 98–99, 114–15, 120–21, 150, 311, 320
Proskauer Rose, 36–37
public speaking, 200

"quantity adjusting" option, 92–93
quants, 138, 145, 241–42
Quantum Fund, 84
quantum mechanics, 363

racism, 10–11, 347
Radcliffe College, 20
Radio City Christmas, 17
Rain Man (movie), 112
Rajaratnam, Raj, 315–17
Rakoff, Jed, 316
Raquette Lake Boys Camp, 12–13
Razak, Najib, 322–24
Reagan, Ronald, 77, 129–30, 218
recording industry cases, 41–44
Red Hat Software, 178
Reebok Sports Club, 198
Reed, John, 318–19

regulations, 345–46, 351
  Clean Air Act, 116
  Clean Water Act, 101
  Dodd-Frank Act of 2010, 310–11
  financial crisis and, 310–13, 346
  Glass-Steagall Act of 1933, 159, 160, 171, 206–7
  IPO and, 152, 180–81
  Sarbanes-Oxley Act, 176, 195, 201–2, 311
Reich, Robert, 295
Rendel, Michael, 329–30, 332
repo (repurchase agreement), 254–55
reputational crisis, 245–46
resilience, 344–57
revaluations (re-vals), 83
rhodium, 60, 116
Riley, Jim, 56, 99, 116
risk, 346–49, 354–56
risk aversion, 124–25, 133, 144–45
risk-management systems, 80–81, 87, 121–22, 163, 241
Robin Hood, 235
Robinson, Jackie, 38
Roche, 291
Rockefeller Center, 47
Rockefeller Foundation, 71, 315
Rock of Gibraltar, 124
Rogers, John
  China trip, 215
  financial crisis, 285, 288, 302, 306, 346
  non-Hodgkin's lymphoma and, 329, 330
  Paulson and, 209
  as secretary of the board, 218, 285, 288, 302, 330
  September 11 attacks (2001), 185
  at the White House, 209, 218, 302
Rolling Stone, 295, 307
Roosevelt, Franklin D., 46, 64, 69
Roosevelt, Theodore, 17
Rose, Charlie, 214–15
Rothschild family, 205
rowing, 22
Rube Goldberg, 243–44

Rubin, Robert, 341
  as co-COO, 76, 78, 79, 97, 98, 107, 114, 137, 138, 189–90, 226
  retirement of, 114, 122, 127, 154
  risk arbitrage, 76, 79, 98
rural electrification, 352
Russia, 2, 9, 177, 352. *See also* Soviet Union
Russia financial crisis of 1998, x, 145, 162–63, 344
Russian Bank for Foreign Trade, 60
Russian Revolution, 318
Russian roulette, 278

Saccente, Jacky Blankfein, 2, 4, 5–6
  brother at Harvard, 18, 19, 24
  personality of, 24–25
St. George's School, 28
Salame, Pablo, 228–29
Salomon Brothers, 65, 130, 137, 150
Salomon Smith Barney, 159
same-sex marriage, 325–26
Sanders, Bernie, 361–62
Sara Lee Corporation, 209
Sarbanes-Oxley Act, 176, 195, 201–2, 311
Saudi Arabia, 58, 74–76, 77, 236
Saudi Arabian Oil Ministry, 58
Save the Children, 235
Scherr, Stephen, 293
Schiphol Airport, 101
Schneider, William, 30
Scholes, Myron, 79, 163
Schultz, Howard, 10
Schwartz, Harvey, 306, 341
Schwartz, Mark, 109, 136–37
SEC (Securities and Exchange Commission), 152, 180–81, 262, 274, 280, 298, 304–5, 329
Securities Database (SecDB), 81
securitization, 246–50
Semlitz, Steve, 109
Senate Permanent Subcommittee on Investigations, 299–301, 308–9
September 11 attacks (2001), 74, 183–89, 348
S.G. Warburg & Co., 159
Shafran, Steven, 294
Shanghai Stock Exchange, 176

Sheinberg, Eric, 117
Shepherd, Cybill, 48
Sherman, Emily, 45
Sherwood, Michael "Woody," 285–86, 290
ShoreBank, 310–11
Shultz, George, 68
Shun Lee West, 109
Siewert, Jake, 320
SIFIs (systemically important financial institutions), 312, 313
Silfen, David, 155
silver futures, 55, 56, 61, 65
Silver, Lou, 178
Simmons, Ruth, 215–16, 308
S. Klein, 3
Smith, Adam, 206, 350
Smith, Greg, 320–22
socialism, 256–57, 350
Solomon, David, 142, 223, 293, 306, 341
Sorkin, Andrew Ross, 297, 322
Soros, George, 84
sound recordings, 41–44
South Africa, 57–59, 116, 177
South African Reserve Bank, 58
South Bronx, New York City, 1–2
South Korea, 90–91
Soviet Union. *See also* Russia
  Cold War, 347, 348
  collapse, 60, 99–100
  Moscow visit, 59–61
SpaceX, 351
Spacey, Kevin, 190
Spain, austerity crisis, 318
Spear, Leeds & Kellogg, 66, 181–82, 190–91
speculative bubbles, 182
Spitzer, Eliot, 180–81
Springsteen, Bruce, 60
stakeholder model of capitalism, 354–55
Standard and Poors's 500 (S&P 500), 75–76, 164, 286
Standard Oil of Indiana, 43
Starbucks, 10
Starrett City, 24
Star Trek (TV show), 304–5
Stecher, Esta, 217–18, 279–80, 285

Steel, Robert, 109, 188–89, 197, 276–77, 294
Story Hall, 34–35
storytelling, 225–26
"strats," 80
Stuyvesant High School, 9
subprime mortgages, 241–55, 258, 267, 297
Sullivan & Cromwell, 118, 217, 306
Sulzberger, Arthur, Jr., 321–22
Sumitomo Corporation, 150
Suskind, Dennis, 52–53, 60–61, 70, 73, 116
Sutton, Percy, 310

Taibbi, Matt, 321
tariffs, 355–56
tax law, 37–48
Taylor, Elizabeth, 46
technology, 92–94, 115, 178, 348, 356–57
Ten Days That Shook the World (Reed), 318
10,000 Small Businesses, 236–37, 238
10,000 Women, 235–36, 238, 261
Tesla, 238–39
Thain, John
  as co-COO, 132, 135, 173, 189–90, 193
  departure of, 197, 217
  financial crisis, 262, 273, 288
  IPO, 155, 160, 165
  at Merrill Lynch, 196, 197, 262, 273, 288
  partnership class, 109, 135
  risk committee, 133–34
  Spear, Leeds acquisition, 181–82
  succession issue, 193, 196–97, 210
Thernstrom, Abigail, 29
Thiel Fellowships, 30
Thiel, Peter, 30
Thomas, K.V., 74–76
Thornton, John
  as co-COO, 132, 135, 173, 187–90, 193–94
  departure of, 196–97
  IPO, 155, 160, 165–66
  partnership class, 109, 135
  September 11 attacks (2001), 187–88
  Spear, Leeds acquisition, 181–82
  succession issue, 193, 196–97, 210
Thucydides Trap, 95–96
Time Warner Cable, 291

INDEX 385

Time Warner Center, 276
time zones, 134, 147
Tourre, Fabrice, 298–99, 310
"tracking risk," 76
trade wars, 355–56
Trading Places (movie), 70–71
Travelers Insurance, 159
treasury securities, 129–30, 163, 179–80
"triple play," 212–13
Trott, Byron, 281–82
Troubled Asset Relief Program (TARP), 273–75, 286–89, 294, 310
True North (George), 305
Trump, Donald, xi, 270, 311, 340–41, 360
Trump Organization, 270
Tsang, Moses K., 126–27
tulip mania, 182
Turnbull, Malcolm, 169
Turow, Scott, 33–34
Twain, Mark, 363

UBS Group, 90, 159, 248, 262
Union Carbide, 356–57
United Jewish Appeal, 10
United Services Group, 188
United Way, 235
Universal Commercial Paper, 97–98
University of California, Los Angeles (UCLA), 42
University of Chicago, 310
University of Delaware, 320
University of Michigan, 70
unlimited liability, 111, 131, 150
U.S. Steel, 206
US Trust, 160
Usual Suspects, The (movie), 190

value-at-risk systems, 122
"vampire squid," 295, 321
Vance, Lee, 170
Vanguard, 191
Vanity Fair, 295
Varadhan, Ashok, 185, 293
venture capital, 175, 178
Verizon, 186
Vietnam War, 26–27, 239, 347
Vince, Robin, 244–45

Viniar, David
  as CFO, 217, 247–48, 341, 343
  financial crisis, 247–48, 252, 285
  global equity funds, 240–43, 244–45
  retirement of, 341
  subprime mortgages, 247–48
Volcker, Paul, 65
Volcker Rule, 311
Volpert, Barry, 188

Wachovia, 189, 276–77, 279–80
Wall Street Journal, 6, 50, 128–29, 197, 317, 323, 329
Wang Qishan, 215
Warren, Elizabeth, 361
Wasserstein, Bruce, 272
Webvan, 178, 179
Weill Cornell Medical School, 110–11, 329
Weill, Sandy, 345
Weinberg, John L., 120, 229
  Exxon Valdez disaster, 101
  IPO, 161
  leadership of, 108–9, 112–13, 127, 190, 226, 337, 341
  note from, on appointment as CEO, 197
  offer of partnership, 108–9
  retirement of, 114, 359
Weinberg, John S., 306
Weinberg, Peter, 277
Weinberg, Sidney, 149, 192, 197, 215, 280, 337
Weiner's Hotel, 4
Weingarten, Reid, 308
Weld Hall, 20
Wellesley College, 35
Wells Fargo, 288
Westbury Hotel, 71
Westlaw, 44
Wharton School, 78
Where the Boys Are (movie), 18
white flight, 11
Whitehead, John, 68, 161, 234, 306, 337, 341
Willumstad, Bob, 271–72
Wilson, Kendrick, 294
Winfield House, 196

Winkelman, Dorinda, 78
Winkelman, Mark
  arrival at J. Aron, 77–82
  background of, 77–78
  bond market crisis of 1994, 125
  departure of, 128–29, 166, 229
  leadership of, 80–81, 87, 93–94, 106–7, 114–15, 122, 135, 226, 227
  Rubin and, 106–7
  technology investment, 80–81, 93–94
Winkelried, Jon, 175–76, 189, 216–17, 285–87
Winthrop House, 28, 178
Witten, Richard, 51–52
Wolfe, Tom, 137–38
Wolf of Wall Street, The (movie), 323
women and diversity, 233–34, 235–37
Working Girl (movie), 47
World Bank, 78, 236, 287
WorldCom, 176, 193–95, 311
World Is Flat, The (Friedman), 213–14
World Trade Center, 55, 183–86, 188, 318, 349
World War II, 4
World Wide Web, 178
Wormwood Scrubs, 148
Wyeth, 291

X (Twitter), 152–53, 360–62
Xi Jinping, 215, 334, 352–53

Yahoo!, 178
Yale Law Journal, 28
Yale University, 13, 17, 32, 52
Yankee Stadium, 12
YES Network, 219
Yiddish, 2, 3
Youngwood, Alfred, 38–39
Yurkiewicz, Felice, 7–8

Zaslav, David, 333
Zehner, Gregory, 170
Zuccotti Park, 318–19
Zuckerberg, Roy, 155